THE LIGHT-GREEN SOCIETY

MICHAEL BESS

The *Light-Green* Society

ECOLOGY

AND TECHNOLOGICAL

MODERNITY IN FRANCE,

1960–2000

THE UNIVERSITY OF CHICAGO PRESS

CHICAGO AND LONDON

MICHAEL BESS is associate professor of history at Vanderbilt University. He is the author of *Realism, Utopia, and the Mushroom Cloud: Four Activist Intellectuals and Their Strategies for Peace, 1945–1989*, also published by the University of Chicago Press.

The University of Chicago Press, Chicago 60637
The University of Chicago Press, Ltd., London
© 2003 by Michael Bess
All rights reserved. Published 2003
Printed in the United States of America
12 11 10 09 08 07 06 05 04 03   5 4 3 2 1

ISBN (cloth): 0-226-04417-3
ISBN (paper): 0-226-04418-1

Library of Congress Cataloging-in-Publication Data

Bess, Michael.
    The light-green society : ecology and technological modernity in France, 1960–2000 / Michael Bess.
        p.   cm.
    Includes bibliographical references and index.
    ISBN 0-226-04417-3 (cloth : alk. paper) — ISBN 0-226-04418-1 (alk. paper)
    1. Environmentalism—France—History—20th century. 2. Green movement—France—History—20th century I. Title.
    GE199 .F8 B47 2003
    333.7′2′0944—dc21

                                                                                    2003009664

♾ The paper used in this publication meets the minimum requirements of the American National Standard for Information Sciences—Permanence of Paper for Printed Library Materials, ANSI Z39.48-1992.

For my wife, Kimberly

CONTENTS

PART I   The Postwar Acceleration

1   NUKES, CONCORDES, AND ANXIETY 11

The French "Special Relationship" with High Technology

CONCLUSION 291

ILLUSTRATIONS

ACKNOWLEDGMENTS

It is a great pleasure to look back over such a long project and to thank the people and institutions whose counsel, information, and support have proved invaluable along the way.

The research for this book, and the writing of it, were funded by four institutions: the John D. and Catherine T. MacArthur Foundation, which provided a Research and Writing Grant for 2000–2001 under its Program on Global Security and Sustainability; the Robert Penn Warren Center for the Humanities at Vanderbilt University, which provided two fellowships, in 1994–95 and 1999–2000; the Vanderbilt University Research Scholar Grants Program, which provided two sabbatical-year fellowships, in 1992–93 and 1996–97; and the College of Arts and Science at Vanderbilt, which gave me sabbatical leaves in 1992–93, 1996–97, and 2000–2001, provided a generous subsidy for publication, and regularly funded my travel to academic conferences. Without the sustained and generous support of these institutions, this project could never have been completed.

I owe a very special debt to Alain Beltran, Jean Carlier, Jean-Pierre Raffin, and Pierre Samuel, both for their insights and comments, and for generously allowing me access to their immense personal archives on environmental issues in French history. Their guidance and assistance was of an order that a researcher usually encounters only in the realm of dreams. My thanks also to the following persons, who consented to extensive interviews: Jean-Luc Benhammias, Brice Lalonde, Laurence Mermet, Théodore Monod, Jacques Noettinger, Sylvie Pétin, François Pharabod, and Antoine Waechter.

Two (initially anonymous) manuscript reviewers for the University of Chicago Press made a major impact on the final product: Mark Cioc, of the University of California at Santa Cruz, and Gabrielle Hecht, of the University of Michigan. Their insightful and constructive criticisms of the first draft proved truly invaluable in the revision process. My heartfelt thanks to both of them!

My research was rendered immeasurably easier and more effective by the assistance of many archivists and librarians in Paris, both at private organizations and public institutions, whom I take this opportunity to thank heartily: Dominique Crimé, at the Agence de l'Environnement et de la Maîtrise de l'Énergie; Robert Boucher, at Les Amis de la Terre; Patrice Prévot at the Aérospatiale Corporation; the librarians at the Bibliothèque de Documentation Internationale Contemporaine (Nanterre); Anne-Marie Roth at the Équipe Cousteau; the Département de la Communication Externe of the Centre National d'Études Spatiales; Corinne Michel and Sylviane Suball at Electricité de France; Daria Robinson at the European Space Agency; the archivists at the news magazine *L'Express* (centre de documentation); Laurence Mermet and the staff at France Nature Environnement; Michel Fansten at the France 2 TV station; Michel Mamon at France Telecom (Bureau de Presse); the staff at Génération Écologie; Suzanne Jouguelet and Mme. Dupuydt at the Institut National de Recherche Pédagogique; the staff of the Institut d'Histoire du Temps Présent; Monique Grégoriou at the Institut Français d'Opinion Publique; the staff of the Centre de Documentation of the newspaper *Libération*; Patrick Henry and Claudine Harasse at the Service de Documentation of the Ministère de l'Environnement; the staff of the Centre de Documentation at the Musée de la Publicité (Union des Arts Décoratifs); Jacqueline Leboucq, in the library of the Muséum National d'Histoire Naturelle; Michel Huet and his excellent staff at the Service de la Communication, Ministère de l'Agriculture et du Développement Rural; the staff of the Service de Documentation, Musée de l'Air et de l'Espace; the staff of the Centre de Documentation, Organisation pour la Coopération et le Développement Économique (OECD); Joel Stehlin in the public relations department of the Peugeot Corporation; Annick Riczker at the photothèque of the Renault Corporation; Mme. Semelle and Mme. Vincenot at the Société Nationale de Protection de la Nature; Francis Boulanger at the press office of the Société Nationale des Chemins de Fer; the staff at the office of Les Verts; and the staff of the Médiathèque at the Cité des Sciences et de l'Industrie at La Villette.

A crucial role in the development of my ideas for this project was played by two year-long faculty seminars at Vanderbilt University's Robert Penn Warren Center for the Humanities. My warm thanks go to Mona Frederick, the Center's Executive Director, for making it a place where interdisciplinary exchange and intellectual enrichment of the highest quality are expertly fostered. The first seminar, entitled "Science and Society," was held in 1994–95. I would like to thank, for their camaraderie and keen critical ideas, my colleagues Arleen Tuchman, John McCarthy, Gisela Mosig, Arkady Plotnitsky, Richard Haglund, Jeffery Franks, Peter Haas, Cathy Jrade, Barbara Kinach, Efstratios Prassidis, and Mark Schoenfield. I would also like to thank the seminar guests, Thomas Hughes, N. Katherine Hayles, and the late Madeleine Goodman.

In 1999–2000 I was fortunate enough to participate in a second seminar at Vanderbilt's Warren Center, entitled "Constructions, Destructions, and Deconstructions of Nature." This seminar, which I co-organized with David Wood of the Philosophy Department, allowed me to spend a year discussing the concept of nature with a literary scholar (Richard Grusin), an anthropologist (Beth Conklin), an astrophysicist (David Weintraub), a classical scholar (Kathy Gaca), an expert on German Romanticism (Laurie Johnson), an art historian (Leonard Folgarait), and a geologist (Jay Noller). To all these people, I owe a major debt of gratitude: the whole conceptualization of this book, from the underlying structure to the minute details, shows the mark of our intensive (and intensely enjoyable) sessions of thinking together. My thanks also to the guests who participated in these encounters: John Compton, Steve Vogel, Holmes Rolston III, Irene Klaver, Chris Drury, David Abram, and Robert P. Harrison. I owe a special debt to my colleague and seminar co-leader David Wood, an inexhaustible geyser of the very best ideas, humor, and surprises. May the Henge be with you!

Two librarians at Vanderbilt University merit a special mention. Joe Mount, and his successor Peter Brush, the history librarians at Central Library, generously allocated funds for the acquisition of several hundred essential new books on environmental topics; their assistance in ferreting out monographs and articles, and their general zeal in helping me find information for this project, made a significant impact on the shape of the final product. My thanks also to the other library staff at Vanderbilt, particularly to Janet Thomason, for allowing me to renew a ridiculously large number of books from home, year after year.

The annual conferences and journals of four academic organizations have proved invaluable in sharpening the conceptual tools with which I have approached this subject: my thanks to the American Society for Environmental History, the Society for the History of Technology, the Society for French Historical Studies, and the International Conference on the History of Technology (ICOHTEC). Special thanks to Jim Williams and Sara Pritchard for introducing me to this latter organization.

Certain ideas in this book have been aired in my published articles over the past decade, and I would like to thank the three journals in which they appeared for permission to use previously published material: *French Politics and Society, Technology and Culture,* and *Environmental History.*

Among the large number of persons who have helped me with this project, and whose kind assistance, critical ideas, or advice sped me along, I would like to single out the following for particularly warm thanks: Susanna Barrows, Robert Belot, Bill Caferro, Joyce Chaplin, Mark Cioc, David Coe, Simon Collier, Paul Conkin, Andrée Corvol, Michel Cotte, Tycho de Boer, Marshall Eakin, James Epstein, Carole Fink, Mona Frederick, Paul Freedman, Robert Frost, Roger Hahn, Joel Harrington, Gabrielle Hecht, Thomas Hughes, Yoshikuni Igarashi, Paul Israel, Martin Jay, Amy Kirschke, Pierre Lamard, Jane Landers, Bruno Latour, Eva Moskowitz, John Opie, Michael Osborne, David Pace, Elisabeth Perry, Lewis Perry, Sara Pritchard, Matthew Ramsey, Veronique Renault, Mark Rose, Hal Rothman, Tom Schwartz, Helmut Smith, Marianne Stevens, Margo Todd, Arleen Tuchman, Meredith Veldman, Frank Wcislo, Spencer Weart, Meike Werner, Tamara Whited, and James C. Williams.

I would like to thank my students at Vanderbilt, both graduates and undergraduates, for the lively and enriching dialogue they have maintained with me over the past decade; this book shows the mark of many ideas they have raised and points they have made, both in and out of class. I would also like to express my gratitude to the staff of the Vanderbilt history department, who have helped me in so many ways over the years: Brenda Hummel, the late Suzanne Koellein, Sally Miller, Lori Cohen, Vicki Crowthers, and Haley Hart.

My literary agent, Mildred Marmur, has nudged my writing along over the years with unfailing good humor and excellent advice; my fervent thanks to her for all the countless ways in which she has helped me. I owe a debt of similar magnitude to Douglas Mitchell, my editor at the University of Chicago Press, who has shown extraordinary solicitude, patience, and insight in nurturing the work of a sometimes beleaguered teacher-scholar. To have Milly and Doug's unstinting moral support during the past decade has truly made all the difference. Hearty thanks also to the superb editorial and production staff of the University of Chicago Press: Tim McGovern, Robert Devens, Claudia Rex, Richard Allen, Mike Brehm, Joe Claude, and Mark Heineke.

Finally, I would like to thank my family for putting up with all the time and energy that this project has taken from them. Kimberly: this book is dedicated to you—a small gesture betokening my boundless gratitude for all you have given me, and continue to give daily to us all. Natalie: you were only ten months old when I first showed you the cold clear fountains in the Place des Vosges, during the initial research trip for this book; I hope that as you grow up you will come to share some of my own passionate love of France, which has only deepened through this study. Sebastian: you are tall enough now to reach my computer keyboard, groping over the edge with your little fingers and judiciously adding letters here and there to my text as I type along; I hope you will grow up to know a France that is even greener and more beautiful, when you get to be my age, than it is today.

> > >

Proposed variant of the standard self-effacing "acknowledgments disclaimer": *All the flaws and shortcomings of this book should of course be blamed on the people listed above. The author cheerfully assumes sole responsibility for the good parts.*

A coelentera, all pulsating flesh, animal-flower,
All fire, made up of falling bodies joined by the black pin of sex.
It breathes in the center of the galaxy, drawing to itself star after star.
And I, an instant of its duration, on multilaned roads which
    penetrate half-opened mountains,
Bare mountains overgrown with an ageless grass, opened and frozen
    at a sunset before the generations.
Where at large curves one sees nests of cisterns or transparent towers,
    perhaps of missiles.
Along brown leaks by the seashore, rusty stones and butcheries where
    quartered whales are ground to powder.
I wanted to be a judge but those whom I called "they" have changed
    into myself.
I was getting rid of my faith so as not to be better than men and
    women who are certain only of their unknowing.
And on the roads of my terrestrial homeland turning round with the
    music of the spheres
I thought that all I could do would be done better one day.

From the poem, "With Trumpets and Zithers" (1965),
in Czesław Miłosz, *The Collected Poems* (Hopewell, N.J.:
The Ecco Press, 1988), 202

PART I

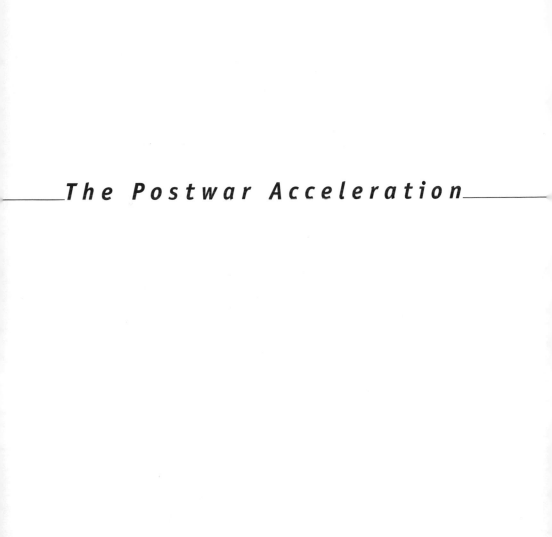

The Postwar Acceleration

Introduction

Ecology is like universal suffrage or the 40-hour week: at first, the ruling elite and the guardians of social order regard it as subversive, and proclaim that it will lead to the triumph of anarchy and irresponsibility. Then, when factual evidence and popular pressure can no longer be denied, the establishment suddenly gives way—what was unthinkable yesterday becomes taken for granted today, and fundamentally nothing changes.
—André Gorz, 1974[1]

This book is about the rise of environmentalism in France during the second half of the twentieth century, and about the emergence, as a result, of a distinctive kind of social order, whose features I sum up with the phrase, "the light-green society." The shade of light green is meant to connote not only moderation, compromise, and half-measures, but also the profound ambiguity that has characterized the reception of ecological ideas among the French citizenry. What is perhaps most striking about the story of French environmentalism is that it can be plausibly read in two sharply divergent ways—as a narrative of success, in which green ideas gradually came to permeate the mainstream culture and economy of this nation; and as a narrative of defeat, in which virtually all the more radical aspects of the original green vision were trimmed down, ignored, or jettisoned by a tenaciously consumerist population.

This book, therefore, is fundamentally about ambivalence—about a society caught between the lure of technology, progress, and abundance on the one hand, and, on the other, the gnawing fear of losing contact with the natural world, of drifting insensibly out of touch with its most cherished heritage and traditions. It is about a society that has stubbornly wanted to have it both ways—traditional *and* modern, green *and* mass-consumerist—at the same time. And it is about the many paradoxes—some would say, contradictions—that have proliferated as a result.

Often, accounts of environmentalist ideas and politics take the form of an implicit morality play, in which two bitterly opposed camps—the critics versus the defenders of industrial modernity—campaign on behalf of a passionate moral vision. What has captured my attention in this project, however, has been something rather less clamorous but far more ubiquitous: it is the vast number of cases in which neither side won a clear victory, but in which, either through political compromise or through the sheer inertia of decision-making processes in a mass democracy, an outcome emerged that borrowed elements from both visions at the same time. What interests me, in other words, is the gradual commingling, over several decades, of these two antagonistic ideological currents—the greens and the technological enthusiasts—to produce something new: the *partial* greening of the mainstream, in which neither side emerged wholly satisfied nor utterly dismayed, but in which a whole new complex of discourses and institutions nonetheless came into being.

In the eyes of the eco-warriors of the 1960s, two possible scenarios loomed over industrial civilization: either humankind would stay on its current course, and thus drift into environmental catastrophe; or else humankind would manage to change course drastically, reinventing the socioeconomic order of modernity, and thus create the sort of ecologically balanced society depicted by Ernest Callenbach in his novel *Ecotopia*.[2] What happened, instead, was neither of the two, but something closer to an unanticipated mixture of both—not a full-scale change-of-course, but rather a significant deflection, a "half-revolution."

The greening of France ran shallow and wide. It ran wide, in the sense that practically every facet of French society eventually came to acquire an environmentalist tint: school-teachers, journalists, government bureaucrats, politicians, industrialists, scientists, citizens' groups, philosophers—everyone eagerly donned the green mantle. Yet it also ran shallow, in the sense that the more radical aspects of the green vision failed utterly to take hold. "Producing less in order to live better"—this had been the battle-cry of the early environmentalists, who envisioned a new society based on cyclical equilibrium rather than endless economic growth. Some of this utopian tension still animates various strains of the *mouvement écolo* in France today, but the green ideas that have gained currency on a national scale remain exclusively the more modest ones. The result is a social order in which virtually every activity is touched by environmentalist concerns—but modestly, moderately, without upsetting the existing state of things too much.

The light-green society of the year 2000, therefore, born as it is of this half-revolution, is fraught through and through with ambiguities, ironic inversions, the blurring of age-old conceptual boundaries. Certainly it lies quite far from what the environmentalists themselves would have preferred; for they perceived their vision of an alternative future as being clear and uncompromising, as resting on an ancient and true distinction between the wild and the artificial. Yet the light-green society turned out very different. The institutions of the central state, fervently repudiated by environmentalists, grew steadily more powerful through the process itself of promoting green aims; the "natural" became an object of rampant commercialization; green political parties, describing themselves as the only genuine alternatives to "politics as usual," jockeyed for percentage points in the polls; new technologies, many of them conceived as eco-friendly, subtly penetrated the land, causing the line between the wild and the artificial to become ever hazier; humankind, often in the name of "saving" nature, intervened in the territory more intensively and pervasively than it had ever done before.

In the eyes of some contemporary French environmentalists, such an outcome represents an abject defeat. Yet this does not strike me as an entirely accurate assessment of what has happened. In the realm of culture, of *mentalités*, I will argue, the shift has actually been profound indeed, for it has entailed nothing less than the reinvention of nature as a fragile and finite space, to be revered and protected by humans. Not since the transition from nomadic hunter-gathering to settled farming, some ten thousand years ago, has such a momentous shift marked the human relationship with the natural world—or so some scholars have quite persuasively argued.[3] Yet it remains undeniable, nonetheless, that in the economic sphere the changes wrought by environmentalism have tended to be much more uneven—at least thus far.

This then will constitute the first half of the book's narrative: how the transformation came about, why it took the forms it did. The second half has to do with the hybrid nature of the result, the strange new landscape into which it has catapulted contemporary France; for this light-green social order turned out to be rife with unresolved (and perhaps unresolvable) tensions. How to protect the environment without simultaneously creating a monstrously bloated state apparatus of legislation, monitoring, and enforcement? Should an environmentally conscious citizenry welcome or curse the cornucopia of "green products" that began flooding the consumer economy in the 1980s, from biodegradable soap to nature tourism? When, and how far, can people use technology to promote green aims, and what status should attach to the proliferating natural/artificial hybrids that result? At what point do the well-intentioned practices of environmental stewardship shade imperceptibly into an ethos of territorial control and management, a form of subtle domination over the land that becomes (in the eyes of some) even more pernicious than the naked exploitation of yesteryear? In sum: can the circle ever be made to fit within the square shape? Can a large-scale, growth-oriented consumer economy ever become meaningfully green? What are the consequences of a "greening" that remains, for profound cultural and economic reasons, stubbornly partial and incomplete?

These are among the difficult questions and dilemmas that the advent of a light-green social order has forced French citizens to confront. They are not, I believe, questions that pertain to France alone. On the contrary, one of my concluding arguments will be that key features of the light-green society can be readily discerned in virtually all modern democracies. In this sense, the case of France has exemplified, with typical panache and vividness, some of the central conundrums of the environmentalist phenomenon that has swept through much of the industrialized world since the 1960s.

> > >

Driving along the narrow backroads of southern France, among the Pyrenees foothills with their scrabbly undergrowth of gorse and sage, you would not expect to find Thémis, the immense solar power station. Here and there you come upon a medieval chapel lost amid the rolling movement of the land, reminiscent of a time when Albigensian heretics were dragged down from the highlands to be questioned and executed;[4] or perhaps a crumbling stone bridge, or a flock of sheep blocking the road, the shepherd plodding behind, staring unconcernedly at you as he goes. But to come up over the rise and see Thémis going full bore, this is a true apparition.

It gathers sunlight to itself. Twenty stories tall, the slender concrete monolith looms over the arid terrain, part minaret, part moon rocket. Two hundred large mirrors arrayed down below, covering an area the size of a soccer stadium, shift infinitesimally on their electric pivots, following the arc of the sun as it tracks across the sky. Each mirror grabs a portion of the harsh noonday light and focuses it toward a single point near the tower's peak, the sun point. You can see the sunbeams reflected upward through the air as your eye moves up the monolith, the rays drawn together over the field of mirrors like an increasingly bright veil.[5] It gets thicker and thicker as the rays converge toward the focal point; you can actually see the sunlight itself, a tangible force concentrated in the air, a vortex around a blinding white center. What strikes you suddenly is the utter silence of this huge machine, no cars on the tiny ribbon of country road, no breeze, only the occasional trill of a quail under the dull-green hillside broom. Somewhere inside the hushed building at the tower's base, 2.5 megawatts of electricity are forming inaudibly, abstractly.

Thémis is a good exemplar of the strange and paradoxical creations that populate the present study. The pinnacle of exotic high tech when first designed in the 1970s, it also epitomized a distinctive kind of machine that sought a renewed closeness to nature, to the underlying rhythms of biological and geological process: man-made, a labyrinth of advanced alloys and mathematical equations, yet designed to harvest the sun's energy like a vineyard or an orchard. Very French, too: for unlike the folksy solar panels cobbled together by eco-enthusiasts in California or Australia—panels designed for micro-applications one rooftop at a time—Thémis was conceived more in the manner of a Louis XIV château: one big central Thing, powerful and imposing, summoning up nature's forces and then bestowing them outward to a grateful citizenry.[6]

The story of Thémis is also emblematic of the broader narrative underlying this book. This experimental solar station was declared a failure in 1986, and shut down the following year. It had proved an interesting and useful failure, declared the engineers of France's state-run electric company, EDF, who had commissioned and financed it; but in the end, they argued, it graphically demonstrated that this kind of solar technology simply couldn't compete for cost-effectiveness with the blockbusting potency of a nuclear-fired turbine.[7] Already since the mid-1970s, EDF had been building nuclear reactors at a furious pace, on a greater scale than any other electric utility in the world. By the late 1980s, when Thémis was taken off-line, France had become something of a renowned pro-nuclear standout among the community of industrialized nations, the country with the greatest concentration of nuclear-powered generators on the planet. French citizens queried by pollsters said repeatedly (and in impressive majorities) that this suited them just fine.[8]

What sort of symbolism does Thémis offer us, then? An appropriately complex symbolism—not a single narrative, triumphant or grim, as in *"the long upward march of ecological consciousness,"* or *"the dashed hopes of green activists,"* but a more multifarious cluster of stories, marked by the breakdown of clear and univocal meanings. Thémis as green technology: a clean, renewable energy source, embodying the profound shift in attitudes toward nature that occurred in the decades following World War II. Thémis as defeated technology: pushed to the wayside by a society unwilling to make the draconian sacrifices that a solar-based energy system would have entailed. Thémis as hybrid: blurring the boundary between the natural and the artificial, part sunlight, part turbine.

The light-green society, I will argue, is ultimately an analogous kind of hybrid. It results from the gradual confluence of two antagonistic currents of postwar history: on the one hand, the headlong rush for technological modernization, and on the other, the environmentalists' radical critique of industrialism. Hence the unabashedly dialectical structure of this book:[9] in Part I, I sketch the contours of the accelerating technological transformation that shook postwar France—its dramatic consequences for both urban and rural society, its profoundly ambivalent reception among the population. In Part II, I describe the genesis and rapid propagation of environmentalist ideas—ideas born largely in critical response to this very modernization process that had swept like a wave over the entire territory.

Then, in Part III, I show how technological modernity and ecological practices came (rather surprisingly) to cohabit with each other, producing the uneasy synthesis that one encounters in France today. Consumer attitudes, government agencies, political and legal structures, industrial production: everywhere, the advent of the light-green society forced the French to grapple increasingly with the world of artifice and the world of nature as mutually interpenetrating spheres. By the early 2000s, an engineer designing a new mechanical device or consumer product could not afford to ignore that product's impact on the biosphere; conversely, an environmental activist could not expect to speak of nature protection without automatically bringing into play a formidable array of green economic practices, environmental laws and regulations, and "eco-technological" interventions. This was not, I will argue, merely a matter of scattered or superficial changes in habits or nomenclature: rather, the realm of the social and the realm of the natural had gradually blurred into each other, in a deep and systemic way.

Finally, in Part IV, as a philosophical "coda" to this tripartite argument, I consider the broader meaning of the light-green social order, the ways in which that social order redefines humanity's "place" within the natural world. If, as my analysis suggests, the case of France reflects a more general pattern of changes that has affected many other industrial democracies—if, in other words, the light-green model promises to become a prominent feature of tomorrow's global society—then what conclusions are we to draw, both for human civilization and for the future of the biosphere itself? The central questions here revolve around the shifting status of nature in an increasingly technological world: the rising tide of artifice, the chances of achieving sustainability, the elusive qualities of a wilderness in retreat—and perhaps above all, the space for human agency in dealing with these vital yet delicate matters, in which the stakes are so frightfully high.

1 Nukes, Concordes, and Anxiety

The French "Special Relationship" with High Technology

If this country does not make the necessary effort to give science the importance it merits and to give those who serve it the prestige necessary for their influence to be felt, it will sooner or later become a colony.
—Frédéric Joliot-Curie, 1945[1]

It is necessary to produce always more and always better, to save and to invest constantly and, even more, to push relentlessly our technical and scientific research, in order to avoid sinking into a bitter mediocrity and being colonized by the activities, inventions, and capacities of other countries.
—Charles de Gaulle, 1964[2]

Ambivalent Modernity

The French, in the decades between 1960 and 2000, encountered a choice that they could never quite bring themselves to make. Like their counterparts in other industrial democracies, they wanted all the comforts of material abundance, the cheery prospect of limitless economic expansion; yet they also wanted a safe, clean, verdant environment in which to enjoy these boons. They feverishly applied themselves in achieving an ever-growing technological mastery over their physical surroundings; yet they wanted their world not to feel "artificial." They held fast to their Concordes, nuclear reactors, computers, cell phones, and *trains à grande vitesse,* yet felt genuine anguish at the passing of traditional society—the France of peasant villages, with its colorful diversity of historic regions, each possessing its own cheeses, dialects, customs, and scenery.

One cannot understand the impact of environmentalism in France, I will argue, unless one takes this ambivalence toward technological modernity as one's basic starting-point. For a great many French men and women, the idea of "écologie" was not merely about protecting species and habitats, but encompassed a broader, more expansive meaning: the critique of industrial modernity itself. It entailed what the French call "une choix de société," a choice about what *kind* of society one wants to live in. The word "nature" became a code-word for something more than woods and rivers: it meant the antithesis of urban, technological society, a haven from the fast-paced, competitive, information-driven lives that so many French citizens had come to lead. In this sense, the key critical ideas of the light-green society formed part of a much older current of unease that went back at least as far as the 1890s—or even farther, some would insist, to the Romantics and their forebear Rousseau: a complex array of doubts and fears about the very underpinnings of industrial civilization.

In this chapter and the one that follows, we focus on the wrenching, almost violent changes that postwar French society was forced to absorb, over a mere three decades, under the bland euphemism of "technological modernization." The changes were rich with paradox: they came swiftly, part of a broader socioeconomic transformation that was sweeping through much of the industrialized world; yet they also resulted from a frenetic national effort, a decades-long mobilization of state and citizenry, tinged by intense hopes and fears. They appeared to spring from a sustained national consensus, marching under the banner of "Progress," yet in fact they were often shaped by fierce ongoing battles among a wide array of shifting social and economic constituencies. They carried the prestige of "the modern" to unprecedented heights; yet they also helped to call forth the ideology of environmentalism—one of the most systematic and influential critiques that industrial civilization had ever faced. In the end, the forces of technological innovation changed France from top to bottom, but they did not themselves come out unscathed: these forces were themselves ultimately modified, reshaped, or absorbed within the new social order that also incorporated their antithesis: the light-green society.

The thundering Concorde, the nuclear reactor, the vanishing peasant—these are the principal dramatis personae of the following two chapters, the recurrent emblems of modernity in urban and rural France. Over time they became symbolic markers for a whole constellation of choices that faced French citizens, choices that came to be deeply intertwined with the rise of ecology as an ideology and as a social movement.

Europe's Nuclear Macho? Perceptions of France as a Relatively "Ungreen" Nation

The first problem that confronts us, in discussing technology and environmentalism in France, is the widely held stereotype that tends to elicit the rather bemused reaction: "Greens in France? I didn't know there were any!" To put it bluntly, the French do not enjoy a very positive image in the eyes of the world's green activists. During the early 1980s, when the German Green Party was clamorously making headlines in the Bundestag, the French environmentalists remained relatively weak and divided. While the Italians, British, Dutch, and Germans were taking to the streets, launching huge demonstrations against nuclear weapons, the French Left kept noticeably aloof. Indeed, to a foreign observer, the primary association between the Socialist government of François Mitterrand and the ecological movement occurred in 1985, when French secret agents blew up the Greenpeace ship *Rainbow Warrior*—and the Socialists' response amounted to little more than a lame attempt at a coverup.

After the Chernobyl disaster in 1986, the French once again stood out among the nations of Europe: day after day, while the Italians, British, Belgians, Swiss, and Germans were issuing iodine to children or banning the sale of lettuce, the French government insisted that its neighbors were overreacting, that the radioactive cloud posed no threat, and that France, with its own dense network of nuclear reactors, remained fundamentally safe.[3] In 1995 and 1996, the French yet again distinguished themselves before world opinion, with a stubborn insistence on pursuing nuclear weapons tests on a remote atoll of the South Pacific, despite a global moratorium on such tests and overwhelming condemnation even from their closest allies. To environmentalists around the world, the French President Jacques Chirac became "HiroChirac"; emotions in the South Pacific region ran hot enough for the Sydney *Morning Herald* to print a banner headline—in French, just to make sure the message reached its intended audience—"Pourquoi les Français sont des Connards" (which translates approximately as "Why the French are Stupid Assholes").[4]

The cumulative effect of these kinds of political behaviors, over the years, has been a widespread perception of the French as one of the world's more "ungreen" peoples—a perception fairly common not just among environmental activists but among many mainstream journalists and academic writ-

ers as well. Here, for example, is the opening of an article by the Paris corre-
spondent for *The Economist,* writing in 1992: "The French have never been
known for pacifism, anti-nuclear protests or concern for the environment.
So the rise of ecologists comes as a bit of a surprise."[5] Or the *International
Herald Tribune* (based in Paris!) in 1995: "One explanation for the French
lack of interest in environmental concerns is that France is among the less
crowded European nations, which gives it a sense of plenty. Another view is
that the rational French have a different sense of esthetics, one that does not
necessarily incorporate raw nature."[6] And yet this perception is false: France
possesses an influential and vibrant green movement, a movement with a
long history and an overall track record that compares favorably with those
of the more celebrated green organizations in Britain, Germany, or the United
States. The French population has enthusiastically embraced many green
ideas and earnestly taken up the cause of *écologie:* opinion polls, electoral results, media coverage, recycling programs, green industries, sweeping legal
reforms—all these indices (and many others) place France among the most
environmentally engaged countries of the world.

How then to explain this apparent contradiction, this disjunction between appearance and reality? The "ungreen" image of the French stems
from a variety of factors: the widely held stereotype about France as an al-
legedly "Cartesian" culture in which reason dominates (and denigrates)
the natural world; a national electoral system that, unlike the German, tends
to block fringe parties such as the Greens from political power; a recurrent pattern of internecine squabbles among French environmentalists.
Nevertheless, the primary reason for France's image as a nation of "anti-
environmentalists" undoubtedly derives from its passionate love affair with
large-scale, high-profile technology in general, and with nuclear technology
in particular. France, in the eyes of green sympathizers around the world, is
not just the homeland of wine, high culture, and *douceur de vivre:* it is the
homeland of the Concorde, TGV, Chunnel, Airbus, Mirage fighter, Exocet
missile, Ariane rocket, and above all of the world's greatest concentration of
nuclear reactors. It is the nation that truculently refuses to stop nuclear tests,
the country whose population repeatedly rallies around its statesmen whenever this aggressively pro-nuclear policy comes under challenge.

In order to put the "ungreen" image of the French into proper perspective,
therefore, we need to understand the special relationship that they developed with high technology—and especially nuclear technology—during
the postwar decades of economic modernization. But we need to make it
clear from the outset that these idiosyncratic cultural traits, for all their importance in French politics and society, can easily mislead. They have misled

some observers, as we have seen, into concluding that the French generally regard green ideas with indifference or contempt—a demonstrably false inference. They can also mislead us by making us lose sight of France's *ordinariness*—the profound commonalities that have linked French postwar experiences with those of Americans, Germans, New Zealanders, and the citizens of many other industrialized democracies. Without a doubt, the light-green society in France was tinged by many distinctive features of national history and culture—the Gaullist quest for technological grandeur, the powerful myth of peasant traditions—and we must first grasp what these were about if we are to understand what the light-green society itself meant to the French. On the other hand, we must also take care to distinguish what was *not* uniquely French in this story, but reflected a much broader set of shifting attitudes toward nature and technology throughout the industrialized world.

The Postwar Boom: Continuity vs. Discontinuity

France was far from unusual in experiencing rapid economic growth during the decades following World War II. By 1975, the nation had witnessed a quadrupling of the gross national product, a quintupling of energy consumption, a vast increase in the mechanization of agriculture and the use of chemical fertilizers and pesticides, a fifteen-fold expansion in the number of automobiles, a twenty-fold increase in the consumption of plastics.[7] The litany of such factors could go on and on: it is typical of most industrialized countries after the war. France's economy grew a bit more rapidly than those of Britain and the United States, a bit more slowly than those of Italy and West Germany—but these differential rates of expansion formed part of a broader groundswell of change that was affecting virtually every Western nation.

Nevertheless, two significant features set France apart. First, the discontinuity from the past proved sharper here than in most other countries; postwar modernization required more upheaval, more uprooting, than it did elsewhere. And second, the underlying mood of modernization was more angst-ridden, the rhetoric of urgency more strident than elsewhere. Both in urban and in rural France, we find these twin themes arising again and again, leaving their indelible mark on the nation's culture.

To speak of the postwar boom years in France as a period of discontinuity, a sharp break from the past, is to invite immediate objections. In the political sphere, the transition from the Third Republic to the Fourth left intact a remarkable number of the institutions and practices associated with the old order of the 1930s.[8] Some French citizens even complained that a virtual "restoration" had taken place in 1944 and '45, a betrayal of the hopes for socioeconomic restructuring espoused by the antifascist Resistance.[9] And certainly it was true that the features of modernization were not new to France: scientific and technological advance, the growth of the welfare state, urbanization, the spread of consumer capitalism, the displacement of agriculture as the dominant feature of the economy—all these processes had been under way since the nineteenth century, and had already made a profound impact on French society and culture.

The key discontinuity, however, lay in the *pace* of change. What took place after 1945 amounted to a sudden and massive acceleration of all these processes, bringing on, in the space of two or three decades, innovations of a scope that had previously taken a century.[10] What had once moved like a glacier now began moving like an avalanche. In nine years, for example, from 1949 to 1958, sales of household appliances quintupled, the number of automobiles and farm tractors quadrupled, the volume of air travel tripled, telecommunications and consumption of electricity doubled.[11] Not only a way of life, but the entire horizon of the possible, shifted.

The French were by no means unaware of what was happening to them. In a classic 1979 study that rapidly became a bestseller in France, *Les trente glorieuses, ou la révolution invisible de 1946 à 1975,* the economist Jean Fourastié opens with a description of two villages, Madère and Cessac. Madère, for Fourastié, provides a perfect exemplar of backwardness: fragmented farm plots worked by primitive agricultural methods, low literacy levels, a community disconnected from the rest of the world, bereft of modern conveniences, a picture of static French country life that could belong to the nineteenth century, and almost as easily to the sixteenth. Cessac, by contrast, although roughly the same size as Madère (500 inhabitants), presents a bustling picture of rural modernity: telephones, cars, TVs, refrigerators—all these are considered normal appurtenances of life by the well-educated inhabitants, most of whom do not work in agriculture at all, but in the tertiary or service sector. The prosperity and dynamism of Cessac present a striking contrast to the millennial torpor of life in Madère. *Eh bien,* Fourastié informs us (obviously savoring the dramatic flourish): they are really one and the same village, separated only by thirty years of remarkable change, 1946 to 1975. Its real name is Douelle, a tiny knot of houses along the winding river Lot, in the remote Quercy of central France: I grew up here, he writes, I lived through this transformation, I can easily document the fact that what transpired here was typical of what was happening in the rest of France as well.

The effect of Fourastié's book, from a literary point of view, was simple but effective, for he had captured a phenomenon that viscerally resonated within the experience of most French citizens. The phrase "les trente glorieuses"—

the thirty glorious years—became part of the national vocabulary. The fact that these years were far from glorious in other ways—Dienbienphu, Suez, Algeria, the ignominious collapse of the Fourth Republic under conditions of near civil war, the cataclysm of 1968–did not detract from the overwhelming obviousness to most French men and women that they had lived through a profound social transformation.

One factor that rendered the transition from Madère to Cessac particularly striking was the sheer extent of Madère's backwardness, the relatively tardy position of France within the European economy of the late 1940s. This may seem a rather strange or even perverse assertion about the nation that had almost conquered Europe a century and a half before, and still fielded Europe's largest army throughout the 1920s and early 1930s—the nation that led Europe in the natural sciences until the mid-nineteenth century, and whose achievements in the social sciences and humanities had continued throughout the twentieth century to place it at the center of Western intellectual life. Yet it was true. The French economy had started upon the process of industrialization a good half-century later than the British, and the gap proved too much for France to overcome throughout the nineteenth century; in addition, though Germany began its own industrial take-off at about the same time as France, it rapidly pulled ahead in the late 1800s, surpassing even Britain as an industrial power by the turn of the century. In the hundred years before World War II, the French economy moved forward in fits and starts, perpetually striving (and perpetually failing) to catch up to its powerful neighbors across the Channel and the Rhine; between 1930 and 1939 France's gross domestic product actually *shrank* by twenty percent, the economy recovering from the Depression more slowly and more painfully than that of any other major industrialized country.[12]

The historian Stanley Hoffmann coined the term "stalemate society" to describe the peculiar nexus of political and economic factors that conspired to thwart modernization under the Third Republic (1870–1940): the disproportionate political weight of the peasantry, the timorous Malthusianism of business elites, the precarious balance among political parties, the rigidity of state institutions.[13] Despite more than a century of industrialization, France on the eve of the Second World War still lagged behind much of Europe in key aspects of its economic life.[14] Specific pockets of cutting-edge modernity certainly existed—one thinks of the pioneering factories of André Citroën, the vigorous aircraft industry in Toulouse, the impressive achievements of the Joliot-Curies in their physics laboratories—but these advanced sectors had to struggle for scarce resources within an overall economic context marked by stagnation and inertia.[15] Antiquated mechanisms for finance capital and investment, a sclerotic and compartmentalized educational system, meager infrastructures for communication and transport, a thoroughly obsolete (albeit picturesque) set of agricultural practices—all these traits of relative backwardness continued to characterize much of France until the mid-twentieth century.

The wake-up call, when it came, was brutal. Within a few short months in 1940, while the world looked on, unbelieving and aghast, the entire rickety edifice collapsed upon itself with a suddenness that left the French people dazed, emotionally shattered. Hitler walked down the Champs Elysées, surveying his massed troops amid the tree-lined avenues of the city he had always despised and now controlled. "For the next four years," notes the historian Alain Beltran, "we lived day-to-day with the very real possibility of ceasing to exist as a national unit, of being dismembered whenever our new masters might wish it."[16]

Here was crystallized the particular French attitude that forms the focus of this chapter: technological Darwinism. It is an attitude whose roots go back much farther than World War II and whose lingering effects have continued to play a decisive role in French politics and foreign policy ever since. "The catastrophe [of 1940]," writes the historian Jean-Baptiste Duroselle,

> caused the crumbling of . . . confidence in diplomacy and the army, of the mistaken belief that France was a great nation of the first rank. The French came out of the trial very bitter, also exhausted, ruined, weakened. But the catastrophe had not only this negative side; it revived a feeling which some condemned and others reduced to an instrument of domestic politics—patriotism. . . . A very strong desire to escape further humiliation had been born.[17]

Technological Darwinism

I derive the term "technological Darwinism" from the phenomenon of social Darwinism—the loose cluster of ideas that emerged in European and American social thought during the second half of the nineteenth century, put forward by philosophers like Herbert Spencer but particularly influential among less distinguished popularizers and essayists like those described by Fritz Stern in *The Politics of Cultural Despair*.[18] At the core of social darwinism lies the notion that all human beings, from individuals to national collectivities, must perpetually compete with each other for scarce resources; those who fail to keep abreast in this endless (and often ruthless) struggle for paramountcy are doomed to vanish from the historical stage. Although numerous racial and other variants of this ideology have existed (one of them explicitly claimed by Adolf Hitler as his own personal philosophy), it is with the blander, more generic sense of this ideology that I am here concerned: the notion that the life of nations is one of relentless competition, that those who do not make themselves strong and independent are condemned to be dominated by others.

This notion constitutes a key strain of public discourse in postwar France. It comes in three forms or variants, which I will call the aggressive, the defensive, and the philanthropic. The aggressive variant, found mostly among thinkers and politicians on the far Right like Jean-Marie Le Pen, stipulates that France needs to actively dominate other nations, other regions of the world, in order to avoid being dominated.[19] Much more commonly, however—and more ubiquitously across the French political spectrum—the tenor is milder, more defensive than aggressive: we need to be strong in order to preserve our own freedom of action, our right to self-determination. Finally, the third variant is the philanthropic one: we need to be strong so that we can share the benefits of our prosperity and unique Gallic culture with other peoples; this strain of thought oscillates between the old *mission civilisatrice* of colonial days (an explicitly racist doctrine) and a more docile and temperate notion associated with the peculiarly French term, *le besoin de rayonnement,* the need for creative self-expression, the desire to shine forth (literally) with the distinctive cultural contribution that one wishes to share with the rest of humankind.[20]

Though all three of these variants are important, it is upon the second, the defensive, that I wish to concentrate here—for it is both the most common and most influential of the three, and it provides one of the keys to understanding postwar French attitudes toward science and technology. The roots of this defensive mentality are complex; they can be traced to the final decades of the nineteenth century, the aftermath of another humiliating defeat at the hands of the Germans.[21] With a mixture of bitterness and grudging admiration, the French looked on as Germany transformed itself between 1870 and 1900 into the foremost commercial and military power of Europe; one could debate endlessly about the sources of German dynamism, about the reasons for France's apparent inability to keep up the pace, about the relative strengths and weaknesses of Gallic or Teutonic culture, but the underlying fact of Germany's preponderance could not be denied.[22]

One might think that the French victory in World War I would have led to an easing of these fears, at least temporarily, but in fact the opposite occurred. The French were grimly aware that Germany had knocked Russia out of the war and held its own for four years against the combined efforts of France and Britain; only the intervention of the immense United States had finally tipped the balance. A terrified victor, France therefore strove hard in the en-

suing peace negotiations to have Germany permanently dismembered, reduced to a more manageable size; but the British and Americans would not
hear of it.[23] After the United States reneged on President Wilson's promise of
a security guarantee for the Franco-German border, all that was left for an
embittered France was to begin weaving a network of diplomatic alliances
with Germany's neighbors in central and eastern Europe; the Maginot Line,
the final and most tangible expression of French apprehensions, began taking shape in the late 1920s.

Fear of being dominated from abroad, however, constituted only half of
this "discourse of anxiety." The other component consisted of profound self-
doubt, the conviction that French society itself was ailing, like a tree rotting
from the core outwards.[24] Nowhere was this more apparent than in the hys-
teria over demographic decline that weighed ever more heavily upon the
French public sphere during the first half of the twentieth century. The decline in births was real enough: French population growth had begun to slow
dramatically in the mid-nineteenth century, and barely hovered at minimal
replacement levels by the year 1914. Then came the slaughter of the Great
War, followed by two decades of actual population *decline*. France was the
first major industrial country to experience such a phenomenon, and it came
at a time when other nations' population numbers were briskly rising, and
when prevailing economic theories closely linked economic vitality with
demographic growth.[25]

These long-running fears provided the historical backdrop for the su-
preme national trauma of World War II. In 1944, therefore, when General de
Gaulle called not only for the reconstruction of his country but for a full-scale
renovation, a basic re-thinking and restructuring, his words did not fall on
deaf ears. Not only statesmen of Left and Right, but also broad segments of
the population, entered after 1944 into a tacit but steely-hard agreement: we
will never let another "1940" happen to us again; we will make ourselves so
technologically strong and so economically vigorous that we will never find
ourselves at any other nation's mercy again. Here lay the essence of technological Darwinism. Rapid and sustained economic growth, in the eyes of
many French citizens, became not just a desirable goal but a matter of maintaining national independence; technology became not just a vehicle for enhancing the quality of life, but a pivotal factor in providing basic economic
and military security. It was true, to be sure, that over the postwar decades
many important groups within French society voiced a deep uneasiness
about the headlong pursuit of technological advance, and feared the effects it
might have on their culture: from Parisian intellectuals to farmers in the
provinces, from nationalist politicians to student activists in the countercul-

ture, the misgivings were as diverse in origin as they were heartfelt. But when the chips were down, for a majority of French citizens, the other fear—of falling behind, of losing national autonomy—ultimately took priority in their feelings.

In discussing the rhetoric of technological Darwinism, we must take care not to reify this concept, as if it were the expression of an undifferentiated and unchanging consensus within French society: for it remained at all times a contested cultural phenomenon, taking subtly different forms in the eyes of many different constituencies over the years. Indeed, one source of its enduring influence probably derived precisely from the fact that it could adapt quite malleably to the worldviews of highly diverse groups of French men and women. A communist like Georges Marchais might put the emphasis on American corporate penetration of the French economy, while a Gaullist like Michel Debré would stress the long tradition of French military and diplomatic *grandeur;* but always the underlying message revolved around a common theme of national independence and the insidious forces that threatened to undermine or erode it.[26]

The Great Renewal

Three fundamental assumptions animated the men who steered France into the new economic era of the late 1940s—figures like the economic planner Jean Monnet, the iconoclastic politician Pierre Mendès-France, and the high civil servant François Bloch-Lainé.[27] First, France would have to overhaul its economy from the bottom up if it hoped to remain a significant player in world affairs; nothing less than an economic revolution would suffice. Second, a key element of this renewal, the foundation of economic and military power in the postwar world, would lie in the domain of scientific and technological innovation. And third, only active leadership by the state could push this scientific and technological innovation with sufficient speed and effectiveness. For a mid-sized nation like France, only strong government intervention could provide the kind of dynamism that would allow French technology (and hence French power) to remain competitive with such giants as Germany had shown itself to be, and the United States and Soviet Union now promised to become.[28]

Thus, the old French tradition of *dirigisme,* of intervention by state officials to channel and reshape the market economy, found a perfect outlet in the postwar ideology of technological Darwinism: for here was a noble cause in which the considerable energies of government planners, statisticians, financial experts, and researchers could be fruitfully harnessed—an exciting confluence of patriotism and scientific discovery. The historian Thomas

Hughes, in his pathbreaking study of technological innovation in the United States since the nineteenth century, coined the term "technological enthusiasm" to describe the powerful cultural current that emerged among American elites—an ebullient, self-confident, yet also deeply pragmatic attitude that sought technological solutions to the manifold social and economic problems of modernity.[29] In France after World War II, this kind of technological enthusiasm took hold with a vengeance—and not only among the policymakers and educated classes. Opinion polls, electoral results, the tone of the mass media: all signs indicated that broad swaths of the French public shared and supported the soaring technological ambitions of their leaders.[30]

To be sure, in France as in America, important undercurrents of dissent, of technophobia and antimodern anxiety, soon manifested themselves, and we will explore these undercurrents more fully in the chapters to come. In the United States, writes Thomas Hughes, especially after 1945, ever-larger numbers of Americans began to question various aspects of industrial society and its underlying notion of linear technological progress.[31] Recent research by cultural historians has suggested that many French men and women during the 1950s and '60s were experiencing the same concerns and misgivings about technology as their American counterparts; yet most of them apparently failed to realize that they in fact *shared* these concerns with their contemporaries across the Atlantic.[32] America, in French imagery, appeared most often as a young and somewhat callow nation that had moved swiftly and serenely into a new era, uncritically embracing even the most extreme aspects of a technological society. In the French case, therefore, anxiety about modernization often tended to take shape as anxiety about becoming "Americanized"—and it contributed to a lasting strain of anti-Americanism in French postwar culture, both among intellectuals and, to a lesser degree, among the citizenry in general.

Nevertheless, this trepidation about France's entry into technological modernity only rarely resulted in an outright rejection of scientific and technological innovation. In the French case, we encounter during the postwar decades a set of attitudes toward technology and tradition that can only be described as profoundly conflicted and contradictory in nature. At the most immediate level, one finds the differing responses of a wide variety of constituencies, some of them retaining a full-bore technological enthusiasm, others shading off along a spectrum of attitudes ranging from cautious optimism to scepticism to outright fear.[33] But even this notion of a spectrum can mislead us, for it fails to capture the fact that conflicting attitudes sometimes animated *the same individual* at different moments. One of the most aggressive proponents of crash-modernization, Charles de Gaulle himself, was also one of the most vocal and eloquent in lamenting the passing of traditional France—the France of Madère, with its slow-paced village life and endearing heritage of ancient habits and ways.[34] This statesman who sought to incarnate the French renewal, the new spirit of postwar dynamism, also delighted in the fact that he was identified in common parlance with his quaint home village—as the man of Colombey-les-Deux-Eglises.

Perhaps the most accurate way to sum up this paradoxical complex of attitudes is to say that many French citizens, in the postwar era, remained lucidly and painfully aware of the cultural costs of modernization; but they told themselves that in the end they had no alternative.[35] "Scientific and technological progress," wrote Raymond Aron in 1968, with a tone of resignation,

> is cloaked in a kind of fatalism. When states decide to make supersonic airplanes in order to gain three hours in the New York–Paris hop—even though the time saved might be lost in the bottleneck between the airport and the center of town—those responsible in both the public and private sectors can only reply with the meaningless phrase, "You can't stop progress." Sometimes it seems that societies themselves have less and less mastery over their destiny as they employ technology to increase their mastery over their physical environment.[36]

And so the French—some with misgivings and some with unabashed eagerness—flung themselves into the adventure of high-stakes technological competition. Their efforts flowed into three partially overlapping areas: first, civilian technologies, such as the Caravelle, Concorde, and Airbus jetliners, the TGV or *train à grande vitesse* (high-speed train), the Plan Calcul computer project, the Minitel computer-telephone, and the Ariane rocket; second, military technologies, like the Mirage fighter aircraft and the *force de frappe,* the French nuclear striking-force; and finally, state-sponsored energy technologies, like the Thémis solar station and the massive network of nuclear-powered electric generators.

For the sociologist Elie Cohen, one of the great innovations inaugurated by France in the postwar decades consisted in the invention of a new kind of enterprise, known as the *grand programme,* or large-scale project. The pattern began in the late 1940s, in the immediate aftermath of the war, and continued through the 1990s (though Cohen believes the era of this kind of state-sponsored enterprise is now over): an ambitious, world-class technological goal, such as the creation of the world's fastest train; a powerful and independent institution to oversee the project, composed of a hybrid between private enterprise and state ownership; lavish financial resources, with state coffers providing an implicit safety net; guaranteed markets for the final product, thanks to state subsidies; and most important of all, an underlying logic of nurturing national technological prowess, strengthening national independence, enhancing the national image.[37] Most of the showcase technologies mentioned above were created by *grands programmes* (the most obvious exception being Thémis, the scale of whose financing qualifies it more for the term *modeste programme*).

In the United States, the closest parallel would be the creation of NASA, the National Aeronautics and Space Administration, in 1958; but NASA remained the exception rather than the rule in America's high technology projects, because the climate of U.S. opinion favored the private sector over government leadership for such purposes (and NASA found its roles steadily trimmed, its mission steadily narrowed, as the decades went by).[38] In postwar France, by contrast, *grands programmes* became a familiar instrument of policy; governments turned to them almost by reflex, by default, whenever French prestige or mastery in a given technological domain seemed precarious.[39] Some of these undertakings, like the development of the TGV, ultimately exceeded their creators' expectations, becoming not only technological showpieces but significant commercial successes (see chapter 7 below); others flopped ignominiously, like the Plan Calcul of the 1960s, France's ill-starred effort to create a national champion in the global computer industry—a sort of "Silicon-sur-Seine."[40] Here it is useful to look in greater depth at one of the more renowned *grands programmes,* the supersonic Concorde, which produced mixed results, and elicited a revealing array of responses from the French citizenry.

Machine/Symbol: The Concorde

Antoine de Saint-Exupéry, the swashbuckling pilot and writer of pre–World War II days, thoroughly captured the French popular imagination in the 1930s with his books *Terre des hommes* and *Vol de nuit:* he described his solo flights through the night skies of Africa, carrying sacks of airmail in a Breguet 14 monoplane with an open cockpit, nothing but brilliant stars everywhere above and dark trackless sands below, the wind in his face, the roar of the engine, the smell of fuel, the sense of power and of infinite smallness.[41] Human hands controlling a magnificent machine: to fly, and to do it well, with style.

Concorde, the world's first supersonic commercial airliner, appears to have exerted a similar hold on broad segments of French culture during the 1960s and '70s. The idea to build such a plane had been circulating among the engineers and planners of the French aircraft industry since the late 1950s; similar ideas had been appearing at roughly the same time on drawing-boards in Britain, the United States, and the Soviet Union.[42] The French aircraft industry had enjoyed considerable success with its creation of one of the world's first jet-powered passenger liners, the Caravelle, in the early 1950s; and now French designers hoped to repeat the *éclat* by breaking through into a truly new era of air travel with a Super-Caravelle, a full-sized supersonic transport (SST).[43] The only problem was money. Even the industrial giants of the United States, like Boeing, McDonnell-Douglas, and Lockheed, had been brought up short by the magnitude of projected development costs for an SST; the French, a fortiori, found themselves completely stymied.[44]

A way out of the impasse emerged at the Paris Air Show of 1961, when British officials came forward with the idea of an aeronautical *entente cordiale*, a joint Franco-British project to build an SST. The French responded eagerly, for the British aircraft industry at the time was roughly three times larger than the French, and the British had already done considerable research on supersonics.[45] The two countries duly signed a treaty in November 1962, pledging to go fifty-fifty on the costs, the work, and the glory.

By and large, the Franco-British teams worked together remarkably well; most aeronautical experts ultimately agreed that this unprecedented cross-Channel collaboration produced a technical triumph, a first-rate aircraft.[46] Nevertheless, frictions inevitably emerged. One revealing tug-of-war went on for four years: it centered on what the new aircraft's name should be. Someone finally came up with "Concorde," but the British balked at the *e* on the end, which would make the entire project sound French. Back and forth between Bristol and Toulouse, London and Paris, tense delegations and nervous memos; in the end, the British gave in. "The *e* stands for excellence, England, Europe, entente cordiale," said the British Minister of Technology Tony Benn with a wry smile.[47]

The problem with Concorde, most analysts now agree, lay not in the technical challenge but in the sanguine commercial projections and assumptions on which the project had originally been based. From a financial point of view, the plane became an unmitigated disaster: it cost approximately ten times more than initially estimated; it failed to attract buyers outside the captive markets of the French and British national airlines, Air France and British Airways; and it continued to require large annual infusions of cash just to keep it flying.[48]

Tempers still flare, thirty years later, when it comes to laying out the causes of this commercial fiasco. Particularly in France, the impression remains strong that the Americans were extremely poor losers, that they could not bear the humiliation of their own failure to build an SST (Boeing having thrown in the towel in 1971), and therefore resorted to all manner of dirty tricks to ensure the commercial failure of this European technological upstart.[49] American airline companies stubbornly refused to order Concordes for their fleets; the Port Authority of New York banned the Concorde from flying into Kennedy airport because of the craft's alleged noise levels; American scientists published articles questioning the safety of flying at the Concorde's high cruise altitudes, citing the possible effects of space radiation; and finally, American environmentalists led an international crusade to ground the Concorde, on account of the plane's possible harm to the earth's fragile ozone layer.[50] The popular weekly magazine *Paris-Match* gave a fair measure of the mood in France with its front cover for December 30, 1972: a bleeding Concorde lying upside-down in the grass like a mortally-wounded bird, the shaft of an arrow projecting starkly from its underbelly—framed by a shrieking headline, "Concorde Assassiné par les Américains?"[51]

In retrospect, despite these Atlantic ill-feelings, the most substantial reasons for the Concorde's commercial failure can be found more simply in a precise set of mistakes made by the plane's designers at the early planning stages. Briefly put, these designers assumed that the excitement and prestige of flying at Mach 2.2 (1,350 m.p.h.) would more than compensate for all manner of other "inconveniences" in the plane's operation: high fuel consumption, relatively short flying range, relatively small number of passengers, sonic booms, and so on. Technical considerations dictated that this narrow-bodied plane could not carry more than 112 passengers (no more than 70 in hot weather), and for a maximum range of 4,039 miles; thus, it could easily trim three hours off the Paris—New York route, but it would have to stop twice to refuel when flying from London to Sydney. Ultimately, the subsonic Boeing 747, also developed during the 1960s, with a range of 10,000 miles, could reach Sydney from London nonstop, and hence *in less time* than Concorde; and the 747 cost *70 percent* less per passenger-seat-mile to operate.[52] Sonic booms, moreover, constituted an unavoidable side-effect of supersonic travel; the Concorde's routes had to include large stretches over water or desert to accommodate the exceedingly noisy transition to supersonic speed. Most countries, therefore, when confronted with a request from British Airways or Air France to fly supersonic craft routinely over their territory, understandably said no—and such refusals could not reasonably be attributed to American intriguing.[53] Already as early as 1978, therefore, a mere two years after the supersonic craft had first entered regular service, production of new Concordes had stopped for good.

How did most French citizens view this story? With aggrieved pride. A nationwide poll conducted in 1975, just as the Concorde was being readied for regular passenger service, asked the French if their country had done the right thing by embarking on this *grand programme*.[54] By a margin of 61 percent (yes) against 27 percent (no), they supported the government's decision to build the Concorde. These opinions cut across professional categories, political orientations, and gender and class divisions: a sizable majority of the French clearly felt that, despite the high cost, the adventure had proven worthwhile.

To be sure, the plane had its detractors. One of the most insistent was the journalist Jean-Jacques Servan-Schreiber, the author well known in France for his bestselling book published in 1967, *Le défi américain*, "The American Challenge." Servan-Schreiber objected to the Concorde because he regarded it as a spectacular waste of money, money that desperately needed to be spent on substantive programs to strengthen European industrial competitiveness.[55] In retrospect, Servan-Schreiber proved at least partly right: the Concorde absorbed scarce funds that could have been spent on a different aeronautics program, the development of the Airbus—a less glamorous, but ultimately more lucrative high-tech undertaking, in which the Europeans would finally succeed by the 1980s at competing with the Americans on their own terms.[56]

Yet most French citizens did not see it this way. To a nation that had taken its share of hard knocks in the preceding decades—the Depression, 1940, Vichy, Dienbienphu, Suez, Algeria—the Concorde offered a powerful opportunity for self-affirmation. The Americans had tried and failed to build their own SST; the Russians, for their part, did build an SST, the Tupolev 144, which looked so much like the Franco-British plane that journalists dubbed it the "Concordsky."[57] Unfortunately for the Russians, the "Concordsky" crashed at the Paris Air Show of 1973, and was ignominiously relegated to cargo service between Moscow and Alma-Ata for the remainder of its short service life. And so the French could say to themselves, as one found them saying in newspapers ranging from the left-wing *L'Humanité* to the conservative *Le Figaro*, "we succeeded where all the others failed."[58]

In this sense, one might conclude that the Concorde served a function in postwar French culture roughly analogous to the role played by the Apollo program in the America of the 1960s; for the emotions felt by American citizens when Neil Armstrong set foot on the moon were not all that far removed from what the French felt when they saw their sleek supersonic aircraft.[59] Expensive it certainly was, and not particularly useful in any direct sense (apart from the development of scientific and technological know-how). But above all, the Concorde gave the French a potent psychological boost, making them feel that they, too, when they applied themselves, could earn a place within modernity's inner circle of winners.

The Role of Nuclear Technology within the National Discourse of Anxiety

It is only with this broad historical and cultural backdrop in mind—the discourse of anxiety going back to the nineteenth century, the postwar mood of technological Darwinism—that one can place French nuclear endeavors in their proper context. For the French are in a class by themselves when it comes to attitudes toward nuclear technology; in their visceral and intense relationship with the invisible forces of the fissile atom, they stand out dramatically among the other nations of the world, nuclear and non-nuclear powers alike.

France was arguably the world's pioneer in nuclear research, the Paris laboratory of Marie and Pierre Curie performing some of the earliest and most pathbreaking experiments on radioactivity and its causes. The Curies' daughter Irène carried on her parents' innovative science, working closely with her equally brilliant physicist husband, Frédéric Joliot-Curie—whose fierce egalitarianism is reflected even in his name, which he insisted on hyphenating to match the change made by his wife after their marriage.[60] (Some wags in the scientific world suggested that adding the name "Curie," for a nuclear physicist, could hardly be construed as a terrible sacrifice.) The Joliot-Curies continued throughout the 1930s to produce first-rate research (despite unbelievably niggardly funding from the French state); they received a joint Nobel Prize in 1934, and were among the élite handful of scientists worldwide who, in 1939, could grasp how close the world was to the possibility of a nuclear chain reaction—and hence nuclear bombs.[61]

Frédéric Joliot-Curie became a convert to communism during these years, and spent the war dividing his time between the Resistance and the struggle to promote French physics; in 1944, with the liberation of Paris, he was named head of the agency that would coordinate French academic research, the CNRS (Centre National de la Recherche Scientifique). A fervent nationalist, he lost no time in shaking up the sclerotic French scientific establishment; for he felt a sense of urgency that he communicated quite effectively to those around him, General de Gaulle included. Joliot-Curie was removed from his powerful position in 1950, a casualty of the deepening Cold War atmosphere; but by this point, France possessed an advanced nuclear research establishment, well funded and staffed by some of the world's best physicists.

The historian Gabrielle Hecht provides an incisive analysis of the first three decades of French nuclear policy in her book *The Radiance of France,* showing the deep link between the unfolding of that policy and the goal of *rayonnement,* the assertion of a unique French identity on the stage of world power.[62] For Hecht, the key to understanding this linkage lies in the concept of "technopolitics," the sometimes clashing, sometimes overlapping strategies used by a wide array of technological actors to harness political ideas— such as the imagery of national uniqueness—in advancing their own individual or group agendas. French visions of national identity, she argues, were bound together in a tight bidirectional relationship with French visions of high technology: the two domains mutually shaped each other over time. Thus, for example, the Gaullist conception of French *grandeur* drew heavily on the prestige conferred by cutting-edge nuclear systems; conversely, those technological systems were themselves shaped and reshaped many times over (from the design stage through to final construction) by the clashing political priorities and shifting political fortunes of the men who championed them.

Perhaps the most striking fact about France's emergence as a nuclear power is that no single meeting or series of meetings, no single group of individuals working together, no single confluence of key events, can be identified as *the* point at which the nation's leadership decided to endow France with nuclear weapons.[63] Rather, what we find is a sequence of incremental "mini-decisions," some technical in nature, some budgetary, some administrative—a long series of tacit compromises and gradual technological advances accumulating, sliding into one another, over a decade and a half. French politicians and scientists in the Fourth Republic appeared extremely reluctant to come out and openly say, "Let's build a Bomb!" Instead, they always opted for keeping the door open, for continuing lines of research and technical development that would leave available the option of building atomic weapons in the future—without committing anyone to an explicit military policy in the present.[64] And so, one by one, the pieces of the puzzle quietly came together: a steady expansion of funding, allowing the newly-created CEA, or Commissariat à l'Energie Atomique, to double its facilities every two years; a decision among scientists in 1951 to build a new generation of high-powered reactors, capable of producing weapons-grade plutonium; a top-secret cabinet meeting in 1954 under the prime ministership of Pierre Mendès-France, giving the green light for exploratory studies of a nuclear bomb; an international environment of increasing East-West tensions, coupled with the chilling prospect of West German rearmament within NATO; growing pressures from the French military, which became ever more keenly interested in the physicists' string of successes. All these develop-ments gradually accumulated, with a weirdly impersonal but also seemingly irresistible momentum.

Only after the collapse of the Fourth Republic and the advent of de Gaulle's new government in 1958 did a French leader finally come forward and forthrightly say, "We have decided to build our own nuclear arsenal."[65] But by that point the decision—it might aptly be dubbed "the-gigantic-decision-that-no-one-made"—had already been working its way into the very core of French institutions for more than a decade. Within less than two years of de Gaulle's announcement, in February 1960, the first French pluto-nium bomb detonated amid the sands of the Sahara; throughout the decade that followed, the nuclear striking-force, or *force de frappe,* absorbed between sixty and seventy percent of France's total budget for military equipment.[66] By 1969, when de Gaulle resigned, France was well on the way to developing a full-fledged strategic triad of nuclear delivery-systems: land-based missiles, submarine-based missiles, and strategic bomber aircraft.

Why did France need such a fearsome arsenal? De Gaulle's answer, driven home in speeches, television addresses, and budgetary debates, revolved continually around the same theme: these weapons provided the key to na-tional autonomy.[67] Both military sovereignty and an independent foreign policy, he argued, hinged on the special status that nuclear arms conferred; henceforth the French territory would become a sanctuary, a haven that no invader could violate without facing incineration. To be sure, international alliances would continue to play a key role, and France would participate vigorously in the activities of the United Nations and other world organiza-tions. But all these activities would rest on a foundation of rigorous military independence. To those sceptics who pointed out that the French arsenal remained considerably smaller than those of the superpowers, de Gaulle replied that it would soon become large enough to threaten *any* aggressor na-tion (including the superpowers themselves) with devastating retaliation for an attack. France, the General assured his audiences, was now safer from military invasion than it had ever been in the whole of its long history.[68]

The French citizenry, over the years, evidently found this logic more and more compelling. If we survey a half-century of French opinion polls from the late 1940s through the 1990s, we can discern a broad evolution or tra-jectory.[69] From the end of the war through the late 1950s, public opinion vacillated on the question of acquiring a French Bomb: some polls came out with majorities in favor, others with majorities against. After the first test ex-plosion of a French nuclear device in 1960, the picture began to change: some polls now showed considerable majorities in support of de Gaulle's nuclear defense policy, but others continued to suggest an evenly divided public. By the early 1970s, the balance had tilted clearly to one side: ever-growing majorities of French citizens were declaring themselves supporters of the *force de frappe* with each passing year, and this trend continued dra-matically throughout the 1980s.[70] Thus, between 1980 and 1983—at the same time as the rest of Europe witnessed an epochal groundswell of peace activism, with antinuclear protestors in the hundreds of thousands swell-ing the streets of London, Rome, Amsterdam, Brussels, and Bonn—France remained stubbornly silent, on the sidelines. French citizens, queried by journalists and pollsters about their conspicuous non-participation in the European pacifist wave, said that they sympathized with the protestors in other nations who were denouncing U.S. and Soviet missiles in Europe—but they resoundingly reaffirmed their support for their own national *force de frappe,* by margins as high as 72 percent ("favorable opinion") against 15 per-cent ("unfavorable opinion")![71]

One key reason for this emergence of a strong national consensus sur-rounding the nuclear striking-force lies in the shifting politics of the French Left. Throughout the 1950s and '60s, both the major French left-wing par-ties, the Socialists and Communists, tenaciously resisted France's develop-ment of atomic weapons; during the 1970s, however, they began to veer away from this position.[72] For the PCF (Parti Communiste Français), the as-tonishing volte-face took place in 1977: adopting a very Gaullist-sounding stance, the party leadership declared that France's independence (particu-larly from the imperialist pressures of American foreign policy) absolutely re-quired a French nuclear deterrent, and that the party would therefore throw its full support behind the *force de frappe* in the budgetary and political deci-sions of the years to come.[73] For the Socialists, the turnaround took place more slowly and subtly; but by 1981, when François Mitterrand gained the French presidency, the Socialist Party had also undergone its own Gaullist conversion. Mitterrand, citing the need for France to conduct its own foreign policy outside the rigid polarity of the Cold War bloc system, concluded that no nation could do this without playing the nuclear card; in the end, he be-came a staunch advocate of maintaining and modernizing the French deter-rent.[74]

Thus, with the main parties of the Left joining the already widespread currents of support for the *force de frappe* on the Right, precious little politi-cal space remained for the development and expression of French pacifist sentiment. France had possessed a fairly vocal and well-organized peace movement since the 1950s, the Mouvement de la Paix; but this was widely (and accurately) identified in French opinion as a puppet of the communists.

"Le pacifisme," therefore, became more a label of contempt and derision for many French citizens than a badge of honorable dissent: it was associated either with the weak-kneed, fuzzy-minded naïveté that had led to Munich— or, worse still, with insidious machinations emanating from Moscow.[75] Independent, non-communist peace organizations remained small and marginal throughout the postwar era.[76]

Some scholars have put forth the argument that the much-vaunted French "consensus" surrounding the *force de frappe* is in fact largely a myth, a convenient fiction invented (and regularly invoked) by Parisian ruling elites because the very existence of such a myth has narrowed the range of debate over military policy and discouraged potential dissenters from airing their views.[77] This argument, however, remains unpersuasive. While it is true that the *force de frappe* had to be pushed upon a divided citizenry by executive fiat during the late 1950s and 1960s, the sheer preponderance of the opinion poll majorities in favor of the French Bomb from the 1970s on cannot be argued away. It also seems implausible to maintain that the French would allow *any* government to ram a genuinely unpopular policy down their throats: again and again, in 1958, in 1968, in 1986, they rose up with massive (and effective) protests when they felt that their opinions were being flaunted by those in power. If the *force de frappe* had truly been unwanted by significant segments of the French citizenry, those dissidents would undoubtedly have organized and risen up (as various groupings could and did do on so many other occasions) to ensure that the politicians paid attention to their wishes.

Still, all this should not lead us to conclude that France is a nation of hawkish hardliners. Indeed, on most issues relating to military security, the French express views that are solidly in line with those of other West Europeans: the dangers of war, optimal levels of defense spending, perceptions of a Soviet threat during the Cold War, perceptions of the East-West military balance, the first use of nuclear weapons in a crisis, the need for international talks and treaties, the pursuit of arms control—in all these areas, the statistics of French opinion polls fit squarely into the mainstream of West European public opinion.[78] Only on two issues do the French stand apart: the *force de frappe,* and the need for NATO. Between 1967 and 1987, West Europeans were asked from time to time whether they considered NATO essential to European security. In all cases, a majority answered "yes." But the margin of support for NATO, averaged over a twenty-year period, once again placed the French in a class by themselves: 71 percent of the British deemed NATO vital to their security, 72 percent of the Dutch, 77 percent of the West Germans—and only 42 percent of the French.[79]

De Gaulle had of course withdrawn France from NATO's unified command structure in 1966, protesting against American dominance over that organization; and a great many French citizens evidently agreed with the General's sentiments, which he expressed in a famous press conference:

> France has retaken possession of its forces and has undertaken to give itself the means of nuclear deterrence. . . . In the hypothesis of a war between the two giants, . . . France would not automatically be the humble auxiliary of one of them; France would arrange for itself the chance to be other than a battlefield for their expeditionary corps and a target for their alternating bombs.[80]

Although it was not clear exactly *how*, in the event of such a crisis, the General's actions would protect France from the grim fate he described here, the underlying intent in his policy remained constant (and was understood as such by the broader citizenry): to preserve French freedom of action as much as possible; to avoid being dragged into a war that was not of one's own making; to escape from a situation in which the strategic destiny of France lay in the hands of decision-makers in Washington or Moscow.

Few indeed were the French men and women who did not find these broad goals strongly compelling: the irreducible psychological appeal of an absolute weapon that was absolutely French. Almost as if by instinct, it was to this core argument that the Socialist Prime Minister Michel Rocard still turned in 1989, the year of the Cold War's ending, as he sought to justify France's nuclear program before a sceptical Australian audience. "Having been invaded three times in less than a century," Rocard explained, "France cannot entrust her security to anyone else. That is why my country has built an independent deterrent."[81] The logic remained as simple and clear in the mind of this socialist as it had been in de Gaulle's mind in 1958, when he first publicly announced France's nuclear ambitions; the General, if he had been present to hear Rocard's speech, would have had good reason for satisfaction at the enduring power of his legacy.

French Perceptions of the *Rainbow Warrior* Affair

In July 1985, the international environmentalist organization Greenpeace collided "full steam ahead" into this Gaullist consensus, with grim consequences for all concerned. Greenpeace's leadership in England had decided early in 1985 to send the *Rainbow Warrior*, the flagship of the organization's peace flotilla, to protest a series of nuclear tests scheduled by the French government on the tiny Pacific atoll of Moruroa.[82] In Paris, the French secret service, which closely monitored Greenpeace's activities, immediately began making preparations to thwart the activists' plans.[83] Here, in this unhappy confrontation, we find one of the more prominent and enduring sources of France's widespread image as an "ungreen" nation; but the real issue, in the end, lay not with the *Rainbow Warrior*'s environmentalist identity, but rather with the threat this small ship posed to the hallowed talisman of French military autonomy.

De Gaulle's government had chosen Moruroa as the new site for French nuclear testing in 1964, after Algerian independence had forced the closure of French test bases in the remote Sahara.[84] The small circle of coral reefs and palm-studded islets, whose colonial relationship with France dated back to the nineteenth century, became the focus of round-the-clock construction work, as engineers built runways, hangars, wharves, and a research complex, as well as blast bunkers layered in meters-thick concrete.[85] The first nuclear test took place in September 1966, a 120-kiloton atmospheric explosion directly observed by President de Gaulle himself (from aboard a French navy cruiser thirty kilometers away). Within days, reports of radioactive fallout began to trickle in from inhabited islands downwind of the explosion; the French government sent in teams of experts, who declared that the area was safe.[86] Throughout the decades that followed, the blasts continued at regular intervals (shifting from atmospheric to underground detonations after 1975); with equal regularity, the peoples of the South Pacific lodged formal complaints and demanded a stop to the French testing program. To no avail: the officials in Paris remained adamant, insisting that the health risks had been brought completely under control, and that the tests were justified by the highest reasons of national security.

It was here that, as early as 1972, Greenpeace's eco-activists found an important cause to champion, with their flamboyant (and dangerous) tactics of direct action around nuclear test sites, harrying the French military with their inflatable Zodiac boats, focusing media attention on the continuing tensions between islanders and government.[87] In Paris, the DGSE (Direction Générale des Services Extérieurs), or secret service, began systematically targeting Greenpeace as a serious threat to the national interest: missions were sent not only to spy on the eco-activists, but also to infiltrate their ranks with undercover agents, and on many occasions to engage in "dirty tricks" ranging from financial obstruction to mechanical sabotage of Greenpeace ships.[88] Until 1985, this rough-and-tumble struggle between the eco-activists and the French spy agency had remained fairly low-key; but here the game turned more serious.

Sometime early in 1985, the leaders of the French secret service got wind of the *Rainbow Warrior*'s planned trip to Moruroa; they gave the go-ahead for two teams of agents to travel to New Zealand and make preparations to sink the ship when it anchored in Auckland harbor. On July 10 the French agents struck.[89] A little after 8:00 P.M. two frogmen in a rubber Zodiac set off across Auckland harbor, headed for the *Warrior's* mooring at Marsden Wharf. Aboard the thirty-year-old converted trawler, the Greenpeace crew were meeting with the skippers of New Zealand's peace flotilla, plotting strategy for the weeks to come. The wet-suited divers drew near, taking advantage of the darkness and the mist, and planted two underwater bombs on the ship's hull, one near the propeller, the other outside the engine room. Then they returned to their bobbing dinghy and silently paddled away. A few minutes before midnight, the explosives went off, ripping huge holes in the *Warrior's* hull below the waterline. It sank quickly, leaving little time for those on board to abandon ship; one of them, a 34-year-old Portuguese named Fernando Pereira, drowned.

The French agents immediately scattered and began leaving New Zealand by various prearranged routes; but two of them, a man and woman named Major Alain Mafart and Captain Dominique Prieur, were arrested the following day by the Auckland police. After three days of questioning, it became clear to the New Zealand authorities that they were dealing with a covert operation emanating from Paris.[90] The French government indignantly denied any knowledge or involvement; its spokespersons suggested that perhaps the KGB had been responsible. Nevertheless, as the police investigation proceeded, and as the French press began pursuing leads within the Paris bureaucracy, the true status of Mafart and Prieur became increasingly hard to deny. On September 18, an investigative reporter for *Le Monde* finally broke through the government's defenses: the newspaper published a story that directly implicated the Minister of Defense, Charles Hernu, in the sabotage operation. Hernu angrily denied the charges, but two days later he and Admiral Pierre Lacoste, the head of the DGSE, tendered their resignations to Mitterrand. The French Prime Minister Laurent Fabius appeared on television to make a somber admission:[91] French agents *had* sunk the Greenpeace ship; they had acted on orders from the Minister of Defense;[92] and a systematic coverup had been attempted. Fabius, claiming that he and Mitterrand had known nothing of all this, formally apologized to the government of New Zealand.

French opinion polls during this crisis painted a clear picture: a wide majority (78 percent) of the nation's citizens felt that bombing the Greenpeace ship had been wrong, that the operation itself had been badly bungled, and that the subsequent coverup was disgraceful;[93] but by equally impressive majorities, they insisted that the nuclear tests in the South Pacific should go on (60 percent), and that the French government was in the right when it took "forceful steps" to ensure that such tests would not be blocked by environmental activists (56 percent).[94] "Sabotaging the *Rainbow Warrior* was not an abominable crime," wrote one editorialist for the popular newspaper *Le Point:*

> Nobody wanted to kill anyone else, and, apart from the ineptitude with which it was carried out, it was a perfectly banal operation. All the great democracies (not to mention the world's dictatorships) regularly carry out operations like this: as long as they are successful, no one loses any sleep over them.[95]

Feeling that they were being unjustly singled out for criticism in the world's press, the French rallied around their government. Although 52 percent of the population believed that Mitterrand and Fabius had indeed known about the sabotage operation from the start, fully 65 percent felt that the president should not consider resigning from his post.[96] Even the French greens, though they issued a few muted public statements condemning the violence done to their fellow activists, ultimately adopted a relatively sullen and passive stance. Any vehement act of protest, they felt, would only alienate potential supporters at a time when the identity of their newly formed political organization was just beginning to gel.[97]

Meanwhile, the French office of Greenpeace, which before the *Rainbow Warrior*'s sinking had been leading a fairly stable existence along the margins of the French environmental movement, suddenly found itself the object of a massive wave of vituperation. Its organizers received mountains of letters from outraged members, who proclaimed that "they were only too happy to support Greenpeace in its fight to save whales and seals, but that they refused to contribute to 'anti-French' actions."[98] Greenpeace-France finally closed shop, broke and memberless, in 1987 (it managed to open again two years later, with a small new staff and renewed chutzpah).[99]

Yet, in the end, there was more to the French reaction than mere patriotism or Gallic pride. Though most French citizens deplored the sinking of the Greenpeace vessel, their strong reactions during the ensuing months stemmed from a more visceral, and absolute, emotion: the conviction that Moruroa was indissociable from the *force de frappe,* and that attacking the *force de frappe* was tantamount to attacking France's most vital source of military security. Greenpeace, by seeking to undermine the nuclear program in the South Pacific, had touched one of the rawest nerves in the French body politic: the desire for national autonomy. In the eyes of most French citizens, their government's actions in vigorously countering this kind of threat seemed a wholly legitimate and essential form of self-defense; to be condemned for it before world opinion seemed grossly unfair, and made them close ranks in a defiant flush of collective anger.

> > >

Overall, one cannot help but be struck by the underlying similarities between the *force de frappe* and the Concorde: a proud will to power, a vibrant technological enthusiasm, resolute state leadership, a decades-long quest for national autonomy. The supersonic plane and the nuclear bomb: if we "decode" these machines, examining them the way an anthropologist might examine a totem or other symbolic artifact from another culture, we uncover two basic strains of postwar French history. At the most immediate level, we find a frantic struggle for respect and rank, but even more profoundly for security and self-sufficiency, waged in the realm of high technology.

At an even deeper level, we find in these two machines the quintessence of the worldview that environmentalism ultimately called into question— the very raison d'être for the rise of ecology as a political and cultural force. The Concorde and the nuclear bomb were embodiments of the word "more" —more speed, more complexity, more power, more economic growth, more prestige. Together they incarnated the Promethean spirit of the *trente glorieuses,* the boom years of rapidly rising technical achievement, of massively expanding intervention in the material world. These machines represented a symbolic mastery over the natural limits that had held back previous generations; they allowed human beings to burst through the sound barrier, to smash atoms, to harness and control elemental forces. In the eyes of the technologists, scientists, and politicians who brought such devices into being, nature was a domain to be explored, analyzed, and dominated, with instruments whose potency would have defied the imagination of a Louis Pasteur or even perhaps a Jules Verne. Nature was there for the taking, and the French, like the citizens of other postwar societies, took all they could.

But behind the Concorde, in its thundering takeoffs, trailed black plumes of smoke, lingering long in the sky —the harbingers of a cultural backlash to come. In the invisible deadliness of the Moruroa test sites, the fallout settling on nearby islands, the spent fuels silently pulsing in barrels underground, lay the intimation of problems without precedent, of gnawing doubts and questions, of rediscovered limits. Even as the *trente glorieuses* extended their powerful reach over the land, a new vision of nature was already forming.

Endangered Species:
The French Peasant

To my mind, the spectacle that overshadows all others, in the France of the past and especially today, is the collapse of a peasant society. An ancient France, a France of bourgs, villages, hamlets and scattered houses survived more or less unchanged until at least 1914 and some would say 1945. After 1945, it fell victim to the *trente glorieuses,* that period of unprecedented expansion which lasted until the 1970s.

Near Céret, where I live, the Aspre valley has now reverted to nature: today only brambles, shrubs, and broom flourish on the poor and untended soil. The population gave up, leaving everything just as it stood, as if evacuating an untenable position in wartime. But before that the position had been perfectly defensible. Life in the Aspre was not wretched: people were poor certainly, and it was a hard life, but that is not the same thing. As one of my friends, born in 1899 in a peasant family, used to put it humorously but accurately: "The only thing we were short of was money."
—Fernand Braudel, 1985[1]

The Rural Future: A Key Issue for the French Greens

Fernand Braudel, perhaps the most famous of postwar French historians, had made his mark in 1949, with the publication of *The Mediterranean,* a monumental study of life around this body of water lying at the crossroads between Africa, the Middle East, and Europe. What set his book apart, and immediately caught the eye of historians around the world, was Braudel's radical redefinition of time and space: instead of studying a nation, a war, a city, or a human biography, he set the boundaries of his research around the shores of an entire sea, spanning cultures, languages, climatic zones, economic systems. To match this vast new frame of reference, he articulated a new scale of historical time itself: the *longue durée* (or long-term perspective), a tracing of cumulative patterns of events over centuries instead of years. His metaphors gripped the imagination. "Civilizations," he wrote,

> like sand dunes, are firmly anchored to the hidden contours of the earth; grains of sand may come and go, blown into drifts or carried far away by the wind, but the dunes, the unmoving sum of innumerable movements, remain standing.[2]

Braudel shifted the balance of historical attention from the feverish "surface" movement of politics and individual life-stories to the ponderous, scarcely perceptible motion of the physical and socioeconomic environment. In another striking metaphor, he likened human beings and their everyday undertakings to ephemeral fireflies leaving pale, brief traces in the air—as compared with the immense time-structures of day and night, and the cycles of the seasons. Carried along on the crest of powerful long-term cycles—economic, social, demographic, environmental—human individuals, with all their hopes, endeavors, and conflicts, remained unaware that so many fundamental aspects of their lives had already been determined in advance. He sought in *The Mediterranean* to correct this anthropocentric distortion, restoring the primacy of a far larger scale of process and change.

And yet, by the time Braudel wrote his last book, shortly before his death in 1985, he had come up hard against a different reality: his tone reflected a new set of facts. For in the space of a few decades—the mere batting of an eye, compared to his customary *longue durée*—his native country had been utterly transformed. Patterns of life that had endured for centuries, even millennia, suddenly mutated or disappeared, like a movie in fast-forward. Populations vanished from the countryside; modes of farming changed and changed again; trade balances shifted; ancient villages became ghost towns; suburbs invaded the abandoned fields; high-tension wires and high-speed train rails sliced through quiet valleys; the very face of the land was recast. Braudel acknowledged this change, but never seems to have explicitly drawn the full theoretical conclusion, namely, that the *longue durée* was a thing of the past, well suited to a preindustrial era perhaps, but thoroughly inadequate to the frenetic pace (and sheer transformative dynamism) of postwar society.

His emotional response to this sea-change was quite clear, however. "Until we have more evidence," he wrote in 1985,

> I shall go on believing that the old peasant way of life survived by combining hard work, wisdom, and comparative comfort in a country which was after all rich in resources. I do not think it is right to look back on it as an epoch of wretchedness and heartache, since retrospectively the survival of the old balance appears to have produced an eminently workable solution. It is by no means clear that today's farming, which is developing in the direction of technology and social change, is necessarily and everywhere the best answer.[3]

Braudel was far from alone in experiencing the upheaval in the countryside with feelings of nostalgia and ambivalence: in memoirs, films, novels, newspaper articles, academic conferences, and countless town meetings, the French made it clear that they perceived the disappearance of the old rural world not just as an economic or demographic change, but as a spiritual loss, a deep wound in the tissue of their civilization.[4]

One cannot fully understand the environmental movement in France unless one takes into account this collapse of a peasant way of life and the strong cultural reaction it provoked. It is hard to overstate the affection felt by the French for their ancestral *paysage;* and the rise of ecology, in the French context, remained inseparable from the wrenching changes that overran this picturesque landscape during the *trente glorieuses.* How to keep the peasant world alive through the 21st century? How to take an anachronistic way of rural life and transform it, so that it retained its old charm yet also meshed successfully with the strictures and demands of a postindustrial economy? These were not just questions for sociologists or regional planners or agronomists: they became hot political issues, drawing upon emotions that ran deep. And in the end, they played a key role in the framing of a distinctively French vision of the relation between ecology and technological modernity.

> > >

In a sense, the fate of the traditional French peasant was sealed during the 1950s, when the governments of the Fourth Republic launched an ambitious plan to modernize the nation's agricultural system—mechanizing the family farms, introducing new high-yield seed strains, and encouraging a massive increase in the use of artificial pesticides and fertilizers.[5] Between 1946 and 1958, for example, the number of tractors churning through the soil of France multiplied ten-fold, from 56,000 to 560,000; in a mere four years, between 1954 and 1958, the number of mechanical reapers, threshers, and other agricultural machines doubled; by the 1980s, the land was being doused with eight times as many chemical pesticides and fertilizers as it had been in 1950.[6] Agricultural productivity grew even more rapidly than the rest of the French economy: a single farmer in 1980 was feeding four times as many persons as in 1950.[7]

If all this modernization was going to work, however, the ancient patch-work of France's countryside would have to give way to a process known as *remembrement*, the consolidation of disparate farm plots into larger units; only huge farms, cutting broad swaths through the land, could hope to com-pete with the economies of scale achieved in nations like Argentina, Canada, the United States, or the Soviet Union. In human terms, the government ex-perts acknowledged, this would mean a drastic reduction in the number of persons working the soil. An entire way of life—indeed, an entire way of see-ing the world—would have to give way to the demands of progress.[8]

As a result, from the 1950s to the 1990s, the population of France's farm-ers fell by 70 percent; the number of farms dropped by half, from two million to about one million.[9] This "rural exodus," as it was called, steadily drained the countryside; in hundreds of villages the same forlorn picture took shape, as declining population forced schools, shops, train stations, and post offices to close, leaving behind only a few old men and women, who waited out their days among decrepit stone houses and uncultivated fields.[10] Here for example was the scene chosen by the journalist Daniel Tacet to open his book, *A World Without Peasants* (1992):

> On December 9, 1987, Marguerite L. hanged herself from a rafter in the hayloft of her barn. Close to her cows. This is how France's peasants die when society makes it clear that they are no longer needed.[11]

Tacet—an expert on agriculture at the conservative newspaper *Le Figaro*—knew that the image of this sixty-year-old farm woman driven to despair by the harsh economic realities of the 1980s would touch a raw nerve among his readers. Indeed, one of the most striking aspects of the postwar rural trans-formation was the sense of helplessness that emanated from most French cit-izens, whether of Left or Right, city or country, as they watched it happening. Ruefully they repeated to each other (and to themselves) the stern dogma of modernization: the mechanisms of a global economy, and the currents of technological progress, are blind and implacable; they do not bend before the private misery of individuals like Marguerite L.[12] It was not until the 1990s—and partly through the persistent activism of the French greens—that one started to see a broader questioning of these harsh gospels of agribusiness and "globalization."[13]

Machine/Symbol: *Le Cheval Vapeur* (Farm tractor, or "Steam-Horse")

A farm tractor, in itself, is not a very exciting machine (unless you happen to be a farmer accustomed to plowing and hoeing by hand). Yet this relatively simple device arguably made an even greater impact on postwar France than the Concorde or the nuclear reactor. Economic relationships, demographic trends, patterns of consumption, cultural heritage—all these domains felt the reverberations caused by this mundane but ubiquitous technological product.

In the discussion that follows I approach the farm tractor indirectly, through the medium of cinema. I do this for two reasons: first, because what interests me here is not so much the machine itself, but the way it changed rural life; and movies, if treated appropriately, as the literary constructions they inevitably are, can help us gain a good deal of insight into the complexities of the rural world. Secondly, in the case of the farm tractor, we have an unusually sophisticated "document" at our disposal, the film *Le Cheval Vapeur,* by Maurice Failevic.[14]

When *Le Cheval Vapeur* first aired on French television in 1980, more than three decades had passed since a similar landmark movie on French rural life had last appeared before the French public: *Farrebique,* by Georges Rouquier (1947).[15] The difference between the two films was a telling one. In the shooting of *Farrebique,* Rouquier and his cinematic équipe had spent an entire year, 1945–46, living with a peasant family in the hilly fringes of the Auvergne. Rouquier adopted the structure of the four passing seasons to guide him in the narrative movement of the film, capturing the daily life on the farm, the dreams and worries of the peasants, the rhythms of nature and human labor. As a director, Rouquier carefully avoided romanticizing the farmer and his family, even encouraging them to speak from time to time in their local *patois,* which would have been incomprehensible to a Parisian. Yet the underlying tone of *Farrebique* is nonetheless one of reverence, of understated homage to an ancient way of life—an existence in which humans still adapted themselves to animals, plants, and stones, not the other way around.

Le Cheval Vapeur was strikingly different. Once again we have a richly textured evocation of French rural life, but this time the tone of the film is bittersweet—with the accent, by story's end, on the bitter. The scene is the late 1950s, somewhere in the remote valleys of south-central France: a classic peasant family, the grandfather (a widower) with his gnarled hands and *béret basque,* the eldest son (who has recently inherited the farm), his wife, and their two children, a boy and a girl. Already the technological advances of the 1950s can be picked out in the background: electric lighting (which had been lacking in the farmhouse of *Farrebique*), a small TV, running water—but still no telephone.

Enter the main character: the farm tractor. First the family debates intensely whether or not to buy such a machine. The grandfather pronounces himself against it, not because of any resistance to the technology itself, but because he opposes borrowing money in order to buy it: he has always avoided any form of debt like the plague. The father objects that some of the other farmers in the region have already mechanized their farms: "I'll never be able to compete with them, if I keep at it with my horse-drawn plow." The mother, who stays quietly in the background (but whose terse opinions are carefully heeded by the men) points out that their son has won a scholarship to continue his education in the nearby provincial town—and unless they buy the tractor, they will be obliged to keep him on the farm to help his father in the fields. This clinches the argument: they will buy the machine, not out of greed for expanding productivity, but out of fear that their neighbors will outstrip them, and out of a desire to free their son for higher education.

Off to the local office of the Crédit Agricole, the state bank established to encourage higher capitalization of farms in remote areas. They get their loan, the tractor arrives, shiny and new. All stand in a semicircle, in the old courtyard before the stone barn, as the father climbs on, nervously following the instructions. The engine roars, he puts it into gear, releases the clutch too quickly—it lurches forward like a bronco. Vast amusement all round. After a few more tries he gets the hang of it. Bouncing on his seat, down to the far end of the yard, then slowly coming around, back past his family, broadly beaming. Progress is good.

But the tractor, it turns out, is not just a machine. It is an element in a larger system, one key component in a more abstract network of interlocking assumptions and institutions. Failevic, the film's director, takes pains to show how the possession of this powerful tool ineluctably entails a new way of living on the land, a new way of seeing the soil, the crops, one's family, one's future. Or, to put it differently, the machine is actually far bigger than it looks, and the tractor constitutes only one small part of it.

Within days of the tractor's arrival, the father has already finished plowing all the old fields that once took weeks and weeks; he realizes he needs to buy or rent new fields if he is going to get his money's worth out of this amazing machine. The family's apple orchard, planted half a century before by the grandfather, has to come down: it is not nearly productive enough to justify devoting precious land to its harvest of scrawny fruits. Failevic lingers long upon the expression marking the grandfather's face, as he watches the tractor pulling down his old trees. Then the proliferation of new needs accelerates: tools and attachments to enhance the tractor's versatility, potent fertilizers to push the yield of the crops, special seed-strains that resist disease and bear a greater harvest. More trips to the Crédit Agricole, more loans.

The grandfather watches all this, distressed, perplexed. "Ils courent tout le temps," he complains—"They're running all the time." Until now, out in the fields, he and his son had taken a long midday break every day, sitting back against a tree, swigging from their liter-bottles of homemade wine and munching on bread and *saucisson,* listening to the buzz of insects, watching the clouds. Now the pressure has become too great: the invisible burden of debt hangs over them, and the word *rendement,* or productivity, becomes a sort of obsession. Every month the interest on the loans adds up and compounds itself: the farm will have to meet its sharply increased goals of *rendement,* or else. In the past, no doubt, the farm had gone through lean years, periods of drought or plant disease during which crops dwindled and belts had to tighten: but now the stakes loom much higher than that, for if the family fails to meet its repayment schedule, the resulting bankruptcy will mean the loss of the farm itself.

The father grits his teeth and works harder; he rises earlier, tending his crops by lamplight in the hours before dawn; his wife comes out in the fields to help; the son comes home for the summer and pitches in; late at night they all collapse in their beds, exhausted. And the labor pays off: the new strains of corn grow tall and straight; at harvest time, the grain piles high in the trailer cart—by far the most abundant yield the farm has ever produced.

And then the dénouement: the father takes the grain to town, where he will sell it to the local distributor. Other farmers are already there, standing around, looking grim. It seems they too have produced bumper crops, and so have the farmers of America and Russia; the world grain markets are glutted; prices have fallen. The manager of the grain depot takes out his calculator: he can offer half the original price. The father stares back at him. He knows this will not even cover his expenses. The loans will default.

Slowly he walks back out to his tractor, stares at the pile of beautiful grain in the trailer cart. He stands there a moment, then abruptly grabs a shovel and begins heaving his grain out into the street, hurling it far into the town square, faster and faster, a silent fury. This corn is useless to him, he finds himself hating it—it is worse than useless, in its very richness and abundance it has cost him his farm. He shovels it desperately away from himself; the other farmers do not try to restrain him. After what seems like a painfully long time, the image freezes and the film credits begin to roll up the screen.

Failevic, in making this movie, did not see himself as the bearer of any single underlying message.[16] One of the film's great strengths lies precisely in its lack of a univocal didactic core: the viewer does not come away with a sense of plausible alternatives, of different choices that might have led to a more felicitous outcome. If the family had refused the tractor and its attendant changes, they undoubtedly would have faced an equally grave set of troubles, resulting eventually in the decline and failure of the farm for lack of competitiveness. Indeed, the harshness of the ending is all the more arresting because one cannot pinpoint the source of this family's misfortune. It was not greed, it was not laziness. The government was doing all it could to help this small farmer modernize and prosper. The machines worked well. The weather was good.

In this sense, Failevic was deliberately remaining faithful to the complex cluster of emotions that most French citizens have felt in confronting the collapse of peasant agriculture. Global economic pressures too vast to be resisted; the speeding treadmill of technological change; the cold logic of capitalism—these lay implicit in the arrival of an innocuous-looking machine, *le cheval vapeur*. On one side of progress lay the exhilarating experience of rising prosperity and material abundance; on the other side lay declining traditions, empty villages, the misery of families and individuals pushed to the wayside.

To what extent did this film present a distorted picture of rural France in the 1950s? Its primary limitation arguably lay in the accent it placed on failure: for it focused on the human costs of modernization, on a family that proved unable to make the leap into a new mode of farming. To be sure, this experience was indeed shared by a great many (perhaps the majority) of France's peasants: theirs was an important story that needed telling, and Failevic told it with great sensitivity. Yet it was also true that some small and medium-sized farms did manage to adapt and survive. High in the Alps and Pyrenees, a few *familles paysannes* simply scraped by as they had always done, tending scattered patches of infertile land with rudimentary horse-drawn tools.[17] Others, on more promising terrain, began experimenting with new crops, such as flowers or fancy vegetables for sale in the specialty markets of the booming cities.[18] Still others bought out their neighbors, one by one, and consolidated these newly acquired lands into successful mechanized farms; they learned to become businessmen, to manage their farms the way an industrialist manages a factory.[19] Capturing this complex diversity of rural experiences was clearly not Failevic's intention when he made *Le Cheval Vapeur*: he wanted his fellow citizens to witness the anguish of the transition, and to glimpse the way of life that was lost.

Not surprisingly, France's farmers vigorously and vociferously resisted the kinds of brutal economic change depicted in *Le Cheval Vapeur*: they did not "go gentle into that good night." Through their influential trade union, the FNSEA (Fédération Nationale des Syndicats d'Exploitants Agricoles), they exerted strong and constant pressure on the politicians in Paris, as well as on the bureaucrats of the European Union, to grant them as many subsidies and tax breaks as possible, cushioning the effects of global competition. They were hampered in this, however, by the fact that the leadership of the FNSEA broadly shared the modernizing, productivist outlook of France's political and industrial elites; thus, the FNSEA, while fighting a rearguard action to ease the transition, was in practice committed to a long-term policy predicated on the gradual phasing-out of traditional peasant farming.[20] Consequently, at several junctures since the 1950s, the owners of small family farms have sought to organize outside the mainstream FNSEA, creating alternative foci of political mobilization. One organization, the Jeunesse Agricole Catholique (JAC), and its outgrowth, the Cercle National des Jeunes Agriculteurs (CNJA), flourished in the 1950s and '60s around a program of local self-help—especially the pooling of small farmers' resources in self-governing, technologically advanced cooperatives.[21] Another group, the MODEF (Mouvement de Défense des Exploitants Familiaux), a more left-wing association, attained a membership of 200,000 during the 1960s and early 1970s; it fought tenaciously to win concessions from the Ministry of Agriculture in defense of small proprietors.[22]

Nevertheless, despite all the peasants' lobbying efforts and struggles for self-organization, they were doomed in the end; for their political leverage steadily declined along with their numbers. Whereas, in 1945, farmers and agricultural workers had comprised 35 percent of France's active population, by 1980 they had dwindled to a mere 8 percent—a figure that brought France close to the demographics of most other major industrial nations.[23] Though farmers could (and did) still launch clamorous demonstrations in defense of their interests, blocking the streets of Paris with tractors, or periodically invading the Ministry of Agriculture with their sheep and goats, their relative influence within French society had shrunk by the 1990s to that of any other minority pressure group. Four decades of rural modernization had produced a rather ironic outcome: the doubling of agricultural output, coupled with the shattering of the farmers' political and economic power.

The Cultural Backlash: In Search of a New Rural Balance

That France's peasants should have loudly lamented the passing of traditional rural life is hardly surprising; but in their lamentation they were far from alone. On the contrary, the entire nation joined them in resisting and decrying the end of the peasant era. Here for example are the opening and closing lines from a song written in 1964 by the popular folksinger Jean Ferrat; it was entitled "La Montagne" ("The Mountains"), and was widely played on French radio during the 1960s:[24]

> Ils quittent un à un le pays
> pour s'en aller gagner leur vie
> loin de la terre où ils sont nés

Depuis longtemps ils en rêvaient
de la ville et de ses secrets
du formica et du ciné

. . . .

Il faut savoir ce que l'on aime
et rentrer dans son H.L.M.
manger du poulet aux hormones.

One by one they leave the countryside
to go earn a living
far from the place where they were born
For a long time they had been dreaming
of the city and its secrets
of formica and movie theaters

. . . .

You have to know what it is that you love
and return home to your apartment block
to eat hormone-fed chicken.

In Ferrat's verses we find all the elements of the postwar backlash against urbanization and the rural exodus: the siren melodies of the city, luring people
from the countryside with glitter and excitement; the authenticity and dig-
nity of the world they left behind; the perversely artificial lives they ended up
leading in their new urban surroundings.

One must be careful here not to confuse this cultural backlash with the
more widespread "back to nature" sentiments that swept through much of
the industrialized world during the 1960s. To be sure, France experienced
the neo-romantic counterculture of the sixties generation as strongly as any
other country, and we will return to this counterculture in the chapters to
come; but Ferrat's song was only tangentially related to it. A love of nature
certainly informed his verses, but it was the human symbiosis with nature,
the distinctive heritage formed over centuries of farming and village culture,
that evoked his strongest emotions.

This theme has reverberated steadily through postwar French society. It
has appeared in movies like Louis Malle's *May Fools* and Bernard Dartigues's
La part des choses, and arguably lay at the root of the enormous success enjoyed by Marcel Pagnol's *Jean de Florette* and *Manon des sources*. It has animated popular novels ranging from the works of Jean Giono to the 1990s
bestseller by Frédérique Hébrard, *Le château des oliviers*. Politicians have
scrapped incessantly with each other in their efforts to claim the rural heritage as their own—from the dubious protectionism of Jean-Marie Le Pen to
the notoriously predictable references made by François Mitterrand to his

own village roots in nearly every television appearance of his long career.[25] Countless town meetings and government blue-ribbon commissions have focused on the rural exodus, and entire sessions of the Assemblée Nationale have been devoted to it.[26] The news media regularly report on questions of rural depopulation and poverty, and academics hold lengthy conferences on the subject. Indisputably, the collapse of peasant society has constituted one of the dominant cultural preoccupations of the postwar era.

What factors rendered the French attachment to peasant traditions so strong and so enduring? Perhaps the key lies in the remarkable malleability of the imagery associated with the "peasant society"—a cultural construction that could hold radically different meanings for different constituencies. To someone like Ferrat, it embodied the antithesis of urban alienation, a touchstone of premodern authenticity. To a politician like Mitterrand, it conveyed a desirable impression of stability, common sense, and demotic roots. But one could also appeal to it from the other end of the political spectrum: those who remembered the Vichy years with fondness would find there, in the land, the reactionary values of religious tradition and social hierarchy. To a student radical of the post-1968 era, the peasant world beckoned with communal values that capitalist society no longer nurtured. To an environmentalist, it held out the promise—or at least the possibility—of a healed relationship with the natural world.

Fernand Braudel, in musing over the powerful hold of peasant traditions on the imagination of his contemporaries, pointed to the exceptionally slow progress of full-scale industrialization in France—the fact that, as recently as the turn of the century, and in some senses even as late as the 1930s, France could still be described as a heavily agricultural nation.[27] What this meant, in practice, was that a great many French citizens (including not a few Parisian urbanites) still possessed direct links with peasant or rural roots— relatives on a farm somewhere, or a country house, or memories of a childhood spent in the countryside. Unlike many other industrialized nations, which had undergone the scission between urban and rural ways of life much earlier and more drastically, France remained permeated with rural traditions well into the twentieth century.

The historian Stanley Hoffmann has offered yet another insight into this phenomenon: the crucial importance of the peasantry in the political balance of the Third Republic. According to Hoffmann, the values incarnated by the peasantry—family, work, thrift—formed the bedrock of the bourgeois ethos on which modern French democracy ultimately rested. Most French citizens, even those who lived in Paris or other cities, felt an enduring kinship with the rural progenitors of their nation's unique "republican synthesis."[28]

Not surprisingly, therefore, in a recent collection of essays that tackles the

exceedingly ambitious project of articulating the French national identity—
Les lieux de mémoire ("The Places of Memory"), edited by Pierre Nora—rural
themes occupy an especially prominent position. Armand Frémont's essay,
entitled "The Land," argues that *pays* and *paysage* began to play more, not
less, important roles in the defining of "Frenchness" at precisely the historical juncture in which peasant farming began its rapid decline:

> Never has the land held such complete fascination for those who no longer live
> by working it—those city dwellers who still want to find themselves con-
> nected with it, part of it. In the years since the Second World War, the land has
> become the focus of an exceptionally abundant literature, both scholarly and
> popular in nature.[29]

As the song by Jean Ferrat suggests, the appeal of the peasant world lay, perhaps above all, in the sense of impending loss—the feeling of a long-familiar
scene being left behind, with only uncertain and disquieting intimations of
the world that would replace it.

Territorial Balancing

The rural exodus was not the only demographic trend that worried the
French in the years following the Second World War: for even as the depopulation of the countryside proceeded apace, the decline of the nation's
provincial capitals appeared to be accelerating as well. In 1947, the geogra-
pher Jean-François Gravier published a book that became an instant sensation: *Paris et le désert français.*[30] Gravier argued that France was becoming a
seriously deformed nation, a macrocephalic invalid: Paris, the megalopolis,
was sucking all the lifeblood from the provinces, leading to a dangerous im-
balance between center and periphery. Gravier marshaled impressive evidence and statistics to bear out his thesis: publishing and education, banking
and industrial management, mass media, political and bureaucratic official-
dom, networks of transportation and communication, fashion and highbrow
culture—all these areas of French life, and many others besides, centered increasingly on Paris. With every passing year the vicious circle grew worse:
the more the nation's talented young people flocked to Paris, the more severe
the "brain drain" in the rest of France, and the more pronounced the decline
of the once-thriving provincial capitals. This single city had become the exclusive focal point of power and opportunity in French society; and the future prospect, for the proud regions surrounding Bordeaux, Marseille, Lyon,
or Strasbourg, appeared to be a slow death by asphyxiation.

Not surprisingly, strong political pressures quickly mounted from outside
the capital to do something about this alarming trend. In 1950, the Minister
of Reconstruction and Urbanism, Eugène Claudius-Petit, steered a new law

through the National Assembly designed to redress the balance between Paris and not-Paris. Thus began what was to become a long road, spanning four decades, of tenacious but frustrating efforts at social and economic reform, seeking, in the words of one politician, to "redistribute economic growth."[31] The challenge was immense, for it sought not only to combat political and administrative habits of centralization that dated back to Louis XIV, the Jacobins, and Napoleon, but also to reverse the effects of a basic economic principle: the simple rule that a successful and dynamic region tends to attract ever more power and money to itself, thereby building on its own momentum, while stagnant regions suffer from precisely the opposite tendency, the ongoing flight of capital and talent toward more promising poles of attraction.

In France, one could sketch out the distinction between these two kinds of regions quite clearly on a map, by drawing a line from Le Havre in the northwest to Marseille in the southeast. This diagonal from Normandy to Provence, dividing the national hexagon roughly into two halves, marked a barrier between two sharply distinct levels of social and economic advancement.[32] Above this line lay two-thirds of the population, three quarters of national economic production, most of the major industrial centers, the major foci of research and decision-making—not to mention Paris itself. Below this line, according to one scholar, lay "the poorer France, more rural, with lower salaries, fewer jobs and opportunities—the France that had little choice but to send its men and women, their hands and brains, to go and work in the rich northeast."[33]

The French government, however, in its efforts to restore regional equilibrium, had a potent tool at its disposal: the postwar institution known as *le Plan*. This was an intriguing hybrid between capitalist notions of free-market non-interventionism and Soviet-style notions of a planned economy; it was developed shortly after the war through the efforts of a small équipe headed by the brilliant technocrat Jean Monnet.[34] Starting in 1947, a government body known as the Commissariat Général au Plan began producing four-year plans that set broad goals for the various sectors of the national economy; but these four-year plans possessed no coercive powers, and adherence to their goals by both private and state-owned firms remained strictly voluntary. Nevertheless, the state planners were influential men (few women were able to gain access to these technocratic circles until the 1970s), and the guidelines they set played an important role in shaping economic legislation and the long-term decisions made by French captains of industry.

During the early 1950s, the Commissariat Général au Plan began systematically incorporating the ideals of regional balancing—the French phrase was "aménagement du territoire" ("territorial housekeeping")—into its qua-drennial presentation of le Plan. Although the economic planners themselves possessed no authority to legislate, they did succeed in encouraging the passage of a broad array of state-sponsored measures designed to put the brakes on the frenzied expansion in the bassin Parisien, and to encourage the regrowth of enterprise in the provinces. A 1955 law forbade the construction of new factories within eighty kilometers of Paris. At the same time, nine urban agglomerations throughout France were baptized as "metropoles d'équilibre"—poles of development that were to serve as economic locomotives for their surrounding regions: Lille-Roubaix-Tourcoing, Nancy-Metz, Strasbourg, Lyon, Marseille, Toulouse, Bordeaux, Nantes, and Saint Nazaire. In these cities the French government offered tax breaks to new investors, subsidized loans, state-funded training for workers, and elaborate infrastructures to accommodate new factories.[35] At the same time, the national transportation network, whose highways and train lines had tended to radiate outward from Paris like rays from the sun, was gradually revamped to allow direct communications among the various regions.[36]

Then, in 1963, these wide-ranging policies were given their own institutional home within the national government, with the creation of a new agency, the Délégation à l'Aménagement du Territoire et à l'Action Régionale (DATAR).[37] The head of DATAR, who possessed ministerial rank, coordinated the government's ongoing efforts at regional balancing; not surprisingly, cartoonists had a field day with the (to say the least) paradoxical nature of DATAR, this agency of decentralization so powerfully orchestrated from the center. Provincial politicians regarded the monies and other forms of support flowing from Paris with understandable ambivalence, for while the state aid was badly needed, it inevitably implied a certain loss of local autonomy. This inherent contradiction in the operation of DATAR was finally corrected in 1982, with the passage of a major piece of decentralizing legislation known as the Defferre Law (after its socialist author, the former mayor of Marseille Gaston Defferre). The Defferre Law enacted several basic reforms: it severely curtailed the power of the prefects, these direct agents of Paris in the provinces, who had once wielded nearly unchallengeable authority; it strengthened the sovereignty of local and regional governments; and it devolved key state functions, such as zoning and social welfare programs, to the local level.[38]

Historians have nonetheless remained cautious in their assessments of decentralization and the progress of aménagement du territoire.[39] While the growth of Paris has slowed over the past few decades, the Parisian basin in the early 2000s still retains its unquestionable dominance over the French economy. The diagonal line between Le Havre and Marseille still marks a division between "two Frances," although the standard of living in the poorer half of the national hexagon has undoubtedly increased. The depopulation of the countryside has continued, but it has begun to slow down; and provincial cities have undergone a rebirth since the 1970s, with broad bands of suburbs spreading out around them. Nevertheless, scholars seeking to interpret these shifting patterns find themselves wondering aloud whether such socioeconomic changes might not have manifested themselves in any case, regardless of DATAR and its manifold efforts. At best, the results can only be described as mixed or ambiguous; for France, as it enters the new century, still tops the list of Europe's more centralized polities. In the frank words of one Spanish legal scholar, invited by his French colleagues in 1992 to address them at one of their periodic conferences on decentralization:

> Compared with the sweeping devolution of power that has taken place in Spain, the measures of decentralization one finds in France seem timid indeed. France has historically been thought of as the homeland of centralism. Seen through the eyes of a foreigner, it very much retains that quality today.[40]

French Uniqueness, French Ordinariness

The Concorde, the nuclear reactor, the disappearing peasant—these figures of French distinctiveness have populated our discussion in the foregoing sections, recurring like leitmotifs in the "great acceleration" that followed World War II. On the one hand, we have charted the contours of a deep structural change that swept through France at the same time as it was moving through most other industrial democracies: the *trente glorieuses* were far from being a uniquely French phenomenon. On the other hand, we have encountered important features that set France apart: the stridency of technological Darwinism in this nation's postwar experience, the passionate attachment to peasant traditions. As with any national case study, we have found ourselves continually tacking between the particular and the general, moving to and fro between the intriguing peculiarities that form an essential element in any national history, and the broader characteristics that reflect cross-national commonalities.

It should not surprise us, therefore, if we encounter this same tension in the story of French environmentalism. At a basic level (as we shall see in the coming chapters), the rise of environmentalism in France ran roughly parallel to the green trajectories of most other advanced industrial nations. But in two significant respects France stood out: attitudes toward nuclear energy and weapons, and the affirmation of a relatively tame, semi-humanized conception of nature. French environmentalists, try as they might, never succeeded in persuading a majority of their fellow citizens about the perils of nuclear technology: even as late as the year 2000, the greens' adamant rejection of all things nuclear remained the principal issue on which their political platform most saliently diverged from the mainstream of French public opinion. When it came to popular perceptions of nuclear technology, the appeal to national autonomy almost always ended up trumping green arguments.

Second, the impact of peasant traditions loomed particularly large in the story of French environmentalism. The rural exodus, the future of agriculture, the balance between town and country, the relation between Paris and the regions—these ultimately became defining issues for the French écologistes. They did not need to proselytize or raise public awareness about these subjects, as they had to do, for instance, with threats to the ozone layer or to the Amazon rainforest. On the contrary, the questions of aménagement du territoire came ready-made, comprising a mature and central current within the civic discourse of postwar France; and the greens found themselves singularly well placed to breathe new life into these issues, taking them up and making them part of their own global vision of a radically restructured social order. French environmentalists, in this sense, were tapping into a distinctively Gallic vision of nature, a vision that accorded a central place to the partially wild, partially humanized character of an ancient countryside. The question of "peasant identity"—of rootedness in a particular spot of land imbued with incommunicable significance—lived on in the France of the year 2000, not only in the nostalgic memories of an urbanized population, but in the futuristic visions of the greens.

These two cultural features—the intensity of technological Darwinism, the strength of peasant traditions—helped define the distinctive identity of the French green movement, setting it apart from those of other nations. Unless we take such features into account, we cannot explain the widespread misperception of the French as an "ungreen" people, the weakness of the antinuclear movement in France, the almost complete absence of Deep Ecology as a strain among the French greens. Nevertheless, these national peculiarities should not cause us to lose sight of the bigger picture. In France, I will argue, the confluence of ecology and technological modernity reflected a much broader reorientation of the relation between nature and human culture that was taking place throughout the democratic portions of the industrialized world. In its broad outlines, the emergence of the light-green society followed a more general pattern, discernible across large swaths of global civilization.

PART II

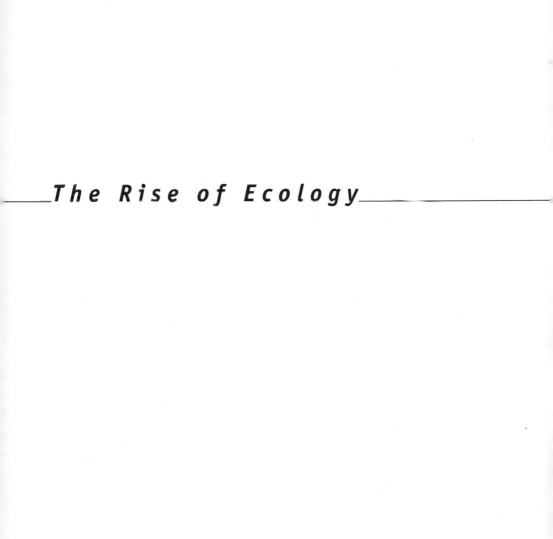

The Rise of Ecology

3   The Prehistory of Ecological Awareness

By my honor I promise that rivers, like revolution, will return to their beds and remain unable to rise during my reign.
—Emperor Louis Napoleon Bonaparte, opening the parliamentary session of 1857[1]

Each epoch tends to project its own favorite metaphors, its own inner fears and desires, onto the nature around it. "The forest is the mirror of society," remarks the historian Andrée Corvol in her book *L'Homme aux bois;* she shows how successive generations of French citizens made use of their nation's woodlands (both the trees themselves and their cultural meanings) in sharply divergent ways: as a form of capital, as a strategic military resource, as a locus for center-periphery power struggles, as an economic safety-net for the peasantry, as a privileged haven for city-dwellers seeking escape from modernity's stresses and strains.[2] In a similar way, Alain Corbin has historicized the trip to the beach—for the coastlines, it turns out, have not always been thought of as appealing places to go. His book, *The Lure of the Sea,* demonstrates how the seaside came to be transformed in the European imagination from a repulsive and frightening place, redolent of pestilential miasmas and reminiscent of the primordial chaos, to a highly attractive site in which the well-heeled classes began to seek the invigoration of the body and the cultivation of spiritual and artistic sensibility.[3]

Corbin's time-frame occupies roughly a century, from 1750 to 1840; but sometimes the reconfiguration of a natural space could take place much more quickly. Simon Schama, in his *Landscape and Memory,* describes how an enterprising fellow named Claude François Denecourt became "The Man Who Invented Hiking": during the 1830s Denecourt mapped out a series of attractive paths through the old royal forest of Fontainebleau, south of Paris, and successfully promoted to that city's bourgeoisie the brand-new idea of the ten-kilometer "promenade dans la nature."[4] What had once been a terrifying, dark, impenetrable thicket, the hiding-place of bandits and wolves, became an enticing world of dappled green light, of enchantment and peaceful contemplation. Seascape, landscape: the dunes and the trees certainly change from year to year, but the meanings and emotions they evoke sometimes change even more profoundly.

Our subject in Part II is precisely such a cultural shift: the reinvention of nature as a bounded and fragile space, requiring intensive human nurturing and protection. The beginnings of this new attitude toward the natural world are already discernible as early as the eighteenth century, and by the year 1900 the nature conservation movements in France and the rest of Europe were undeniably in full swing; but it was not until after World War II that this new conception of nature became a true mass phenomenon, a central feature in the cultural landscape of modernity.

Let us consider for a moment the advertisements shown in figures 1 and 2, in which the central image is the angular silhouette of a factory with its smokestacks spewing black clouds.[5] It is hard to believe that, early in the twentieth century, someone in the advertising business could have chosen such an image to elicit a positive and admiring reaction from the French reading public. Yet this was a common and recurring motif in advertisements throughout the industrialized world (not just in France!) during the years after the First World War. Evidently, the mentality of that period associated the harsh rows of belching chimneys with bustling productivity and prosperity, and with the comforts that they brought with them. The idea that all that smoke had to be going somewhere, and that it might eventually accumulate in sufficient amounts to render the air unbreathable, does not seem to have occurred to the citizenry of that era. The factory churning out its products—and its byproducts, like smoke—was the quintessential symbol of technological progress, an aspect of modernity that most people eagerly embraced.

And yet, within the space of the next fifty years, from 1920 to 1970, that symbol's emotional valence had undergone a complete reversal, from cele-

Figure 1. Advertisement for Pompes Worthington (1918). (Courtesy of Editions L'Usine Nouvelle, Cent Ans de Publicité Industrielle, 1991.)

bration to opprobrium; the sky above the factory had been reinvented as a vulnerable, delicate space, and the factory recast as the aggressor. What is perhaps most striking about this reversal of values is the fact that technological progress itself was never cast aside, but lived on quite successfully into

Figure 2. Advertisement for Fabriques Réunies d'Emeri et de Machines (1919).
(Courtesy of Editions L'Usine Nouvelle, Cent Ans de Publicité Industrielle, 1991.)

the new era. In France (for reasons we have already begun to explore in the preceding chapters), the post-1945 generations clung tenaciously to the underlying ideas of scientific advance and technological innovation; these ideas, they felt, should not be abandoned, but rather reformulated, radically recontextualized. A machine was not a bad thing in itself: what mattered was the place occupied by the machine within a broader network of reverberating ecological and social relationships. Technological progress could be reengineered, so that it might harmoniously coexist with the spontaneous rhythms of the natural world—or so the postwar generations ardently willed themselves to believe.

Environmentalism and Ecology: Working Definitions

The words, "environmentalist," "ecological," and "green" are often used, both in scholarly and non-scholarly discourse, as if they were loosely synonymous. The problem is compounded for someone studying France, for the word "écologiste" in French means exactly what the word "environmentalist" means in English: an activist devoted to a program of social change. Though each of these three words tends to have different connotations from the others, I will accept this de facto overlap in their meanings, and use them as if they were roughly interchangeable. Where I need greater specificity, such as, for instance, in speaking of ecology as a scientific discipline, I will make this clear in the text.

The notion that it is sacrilegious, or just plain stupid (or both), to lay waste to the place where one lives—for instance, by chopping down all the trees—has been around for several thousand years. Around 300 B.C., for example, the Athenian writer Theophrastus, one of Aristotle's favorite pupils, worried about the possibility of severe climate change that might result from the systematic deforestation going on in his native Greece.[6] Everywhere humans have settled, they have had to come to grips with the patterns and cycles of the natural world from which they derived sustenance; in every case they have formed a relationship with that world, and a cultural representation of it, often marking its boundaries and characteristics very differently from the way this has been done in the West. Thus, in a sense, it is legitimate to think of the rich heritage of environmentalism as growing out of all these far-flung traditions—the Taoist conception of the circular flow of cosmic energy, the ancient Ayurvedic knowledge of herbal healing, the Native American vision of land and sky as being structured by cardinal directions, the Amazon tribeswoman's easy sense of continuity between the human and the nonhuman. Indeed, this is precisely the point made by some proponents of Deep Ecology, who wish to broaden the base of our understanding of nature beyond the "physical environment" as typically construed by contemporary Western science.[7]

Though this wide-ranging anthropological approach has much to commend it, I will maintain a narrower focus in the chapters that follow, basing my narrative on a more historically specific definition of the term, "environmentalism." The reason for this narrower focus is that French environmentalism, while it may certainly have absorbed certain elements from ancient or extra-European sources, nonetheless resides squarely within the cultural tradition whose roots go back to the eighteenth-century Enlightenment. Both in its epistemological framing of its object, which is grounded in the natural sciences, and in its political and moral orientation, which is solidly anchored in the language and habits of the liberal European left, French environmentalism is a movement whose identity is unabashedly Western and modern. Its history runs roughly parallel to the development of European and global industrialism, to which it is explicitly linked by green theorists and green activists alike. To borrow a metaphor from medicine: if industrial economies running out of control can be likened to a disease of modern civilization, then environmentalism has emerged as one proposed cure; and any attempt to discuss the cure as something separable from the context of this specific disease is bound to rob it of its basic meaning.

Our working definition will therefore be as follows. Environmentalism connotes a new vision of the human place within nature, a cultural transformation of nearly Copernican proportions: from a world perceived as infinite in its resources, a world for humans to master and put to use without restriction, to a world perceived as finite in both its resources and its resilience, a fragile world requiring from humankind a newfound mentality of self-restraint and even of active protectiveness. It arises out of a generalized attitude of respect for our natural surroundings, and of concern about how best to preserve those qualities that are essential to "naturalness"—whether because those qualities are deemed to possess intrinsic value, and are hence worth preserving for their own sake, or because their preservation is linked to the furthering of human aims and welfare.[8]

Implicit here lie four ideas that together make up the core intellectual content of environmentalism: the concepts of finitude, interconnectedness, systemic rupture, and global socioeconomic transformation. (We return to these ideas in chapter 5, where we discuss contemporary French environmental thought in greater depth.) The first of these, finitude, is generally associated with the "discovery" that the world's resources and space are limited, and that, if the planet's energy and raw materials are increasingly transformed into garbage, effluents, and heat, our "spaceship earth" will someday become uninhabitable; it is a discovery whose roots go back to the time of Malthus, but whose specifically environmentalist dimensions are most often situated by historians in the mid-twentieth century. The second concept, interconnectedness, goes back farther, to at least the early 1700s. It centers on the notion that the phenomena of the natural world are actually far more closely related to each other than we at first tend to think: like far-removed points in a spider's web, they are linked across space and time through causal connections that are often extremely complex and hard to discern. In this sense, they constitute large-scale natural "systems" whose integrity, equilibrium, or dynamic evolution a patient human observer can reveal. These systems, however, range from the robust to the delicate: in some cases, an impinging external force, such as an asteroid impact, or the cumulative pressure of encroaching human activities, can cause a natural system to collapse or undergo radical alteration. Here then we arrive at the third concept, that of systemic rupture—a fundamental dislocation in one or more natural systems, entailing consequences that under some circumstances may even threaten the continued survival of human beings themselves. Hence the fourth and concluding idea, of global socioeconomic transformation: if humans want to forestall these kinds of systemic ruptures (at least those that they are instrumental in causing), they need to change their own collective patterns of behavior. In many cases, because of the large scale and complex nature of the systems under threat, this is believed to require a major rethinking and reorganization of human economic activities—with an attendant need for profound social and cultural changes to speed the transformation along.

Environmentalism, then, is simultaneously descriptive and prescriptive: it flows from a specific kind of analysis of the physical world, and it leads to a concomitant set of tangible imperatives in human society. Since what lies at stake here is nothing less than human survival and the human place within nature, it should not surprise us that both these aspects of environmentalism—the descriptive and the prescriptive—are fraught with unresolved questions and intractable disagreements. What really constitutes a natural system? How do we know for sure that such a system is approaching rupture? How do we weigh the costs of drastic self-imposed social change against the alleged benefits of a forestalled systemic collapse? This explicit commingling of science and ethics, of nature and politics, places environmental issues among the most inherently controversial subjects in contemporary society.

To make matters still more complicated, the academic discipline on which environmentalism rests—the science of ecology—has itself undergone a dizzying series of conceptual shifts in the centuries since it first emerged. The word "ecology" was first coined by a German biologist, Ernst Haeckel, in the mid-nineteenth century; but most historians agree that the roots of ecology as a science go at least a century farther back, into the heart of the Enlightenment. Donald Worster, in his *Nature's Economy: A History of Ecological Ideas,* traces a long succession of scientific visions, each of them constructing nature in its own distinctive way, each of them profoundly influenced by the underlying assumptions and philosophical penchants of the prevailing Zeitgeist: the rigorously logical nature of Linnaeus, a static, orderly, mechanistic kingdom well suited to this man's obsessively taxonomical mind (as well as to the Age of Reason in which he operated); the exuberant, upwelling, protean, teeming nature of the Romantic Thoreau; the grim nature of Darwin's understanding, in which scarcity and competition ruthlessly plucked out hapless individuals and species and consigned them to oblivion; the harmonious balance of nature conceived by early twentieth-century American conservation scientists, who hoped to restore the wilderness to its bygone symmetries; the self-organizing Gaia envisioned by some postwar ecological enthusiasts, a single planetary superorganism; and most recently the eerie nature of chaos theory, in which no stable underlying order can be discerned, but only an unpredictable ebb and flow, an uncertain syncopation of cosmic lulls and catastrophes.[9]

Our working definition of "ecological science," therefore, has to remain broad enough to embrace this extraordinary malleability of the concept of nature in the hands of successive generations of scientists—for it has shown itself to be a concept that twists and shifts and undergoes one metamorphosis after another, evolving over the years like Darwin's finches on the Galapagos Islands. Ecological science, for our purposes, will mean the systematic study, using empirical and quantitative methods, of patterns of life as they emerge and develop over time; of the relations among different species of fauna and flora as they inhabit portions of the territory; of the global systems and meta-systems that affect the flourishing and evolution of life forms, ranging from chemical reactions at the microscopic level to climatic movements spanning continents; and finally of the impact that human society has exerted on these systems.[10] In France, as in other Western nations, the history of environmentalism has followed on the heels of this long, tortuous evolution in the scientific representation of nature. Before there could be environmentalism, there had to be a concept of environment itself; and it is to the early progenitors of this idea that we now turn.

Nineteenth-Century Precursors in France: From "Acclimatation" to Conservation

French naturalists lay at the forefront of the development of the life sciences in Europe: such figures as Buffon, Lamarck, Cuvier, Daubenton, and Jussieu formed part of an international scientific community that, between the mid-eighteenth and mid-nineteenth centuries, were paving the way for the nascent sciences of biology, zoology, or geography as we know them today.[11] France under the Ancien Regime already possessed an impressive Jardin des Plantes in Paris, an institution founded under Louis XIII, devoted to the preservation and study of medicinal plants from around the world. This institution had its purview significantly expanded in 1794, during the waning years of the Revolution; it was renamed the Muséum National d'Histoire Naturelle. Throughout the nineteenth century the Muséum constituted the central institution in the development of the life sciences in France.[12]

In 1841 a young zoologist named Isidore Geoffroy Saint-Hilaire became the Muséum's Professor of Mammals and Birds.[13] Geoffroy Saint-Hilaire was a rather unusual fellow among the elite community of French scientists, because he was not afraid to get his hands dirty, and actually *enjoyed* going out to the Muséum's research farm near Paris to work directly with the animals about which he wrote—cross-breeding them, studying their ailments, classifying them. He also believed that scientists were not doing enough to improve the lives of their fellow citizens, and resolved to use his position to promote the practical application of zoology in ways that would directly benefit French society. In what ways could zoology render itself useful? For Geoffroy Saint-Hilaire, the answer came as he catalogued the immense variety of animal specimens housed in the Muséum: birds, mammals, and myriad other creatures from all over the world. Many of these animals were put to excellent use in their native lands, where the locals used them for food, labor, or clothing. Why not select the most promising from among these exotic species, and bring them to France—in effect, transplanting them into a new home where they might make a major contribution to the national welfare? The trick, of course, lay in ensuring that these animals could successfully make the transition to a new climate and new surroundings; and here was born Geoffroy Saint-Hilaire's lifelong *idée fixe,* the theory of *acclimatation.*

French zoologists at the time were divided into two schools of thought: the followers of Georges Cuvier, who held that species were fixed, and rigidly adapted for survival in one type of environment; and the followers of Geoffroy Saint-Hilaire, who held that nature was more flexible, and that a species could adapt successfully to a new environment, provided the new conditions were not too radically different from the original ones.[14] Geoffroy Saint-Hilaire, determined to make *acclimatation* a reality, began seeking political and financial support for his idea among French aristocratic and business circles; and by the early 1850s his enthusiastic sales pitches had not only convinced a wide group of prominent citizens, but had won over the new Emperor Louis Napoleon himself. In 1854, the emperor personally presided over the creation of a new scientific organization, the Société Impériale Zoologique d'Acclimatation, with Geoffroy Saint-Hilaire as its first president. That society still exists today, its name having been changed in the twentieth century to Société Nationale de Protection de la Nature; it remains one of France's premier contemporary institutions for environmentalist action, education, and lobbying.

Nevertheless, the words "protection de la nature," in the organization's name should not mislead us; for the mentality of Geoffroy Saint-Hilaire and his nineteenth-century successors was (not surprisingly) rather far removed from that of a contemporary green activist. Underlying Geoffroy Saint-Hilaire's efforts lay an unabashedly homocentric vision of the human place within nature—a vision in which a scientist's highest calling was to understand nature's inner workings, the better to harness its bounty toward human ends. This was precisely the mentality that had already led to various efforts at "nature protection" in France's long history: the Code Forestier Royal, first promulgated in 1346 by Philip VI, designed to regulate the felling of trees in the king's forests; or the sweeping Ordonnance de Colbert of 1669, which comprised more than five hundred articles of forestry law.[15] These acts of legislation were not intended to protect nature for its own sake; rather, they laid out the rules for the long-term conservation (and expansion) of a crucial economic and military resource, namely, wood. "France will perish for want of wood," an anxious Colbert told Louis XIV.[16]

Similarly, in the nineteenth and early twentieth centuries, one should not

read too much into the various pioneering actions taken in the name of nature conservation. If clearcutting certain slopes in the Alps was forbidden, it
was mainly because of the resultant danger of avalanches; if certain rivers
were zealously protected from silting or erosion or urban encroachments, it
was because of the concomitant danger of floods: in virtually every case, the
principal point of reference remained human welfare.[17] This fact helps us to
understand better Geoffroy Saint-Hilaire's efforts at *acclimatation*. A twenty-
first-century zoologist might find it puzzling that someone, in the name of "la
protection de la nature," would seek to introduce yaks from China into the
valleys of the Alps, South American alpacas into the plains of southern
France, and—most wondrous of all—kangaroos into the Pyrenees![18] The
notion that these French regions comprised natural wholes of their own, and
that the large-scale introduction of exotic species might cause significant dis-
ruptions—this evidently lay beyond the conceptual reach of the Société Zoologique d'Acclimatation. Yaks meant milk, and meat, and a hardy form of
labor to pull plows; alpacas meant high-grade wool. If these species could
become part of the "new nature" of rural France, so much the better. As for
the kangaroos, Geoffroy Saint-Hilaire reasoned, if they could adapt successfully to the arid scrubland of the Pyrenees foothills, and proliferate in the
wild, their eventually abundant numbers might help revive the local leather
industry, which had long been languishing. (Needless to say, this particular
idea never got off the ground.)

This anthropocentric mentality, moreover, was not peculiar to France.
According to the historian Raymond Dominick, it equally characterized Germany around 1900: "Most rationales presented by the early German conservationists appealed purely to the interests of homo sapiens. . . . Many human
beings saw no significance in the demise of a species other than their own,
unless that species had something tangible to offer humankind."[19] And in
the Progressive-era United States, according to Donald Worster,

> the conservation program that emerged under Gifford Pinchot's leadership in the
> early years of the twentieth century paid little attention to ecological complica-
> tions. It was primarily a program aimed at maximizing the productivity of those
> major resources in which man had a clear, direct, and immediate interest.[20]

All of which is not meant to denigrate turn-of-the-century conservationism,
for despite its limitations, it marked a major step in the dawning awareness
among Westerners that human activities were taking a growing toll on the
natural environment, and that corrective measures would be increasingly
needed. Even though conservationist policies were still couched in a homocentric language of "resource management," they nonetheless constituted a

substantial shift from a world in which those resources had been blithely taken for granted.

From Utility to Beauty: The Early Twentieth Century

The other great current of nineteenth-century Western culture that helped pave the way for environmentalism was, of course, Romanticism. Though confined (at least initially) to intellectual elites, this enormously fertile movement in the arts and philosophy brought about a far-reaching reevaluation of the natural world and the human place within it.[21] The rejection of the mechanistic models prevalent in eighteenth-century rationalism; the revalorization of feeling and subjectivity in the human relationship with landscape; the poetic visions of organic unity in nature, and of human beings as forming part of that unity; the critique of utilitarianism, with its purely instrumental attitude toward the earth's places and creatures; the sense of the sublime, through which certain spectacular natural scenes were believed to offer glimpses into a sacred level of reality—all these characteristics went hand-in-hand with a profound sense of reverence for the wild and nonhuman world, bringing forth a new language and new metaphors through which humans could apprehend their surroundings. The Romantic sensibility was certainly not "ecological," in the twentieth-century sense of the word; but it took Westerners a step closer to such an ecological worldview by offering powerful new grounds for appreciating and valuing nature.

This gradual shift of mental horizons found one of its first tangible manifestations in the New World, with the creation by the United States of Yellowstone Park in 1872. This *was* something new: to take a large chunk of territory (granted, the Americans had plenty of it) and set it aside, barring further development of its resources, not because this piece of land might somehow prove useful, but because in its pristine state it possessed certain intangible aesthetic qualities that were deemed worth protecting.[22] True, the French could take pride in the fact that, as early as 1858, their own forest of Fontainebleau had been designated a protected area by a decree of Louis Napoleon.[23] But Yellowstone was manifestly different, both in sheer scale and in the strictness of protection envisioned. Whereas Fontainebleau would always remain something akin to a large suburban garden-park, criss-crossed by paths and heavily frequented by urban visitors, the creation of Yellowstone took a vast wilderness and declared it off limits to any further large-scale introduction of human artifice. It was the remoteness and wildness itself that formed the object of the park's existence: the "natural resource" in question was not primarily utilitarian but aesthetic.

In the decades that followed, the example set by Yellowstone stimulated and emboldened nature lovers in other nations to press successfully for the creation of similar parks of their own—in 1879 in Australia, in the mid-1880s in Canada, in the 1890s in New Zealand and South Africa, in 1909 in Sweden, in 1914 in Switzerland. One historian is even moved to speak of a worldwide "national park movement" during these years.[24] However, it is problematic to speak of all these parks as if they were truly comparable creations, because their legal status differed enormously from nation to nation, as did the degree to which they were effectively protected from human encroachments. It was not until the late 1940s that global organizations and conventions were formed to provide common guidelines and some degree of legal uniformity for the world's nature preserves and parks.[25]

In France, as in Switzerland, the first area designated by the term "national park" was set aside in 1914, just on the eve of World War I: a rather niggardly tract of 5,000 hectares (about 20 square miles) surrounding the spectacular crags of the Mont Pelvoux in the Alps (this was later integrated into a much larger entity, the Parc National des Ecrins). Two years earlier, in 1912, a remote cluster of rocky islets off the coast of Brittany had been grouped together as a sanctuary for wild seabirds—the Réserve Naturelle des Sept-Îles. These pioneering creations resulted from concerted action by two very different constituencies: on the one hand, scientists and nature-lovers, acting under the aegis of organizations like the Société Zoologique d'Acclimatation and the French League for the Protection of Birds; and on the other hand a broader (and more politically powerful) group of organizations, the largest of which were the Touring Club of France and the Alpine Club of France.[26]

If the creation of wildlife preserves had depended on scientists and bird-watchers alone, it would most likely have failed, for they only amounted to a small and relatively marginal constituency. But what had also begun to happen, as Europe rapidly industrialized in the final decades of the nineteenth century, was a profound set of interconnected shifts in both economy and culture. Rising prosperity and education levels, coupled with improved technologies of transportation, had given rise to a sizable leisure class eager to engage in travel and tourism. These newly mobile masses of people soon found it expedient to join forces in organizing excursions and trips; and as they wandered, and compared notes with each other, they began to create a common European culture of "beautiful spots" that became *de rigueur* for any cultivated traveler.[27] They wrote travel books and guidebooks, drew sketches, took pictures; and the spots they visited ultimately fell into two categories: historic and artistic landmarks, and natural sites of special scenic beauty. In this way the aesthetic value of nature, already precious to the poets and cultivated elites of the Romantic era, was now being claimed as part of the birthright of Europe's burgeoning tourist masses. By the turn of the century, therefore, one could find the value of a scenic location being placed on a par with the value of a historic battlefield or major art museum: all three types of sites came to be telescoped together, in the eyes of cultured Europeans, as forming part of a common national heritage.[28]

In England, this development helped give rise in 1895 to the birth of that remarkable entity, the National Trust—a powerful organization devoted to the acquisition and preservation of England's finest historic, artistic, or natural treasures. In other European countries, like France, where no such institution existed, the task of pushing for the protection of such treasures devolved into the hands of private organizations, the largest of which in the French case were the Touring Club and the Alpine Club. Confronted with decaying national monuments and artistic sites, or with factories marring the picturesque charm of France's rural valleys, these clubs helped mobilize an influential lobby in the Parisian corridors of power. They formed a loose alliance with scientists, who provided alarming statistics about the disappearance of European flora and fauna, and with nature-lovers, who pressed for the protection of specific animals, such as birds or whales; and together they formed a pressure-group that commanded the politicians' attention.[29]

Still, the progress was halting. In 1923, the First International Congress for the Protection of Nature was held in Paris, under the sponsorship of the Muséum, with 309 delegates attending from some two dozen nations (including the U.S.). Scientists at the congress addressed the need for greater international coordination, and for the creation of a permanent body to oversee global efforts at nature protection—but in the end, such a body failed to materialize until after World War II.[30] In 1927, the French government granted to the Société Zoologique d'Acclimatation the right to create and oversee a 15,000-hectare nature preserve in the Camargue wetlands, near the Rhone delta.[31] Throughout the late 1920s a series of decrees issued by France's colonial bureaucracy banned such practices as dynamite fishing in New Caledonia, and created large nature preserves in the Antarctic and in the Algerian desert. In 1930 the first comprehensive law on the preservation of French historic, artistic, and natural sites was passed by the Assemblée Nationale; but it provided insufficient funds for monitoring to ensure that the law was being obeyed, and only mild penalties for those who flouted it.[32]

Nevertheless, despite this somewhat mixed record of partial successes and disappointments, one could clearly see a new language emerging—a language of aesthetic values and intergenerational responsibilities that already foreshadowed the "green" discourse of the postwar era. In 1931, for example, the Muséum organized a second international congress on nature protection; its keynote address, delivered by Professor A. Gruvel of the Muséum, is worth quoting:

> We believe that a nation's natural sites, with their picturesque beauty, should be counted among its greatest treasures. They form the personality of a country, and are crucial to the dignity and welfare of its population. They must be preserved for future generations, and not just for one people, but for all humanity. We believe that every government has the duty to protect the natural riches of its territory, using all the means necessary to ensure that this is done effectively and thoroughly.[33]

The emphasis on the word "beauty" in this speech—particularly since it is made by a scientist—is especially striking. By going beyond the conservationist discourse of nature's utility as an economic resource, and emphasizing instead its aesthetic qualities as part of the national heritage, the nature protection advocates of the early twentieth century took a major step toward the recognition within nature of intrinsic value—a value independent of human aims or needs. To be sure, the transformation of mental horizons still remained incomplete, for the saving of a mountain forest or coastal wetland because its beauty affords pleasure to humans still bespeaks, in the end, a homocentric logic. And yet, in the very act of recognizing such beauty, one has already moved closer to endowing that forest or wetland with a value that it possesses in its own right, simply by being what it is. One cannot help but feel a certain respect for a natural site that one apprehends through this aesthetic mode, as well as a sense of responsibility for the flora and fauna that collectively render it unique and memorable. One has therefore taken a partial but substantial step toward an "ecocentric" system of values, in which natural entities are regarded as possessing worth in and of themselves.[34]

Still, we must be careful not to conclude, from the foregoing discussion, that Europeans in general, and Frenchmen in particular, were already "going green" in the interwar years. Far from it. The vocal advocates of nature protection remained, until the 1960s, a relatively marginal group; the majority of Europeans simply did not give such matters much thought, still holding fast unquestioningly to their faith in economic and technological progress, completely unaware of any possible complications or nasty systemic side-effects. After all, the advertising images shown earlier in this chapter—enthusiastic depictions of factories belching smoke—dated from as recently as the 1920s. Even among the era's true believers in nature protection, one still encounters rather sobering documents, such as the elegantly printed menus from annual banquets held in Paris between 1905 and 1921 by the members of the Société Zoologique d'Acclimatation, featuring:

> *Hors-d'Oeuvres*
> * Pastries stuffed with sea turtle liver *foie gras*
> * Omelettes of ostrich eggs
> * Indian Ocean crab salad
> *Main Course*
> * Stewed camel
> * Indian python
> * Patagonian guinea-pig curry
> * West African crawfish
> * Madagascar mountain goat *à la broche*[35]

The fine line between saving wildlife and eating it, apparently, still had to wait a few more decades.

1945–1960: Warnings Unheeded

In France, as we saw in chapter 1, the experience of the Second World War constituted a searing national trauma whose psychological consequences still remained potent five decades later. It propelled the French into the *trente glorieuses,* the headlong rush for modernization that utterly transformed the French economy (and territory) between 1945 and 1975. With the nation's energies focused on the demands of the postwar economic boom (and on the grave problems posed by Indochina and Algeria), the 1940s and '50s were relatively quiet years for French environmentalism. In 1948, the French scientists who had organized global conferences in 1921 and 1931 hosted an international meeting of conservationists at Fontainebleau; out of this meeting came a new organization, the International Union for the Conservation of Nature (IUCN), which by the year 2000 would count 10,000 scientists from 76 countries among its membership, and play a key role as a global clearing-house for environmental education and action.[36] Nevertheless, the IUCN's activities remained relatively low-key throughout the 1950s and early '60s, because the scientists who comprised its membership continued at this time to believe that their primary role was the impartial observation of nature, and not political activism on behalf of an environmental agenda.

Thus, in 1952, Roger Heim, the director of the Muséum National d'Histoire Naturelle, published a pioneering book, eloquent and amply documented, entitled *Destruction et protection de la nature,* in which he laid out the emerging environmental crisis in its broad outlines, from the disappearing fauna and flora of Europe to the problems of global pollution and overpopulation.[37] But the book was mostly read only by fellow scientists, and his pleas for strong governmental action went unheeded. Heim, like other scientists, would have considered it highly inappropriate to call a press conference and publicize his findings in a dramatic way; for in the 1950s, this would have branded him among his colleagues as a disreputable self-promoter.[38] The result was that, while a small elite of scientists clearly recognized the grave environmental consequences of rapid modernization, this knowledge remained entirely outside the awareness of the broader public.

There was, of course, one man in these years who was not afraid of such self-promotion, and who eventually became France's most famous environmentalist: Jacques-Yves Cousteau. The great irony of Cousteau's career is that, of all French public figures, his name is far and away the most likely to be recognized around the world, as a link between the words "France" and "nature"—and yet, he ultimately became something of a pariah among French greens, and his achievements are completely ignored in virtually all the French environmentalist literature. The principal reason for this is that Cousteau insisted throughout his long career on maintaining his independence of action, doing things his own way, refusing to form political alliances, and above all, repeatedly rebuffing France's environmentalists when they begged him to become their standard-bearer. Instead, he created his own organizations and promoted them with tenacity, zeal, and skill—as well as a great deal of gimmickry and slick salesmanship. Many French environmentalists came to regard him as a "sellout"—someone who had placed his own personal success and fame above all other ideals and considerations.[39]

Cousteau was already a man in his forties when he presented his first feature-length film, *The Silent World*, at the Cannes Film Festival in 1956. He had loved the sea ever since his childhood, and had been tinkering since the 1920s with various technologies that would allow him to stay longer and longer underwater, and to record what he saw on film. In the late 1930s the breakthrough came, when he invented (and patented) the aqualung. Freed by this remarkable device to move about in the water as he wished—he referred to himself and his collaborators as "menfish"—Cousteau showed an innate flair for weaving his underwater pictures into an exciting and imaginative storyline, simultaneously imparting a feeling of danger, adventure, and scientific discovery. Before the screening of *The Silent World*, the public's only experience of underwater movies had consisted of murky images wafting to and fro in a bubbly fog; now they were presented with crystal-clear seascapes in full color, shipwrecks and coral reefs, a phantasmagoria of weird fishes and plants, all revealed by these men floating weightlessly in a suspension of dappled blue light. Small wonder that the film won the grand prize at Cannes, and an Oscar in 1957![40]

Cousteau used the money from the film to buy a World War II–era U.S. navy minesweeper, known simply as the *J-826;* he rechristened it *Calypso,* and proceeded to fit it out as a floating base for undersea exploration. Over the decades that followed, he traveled around the world, making dozens of feature films and documentaries, writing books, dreaming up one adventure after another and then allowing his audiences to participate vicariously through the media of TV and film. He became, in the words of one biographer, a "living legend," his name virtually synonymous with the undersea world. It was not long, moreover, before Cousteau discovered that in many parts of the planet his cherished seascapes were seriously ailing: pollution, ocean dumping, and rapacious fishing practices were taking a heavy toll on the aquatic environment. Thus it was that he became an "environmentalist"—not as someone who read about the ecological crisis in books, but as someone who encountered it in daily life. His films began documenting, for a worldwide audience of millions, the damage that humans were causing to fragile marine ecosystems. In 1974 he formed the Cousteau Society, a membership organization devoted to educating the public about marine environments; the society continued to remain active after Cousteau's death in 1997.[41]

What appears to have rankled, among many French greens, was Cousteau's insistence on calling himself an environmentalist, when in fact he often depicted other environmentalists as doctrinaire and uncompromising extremists. To take but one example: in 1987 the French government, acutely sensitive to mounting public protests over its nuclear blasts on the Pacific island of Moruroa, asked Cousteau if he would be willing to conduct a series of radioactivity tests inside the atoll's lagoon. The captain agreed, and the *Calypso* and its crew duly spent five days taking measurements from samples of water, sediment, and plankton. Cousteau then issued a report, triumphantly publicized by the French government, stating that all man-made toxins in the lagoon were well within acceptable limits, and that the marine habitat remained healthy. Enraged environmentalists from around the world lambasted Cousteau as a dupe whose divers lacked the proper scientific expertise for conducting such tests, and who had been cynically used by the French government to legitimize its continued nuclear blasts. According to Cousteau's biographer, Richard Munson, this episode was no exception:

> When [environmental] activists decried the destruction of the planet's ozone layer, the Captain argued that the protective gases had not noticeably diminished. When they protested about accelerating nuclear contamination, he noted that his work with the International Atomic Energy Agency had de-

tected no increase in the radioactivity of the oceans. And when asked about the fate of the seas in general, he said, "The majority of scientists see no hope. In this they are more pessimistic than I."[42]

Adding insult to injury, Cousteau initially responded favorably when France's environmentalists invited him in 1981 to stand as the green candidate for the nation's presidency; but, after two weeks of national headlines and much media publicity for himself and his organizations, he abruptly announced that he had changed his mind. He could be more effective, he explained, by working outside the political system. To many greens, this "gran rifiuto" seemed simply unforgivable.

If one takes a long view, however, it would seem downright perverse to deny that Cousteau made as great a contribution to global environmental awareness as any other man or woman. It was not so much the technical breakthrough of his films that made the difference; for sooner or later the technology of underwater photography would undoubtedly have advanced just as far, with or without Cousteau's participation. What really set Cousteau apart was the talent with which he conceived and created his movies, casting them in a way that garnered him an eager and loyal audience numbering in the hundreds of millions. Over the years, film after film, adults and children throughout the world followed that familiar aquiline face, savoring the spirit of the *Calypso*'s voyages, learning to know the sea in a way that was interesting, exciting, and deeply affecting. Cousteau's love of the sea was infectious, and he passed this love successfully to an entire generation. For this, regardless of his personal shortcomings, he must be duly recognized.

> > >

In the century between 1850 and 1950, French visions of the human place within nature had shifted dramatically: from Geoffroy Saint-Hilaire and his dreams of *acclimatation* to Roger Heim and his *cri de coeur* about disrupted ecological equilibrium and the need for urgent measures of nature protection. When Geoffroy Saint-Hilaire headed the Muséum National d'Histoire Naturelle, the emphasis still lay on an unabashedly homocentric worldview, in which the planet's territories and biota were regarded primarily as so many assets waiting to be picked up and used. By the time Roger Heim took the helm at the Muséum, the underlying set of assumptions had changed not once but twice: first incorporating an appreciation of the natural world's intrinsic beauty, and then moving into a framework in which the diversity of nature's creatures, and the fragile balances among them, were valued for their own sake.

By the mid-1950s, therefore, one could say with some accuracy that modern environmentalism had already been born: but its birth went largely un-noticed. The scientists and nature-lovers who fretted about the future of the world's ecosystems had already begun to sound the alarm; but they were few in number, their voices drowned out by the ambient roar of the *trente glo-rieuses*. It would take a radically new political and cultural climate—the fer-tile turmoil of the 1960s—before those voices finally made it through into public awareness.

4 The Unexpected Trajectory of Environmentalist Success

Comme un arbre dans la ville
J'ai la fumée des usines
pour prison et mes racines
on les recouvre de grilles
Comme un arbre dans la ville

Like a tree in the city
I am imprisoned in factory smoke
and my roots are encased
in iron grills
Like a tree in the city

—From the song, "Comme un arbre" by Maxime Le Forestier, 1972[1]

1960–1974: Taking it to a New Level

It was only in the 1960s that environmental activism, in France as in other industrialized democracies, began acquiring the features of a modern grassroots movement, with a growing popular following, a diversified and vigorous organizational base, and a distinctive agenda of its own. At the beginning of the decade, the notion of safeguarding an endangered environment was still confined to the margins of society; by 1969, "la protection de la nature" had become a familiar phrase not only in the French mass media, but in political circles as well.

What had happened? Why did this particular decade become the pivotal one for the nascent movement? Clearly, in addressing these questions, it is not enough to point to the *Torrey Canyon* oil spill of 1967 off the coast of Brittany, the translation of books like Rachel Carson's *Silent Spring* in 1968, or the campaign to save the Vanoise national park in 1969. Even if we acknowledge the importance of these events in the history of French environmentalism, we are left with more unanswered questions: Why did this particular oil spill and this particular endangered park become popular "causes," when similar events in the past had utterly failed to arouse the public imagination in a similar way? Why did Carson's *Printemps silencieux* become a bestseller, when Roger Heim's *Destruction et protection de la nature,* which was also gripping and well written, had languished in obscurity? What had changed, in the *mentalités* of the French citizenry, and why?

When one poses these questions to the French greens themselves, one sometimes finds the following sort of answer. The main reason for the rapid rise of environmentalism, we are told, lies in the postwar economic boom itself: the sheer scale of humankind's impact on nature increased so dramatically during these years that it was finally noticed by even the most obtuse segments of public opinion. One might call this the "dead fish explanation," because it typically rests on the following sort of anecdote:

> For years I had gone fishing in the brook behind my grandparents' farm. Then, in the 1950s, I began to notice that I was catching fewer and fewer fish. By the 1960s the fish were gone, and a vile yellow scum was accumulating along the stream where once, as a child, I had spent my happy summer days.[2]

The problem with this "dead fish explanation" lies in the fact that it is sometimes presented as an "objective" causal factor, measurable by clear statistics: an increase in pollution results in a concomitant increase of ecological awareness. Yet, as we saw in our earlier example of the 1920s advertisements featuring belching smokestacks, this connection is by no means so straightforward: for pollution, while quantifiable, also lies partly in the eye of the beholder. A smoking factory can possess a negative or positive valence; dead fish in a brook might pass unnoticed by one generation, then become charged with ominous meaning for another. What we need to understand, therefore, are not only the physical and social changes themselves, but also the channels of cultural mediation through which they are interpreted and given meaning.[3] When, and why, does a stream full of dead fish—or a fac tory pouring out smoke—come to be perceived as a harbinger of more pervasive and insidious dangers?

In approaching this fundamental question, with specific reference to the 1960s, we can single out four distinct types of causal factors, each interacting dynamically with the others in producing the gradual shift.

The first has to do with the profound cultural ambivalence already described in chapters 1 and 2—the particularly intense manner in which France found itself caught between technology and tradition, modernity and history, soaring Concorde and vanishing peasant. Torn between the lure of consumer society and the fear of losing national specificity, between the specter of falling behind other nations and the attractions of an ancient rural *douceur de vivre,* the French flung themselves into the modernization process, while experiencing all its stresses and contradictions in an especially vivid and acute form. Without a doubt, this ambivalence toward modernity, which one could find among virtually all segments of the French population, constituted a key precondition for the rise of environmentalism; it formed part of the broader context of postwar *mentalités* that rendered environmentalist ideas meaningful and attractive to ever-growing numbers of citizens. (We return to this subject with a fuller discussion in chapter 5.)

A second factor lay in the emergence of a new form of activism: a sharpening sense of purpose among the scientists and nature conservation groups who had, in previous decades, taken a much more docile and conventional approach. This phenomenon was by no means peculiar to France; across the Atlantic as well, writes the historian Rae Goodell, the attitudes of American scientists toward political involvement and social responsibility were swiftly changing:

> In the 1940s most scientists stuck to their laboratories and avoided the taint of politics. In the 1950s it became fashionable to make occasional trips to Washington and give behind-the-scenes advice to government officials. In the late 1960s the behind-the-scenes "inside" advisory system lost its enchantment and effectiveness, giving way to a rash of alternative, "outside" activities in Congress, courts, and the press.[4]

It was in 1968 that French scientists and nature-lovers finally mobilized to create the FFSPN (French Federation of Nature Protection Societies), an influential lobbying group and national focal point for environmental action: this federation eventually grew to embrace more than three dozen national organizations and some forty-five regional associations, each of them focusing on some aspect of environmental protection. According to the scientists who founded the FFSPN, the forming of such an organization in the late

1960s only became possible because a gradual change of mentality had taken place, a decade-long process of radicalization that one of them, the chemical engineer Philippe Lebreton, described in straightforward terms: "It was no longer enough to occupy ourselves with the mere study of nature. We realized that we needed to take the initiative in organizing ourselves to protect it."[5] These scientists began writing books and articles of a much more alarmist and militant tone than Roger Heim had used a decade before— books such as Jean Dorst's *Avant que nature meure* ("Before nature dies"), published in 1965.[6] Meanwhile, translations were becoming available of bestsellers written by foreign scientists, such as Carson's *Silent Spring,* which began reaching French audiences in 1968, and Barry Commoner's *Quelle terre laisserons-nous à nos enfants?* ("What kind of planet will we bequeath to our children?"), published in 1969.

Here a third factor came into play: the counterculture of the 1960s, which simultaneously exerted a profound formative impact on the early environmental movement, and in its turn adopted many of that movement's ideas.[7] When historians and sociologists, writing in the 1990s or later, interviewed green activists and asked where the roots of their environmentalist engagement lay, most of them pointed unhesitatingly to the sixties—to the broader spirit of *contestation,* or fundamental questioning, that permeated the student movement and culminated in the revolt of May 1968. In this regard, however, we confront a bit of a paradox: for, on the surface of it, the "Events" of May '68 do not look very green at all.[8] If we survey the themes that seem to have preoccupied the *soixante-huitards* (activists of '68), if we scrutinize their manifestos, posters, and graffiti, we cannot but note that the words "nature," "pollution," or "environment" appear only rarely, and (relatively speaking) on the periphery of awareness.[9] In the *Petit dictionnaire de la révolution étudiante,* compiled by Alain Buhler in 1968, for example, one finds no reference to any words along these lines; the only entry that might plausibly be considered environmentally related is "société de consommation" (consumer society). But the definition given to this term is itself revealing in its emphasis:

> Denounced by Marcuse and by the majority of European student movements, consumer society constitutes the most insidious and refined form of industrial capitalism. The object-symbol of a high standard of living becomes an end-in-itself for the individual, and not a means toward achieving happiness. It imprisons the individual in an infernal circle of installment buying.[10]

The focus here is on the alienation caused by consumerism for human beings as social and cultural entities—and not on the harm done by consumer society to the natural world. Similarly, one famous dictum of May '68 was *"Sous les pavés, la plage"*—"Beneath the paving stones, the beach"—but to interpret this as an environmentalist slogan, in the literal sense of the term, seems to miss the point entirely. The beach referred to here was more likely meant to connote the spontaneous dimension of human free play and imagination, lying trapped below the metaphoric paving stone, the encrustation of urban modernity, with its rigid conventions and artificiality.

Thus, we will search in vain for any explicit current of environmentalist concern in the events of May '68;[11] but this does not mean that the upheaval of that month did not profoundly affect the nascent environmental movement. On the contrary, May '68 arguably constituted the preeminent turning point in French politics from which French environmentalism most directly profited and grew—and from which it derived much of its anti-statist and anti-consumerist character. At the most obvious and immediate level, one subset of the disaffected youth of '68, disillusioned with the reimposition of Gaullist order, simply fled the modern Babylon of Paris and set up communes in the hidden valleys of the Cévennes or the stark plateaus of the Lozère. This came to be known in French as the *Baba cool* legacy of '68—where "Baba cool" translates roughly as "organic hippie New Age"—and though in itself it proved relatively ephemeral, its broader cultural influence did not. This neo-ruralist cultural strain, with its revalorization of all things "natural," helped contribute to a much broader reorientation of patterns of consumption and leisure that took place within the mainstream French society during subsequent decades—from foods to cosmetics to the ideal vacation (see the more detailed discussion in chapter 8).

In a more specific sense, moreover, the impact of May '68 upon French environmentalism can be found in the way the greens conduct their politics to this day.[12] Their emphasis on decentralization, on grassroots meetings, on the mandatory rotation of leadership positions; their resistance to formal institutionalization; their distrust of hierarchy; their rejection of politics as the province of a professional political establishment; their desire to invent a new and fluid form of political power—all these ideals can be traced to the spirit of democratic renewal that pervaded May '68.[13] Moreover, whereas the French "culture of dissent" of the 1940s and '50s had generally been polarized along straightforward left-right political lines, the new wave of dissent that erupted in the sixties often rested on a rejection of both Left and Right as equally outdated positions.[14] After the sixties, organized grass-roots dissent became far more polyvalent, and potentially more "respectable," than it had been before; it became possible for eminent scientists and well-known academics to throw themselves into environmentalist organizing and lobbying, without necessarily falling into the powerful force-field of conventional party politics.[15]

But the deepest link of all between the greens and May '68 lay at the level of underlying philosophy or (to use a looser term) *Weltanschauung*. Both these cultural movements called into question not just this or that political regime, this or that industrial practice, but rather the whole civilization of modern industrialism, as it has emerged in the past three hundred years. They both centered on the notion that human beings in the late twentieth century faced a fundamental choice about what kind of society they wanted to live in. Though the inflections were clearly different in the two movements, it was this globalism (and radicalism) of view that bound them together—this insistence on questioning not merely the means, but the underlying ends, of all governance, production and consumption.[16]

We are now better placed to return to our initial question: How does a stream full of dead fish come to be perceived as a harbinger of more pervasive global dangers? The answer lies in the threefold cultural transformation that marked the sixties generation: a widespread ambivalence toward technological modernity; a sharpening sense of militancy among scientists; and a potent new form of radical dissidence manifesting itself in the counterculture. It is only with this broad backdrop in place that one can point to a fourth and final factor, namely, the specific physical threats to the environment that took place during this decade—events that, unlike similar threats or catastrophes in previous decades, were now seized upon by French public opinion in an entirely new way. In 1967, an oil tanker steaming toward the English Channel, the *Torrey Canyon*, caught fire and spewed crude oil along the beaches of Brittany; henceforth the *marée noire,* or black tide, with its arresting imagery of tar-coated sea birds, became part of the nation's popular vocabulary. This was by no means the first such oil spill that Europeans had witnessed; but it now came to be seen not as an isolated tragedy, but rather as a symptom of a broader *system* of energy use that would inevitably continue to produce such tragedies, through the very nature of its functioning. For the first time the questions were raised: Do we really have to do things this way? What would it take to change the system that produces this kind of outrage?[17]

Two years later, in 1969, a government agency rather insouciantly announced that one of France's most beautiful national parks, the Vanoise, created only six years earlier in a remote stretch of the Alps, would be rezoned to allow the building of a major ski resort.[18] The story of the Vanoise park went back to 1922, when the Italian king donated a large plot of his private alpine hunting lands for the creation of Italy's first national park, the Gran

Paradiso. Since the Italian parkland was delimited on its northwestern edge by the national boundary between France and Italy, the Société Zoologique d'Acclimatation immediately began pressing for an adjoining park on the French side—an act that would effectively double the area under protection, affording the region's wildlife a considerably more diverse habitat. For forty years the bureaucratic struggle dragged on, and finally, in 1963, the Vanoise became a legal reality: 53,000 hectares of mountain peaks, desolate highland valleys, and pristine lakes. Moreover, since France had meanwhile become a member of the IUCN, the new park's protective statute was considerably more stringent than that of previous French nature preserves; it was hailed officially as France's first "real" national park. Champagne flowed at the offices of the Société Zoologique d'Acclimatation (which had recently changed its name to Société Nationale de Protection de la Nature).

But powerful real estate interests had also been eyeing the alpine slopes, with a very different frame of mind. Skiing was fast becoming one of France's most popular sports, and there was a mountain of money to be made in the development of ski villages, complete with lifts, hotels, restaurants, discotheques, and boutiques. Even before the creation of the Vanoise park, a consortium of businessmen and local politicians (led by a man named Pierre Schnebelen, whose name means "snowball" in Alsatian dialect!) had been pressing the regional and national governments for permission to "mine the white gold"—promising jobs, international tourism, and a major infusion of cash into one of France's poorest rural backwaters. This intensive lobbying effort finally paid off in 1969, with an administrative decision to bend the park's rules and allow the ski project to proceed.

To the newly-created FFSPN, this meant war. A group of indignant scientists and journalists formed an organizing committee, led by the writer Jean Carlier, and launched what amounted to France's first nationwide campaign on behalf of a natural site. They wrote letters to the editors of the major newspapers, gave speeches on the radio, circulated petitions, and contacted their scientific colleagues in other nations, who duly wrote letters directly to the President of France, Georges Pompidou. Within a few months' time, the chorus of angry denunciations was making daily headlines, like the following in the widely respected (and usually pro-business) *Figaro:* "The Vanoise scandal: a paradise for wildlife and nature lovers, France's first nature reserve will be sacrificed to political and financial interests."[19] Even the communist newspaper, *L'Humanité,* which had initially supported Schnebelen's project because it would bring jobs for the alpine region's working class, changed its tune and began ardently defending the park.

President Pompidou, newly installed in office after de Gaulle's resignation, was undoubtedly taken aback by the sacks of protest letters delivered daily to the Elysée palace: such an upwelling of sentiment in defense of a remote natural site—described by the ski resort developers as "a few empty mountain valleys and a few mountain goats"—had never before occurred in his country. But he was a perceptive man, and he quickly recognized the latent political force behind this popular campaign. He therefore quickly rescinded the go-ahead for Monsieur Schnebelen's ski resort, restored the park's original status, pronounced himself an ardent protector of nature—and ordered his aides to begin drawing up plans for the creation of an entirely new government body, the Ministère de la Protection de la Nature et de l'Environnement.

To Pompidou's credit, one must first acknowledge that this was an extraordinary act.[20] No other nation had yet accorded cabinet-level authority—a whole government ministry—to the principle of nature protection. It would have been easy for the president to gain favorable press with a much more modest innovation, such as the creation of a state-funded environmental agency; but instead he opted for an entirely new institution at the summit of state power. The new ministry duly began functioning in 1971, with Robert Poujade, a stalwart of the Gaullist political establishment, at its head (not to be confused with Pierre Poujade, the cantankerous Provençal grocer who had launched a short-lived populist revolt in the 1950s).

Nevertheless, in actual practice, the new ministry found itself hamstrung from the start: its budget was set at one one-thousandth of annual state expenditures, a derisory amount.[21] As a bureaucratic newcomer, it was regarded either as a modest threat, or (worse still) as something of a joke by other cabinet-level officials. Poujade got some helpful advice from his ministerial colleagues. Edgar Faure, a former prime minister, told him:

> It's going to be hard, and what's more, you won't be given adequate means to accomplish much, so above all you must talk, talk a lot, bring up ideas, get lots of ideas circulating. If you need any I can give you some.[22]

And another official:

> Basically, your job as Minister of the Environment will be to go around making life difficult for (*embêter*) the rest of us. Risky business![23]

Poujade, who took his assigned role very seriously, struggled for three years to build his organization into an effective instrument of public policy; he finally resigned, disgusted, in 1974, writing up his experiences in a memoir entitled *The Ministry of the Impossible*.

Still, even at its inception, the Ministry of the Environment did possess real powers that should not be underestimated. The sociologist Florian Charvolin has shown that this institution was not given, ex nihilo, an entirely new set of tasks; instead, it grouped together, under the novel term of "environment," a wide-ranging series of existing agencies and bureaucracies that had already been dealing with various aspects of territorial or health-related public policy for decades. Its jurisdiction took shape like a patchwork quilt, cobbled together in bits and pieces, from functions formerly carried out under the aegis of the Ministries of Agriculture, Industry, Cultural Affairs, or *Aménagement du Territoire*. It comprised an extremely heterogenous set of activities, from building nature trails to disposing of abandoned vehicles, from setting emissions standards for home furnaces to conducting experiments in wildlife habitats, from noise abatement in cities to rural mapmaking to implementing nature-education programs in secondary schools.

What was truly new, Charvolin argues, was for all these diverse aspects of everyday governance to be brought together under a single umbrella concept, "the environment."[24] From Pompidou's rather narrow initial theme of "protecting nature," the ministry, in actual practice, found itself increasingly embroiled in virtually all areas of French citizens' interaction with their physical surroundings. As Poujade saw it, the word "environment" possessed an "imperialist" quality: by its very essence it brought out countless connections among people and things, forcing the ministry's officials into ever-broader engagement with the most seemingly disparate aspects of French society.[25] This tendency toward a wide-ranging and multidisciplinary purview was to grow in significance over the decades that followed, as the ministry gradually defined an overall mission for itself and consolidated its position within the corridors of power (see the discussion in chapter 9).

But it was not just in France that the early 1970s were proving seminal for the emergence of environmentalism. Like a microscopic culture multiplying on a petri dish, the movement started out as a series of small and unconnected specks in the 1960s, only to flower forth dramatically in the first half of the new decade. In 1967 an international group of businessmen and scientists had met in Rome, at the invitation of Aurelio Peccei, an intellectually oriented manager in Italy's FIAT conglomerate; the group, which came to call itself the Club of Rome, shared a common penchant for statistical analysis and a common anxiety about humankind's future.[26] Working together over the next five years, they conducted a wide-ranging survey of global industrial development, using scientific and mathematical models to project current trends into the long-term future. What they saw alarmed them profoundly: a grim scenario of Malthusian collapse and environmental catastrophe. In 1972 they published their findings in a slender volume, *The Limits to Growth,* which was quickly translated into many languages and made a sensation throughout the world.[27] Its success was undoubtedly due to two main factors: it presented what appeared to be cold, hard facts, arrayed in sophisticated graphs and charts; and (equally importantly) it offered not only gloom but hope, forcefully making the argument that all was not yet lost, and that a sustainable world economy still lay within reach, if only humankind made the right choices in the present.

The United Nations, too, played a key role in raising global environmental awareness. In 1970, UNESCO (the United Nations Educational, Scientific, and Cultural Organization) created a new international program entitled "Man and the Biosphere," devoted to the promotion of ecological studies at 352 "biosphere reserves" throughout the world, and to the dissemination of the resulting information to scientists, government bodies, and the public.[28] Then, in 1972, UNESCO convened a major international conference of scientists, diplomats, and public health experts in Stockholm—the first such world gathering specifically devoted to the environment. The conference proceedings were widely covered in the media, resulting in the publication of a sobering official report on the state of the planet, and in the creation of a new agency, the UNEP (United Nations Environmental Program), which became an important player in international environmental protection.[29]

These "global" events were of course being echoed in individual nations: for example, with Earth Day and the creation of the Environmental Protection Agency in 1970 in the United States, the formation of Friends of the Earth organizations in many countries after 1969, or the founding in Germany in 1972 of the influential *Bundesverband Bürgerinitiativen Umweltschutz* (Federal Union of Citizens' Initiatives for Environmental Protection).[30] France was no exception.[31] A French branch of Friends of the Earth—Les Amis de la Terre—was formed in 1971 by a group that soon came to be dominated by the ebullient personality of a twenty-five-year-old Parisian activist named Brice Lalonde. Lalonde, who would go on to become one of France's most prominent environmentalists, had been a student leader in May '68, and had been gravitating increasingly toward eco-activism ever since. Under Lalonde's guidance, Les Amis de la Terre organized its first major demonstration in 1972—a festive gathering in Paris of 20,000 bicycle-riding persons of all ages, seeking to "send a message" to their fellow citizens that automobiles were slowly choking to death their lovely capital city. It was called *la Vélorution*—a play on the French words for bicycle ("vélo") and revolution. Parisians had in fact been fighting bitterly with each other over a government proposal to run a new four-lane highway, right at the water's edge, along the left bank of the Seine in the city's historic fifth and sixth arrondissements—

and Lalonde's cheerful *Vélorution* gave an early example of his complex personality at work: superb organizational talents, a light-hearted and casual style that contrasted pleasantly with the "gloom and doom" seriousness of many other environmentalists, and (above all) an unerring flair for garnering media attention. (The proposed *autoroute rive gauche* was eventually defeated, and environmentalists could legitimately claim part of the credit for this early victory.) Les Amis de la Terre soon boasted several thousand members in two dozen local chapters throughout France; it began publishing its own eco-activist journal, *La Baleine* ("The Whale") in 1972.[32]

With the advent of this new organization, environmentally minded French men and women now faced a choice between two very different kinds of activism. On the one hand, they could join the FFSPN or one of its member organizations—national bodies like the Société Nationale de Protection de la Nature, regional groups like Picardie Nature, or thematic associations with such picturesque names as the Friends of Skunks, Foxes, and Other Persecuted Creatures (based in Paris); or the Association of Apple Munchers (Belfort). To join one of these organizations would mean working alongside scientists and nature-lovers, engaging in a style of activism that focused primarily on educating the public and pushing for new environmental legislation. Or, alternatively, a concerned citizen could join Les Amis de la Terre and participate in a more aggressive, free-wheeling style of activism, ranging from street demonstrations to direct action at endangered sites; these campaigns could be expected to aim at a broader array of causes than "nature protection" in the strict sense (the *Vélorution* being a good example). A typical exploit, for Les Amis de la Terre, was Lalonde's trip by sailboat in 1973 into the Moruroa lagoon in the South Pacific—an act of civil disobedience, carefully orchestrated amid a blaze of media coverage, that would have been unthinkable for most members of the more conservative FFSPN (though they might abhor the nuclear testing with equal ardor). Although these two green constituencies were to clash from time to time over the years, their efforts in many ways complemented each other; in the long run, it is probable that the overall cause of French environmentalism benefited from the implicit division of labor that they created.

To speak only of these relatively small membership organizations, however, would be to miss a broader point about the shifting horizons of French popular culture in these years. Whether one went to the bookstore or the movies, or turned on the radio or TV, one could not help but encounter a new set of ideas in circulation: in the following lists of titles, one sees the outlines of a relatively swift transformation of attitudes, like a photographic image emerging on a developing print. In bookstores: Jean Baudrillard, *La société de consommation* (1970); Pierre Aguesse, *Clefs pour l'écologie* (1971); Pierre George, *L'Environnement* (1971); Jacques Vernier, *La bataille de l'environnement* (1971); Serge Moscovici, *La société contre nature* (1972); Marcel Clébant, *Croisade pour la mer* (1972); René Dubos, *Nous n'avons qu'une terre* (1972); Ivan Illich, *Energie et équité* (1973) and *La convivialité* (1974); René Dumont, *L'Utopie ou la mort* (1974); Prof. Mollo-Mollo [Philippe Lebreton], *L'Energie, c'est vous* (1974); André Gorz, *Ecologie et politique* (1975); Philippe Saint-Marc, *Socialisation de la nature* (1975).[33]

The following films and documentaries, meanwhile, were airing on television or showing in French theaters: *Nature morte* (1968); *La France de demain* (1972); *La vie ou la mort* (1973); *Le retour du saumon* (1974); *Au rhythme de la nature* (1974): *Terres humaines* (1974); and *Les parcs nationaux* (1977).[34] And on the radio during the late 1960s and early '70s: Johnny Halliday, "La pollution," and "Rendez-moi le soleil"; Antoine, "Touchez pas à la mer"; Pierre Perret, "Donnez-nous des jardins" and "La cage aux oiseaux"; Yves Duteil, "Sur une mappemonde"; Jean-Pierre Lang, "J'aime bien ma terre"; Jules Beaucarne, "Front de libération des arbres fruitiers"; Georges Brassens, "Auprès de mon arbre"; Michel Delpech, "Le chasseur"; Georges Moustaki, "La mer m'a donné" and "Le temps de vivre"; and Maxime Le Forestier, "Comme un arbre."

Nationwide opinion polls clearly reflected this growing environmental awareness. A 1967 survey asked French citizens how they regarded the year 2000: when it came to environmental issues, an average of 70 percent thought that most problems, such as pollution, overpopulation, and noise, would still plague France at the end of the century as much as they did in the present.[35] In a 1972 survey, 50 percent of respondents said they believed that technological progress was generating forms of pollution and environmental degradation that would, on balance, *outweigh* the very benefits that progress had brought with it.[36] Another poll, conducted in 1976, posed a broad philosophical question: "Do you think that technological progress is rendering our society and our lifestyle so artificial as to endanger the survival of coming generations?" Fully 76 percent answered in the affirmative, while only 18 percent disagreed.[37]

The sociologist Ronald Inglehart, in a pathbreaking study based on similar polls conducted throughout Europe in 1972 (and eliciting similar results), drew the following broad conclusion: Europeans during the 1960s and '70s were making a transition from a "materialist" to a "post-materialist" set of values.[38] By "materialist" values, Inglehart referred to a cultural orientation, prevalent among broad segments of the 1940s and '50s population, that prized physical comforts and job security as the primary goals for most households. The immediate postwar generation, having experienced the wrenching upheavals of wartime, became fixated on achieving the perquisites of basic material security. By contrast, the children of that generation, who grew up in an environment of relative prosperity and stability, found themselves in the enviable position of being able to take the material aspects of daily life for granted; their psychological and emotional needs, and their moral orientation, therefore shifted in a new direction, toward the intangibles that are often referred to as "quality of life." Leisure time, aesthetic concerns, questions of meaning and identity, fulfilment at one's job, friendships and social relationships—all these constituted, for Inglehart, a "post-materialist" set of values that emerged with the sixties counterculture, but that also had broader implications for the European mainstream.

Environmentalism, of course, provided exactly the kind of social and political engagement that a "post-materialist" generation would find compelling: a willingness to scrutinize critically the engines of economic growth, and to pose instead a new set of questions about the costs of that growth, both to the natural world and to humans as well. These costs might be quite concrete, as in the case of water pollution, or much more ethereal in character: a paucity of green spaces in one's city, a diffuse sense of alienation from one's rural roots. In either case, Inglehart concluded, the 1960s and 1970s marked a period when Europeans began, in unprecedented numbers, to experience a new anxiety about modernization—anxiety not so much that modernization would fail, but that its very success would produce a profoundly flawed social order that was also dangerously out of balance with the rhythms of the natural world.[39]

Nevertheless, in France as in other European countries, only a small minority of citizens felt moved to express these anxieties in some form of concerted activism along the lines of Les Amis de la Terre: those who did so found that they constituted, rather self-consciously (and perhaps proudly), a "green fringe" of French public life (see figures 3, 4, and 5). They had their tiny organizations, most of them impoverished and ephemeral; they had loose ties (and ongoing arguments) with their friends on the Maoist left or in the "left-libertarian" trade union, the CFDT; they had several vivacious and mordant journals to choose from—*La Gueule Ouverte, Survivre et Vivre,* and *Le Sauvage* (all of which concentrated on green issues) and *Charlie-Hebdo,* which appealed more broadly to the non-Communist left. They read Sartre, Illich, Ellul, and Gorz, and relished the sardonic, outrageous humor of the cartoonist Jean-Marc Reiser, creator of the unforgettable character Gros Dégueulasse.[40] (See chapter 5 for a more detailed discussion of the greens' intellectual horizons.)

But they remained relatively few in number. In April 1971, a group of ac-

Figure 3. Poster: "Nuclear Society, Police Society: No to Nuclear Energy" (1978).
(Courtesy of Musée de la Publicité [Union Centrale des Arts Décoratifs].)

tivists based in Alsace, organized France's first antinuclear demonstration,
outside the civilian nuclear power station being built at Fessenheim; some
1,500 persons showed up. A few months later, in July, the numbers were better: 15,000 demonstrators protested at the Bugey reactor site, along the
Rhone.[41] In November 1971, many of the same persons met again, this time
not at a nuclear site, but on the remote plateau of Larzac in central France,

Figure 4. Poster by Raymond Savignac: "No to the Left Bank Highway" (1973). (Courtesy of Musée de la Publicité [Union Centrale des Arts Décoratifs].)

where the French army had announced its intention to extend one of its firing grounds, against the repeatedly expressed wishes of local peasant municipalities. The Larzac campaign quickly took on a broader symbolic meaning, as it became clear that the French state would not budge on this issue: in July 1972, 20,000 persons—environmentalists, peace activists, Maoists, anar-

"Poor old guy . . ."

"You want me to console you?"

"There you are, all tarred, blackish, and sticky. Well, inside my lungs it's the same thing."

"With all the cigarettes I smoke every day, I have two critters like you in my lungs!"

"And for you, the tar's free, but as for me, I have to pay for it—a lot!"

"Good, well, with that, you're on your own! You must feel better now!"

Figure 5. Cartoon with Gros Dégueulasse by Jean-Marc Reiser, mid-1970s. (Courtesy of Michèle Reiser and Éditions Albin Michel.)

chists—converged on the site, portraying the conflict as a classic David and Goliath showdown. (The struggle went on, year after year, until 1981, when the newly elected President François Mitterrand finally forced the army to throw in the towel.)[42]

For the most part, French public opinion followed these developments with interest—even, for many on the Left, with a certain sympathy. Just how much sympathy was a matter of considerable debate among environmentalists at the time; and this question led to the idea of testing the waters by putting forward an environmentalist candidate in the national presidential elections of 1974. A series of meetings held in the house of Jean Carlier (who had led the Vanoise campaign), eventually settled on the name of the eminent agronomist, René Dumont. Dumont, seventy years old, was already internationally famous for his pioneering studies of Third World poverty; his attention had turned in recent years to the ecological crisis, and he had just published a dramatic book entitled *Utopia or Death,* in which he brought to-gether the grim statistics of the Club of Rome with an open advocacy of dra-conian solutions bearing the heavy influence of socialism.[43] Indeed, in the eyes of some environmentalists, Dumont was "more red than green."[44]

With the irrepressible Brice Lalonde acting as campaign manager, the en-vironmentalists flung themselves for the first time into national politics. Not without misgivings: they worried that Dumont's campaign would divide the Left and hurt the Socialist candidate Mitterrand; they worried that running for election would embroil them in the dubious traffickings of party politics; they worried that, if they did unexpectedly well, this very success might cause them to lose their identity as *contestateurs,* as a fundamentally anti-establishment ideological grouping. They needn't have agonized too much. When the results came in on election day, Dumont received 1.3 percent of the vote; the election went on to a second round, in which the center-right candidate, Valéry Giscard d'Estaing, emerged victorious. Most greens re-garded their electoral performance as a modest success.[45] In their first sortie into national politics, their candidate had surpassed several other left-wing contenders, and placed green ideas for the first time on the political map. On the other hand, with only one percent of the population in their camp, they clearly had their work cut out for them.

1974–1981: Eco-Quixote vs. Electricité de France

Greenpeace-France, as we saw in chapter 1, ultimately ran aground and sank on the shoals of the *force de frappe.* During the late 1970s, the French environmental movement as a whole nearly suffered the same fate when it tackled France's civilian nuclear industry. In this latter case the dissidents' numbers were notably greater—protest demonstrations against nuclear-generated electricity attracted far more participants than the embarrassingly feeble gestures against nuclear weaponry—but in the end the French popu-lation's attachment to the atom proved still more potent and durable. The environmentalists, still rather new to the politics of confrontation, made se-rious mistakes that cost them dearly; the state, for its part, bore down on them with relentless and overwhelming pressure—as in the Yeats poem, "a gaze blank and pitiless as the sun."[46]

Like the Concorde, the French nuclear reactor network constituted a re-markable technological achievement—a victory of political tenacity as much as a feat of engineering. The contrast with the United States is particularly in-structive: for in the U.S., the attempt to build a supersonic airliner failed for economic reasons, and the attempt to build a dense nationwide grid of nuclear power plants failed for political reasons. In France, both projects were tackled and successfully realized. By the mid-1990s, nuclear reactors were producing 80 percent of France's electricity, with a good deal left over for sale to Germany and Italy. The superlatives piled up most remarkably: more reactors per kilometer of territory than any other nation; the most advanced fuel-processing facilities in the world; the largest fast-breeder reactor; more of its total energy output coming from nuclear technology than any other country; the largest stockpile of nuclear waste per number of inhabitants; the highest level of public debt attributable to nuclear construction.[47] Both the supporters and the detractors of Electricité de France (EDF), the state-run utility company, could agree on one thing: when the French undertake one of their trademark *grands programmes,* they really do mean *grand.*

The roots of France's civilian reactor program extend back into the late 1940s, to Frédéric Joliot-Curie and the creation of the Commissariat à l'Energie Atomique (see the discussion in chapter 1). Although this eminent physicist vehemently opposed the harnessing of the atom for warlike purposes, he embraced the civilian potentialities of nuclear energy with unabashed ardor; and in this attitude he was fairly typical among French physicists.[48] Even after Joliot-Curie's political fall in 1950, therefore, the Commissariat à l'Energie Atomique (CEA) remained eagerly oriented toward the development of cutting-edge reactor technology. In the eyes of the Fourth Republic's politicians and technocrats, the possibility of nuclear energy seemed almost too good to be true; for France had historically found itself hobbled, in its quest for industrial growth, by the poor reserves of coal and (later) oil that could be found on its territory. In 1938, French coal production had peaked at roughly 25 percent of German production and 20 percent of British production—a terrible handicap to the French economy in its struggle for modernization. How then could France hope to carry out its ambitious plans for postwar economic resurgence, unless the "energy equation" could somehow be solved? And then, out of the mysterious entrails of the atom, a possible deus ex machina: vast amounts of cheap energy based on uranium, a mineral found in relative abundance at several remote locations in southwestern France! The text of a 1957 energy bill in the Assemblée Nationale neatly summed up the prevailing attitude: "France, which was not able to win completely either the coal battle of the nineteenth century or the oil battle of the first half of the twentieth century, intends to confront the nuclear age with the certitude of success."[49]

The first French nuclear reactor, nicknamed Zoé, went critical in 1948; the first nuclear-electric generator, a modest forty-megawatt installation at Marcoule, in northern Provence, went on line in 1956. Thereafter the French built larger and larger reactors, with another six coming on line by 1965; in that year, the pace was stepped up even further, with a commitment to produce 500 megawatts of nuclear-generating capacity per year. Electricité de France (EDF) had been an increasingly enthusiastic proponent of the nuclear cause since the 1950s. As the nation's largest government-owned enterprise—some referred to it as a veritable state within the state—EDF employed more than a hundred thousand workers; its highly centralized structure allowed it to set nationwide standards for both the generation and distribution of electric power.[50] The elite corps of engineers and economists who ran EDF had become convinced that future French economic growth hinged on ever-expanding energy consumption, and that a hefty portion of this energy should flow from EDF's own expanding network of nuclear reactors rather than from imported petroleum. With their considerable political clout, they accordingly pressed within the government for an ever-greater commitment to atomic power.

Then came the OPEC oil embargo of 1973: within the space of a few months, the price of petroleum quadrupled. The French government, which had been banking heavily on its carefully cultivated relationship with the Arab world, found itself lumped together with other Western countries in the OPEC choke-hold; French citizens faced long gas lines, rising inflation, economic recession, and cold winters. The sobering experience of strategic vulnerability that had long lain implicit in the West's energy dependency now became a very real fact of life.[51]

Suddenly the EDF lobbyists within the corridors of power had the undivided attention of the politicians. Pierre Messmer, the French prime minister, decided that he wanted to tackle the crisis with a Gaullist élan worthy of the late General: for several months he convened intensive meetings among EDF and CEA experts, finance personnel, industry representatives, and government ministers, weighing the various options; then, on March 6, 1974, he went on television to address the population. "France," he explained, in the resolute tone of someone who has made a Big Decision,

> was not favored by nature in its energy resources. No oil, less coal than England or Germany, far lower gas reserves than Holland. But our great opportunity lies in nuclear power, a domain in which our country has made itself a leader since the Second World War. In our quest for greater self-sufficiency in energy production—or, shall we say, for a lower degree of dependency—we shall give the priority to nuclear-generated electricity. The effort will cost a great deal, and I personally commit myself to seeing it through to success.[52]

The Messmer Plan, as it came to be known, left everyone breathless with its draconian boldness, for it amounted to a complete restructuring of France's energy cycle—a wager on a time-scale of half a century, with the nation's fundamental economic and physical security in the balance. Sixteen new nuclear power stations would be built in the following two years, by 1976–a *quadrupling* of the highest rate of construction yet sustained. Then, in successive years, the pace was to continue, with 32 new plants scheduled over the following decade. The total investment, as forecast by the Ministry of Finance, amounted to 177 billion francs, or nine percent of one year's GDP—the equivalent of building 16,000 kilometers of highway.[53]

To a non-French observer, perhaps the most striking aspect of Messmer's energy plan was that it did not come up for formal discussion by the Assemblée Nationale until May 1975, more than a year after it was launched—by which time the accelerated building program was already well under way. Because of the highly centralized and top-heavy structure of the French state, a relatively small group of technocrats and politicians effectively made a choice for all of France, steering the nation resolutely onto the nuclear road, with consequences that would decisively affect the population and the territory for at least a century to come. Whether one approved or disapproved of nuclear power, this in itself constituted an undeniable, and quite remarkable, fact.[54]

Machine/Symbol: The Nuclear Reactor

"It's very simple, a nuclear power plant: it's like a coal-burning plant in which we have a reactor instead of a fire under the boiler!" So spoke an EDF regional manager to Pierre Massé, the head of EDF, in the late 1960s. Massé was horrified. This, he felt, was precisely the sort of cavalier attitude that could sooner or later lead to disaster. Massé made it one of his primary missions, during his three years at the utility's helm, to ensure that no one among the technical staff could ever think such casual thoughts about the enormous powers over which they were presiding.[55]

And yet, in a sense, EDF's callow regional manager had a point: a nuclear-powered generator does function in much the same way as a fossil-fuel powered generator. In both cases the object is to create heat (large amounts of it) with which water is boiled; the resulting high-pressure steam is then piped through a nozzle, imparting its force to the vanes of a spinning turbine; the turbine passes its rotational energy to a shaft which drives an electric generator. Of course, Massé was also right to be horrified: for while creating heat by burning a fossil fuel is relatively straightforward, creating heat through a nu-

clear reaction is entirely another matter. At every stage of the nuclear production line, risks accumulate and complex technological obstacles must be
overcome.

First the raw uranium ore must be mined and purified, then it must be
concentrated into dense packets and enriched, boosting its fissile qualities:
already in both these stages, one is dealing with a radioactive substance, and
hence with an intrinsic element of danger. Inside a nuclear reactor, the enriched uranium is allowed to "go critical," which means that a chain reaction
takes place: one atom splits and releases two neutrons; the two released neutrons in turn strike two other atoms, both of which split and release two
more neutrons apiece; these four neutrons in turn strike four more atoms,
causing them to split and release eight neutrons . . . and the exponential
cycle is off and running, 16, 32, 64, 128, 256, 512, 1024, and so on. All this
happens in a fraction of a second; and each time an atom splits and releases
two neutrons, it also releases energy in the form of heat. To control this
process inside the reactor core, rods of graphite or other neutron-absorbing
elements are mechanically inserted or withdrawn, thereby allowing the reactor's operator to slow down the fission process or to accelerate it as he or she
desires. The heat from the nuclear fission is passed on to a large volume of
water flowing in pipes around the reactor core—and thence to the turbine
and generator. This water therefore fulfils a double purpose: it extracts us-
able energy from the fission process, and it cools the reactor core, keeping
it from burning too hot and melting. After a certain amount of time inside
the reactor, the uranium fuel becomes spent, and must be replaced. The
spent fuel, a highly radioactive substance, is then taken to a reprocessing
plant, where it is chemically treated to render it more stable, and finally
melted into a vitrified form. The resultant glassy waste, one of the more toxic
substances known to science, must be stored indefinitely: its poisonous
qualities will persist for thousands of years.[56]

Massé, who was no fool, lucidly realized how many ways something
could go wrong with this process: transportation, reactor design, mechanical
failure, human error, bureaucratic glitch. He also felt confident that EDF was
entirely up to the task, as long as the necessary safeguards, backup systems,
and training programs were rigorously maintained. It added up to a long-
term wager of sorts—a high-stakes wager that France's technological and administrative mastery could outweigh the risks, and that the nation could
therefore liberate itself (at least partially) from its dependency on fossil fuels.

One of the fundamental ironies of this nuclear wager emerged at about the
same time as Massé presided over EDF, between 1966 and 1969. It came to
be known as *la guerre des filières,* or the war over designs, and it culminated

in a rather astonishing twist in the discourse of national autonomy: starting in 1970, nearly all new French reactors derived from an imported American blueprint. The roots of this paradoxical outcome went back to the late 1950s, when a growing rivalry had emerged between the CEA (Commissariat à l'Energie Atomique) and EDF over which of these two state agencies would oversee France's passage into the industrial phase of the nuclear era.[57] Both organizations judged themselves to be better qualified for the job, the CEA because of its pioneering role in nuclear research, EDF because of its long experience in managing large-scale technological systems. The rivalry became bitter and intense—a classic exemplar of what the historian Gabrielle Hecht has dubbed "technopolitics," the deep mutual interpenetration of engineering decisions and political calculation in the shaping of technological systems.[58]

In the end the *guerre des filières* came to hinge upon a choice between two reactor designs: a model preferred by EDF, based on the use of enriched uranium as fuel and pressurized water as a coolant (hence the designation PWR, or Pressurized Water Reactor); and a model favored by the CEA, based on the use of natural uranium as a fuel and an inert gas as a coolant (generally referred to as the gas-graphite reactor). Throughout the 1960s the CEA had the upper hand in this bureaucratic struggle. Its gas-graphite reactor had been designed and perfected by French scientists; it used natural uranium, a fuel that could be mined relatively easily within the national territory; and (last but not least) this design produced, as a normal phase of its functioning, a form of plutonium that worked well in nuclear weapons. EDF, by contrast, argued that the PWR reactor was safer, and, above all, much cheaper to build and to operate. What was more, the PWR design had already established itself as the preferred technology in most other nuclear nations, especially the United States; this meant that France, if it wanted to manufacture and sell reactors on the international export market, would have to adopt the prevailing PWR design if it wanted to compete successfully in this lucrative industry.

For President de Gaulle, who followed the arguments of both sides with regal detachment, the CEA's position ultimately came to seem unassailable: the gas-graphite reactor was a French technology; it would produce electricity with French nuclear fuel, while simultaneously turning out French plutonium for use by the military. National autonomy carried the day, and he overrode the pleas of EDF.

But then, in 1969, de Gaulle abruptly resigned, and his prime minister, Georges Pompidou, assumed the presidency. Since Pompidou was an economist by training, EDF saw its chance to launch a full-scale flanking maneuver. National autonomy, the EDF leaders argued, remained as important as ever: but a *true* form of national autonomy required strong commercial competitiveness on international markets, not just a stubborn adherence to the "made in France" label at any cost. It was true, they admitted, that the PWR technology was more American than French; but France could adopt this technology, master it, and eventually compete strongly with the Americans at their own game. Only in this way, and not by clinging to the flawed (so they argued) gas-graphite design, could French technology remain at the forefront of the world's nuclear industry.[59] Such was the bureaucratic clout of EDF that, within a year, in 1970, Pompidou had thrown his support behind the PWR design and consigned the CEA's plans to extinction.

When the Messmer Plan went into effect four years later, therefore, most of France's new reactors were PWR models built under license from the American firm Westinghouse! This fact, deliberately downplayed by the government, remained largely unknown to the French public. What was more, EDF had taken yet another, and more considerable, gamble: all the new reactors stemmed from a single design. The benefits of this policy appeared considerable: economies of scale in production and construction, interchangeability of parts, and uniform training programs for EDF reactor personnel. Nevertheless, the system's one major drawback could also prove monumental: if the Westinghouse design should ever develop unforeseen problems, the whole of France's electro-nuclear industry might find itself hobbled at one stroke.[60]

It was an awesome gamble; and in some respects it could be regarded as having paid off handsomely over the ensuing two decades. Each time the Westinghouse contract came up for renewal over the years, French design components were systematically inserted, and the French share of ownership steadily increased.[61] Meanwhile, the French nuclear industry had developed its own uranium enrichment plants, its own uranium mines in Africa, its own waste-processing facilities. COGEMA, Framatome, and Alsthom, the key companies in French nuclear manufacturing, led the world with their cutting-edge technology. A huge fast-breeder reactor at Creys-Malville, based on a new design that burned nuclear waste as its fuel, began functioning (after numerous setbacks) in the early 1990s.[62] France had made itself a world leader, if not *the* world leader, in virtually every aspect of the nuclear fuel cycle. De Gaulle would have been pleased.

> > >

How did the French people feel about the Messmer Plan? By and large, with the exception of a sometimes sizable minority, they accepted it. Resistance to the nuclear project came from three main sources: the environmental movement (to which we return in a moment); committees of scientists and economists who questioned the project on technical grounds; and the opposition parties of the Left. Of these three, the most important by far would have been the Socialist Party—*if* it had forcefully taken up the antinuclear cause. But it didn't. The Socialists remained divided over nuclear energy between 1974 and 1981, with one faction arguing that nuclear electricity was essential to economic growth and hence to workers' prosperity, while the other faction opposed nuclear technology on grounds that largely echoed the arguments of the scientists and ecologists.[63] Socialist opposition to the Messmer Plan therefore remained rather muted throughout the 1970s; what was more, when the Socialists finally won a major election victory in 1981, it was their pro-nuclear faction that decisively got the upper hand. The newly elected president François Mitterrand promptly canceled a few nuclear power plants as a sop to his environmentalist allies, but otherwise maintained the vast nuclear program untouched. In retrospect, the profound continuity between the conservative governments of the 1970s and the left-wing governments of the 1980s in this regard constitutes a striking feature of that period's political history.[64]

Opinion polls from these two decades suggest that the Socialists, in adopting their openly pro-nuclear stance, were bowing to a clear electoral reality: like the *force de frappe,* the civilian nuclear industry had been gaining popularity during the 1970s (and like the *force de frappe* it continued to do so throughout the 1980s).[65] In 1974 and 1975, approximately 55 percent of the population declared themselves in favor of the nuclear-electric program, versus 33 percent who opposed it.[66] In 1981, at the time of the next presidential election, the ratio held firm, with 62 percent declaring themselves pro-nuclear and 37 percent antinuclear.[67] Once again, as with the *force de frappe,* these kinds of polls placed France in a unique position amid the nations of Europe: like a lone star in the statistical firmament, French opinion stood at the top ranking of pro-nuclear nations, with a ratio between positive and negative opinions that hovered a full 18 percentage points above the European average.[68]

This should not mislead us, however, into believing that the French government and EDF were mere passive spectators in the evolution of French opinion. Far from it: a great deal of active manipulation, cajoling, and antidemocratic chicanery went into the building and reinforcing of this pro-nuclear consensus.[69] Mayors and city councils of towns located near proposed reactor sites were offered extremely generous funds for parks, gymnasiums, and schools, as long as their communities docilely went along with EDF's plans.[70] Public hearings on proposed reactors were held at inconvenient times and locations; then, when the locals' questions and objections had been recorded, they were blithely ignored anyway.[71] A heavy veil of state secrecy enveloped all aspects of the nuclear industry, from financial outlays to construction to operating procedures to the maintenance of public safety.[72] Scientists outside EDF were refused access to technical information; when they insistently pursued such information, their requests were endlessly deferred; when they went public with their frustrating experiences, they were branded as extremists by the government.[73] Films showing both sides of the nuclear debate were banned from French television.[74] Accidents in French reactors were regularly presented to the public as minor glitches—with no opportunity for external watchdog groups to verify EDF's safety record.[75] Around some nuclear sites, the political influence exerted by power-plant managers extended far enough to ensure that their own employees would be elected as local mayors and town councillors.[76] "In the mid-1970s," admitted one EDF economist,

> most of us thought it unlikely that our full program would succeed. There were too many possibilities: opposition from the Ministry of Finance, the scientists [in the antinuclear movement], a victory by the left in 1978, hesitation on the part of the government. . . . [But part of our tactic] was never to speak those doubts. We had to be confident and not admit there was any alternative. There could be no choice about *le nucléaire*.[77]

This, then, was the formidable set of obstacles that France's environmentalists and antinuclear scientists faced when they took on EDF in the early 1970s. As they saw it, they had two basic strategies at their disposal: on the one hand, to educate the French public about the dangers of the nuclear industry, putting the government and EDF on the defensive; and second, to engage in frequent and militant forms of direct action at nuclear sites, since this would attract much-needed media attention as well as slow down the frenetic pace of construction.

The government responded to the first strategy by calling upon its own prestigious corps of engineers and experts to parry each line of antinuclear argument as it arose. When environmentalists claimed that the reactors were fundamentally unsafe, they countered that the industry's risks could be brought within acceptable limits through a system of appropriately overlapping security procedures and failsafe techniques.[78] When the greens asked about nuclear waste, the government scientists assured the public that these wastes were being stored in a top-security underground facility in Normandy, and that research was under way on a permanent solution, such as burning the waste in a new generation of fast-breeders. When the greens protested about "the road not taken"—the lack of serious commitment to developing alternative energy sources (including conservation)—the government experts had a ready response: as long as the French people wanted an economy based on growth, this continuing growth would require ever-greater quantities of energy. If the French wanted to keep their position as the world's fifth-largest industrial economy, they argued, alternative energy sources could only provide a relatively small slice of the overall "energy pie"—and sooner or later, since fossil fuels must inevitably run out, this left no alternative but le nucléaire.[79] At this point the greens could call into question the notion itself of endless economic growth—but this in turn opened them to being portrayed as Luddites or utopians who were totally out of touch with the aspirations of mainstream French society. The arguments went back and forth, but they ultimately failed to make much impact on public opinion: the fact that eminent scientists could be found championing both sides of the debate did not help.

As for the environmentalists' second strategy—direct action—this ultimately proved a disaster.[80] In mobilizing their demonstrations during the mid-1970s, the relatively inexperienced greens gladly accepted the participation of "veteran" dissenters from various strands of the radical or anarchist left. These militants, steeped more in Bakunin, Fanon, and Marcuse than in Rachel Carson, regarded antinuclear protest as an excellent way to do battle with their sworn enemy, the central government: their long-term aim was not just to halt the Messmer Plan but, as their favorite phrase went, "to smash the state apparatus." In the meetings of the antinuclear movement as it planned demonstrations, this small but influential group of militants pushed successfully for ever more confrontational tactics, casting scorn on the peaceable protests of the early '70s, and calling for site occupations, sabotage, and frontal engagement with the police. Such tactics, they argued, would force the state into the kind of repression that, aired nightly on television, would turn the tide of public opinion in their favor.[81]

The majority of environmentalists, who had little taste for these tactics, thus found their movement increasingly hijacked by an extremist minority who were all too ready to engage in violence. Green leaders could plead all they wanted for peaceful and orderly conduct, but it only took a few individuals throwing rocks (or Molotov cocktails) at the police to precipitate a melée. Too many times, during the mid-1970s, as antinuclear demonstrations were covered on the nightly news, France's television audiences witnessed scenes of disorder, property damage, and sometimes outright violence. All this, of course, played right into the hands of the government, which could now come forward as the defender of public order against a wild mob of extremists.[82] And defend it most certainly did: with police dogs, barbed wire, tear gas, truncheons, and charging phalanxes of CRS agents— the dreaded Compagnies Républicaines de Sécurité (a sort of Rambo battalion of police crowd control).

This politics of confrontation finally came to a head on July 31, 1977, when 30,000 chanting demonstrators converged on one of France's most controversial reactors, Super-Phénix, the huge fast-breeder outside the village of Malville, not far from Lyon. Earlier that year, a meeting of antinuclear organizers had issued the following declaration:

> Legitimate defense against *Super-Phénix*! Green light to any action that will slow down the reactor's construction. We must undermine this project by any means necessary and on all available occasions. EDF has turned Malville into a fortified camp surrounded by electric fences and police dogs: we must attack this citadel from all sides![83]

On the morning of July 31 it was raining. Overhead, police helicopters circled. The CRS corps allowed the demonstrators to gather in a cul-de-sac of the village below the reactor site, then charged. From one side came Molotov cocktails, from the other side tear-gas canisters and concussion grenades. The demonstrators fell back and began fleeing, but found themselves caught in a crush of bodies. The CRS agents waded into them, truncheons flying; as protestors escaped into the fields beyond, the CRS followed, clubbing them into the mud with brisk efficiency. When the day was over, more than a hundred demonstrators came away bruised and bloodied; one protestor had been killed, three maimed, and five policemen seriously injured. Both sides accused the other of deliberately provoking the incident.[84]

The event marked the end of a certain style of environmental activism in France; for large sectors of the French citizenry strongly supported the government in its tough stance—almost half of the Socialist Party's voters, and 80 percent of the voters on the center and center-right.[85] The antinuclear demonstrators, goaded on by a violent minority within their midst, had been effectively typecast before French public opinion as extremists and anarchists.[86] It took several years for the ecological movement to nurse its wounds, reorganize itself, kick out the anarchists, and come back again, this time with a more moderate strategy: to enter national politics as a full-fledged, institutionalized competitor.

As for the nuclear reactors, they went on being built. One of the ironies of EDF's nuclear program was that it ultimately became *too* successful, producing far more electricity than French consumers and industry could use. This posed a serious problem, because the government's economists had counted on a steeply rising demand curve to boost EDF's revenues and hence provide enough income to service the enormous debt incurred by nuclear construction. When demand slackened in the late 1970s, partly because of conservation measures enacted after the oil crisis, EDF found itself forced to launch a new campaign, summed up by the publicity slogan, "tout électrique, tout nucléaire"—all-electric, all-nuclear.[87] The idea was simple: to lure French society away from the use of oil, coal, and gas, and to reorient it progressively toward an increased reliance on nuclear-generated electricity. This meant, above all, warming the homes and offices of France with electric heaters rather than fossil-fuel furnaces—a tough challenge for EDF's salesmanship, because electricity (as compared with fossil fuels) is an inherently inefficient vehicle for creating heat. Yet EDF saw no alternative, and thus resolutely embarked on a crusade to "electrify" French consumption patterns. To those who objected that this meant promoting a systematic waste of energy resources, EDF's spokespersons retorted that it was better to rely on an inefficient heating source produced within the national territory, than on a more efficient heating source imported from abroad. Between 1974 and 1984, the consumption of electricity in French households doubled.[88]

Perhaps the greatest irony of all, however, lay in the financial bottom line; for building and maintaining France's nuclear power grid proved enormously expensive, and though EDF recouped a small portion of its outlays by selling surplus electricity abroad, the overall financial picture for nuclear power remained bleak. Between 1973 and 1984, as the Messmer Plan surged ahead, EDF's cumulative debt rose by 650 percent.[89] Much of this headlong borrowing spree took place overseas, as EDF became a world-class player in international money markets. By the mid-1980s, EDF's foreign indebtedness stood at 93 billion francs, or 15.6 percent of total French foreign debt. the giant utility weighed in as the third largest borrower on the U.S. market, after Ford and General Motors. "Each time one of our clients pays 100 francs," lamented EDF director Marcel Boiteux in 1986, "25 francs go to paying the interest on debts."[90] According to one group of scholars,

> Building the huge French nuclear industrial complex, usually presented as the key to energy independence, has in fact been one of the many international factors in the devaluation of the franc, and one of the main causes for the growth of the French foreign debt and the financial *dependence* of France.[91]

What was worse, from a long-term perspective, was that EDF's financial squeeze could only become tighter and tighter, because the deferred costs of storing nuclear waste and retiring old reactors from service had barely begun to make themselves felt. A nuclear reactor lasts, on average, thirty years; then it must be dismantled, and its (highly radioactive) components properly disposed of. This expensive phase of the nuclear energy cycle had never figured explicitly in EDF's cost calculations; but by the early 2000s, with the first generation of senescent reactors ready to shut down, the long-postponed reckoning could no longer remain hidden from view.

1981–1989: Entering the Political Fray

In the aftermath of the drubbing received at the hands of EDF and the French state, the French greens experienced what can only be described as their political nadir. Racked by bitter internal divisions, and effectively portrayed as wackos or political extremists in the eyes of large swaths of the French public, they were forced in the late 1970s to ask themselves fundamental questions about their long-term goals and the best strategies for achieving them. Clearly, the tactics of head-on confrontation and civil disobedience had failed miserably; but would more conventional paths of political action work any better?

Most environmentalists, coming as they did out of the pullulating counterculture of the 1960s, felt a profound frustration with France's political establishment and electoral system. To them, this system added up to a travesty of democracy—manipulative, elitist, unresponsive, overcentralized, too often in the pocket of big business. The major question facing them, therefore, was twofold. Should they try to become regular players in this political game, or remain resolutely outside the system? And if they decided to enter politics, in the name of gaining influence and public recognition for their ideas, could they do so without sliding down a slippery slope of compromises until they were no longer meaningfully different from the parties they scorned? To put it simply: could they realistically hope to invent a new way of doing politics?[92]

The greens first confronted these questions in the 1970s, and they continued to wrestle with them right through the next quarter-century and into the new millennium. If one takes a somewhat long view of these years, the pattern that emerges might be summed up as follows: the environmentalists started off in the 1970s and '80s by rigorously setting themselves apart from all other parties, conducting their business in radically innovative ways. Then, in the 1990s, they gradually began to scale back their most distinctive practices, and to acknowledge the need for more traditional forms of power.[93] By the turn of the millennium, this "normalization" process was well under way: for although it was true that the environmentalists still played by different rules than other political parties, they were now playing closer to the mainstream than they ever had done before.

After the presidential elections of 1974, Dumont's campaign committee quickly dissolved itself. Although some activists wanted a stable political organization to coordinate their efforts over the coming years, the majority found this idea repugnant: organizations, they believed, had a way of corrupting those who served in them, because power often became for these people an end in itself. Hence the preference, among most green activists, for what were called "biodegradable" political committees: cobbled together on an ad hoc basis, to serve a specific electoral purpose, then routinely disbanded. This came to constitute the first major issue of principle that the environmentalists confronted: to form, or not to form, a political party.[94]

The problem was that, while the system of biodegradable committees succeeded admirably at preventing any undesirable sclerosis among the greens, it also prevented them from building expertise and momentum from election to election. In France, this posed a particular problem, because elections took place there almost every year, each time focusing on a different level of government: municipal, cantonal, regional, parliamentary, presidential, and (after 1979) for the European Parliament. Thus, the greens found themselves forming biodegradable organizations to contest such elections in 1977, again in 1978, twice in 1979, and then again in 1981—the results, until 1981, hovering around one or two percent of the vote. Each time, moreover, they had to start over from scratch, resulting in a high degree of "burnout" among the activists conducting the campaigns.

The 1981 presidential election brought many of these issues to a head. Brice Lalonde, the green candidate, campaigned on a platform that included curbing pollution, cutting back on energy consumption, and other such environmental measures, but also advocated a global redistribution of wealth between rich nations and poor ones, and proposed, within France itself, to combat unemployment through a complex system of reduced working hours and job-sharing.[95] Overall, this unabashedly idealistic stance was designed to appeal to a large constituency of voters, primarily on the Left, who shunned the Communists because of their Stalinist heritage, but who regarded the Socialists as having compromised too heavily with the entrenched interests of the Establishment. The strategy evidently worked, for Lalonde received 3.9 percent of the vote in the 1981 election—three times more than Dumont a mere seven years before. The greens had become the fifth-ranked political force in France.[96]

Nevertheless, this achievement was being rapidly overshadowed by the greens of West Germany, whose breathtaking rise in the early 1980s brought them into the Bundestag and into headlines the world around. The French electoral system, by contrast, was explicitly designed to keep small fringe parties from gaining access to parliament: unless the French environmentalists could get past the legal threshold of five percent of the vote, they would remain shut out of the Assemblée Nationale indefinitely. Between 1981 and 1984, therefore, more and more environmental activists began to reconsider their refusal to form a permanent political party. Many of them felt betrayed by the Socialist leader Mitterrand, who had won the presidency in 1981 partly by promising all manner of environmentalist legislation—but whose actual policies in office, such as the continuation of the Messmer Plan, seemed indistinguishable from those of his right-wing predecessors. The idea began to surface, at environmentalist gatherings, that it was no longer enough to seek to influence the Socialists; rather, it was time to create a new ecological party that would *replace* the Socialists as the major political force on the Left.

The result, after considerable wrangling and maneuvering, came at a meeting in January 1984 at Clichy: the birth of *Les Verts*. (I will henceforth reserve the capitalized "Greens" to refer to this party, and continue using the lower-case "greens" as a synonym for environmentalists in general.) But this was to be a political party unlike any other: it would maintain a tight thematic focus on environmental issues; it would not form tactical alliances with other parties; its national structure would remain decentralized and loosely federative, with annual meetings setting a common policy; its leadership would come from a committee rather than from any single personality; it would guarantee equality between men and women; and it would feature mandatory rotation of all leadership positions within the party and of all elected positions gained by the party. The old spirit of May '68 had come alive again—the dream of reinventing political power in a way that kept it fluid, open, and non-hierarchical.[97]

Unfortunately, the gap between dream and reality proved hard to bridge. Brice Lalonde, irked at his failure to gain the leadership of the new party, retreated to his original organization, Les Amis de la Terre, and announced his intention to begin contesting elections with a separate environmental list of his own. Les Verts, he said, were simply too doctrinaire for his taste: France needed a more moderate and reasonable green alternative. To the fury of his erstwhile comrades, Lalonde's new grouping won 3.4 percent of the vote in the European elections of 1984–matching exactly the 3.4 percent won by Les Verts! What should have been a triumph for the greens—an eyebrow-raising 6.8 percent result—had been neatly split in half. Here began a bitter and damaging rivalry that would last more than a decade, well into the 1990s—effectively locking the environmentalists out of the French parliament, as well as wasting their energies in bickering and mutual recriminations.[98]

Nevertheless, at all levels of governance except the national parliament, the environmentalists—both Les Verts and Lalonde's group—were now winning votes in unprecedented numbers. Many French left-wing voters in the mid-1980s were becoming "DDS" ("Déçus du Socialisme"—"Disappointed with Socialism"), as Mitterrand's party increasingly gave the impression of a senescent and soulless entity, racked by internal scandals and schisms of its own; for growing numbers of these DDS individuals, the greens seemed to offer a fresh start and a new political home.[99] In 1986, an Alsatian ecological scientist named Antoine Waechter emerged as the most influential voice among the collective leadership of Les Verts; beneath an earnest and understated demeanor, he combined personal qualities of steely determination, high ambition, and uncompromising adherence to the green ideology.[100] Other parties, sensing the growing popularity of environmental issues, began making overtures to the Greens about forming political alliances, but Waechter adamantly reaffirmed the original party policy: "L'écologie n'est pas à marier!" ("Ecology is not going to marry anyone!").[101] This strict adherence to principles, as well as the party's vibrant internal democracy, appealed to many voters, who had grown fed up with the cynicism and opportunism that seemed to afflict conventional politics.

Then came Chernobyl. As in the rest of Europe (indeed, the world), initial responses after the reactor meltdown on April 26, 1986, were conditioned by the lack of hard information available outside the Soviet Union; rumors and counter-rumors stoked the alarm of populations far and wide, and in this the French were no exception.[102] The French government, however, distinguished itself early on among the world's public authorities for its systematic downplaying of the dangers that the accident posed. French officials gave terse, blandly reassuring comments in their press releases and circulars, urging the population not to worry. While governments of most other West European nations took extraordinary measures of civilian protection, from evacuations to destroying foodstuffs to issuing iodine to children, the French authorities repeatedly and vehemently denied that such moves were necessary. "The West German press," wrote a reporter for *Le Monde* on May 9,

> is becoming more and more astonished at the total lack of official reactions and precautionary measures in France. This perfect serenity of our nation stands out as an exception in Europe. Many Germans are becoming convinced that the French government is hiding the truth [about Chernobyl], so that it will not have to answer difficult questions about its own nuclear programs.[103]

When several weeks had gone by, and a tentative balance sheet of the Chernobyl disaster could be drawn, French citizens were consternated to discover that they had been duped. Contrary to the benign portrayal of events given by their government, a far more somber picture emerged: thirty-one persons had died near the burning reactor, 100,000 Ukrainians were being evacuated, and a cloud containing approximately 100 million curies of radionuclides had spread over large swaths of Western Europe, including significant portions of France. Voicing the outrage felt by many French men and women, *Le Monde*'s editorial for May 13 lashed out against the French nuclear establishment:

> Today the government is experiencing the backlash from all the disinforma-
> tion it has sown since the accident. One can accuse the Soviet Union of having
> dragged its feet in informing its neighbors about Chernobyl, but the other na-
> tions of Europe, which possessed equally as little information as France, acted
> vigorously in taking precautions to protect their populations and minimize the
> effects of the radioactive cloud. Our government did not assume this responsi-
> bility. . . . When it comes to the atom, French leaders act as if they were para-
> lyzed.[104]

Opinion polls clearly reflected this anger and sudden loss of faith in the reliability of government assurances. Among those questioned, 52 percent felt that nuclear construction should stop; 68 percent believed that a Chernobyl-style disaster could happen in France; 79 percent thought that they had been lied to by the French authorities; 93 percent felt that they lacked adequate information about the nuclear industry.[105]

At EDF, it was time for a major reassessment of attitudes. Whereas the watchword thus far had been, in effect, "What they don't know won't hurt them," now a new policy came into effect—a sort of French *glasnost*. Nuclear watchdog agencies within the government were given greater autonomy from the CEA and EDF; accidents in French reactors were classified according to a "scale of seriousness" and regularly reported to the media (roughly 250 such incidents per year); emergency evacuation plans and other contingency measures were made public for the first time; and EDF embarked on a comprehensive effort to educate the French citizenry about how reactors worked and what risks their operation entailed.[106] In all these ways, the Chernobyl catastrophe exerted strong pressures for a relative democratization of France's electro-nuclear industry.[107]

Somewhat ironically, this new strategy of informing the public rather than concealing the nuclear risks appears to have worked strongly in favor of EDF. By the early 1990s, the Great Fear caused by Chernobyl had largely faded, and opinion polls indicated a broader base than ever of public support for *le nucléaire*—fully 80 percent in favor of continuing with nuclear-generated electricity. In poll after poll, a majority of French citizens declared itself well satisfied with the safety of French reactors, the competence and training of technical personnel, and the ability of EDF to contain any likely accident that might occur. The treatment of radioactive wastes and the long-term mainte-nance of the nation's fifty-odd nuclear reactors remained matters of consid-erable concern, but, once again, a majority of those polled felt confident that the scientists and technicians were not lying to them when they said that the system was safe, and that they had matters well under control.[108]

In the short run, however, Chernobyl gave France's environmentalists a significant boost. It was not so much the nuclear issue in itself, but the fact that the "écolos"—as they were affectionately called—were the only ones systematically addressing such issues, that appears to have made an impres-sion on French voters. With the Socialists in steady decline, and the French Communists thrown completely off balance by Mikhail Gorbachev's ongoing Soviet reforms, a power vacuum was opening up on the French Left. Then, in 1988, the Socialist Prime Minister Michel Rocard, seeking to beef up the party's green credentials, appointed Brice Lalonde as the new Minister of the Environment; this immediately benefited Les Verts by diverting Lalonde's en-ergies (temporarily) away from electoral competition. The breakthrough for the Greens came the very next year, in the municipal and European elections of 1989. At the municipal level, 1,369 green candidates were elected to sit on town councils all over France; Les Verts had received between 10 and 25 per-cent of the vote in many French cities. At the European level, the Greens got their highest score ever, with 10.6 percent of the national vote. They now surpassed the West Germans, for with their nine elected representatives at Strasbourg, Les Verts boasted the largest national green grouping in the Eu-ropean Parliament.[109]

1989–present: "Tous Verts!"—"We are all environmentalists!"

Not surprisingly, these were giddy times for the French greens. Pundits and editorial commentators began speaking of a "green wave" that had swept the nation. In 1992 the journalist Roger Cans, Le Monde's long-standing spe-cialist on environmental topics, wrote a book entitled Tous Verts!—a cry of frustration at the facile manner in which everyone in French society (or so it appeared) had suddenly discovered his or her own profoundly green convic-tions.[110] He was right: by the 1990s, France was a nation in which few areas of public life remained untouched in one fashion or another by the green ide-ology.

Nevertheless, to speak of a "green wave" can also be misleading. Certainly this term makes sense in the political sphere, where fashions wax and wane rather easily, and where environmentalism had suddenly become "all the rage." But the term serves less well in capturing the complex reality of the French economy and society as a whole—for in these broader spheres, it was not so much a green wave that broke over France, but more like a green drizzle that had been falling steadily over two decades, and that had thoroughly drenched the nation by the 1990s. It *seemed* like a wave, no doubt, because French men and women rather abruptly became aware of green issues to an unprecedented degree; but in fact the changes had been unobtrusively accumulating over a much longer period.

France's major newspapers and other mass media had been regularly covering environmental subjects since the 1970s. Significant environmental legislation had passed in virtually every year since the creation of the Ministry of the Environment in 1971–from pollution controls to the creation of new wilderness reserves, from stringent environmental impact studies to the founding of ecological research institutes. New environmental regulatory agencies had sprung up, at all levels of government. School textbooks had started in the late 1970s to incorporate long sections on "la protection de la nature." Within the broader culture, French scholars and journalists had written dozens of books on green topics, and several green journals had been circulating since the late 1970s. Supermarkets, starting with the large chain *Monoprix,* had been offering their customers "environmentally oriented" products since the early 1980s; large-scale recycling programs had started around the same time in most French cities. Industrial firms had been taking care to cultivate a "green profile" for themselves since at least the mid-1980s. Meanwhile, the FFSPN and other nature-protection societies had been far from dormant: they had organized locally and nationally over the years, rallying and marching to stop dam-building on the Loire river, to save the Pyrenean brown bear, or to prevent the digging of a major new canal linking the Rhine and Rhone rivers. Opinion polls had both reflected and encouraged this trend: over the years, the French placed "quality of the environment" higher and higher in the priority of their concerns, until by 1990 it ranked second only to "unemployment."

This broad panoply of relatively quiet changes (taken up at greater length in Part III of this book) formed the backdrop to the clamorous success experienced by green political activists in the early 1990s. But even in the political sphere, it is important to note that green activists had already been serving as elected officials since the municipal elections of 1977, when thirty of them first entered city councils throughout France. And the numbers had been steadily rising ever since: 300 écolos entered office in the municipal elections of 1983, along with three regional councillors elected in 1985.

These individuals had not only grown accustomed to raising green issues in the city halls and regional assemblies of France, but had also—and equally significantly—accustomed the officials of other parties to hearing those issues raised and addressing them knowledgeably. It was a gradual, and mutual, apprenticeship that slowly tinted the mentalities of local government with a deepening environmental awareness.[111]

Still, few were prepared for the sudden and ubiquitous popularity that swept up green ideas and issues in the early 1990s—perhaps least of all the greens themselves. The first thing that Brice Lalonde did, as he observed the rising fortunes of his rivals, was to announce in 1990 the formation of his own new political party, Génération Ecologie. France needed a second green organization, he explained, for reasons that echoed the split between Realos and Fundis in Germany: one green grouping (his own) would be pragmatic, flexible, constructive, and open to cooperation with other parties in the pursuit of tangible environmental results; the other grouping would continue its hard-line policies—doctrinaire, intransigent, and sectarian. Not surprisingly, Les Verts quickly condemned this comparison, portraying Lalonde as a power-hungry and unprincipled opportunist.[112] Nevertheless, despite the sniping and bickering, French voters were apparently in the mood to forgive them, for in the next major elections, held at the level of regional governments in 1992, the "green wave" continued: 6.8 percent of the vote to Les Verts, 7.1 percent to Génération Ecologie, resulting in the election of some 100 regional councillors for each party (compared with just three in 1985). In addition, Marie-Christine Blandin, representing the Greens in the region of Nord-Pas-de-Calais, was elected to the powerful post of Regional President, which she would hold for six years; for the first time, an entire region of France would be governed by a coalition in which the leaders were écolos.

This proved to be the apex of green electoral power for the first half of the 1990s. Although Lalonde and Waechter tried to mend fences, and even signed an accord in the name of minimizing future quarrels, the breach between them took a heavy toll among voters—who evidently were beginning to believe what both parties said about each other. The result, in the national parliamentary elections of 1993, was a bitter disappointment: 4.1 percent of the vote for Les Verts, 3.6 percent for Génération Ecologie. Despite a combined total of 7.7 percent, the schismatic environmentalists had once again failed to cross the fateful 5 percent threshold for entry into the French parliament. And worse lay ahead. The following year, in the European elections, the greens received a dismal 2.9 percent of the vote, all nine of their representatives had to pack their bags and leave Strasbourg.[113]

It was a sobering moment. During 1994 and 1995 a great deal of soul-

searching went on, especially among Les Verts, and the result was the gradual emergence of a new leadership—and a new doctrinal flexibility—within
the party. The most prominent figure in the new leadership was a woman
named Dominique Voynet, a 37-year-old medical doctor from the Franche-
Comté who had long been active in politics, having represented the Greens
in the European Parliament, the town council of Dole, and the regional council of the Franche-Comté. In 1993 she was elected as one of the Greens' four
influential *porte-paroles,* or spokespersons; and in this capacity she began
making a case for reconsidering some of the party's long-standing practices.
The a priori refusal to engage in political alliances, she argued, had condemned the Greens to the margins of French politics; it was time to begin
working together constructively with other progressive political forces.
Equally damaging, in her view, was the insistence on placing environmental
issues at the center of the Green political identity; for as long as this remained
the case, most voters would see Les Verts as a "single-issue" party and would
refuse to entrust them with the broader powers of high office. The Greens,
for Voynet, needed not just an environmental and economic platform, but a
comprehensive social vision and a realistic foreign policy, if they wanted to
be taken seriously as contenders for national power; defending fauna and
flora should continue to play a key role, but so should defending the homeless, the unemployed, immigrants, women, and the Third World's down-
trodden millions. "Green" should connote more than just a clean natural
environment: it should also mean a just and peaceful *human* environment.[114]

This line of argument—downright heretical to the party's ideological
purists—increasingly carried the day. In 1995 Voynet was chosen by the
Greens as their candidate for that year's presidential election; she received
3.3 percent of the national vote. But the real turning-point came in the parliamentary election of 1997. The Greens struck a deal with the Socialist
leader Lionel Jospin, stipulating that in certain districts where a Green candidate had a strong chance of winning, the Socialist candidate would stand
down in favor of the Green; in return, the Greens would vote for the Socialists everywhere else.[115] The result was that, with Socialist support, six
Greens were finally elected to the Assemblée Nationale. What was more,
Jospin invited Voynet to join his government at the head of an enlarged Ministry of the Environment—an institution that would henceforth include the
powerful bureaucracy of DATAR, or Aménagement du Territoire. Her first
acts, as minister, were both symbolic and very concrete: she ordered the immediate shut-down of the fast-breeder Super-Phénix at Creys-Malville (thus

exacting vengeance, at two decades' remove, against EDF and the pro-nuclear establishment); and she canceled the controversial Rhine-Rhone canal project.[116] The Greens had truly entered the central corridors of power.

Then, in 1998, another symbolic *coup de théâtre:* Daniel Cohn-Bendit, the most famous student leader of May '68, returned to France after thirty years of exile in Germany. The son of German Jews who had fled to France in 1933, Cohn-Bendit was born in France in 1944 and raised as a bilingual, and indeed "bi-national," young man. ("When I watch a soccer match in France, I root for the Germans, and when I watch in Germany, I root for the French.")[117] De Gaulle's government had expelled the young firebrand in 1968, citing his "subversive activities" at the Sorbonne; he had since made a name for himself as a left-libertarian intellectual in Germany, dividing his time between political activism and serving as cultural attaché to the mayor of Frankfurt. Now, in 1998, he was returning to his second home—to join Les Verts and head their list of candidates in the upcoming European parliamentary elections of 1999. (The European Union allows its citizens to stand for these elections in any of its member nations.)

The French Left—and youths of all political stripes—responded to this icon of the countercultural past with unbridled enthusiasm. "Dany le Rouge," as he had been affectionately called in 1968, now became "Dany le Vert"— and his charismatic presence added even more potency to what was already a thoroughly energized Green party.[118] In the June 1999 elections for the European Parliament, the Greens got 9.7 percent of the French vote, and sent a delegation of nine representatives, headed by Cohn-Bendit, to Strasbourg. Equally importantly, they had become the second-ranked partner in Lionel Jospin's governing coalition, and could now feel justified in demanding a greater share of power from the Socialists.[119] Green elected officials were now active at every level of governance: from town halls to the national parliament, from government ministries to the supranational institutions of Europe.

What this "entry into power" would mean, for the Greens' future electoral support—and indeed, for their very identity as a political grouping—remained to be seen. Some, like Waechter, believed that his party had sacrificed its soul in a Devil's Bargain, and had now become dependent on the Socialists for its existence.[120] Others, like the influential Green economist Alain Lipietz, felt that this broadening of perspectives was long overdue, and looked forward with enthusiasm to the creation of a new "green-progressive" pole in French public life.[121] This debate, which in fact had already arisen as early as René Dumont's campaign for the presidency—"Are we more red or green at heart?"—seemed likely to continue raging (and dividing the greens) for the foreseeable future. But one thing was clear: green visions, in all their fractiousness and heterogeneity, had become by the year 2000 an integral part of French modernity. They had influenced the mainstream, and had in turn been altered by their interaction with the mainstream.

To a more systematic overview of those green visions, we now turn.

5 Nuances of Dark Green

The Intellectual Horizons of French Environmentalism

The connection between "more" and "better" has been broken. "Better" may now mean doing with less. It is possible to live better by working and consuming less.

—André Gorz, 1975[1]

A Revolution against the Industrial Revolution

One of the most exciting aspects of green thought lies in the sheer brashness of its vision, the intellectual sweep that embraces not only centuries but millennia. According to this vision, three epochal turning-points have marked the human relation to nature: the transition, some ten thousand years ago, from hunter-gathering to settled farming; the Industrial Revolution, some 250 years ago; and the ecological revolution, through which we are all living today. Whether or not one agrees that these three transformations have been among the most important ones in human history, this broad formulation does help to put things into perspective. Environmental thought thinks big.

The first of these three transitions has been given its most memorable description by the historian Max Oelschlaeger. In his book, *The Idea of Wilderness*, Oelschlaeger speculates about what must have happened in the transition from the Paleolithic to the Neolithic, the momentous passage from the way of life of the hunter-gatherers to that of the early agriculturists:

> The agriculturist necessarily defines "fields" (areas cleared of natural vegetation), "weeds" (undesirable plants intruding upon fields), and "crops" (desirable plants suited to human purposes). In contrast, the hunter-gatherer lives on what is conceptually the "fruit of the earth"—fields, weeds, and crops simply do not exist. Furthermore, whereas the hunter-gatherer is at home anywhere in nature, the farmer creates a human settlement that is "home" as distinct from the "wilderness"; and nature harbors threats to home and field, as in the predations of the barbarians or "wild men" who roam about nature, "wild animals" such as wolves and cats that prey on desirable domesticated animals such as sheep and goats, and "wild insects" such as locusts that eat grain. And, finally, the product of the agriculturist is no longer conceived as the fruit of the earth but rather won, at least in part, from nature through sweat and toil.[2]

A deep cleavage or rent moves through nearly every aspect of the human life-world when the hunter-gatherer stakes out a piece of land and begins working it as his own. Even if no specific individual ever experienced this transition in its fullness—making the move in a single lifetime from hunter-gathering to farming—certainly the contrast between the two cultures over a series of generations must have become quite striking. On one side of the divide we find a nomadic pattern of life in which all of nature is potentially home, and all of nature's creatures are potential food; on the other we encounter a sharply dualistic world, in which the settlement and its members lie at the center, and outsiders of all kinds begin to proliferate in the surrounding environment: animals that are ours or not ours, humans who are from here or not from here, places that are familiar and places that are wild and strange, plants desirable or undesirable, soil that I work on and soil that I allow to do as it will.

One needs to be cautious here, for certainly the life of the Paleolithic hunter-gatherers should not be idealized as a paradisiacal "living off the fat of the land," an Edenic world in which dualistic distinctions between good nature and bad nature might not have existed.[3] Stinging nettles were probably shunned with the same alacrity by the denizens of both the Paleolithic and the Neolithic. But the world of the hunter-gatherers was necessarily a less sharply differentiated one, because it lacked the new points of reference described by Oelschlaeger above, of home, crop, pest, wilderness. The whole relationship to the natural world undergoes a metamorphosis when human beings begin working a fixed spot in the territory. One exerts one's will upon nature, shaping it far more systematically than before, channeling water, pulling out weeds, flattening soil—a relationship both of nurturing and of command, an injection of human will into the surroundings. Instead of foraging for edible plants and stalking elusive game, and then moving on, the agriculturist stays put, reshaping the local nature to make it fit human needs. Instead of taking what nature happens to offer and making the best of it, the agriculturist begins more actively manipulating nature, making it produce desirable things in as great a quantity as possible. From coexistence with nature to domination over nature: the first major steps were arguably taken along these lines. The human place within the natural world had changed.

It changed again, arguably in an equally momentous way, during the two centuries following 1750 in Europe. The shift was twofold, entailing a cultural "disenchantment" of nature at the same time as a tremendous escalation in the technological manipulation of nature. Historians use the word "disenchantment" to connote the complex reorientation in European attitudes that took place around the seventeenth and eighteenth centuries: a steady decline in the portrayal of the physical environment as possessing venerable supernatural, spiritual, or organic qualities, and a growing tendency to regard the earth and its creatures as being simply forms of mechanistically structured matter, subject to empirically ascertainable causal laws, and available for humans to manipulate and put to use as they saw fit.[4] This new attitude helped pave the way for the sweeping transformation that a dumbfounded Karl Marx was already describing as early as 1848:

> The bourgeoisie, during its rule of scarce one hundred years, has created more massive and more colossal productive forces than have all the preceding generations together. Subjection of Nature's forces to man, machinery, application of chemistry to industry and agriculture, steam-navigation, railways, electric telegraphs, clearing of whole continents for cultivation, canalization of rivers, whole populations conjured out of the ground—what earlier century had even a presentiment that such productive forces slumbered in the lap of social labor?[5]

And what presentiment—we might add—could Marx himself have had that the century following 1848 would witness not only a continuing expansion of these processes, but a constant *acceleration* in that expansion, utterly dwarfing the changes he had experienced in his own lifetime? If one takes but a single measure of twentieth-century industrial society at work—total world levels of energy consumption—a graph for the period 1900–1993 speaks most eloquently: about 10 quadrillion BTU's per year in 1900 (a BTU, or British Thermal Unit, being roughly equivalent to the amount of energy contained in a burning match); 30 quads (quadrillion BTU's) per year in 1920; 50 quads in 1940; 110 quads in 1960; 220 quads in 1980; and 360 quads in 1993 (23 percent of this consumed by the United States alone!).[6] If the graph that depicts this were the side of a mountain, it would be much too steep for skiing.

During the late 1960s and early 1970s, a widely dispersed, unconnected, and heterogeneous array of thinkers began to examine this furiously accelerating economic growth with a critical eye: people like Arne Naess in Norway, Barry Commoner in the U.S., E. F. Schumacher and Edward Goldsmith in Britain, André Gorz and Jacques Ellul in France, Ivan Illich in Mexico, the scientists and economists associated with the Club of Rome, and many others.[7] For all the diversity of their perspectives, these writers began cobbling together a common basic analysis of what was happening.

If one scrutinized the major political systems of the twentieth century, they argued, one could discern a rather striking common denominator. Liberal capitalism, Fascism, Communism: all these systems, or ideologies, had in common the assumption of an industrial economy, perpetually expanding its size, its markets, its output, its diversification, its consumption. Growth, Development, Intensification, Expansion: these were the watchwords in Moscow as in Detroit, in Bombay as in Berlin. Make more, make it better, make it more efficiently, offer it to more and more people.

The green thinkers used the word "productivism" to describe this type of industrial system—a system predicated on an implicit model in which a linear trend of ongoing upward growth projects indefinitely into the future. There might be dips and troughs, depressions and cyclical adjustments, but the productivists' fundamental assumption remained always the same: economic growth, over the years, meant increasing prosperity and well-being for more and more people; a cessation of growth could not but mean misery and crisis.

To the green thinkers, this linear model seemed fundamentally flawed, because it rested on two problematic assumptions: first, that nature, or "natural resources," were free and unlimited (or could be treated as such); and second, that the planet's capacity for absorbing the byproducts of industrial growth, such as heat, garbage, and pollution, was similarly unlimited. Both these assumptions, they argued, were demonstrably false: the planet's resources and resilience were actually approaching their limits alarmingly fast.

The only solution was to inaugurate a fourth epoch in the human relationship with the natural world: a new economic system that moved beyond the linear model of continuous growth; a new attitude toward nature that moved beyond the domineering mentality first established in the Neolithic and aggressively intensified in the Enlightenment. What the green thinkers proposed was nothing less than a revolution against the Industrial Revolution itself: a new economics based on a steady-state model, in which resources were only used to the extent that they could be fully restored and replenished; a new mentality in which nature's rhythms were respected and actively protected by humankind. Where the old model had been linear, the new one would be cyclical or circular; where the old watchwords had been "infinite growth," the new ones would be "sustainable equilibrium."[8]

The green thinkers realized that this would not be easy. Retooling an economy, on such a radical scale, ultimately means retooling an entire civilization: they freely admitted it. But they argued that humankind had no choice. As expressed in the rather blunt title of René Dumont's first environmentalist book, published in 1974, it was simply a matter of "Utopia or Death." They knew that the transformation they sought in world affairs would take many generations to become a reality; and they acknowledged that they could not clearly picture how the end-result would take shape. What they were undertaking was a struggle in a general direction, a direction they regarded as being superior from a moral point of view and smarter from a practical point of view: a complete shift in the way resources were used, wealth was produced, and goods were distributed, on a planetary scale.

The Two Main Currents of French Green Thought

In France, as we saw in chapter 4, this revolutionary new ideology took hold quickly—especially among certain intellectual and associative circles that had already been moving in a similar direction during the 1960s. Two distinct styles of French environmentalism emerged at this time, two casts of mind that can still be said to characterize the greens in France today: for lack of better terms, I will call them "nature-centered environmentalism" and "social environmentalism." These are best thought of as Weberian ideal types, constituting two opposite ends of a broad polar spectrum, with the majority of French greens falling somewhere in between.

Nature-centered environmentalism tended to emphasize the tangible threats posed to the biosphere by the onward march of industrialization: this or that mountain lake or rare species of mammal under pressure from hunters or real-estate developers, the ominously shifting migratory patterns of birds, the deteriorating quality of groundwater, the long-term dangers of global overpopulation. This current of green activism came out of the well-established tradition of nature conservation: its proponents included many scientists, well-to-do nature lovers, members of organizations like the venerable Ligue Pour la Protection des Oiseaux, or the FFSPN (which was to change its name in the 1990s to France Nature Environnement). Its background was for the most part socially "respectable," its ideology cautious and intellectually meticulous. Its tone was one of understated indignation.

Social environmentalism, by contrast, emphasized the two-way connection between issues of "nature protection" and the most intractable problems of human society, such as poverty, inequality, violence, and alienation. The proponents of this style of green activism tended to become frustrated with sharply focused efforts to save a particular species or endangered site; for while readily acknowledging the importance of the countless threats to nature described by their scientific colleagues, they nonetheless felt that a lasting solution to such ecological problems could only be found in a deeper transformation of the entire economy and culture of industrial civilization. They insisted, moreover, that not just "wildlife" issues but also the quality of life in the human world should take a high priority in the greens' agenda: the grim suburbs of Paris or Marseille, in their view, were just as badly in need of "saving" as the Amazon rainforest. This current of activism grew directly out of the anti-establishment movements of the sixties, bringing together dissident intellectuals, students, trade unionists, libertarian leftists, and a broad array of others who wanted to see the French status quo shaken up. Its tradition could be traced back (somewhat loosely) to the early nineteenth-century utopian socialists; its proponents saw in the word "écologie" a talisman for the renewal of ancient struggles on behalf of ideals of social restructuring and human redemption. Its tone was one of bitter outrage and, at the same time, of fervent hope and idealism.

One of the earliest intellectual progenitors of the nature-centered environmentalists was not a Frenchman but a French-speaking Swiss artist and ecologist, Robert Hainard.[9] Born in Geneva in 1906, Hainard developed a passion for the mountainous countryside of western Switzerland and eastern France, whose fauna and scenery he depicted in thousands of etchings and lithographs. His first book, *Et la nature?* ("What About Nature?") was published in 1943, and laid out, in a prescient fashion, a vision of nature that an American like Aldo Leopold would no doubt have recognized as thoroughly "ecocentric." Defining nature as all that which lies outside of human shaping, control, or influence, he pleaded for the preservation of his beloved countryside from the onslaught that was already assailing it in the 1940s. Though Hainard remained relatively unknown to the broader French public, his influence among circles of French scientists and conservationists was substantial: he is cited by many of them as the writer who, more than any other, taught them to look at nature with a new reverence and appreciation.

The scientist Philippe Lebreton, a chemistry professor at the University of

Lyon, also played a key role among the nature-centered environmentalists. His book, *La nature en crise* ("Nature in Crisis"), published in 1986, provided an exhaustive reference source on the "state of the environment" in France, long before the Ministry of the Environment began publishing periodic reports on the subject. Lebreton was also one of the pioneers of ecological politics during the 1970s, helping to promote René Dumont's presidential bid in 1974, and himself running for election several times during that decade. But the most successful nature-centered environmentalist in French politics was undoubtedly the Alsatian ecological scientist Antoine Waechter.[10] It was Waechter who, after the formation of Les Verts in 1984, steered the new party resolutely away from alliances and deals with other progressive groups on the Left, insisting on the need for a "pure" and distinctively environmentalist platform. This strategy, following logically from Waechter's own training as a naturalist, proved highly successful during the late 1980s and early 1990s, allowing the Greens to carve out a clear-cut identity and a stable niche for themselves on the French political scene. The strategy began to show its limitations, however, during the mid-1990s, as the competition from Génération Ecologie and from the newly revitalized Socialists threatened to consign Waechter's purist Greens to a perpetually marginal role.

Overall, the nature-centered environmentalists played a central part in assuring the success of France's green movement. Their campaigns to educate the French public, the lobbying efforts they mounted, the books, articles, and editorials they wrote over the years—all these added up to a sustained and profound leavening of French perceptions of the environment. If one looks for example at France Nature Environnement (the renamed FFSPN, or FNE), one cannot but be impressed by the sheer breadth and scope of its activities. By the year 2000 its federal structure comprised fourteen national associations and about 3,000 local societies with a total membership of 850,000 persons.[11] With a central coordinating agency in Paris, and a dense capillary network of regional and community groups throughout the nation, the activists of FNE divided their efforts into sixteen thematic areas such as natural habitats, recycling, forests, agriculture, transport, tourism, marine life, water resources, or biotechnology. Each of these thematic areas became the purview of a specialized task force that established its own nationwide network of experts and citizens, monitoring developments in its assigned area, writing reports for the rest of the membership, and calling for concerted action when the need arose. The result, accumulated over many years, was a steady increase in the number and size of protected natural sites, in the sophistication of environmental laws, in the power and effectiveness of environmental regulatory bodies.

But the influence of FNE went beyond lobbying and public campaigning. Many of its members agreed to sit on the boards of the powerful state agencies through which the French government honed and implemented its environmental policies—committees like the National Council on Water Usage, for example, whose rather dull bureaucratic name concealed enormous nationwide clout, or the Council on Nuclear Information and Security, which possessed substantial advisory and regulatory authority. To serve on such governmental commissions gradually became part of the everyday duty of many prominent French environmentalists; it was a modus vivendi with the state that came to be accepted as normal for both the government insiders and the activists themselves.[12] Here, once again, the nature-centered environmentalists unobtrusively but profoundly contributed to the shaping of their country's environmental profile.

Social Environmentalism: Four Interlocking Agendas

Most social environmentalists enthusiastically applauded the ongoing achievements of their nature-centered colleagues. Nevertheless, they also branched out into new territory of their own. Arguably one of the first and most important social environmental theorists in France was André Gorz, a left-wing journalist who worked for *Le Nouvel Observateur* and with Sartre's review *Les Temps Modernes* during the 1960s and 1970s. Gorz contributed regularly to the green and left-wing newspapers of the 1970s, such as *Charlie-Hebdo, Hara-Kiri, La Gueule Ouverte,* and *Le Sauvage;* his articles were assembled and published in 1975 as a book, *Ecologie et politique,* which rendered him even more influential. For Gorz, modern industrial society (both capitalist and state-socialist) had fallen for the fatal seductiveness of the word "more." Lured on by the ever-receding mirage of attaining fulfilment through material abundance, the peoples of the industrialized world had fallen into a trap: they had built a society founded on hierarchy, exclusivity, and the exploitation of nature and other humans, while discovering, to their frustration, that the very structure of their lives precluded a satisfying social existence. The only way out, in Gorz's view, lay in a complete reorientation of both ends and means: a new society, in which only those goods were produced that could be equitably enjoyed by all, and whose production would not exhaust the material resources of the environment. To choose, voluntarily, a more simple lifestyle with less work and more free time; to ensure equality of access to goods and services for everyone; to do so in an ecologically sustainable way—these became the principles by which Gorz organized his utopian vision.

One of the names that recurred in Gorz's writings was that of Ivan Illich, a Viennese-born social theorist who had been a Catholic priest in New York and Puerto Rico, before founding an innovative research center for social thought in Mexico. Gorz introduced French-speaking audiences to Illich's work—particularly his most famous book, *Tools for Conviviality*, which began with the following provocative words:

> During the next several years I intend to work on an epilogue to the industrial age. I want to . . . show that two-thirds of mankind can still avoid passing through the industrial age, by choosing right now a postindustrial balance in their mode of production—[a balance] which the hyperindustrial nations will be forced to adopt as an alternative to chaos.[13]

The key idea here, as in Gorz's thought, was that of the self-defeating or counterproductive nature of modern industrialism: the increasingly frenzied but irretrievably fruitless productivity going on in contemporary society. The harder one worked, the more activities one undertook, the less fulfilled one became: this system must someday break down, both because it failed to deliver what it promised, and because its internal contradictions would lead it toward an ultimate collapse. Both Illich and Gorz provided detailed "case studies" to back up their critiques, analyzing educational programs, health care, and energy policy to illustrate the contradictions and overall illogic of these large-scale systems within modern society. And both writers (but particularly Gorz) continually returned to the lack of environmental sustainability as the final and most glaring contradiction of all.

Another thinker who had been exploring these themes was, of course, Jacques Ellul, whose many writings over several decades were summed up by his last book, *The Technological Bluff* (1990).[14] Although Ellul never joined France's environmentalists as an activist in his own right, his works nonetheless made a substantial impact, because they provided a sophisticated set of conceptual tools for subjecting technology to systematic critical scrutiny. Perhaps the most important of Ellul's contributions lay in his refusal to consider a technological product, such as a nuclear reactor or an automobile, in isolation from the broader network of assumptions, practices, and institutions that rendered it functional. Though this kind of approach has since become common among historians of technology, Ellul was already pioneering it as early as 1964: "Modern technology," he wrote, "has become a total phenomenon for civilization, the defining force of a new social order in which efficiency is no longer an option but a necessity imposed on all human activity."[15]

For example, in speaking about the automobile, Ellul considered not only the machine itself, but the economic aspects of purchasing such a vehicle and rendering it available to the masses, the philosophical arguments about the freedom of movement that this machine conferred, the social status associated with owning an automobile, the underlying assumptions of a society that was seeking ever-greater speed in its transportation and communications, the environmental implications of the machine once it entered mass-production, the broader costs of road systems and their maintenance, the implications for public health because of accidents and pollution, the constant renewal of models from year to year, the waste of energy as compared with mass transportation—in short, the automobile not as an isolated artifact, but as a "total social fact," an embedded part of a much larger meta-system of objects, persons, habits, expectations, values, and institutions. Above all, what Ellul most passionately challenged was the widespread ideology that identified progress with technological advance—as if any and all technological innovation constituted ipso facto a step forward in the realization of basic human values. *Au contraire,* he argued, something very different proved all-too-often to be the case. Many alleged technological "advances" revealed themselves under scrutiny to be either unnecessary or downright harmful: they caught up human beings in a web of interconnected practices and expectations from which it became extremely difficult to escape. Who, he asked, in a society like the United States, could now afford *not* to have a car?

We need to be cautious, however, in assessing Ellul's impact on France's greens. On the one hand, he undoubtedly played a major role in unmasking the triumphalist ideology of modern scientific and technological advance, showing the many absurdities and contradictions in the contemporary deployment of machines and the values they embodied. This was to prove extremely helpful to greens throughout the world, particularly in making the distinction between "unsustainable technology" and "appropriate technology." On the other hand, it was rare to find in Ellul's writings any sense that modern technology could *ever* be anything other than harmful or insidiously oppressive. Many greens apparently did not share Ellul's pervasive pessimism, and concluded that some technologies, after careful consideration of their local and systemic effects, could indeed be given a green stamp of approval. Ellul, for example, lambasted computer technology, portraying it as a gimmick that distracted people from the business of living their real daily lives. Most greens did not share this interpretation, and came instead to regard the computer as a relatively energy-efficient, affordable machine that allowed people to "telecommute" to work, link up with one another in de-centralized grassroots networks, or offer each other exciting vistas of recreation, education, and creativity.[16] Thus, many greens simply chose to pass over or ignore this rather curmudgeonly and perhaps excessively gloomy side of Ellul's thought.

Gorz, Illich, and Ellul embodied what might be called the critique of industrial modernity among social environmentalists. A second strain of social environmentalism found its most eloquent (and passionate) expression in the work of René Dumont: *tiers-mondisme,* or advocacy on behalf of the wretched billions of the Third World.[17] Dumont's credentials for articulating this position were impeccable, since he had established himself as a world-famous agronomist and economist decades earlier, and had been crying out for a global redistribution of wealth long before it became fashionable. The key to Dumont's analysis lay in his interpretation of the Third World's woes as symptoms of a broader, and truly global, economic crisis. Overpopulation, illiteracy, infant mortality, mass migrations, intractable poverty—all these were to be understood not just as problems of "underdevelopment" in one part of the world, but as a more comprehensive problem of unbalanced and irrational development on a planetary scale. Global capitalism, he argued, had presented humankind with two interconnected and deadly threats: the threat of demographic collapse emanating from the southern hemisphere, and the threat of ecological collapse emanating from the northern hemisphere. A catastrophe was looming, he maintained, unless human beings empowered their governments to take draconian measures along three distinct (but closely linked) gradients: rolling back population growth; redistributing wealth and resources more equitably across the world; and phasing in a more ecologically sustainable mode of production.

Dumont's urgent message became an integral part of the green political agenda over the decades that followed. By the late 1990s, the official platform of Les Verts included the following: cancellation of Third World debt (except in cases where such action would favor dictatorial regimes); sharply increasing annual development aid (to at least one percent of the European Union's aggregate Gross Domestic Product); preferential opening of European economies to imports from poor countries; new taxes on global financial transfers, with the proceeds of these taxes going to a fund for worldwide sustainable development.[18] The idea behind all these policies boiled down to a simple one: the human suffering in poor countries was not just morally intolerable; it also constituted a deadly threat to the survival of humanity as a whole. Global poverty threatened ecological balances as much as the headlong rush of unrestrained industrial production: both had to be brought under control through a single, integrated set of drastic reforms on a planetary scale.

A third strand of social environmentalism tackled the vexed problem of the *exode rural,* the dramatic depopulation of France's (and Europe's) countrysides in the decades after 1945, under the impact of agricultural modernization and the rise of the tertiary and information sectors of contemporary economies. By the year 2000, approximately 90 percent of French men and women lived in cities or suburban agglomerations (see the discussion in chapter 2).[19] Perhaps the most influential green thinker on this issue was Bernard Charbonneau, a schoolteacher from the Landes region, south of Bordeaux. In all his books, but particularly in one entitled *Sauver nos régions: Ecologie et sociétés locales* ("Saving our Regions: Ecology and Local Societies"), Charbonneau returned continually to the same fundamental dichotomy: on the one hand, the picture of a grim future, in which anonymous crowds of people inhabited identical apartments in virtually indistinguishable cities, consuming the bland, mass-produced harvests of a featureless countryside; on the other hand, the defensive vision of France as it might yet be, a nation of thriving and diverse local communities, in which human beings could still savor the heterogeneity of products and traditions that could only come from a sense of rootedness in one's own native land.[20]

Charbonneau was an unabashed "regionalist," in the sense of wanting to reverse the distortions of overcentralization that had caused France's ancient provinces to revolve increasingly around the Parisian megalopolis. Yet he poured scorn on the regional separatists and purveyors of folklore who hoped to restore their localities' former greatness through a combination of nostalgia and greedy scrambling for economic concessions from the national government. Instead, he advocated a full-fledged transformation of agricultural production, distribution, and consumption, with the long-term aim of dismantling the system of large-scale agribusiness, breaking down the sharp division between rural and urban worlds, and restoring vitality to regional and local economies. Only this, he believed, would add up to a real and lasting decentralization.

To begin with, he argued, the government needed to reverse its present system of agricultural subsidies, which disproportionately benefited the largest farms, and begin subsidizing those small-scale farmers who chose to stay in mountainous regions or in other areas of relatively low productivity. Both France and the EC should adopt fiscal measures that encouraged the return of polyculture, so that each region would once again be growing a wide variety of local fruits, grains, and vegetables. Most consumers, he wagered, would be willing to pay a bit more at the grocery store, if their foods tasted better and were locally grown in a countryside that was still beautiful to visit on weekends and holidays.

Far from fearing technology, Charbonneau advocated its cautious but widespread application. Each of its uses and forms, he argued, should be rigorously subjected to critical scrutiny, so that technological mastery became not an end in itself, but served as a means to the higher end of "qualité de la vie," or quality of life—a concept that he understood above all as care for one's surroundings, growing out of a sense of long-term identification with one's home locality. For Charbonneau, this utopia beckoned as a patchwork of mid-sized towns and small settlements, communicating and trading with each other on a global scale for some purposes, yet also firmly connected to the diverse countrysides that sustained them—marshlands, deserts, forests, wheat fields, mountain slopes, seasides. Such an urban-rural hybrid, he believed, held out the prospect of an antidote to a homogenized modernity of suburban malls and featureless consumerism: it offered, by contrast, the ideal of distinctive local cultures grounded in the endless differences of landscape. (A more detailed description of this vision follows in chapter 6.)

The fourth current of social environmentalism tackled the thorny questions of mass electoral mobilization, national political power, and "green government." Its proponents envisioned transforming the greens from a rather narrowly based political grouping to a major new force on the French Left—the key player in a broad progressive coalition that would replace the unpalatable Communists and the increasingly stale and compromised Socialists. One could point to many greens as the standard-bearers of this viewpoint over the years, from the hard-bitten Breton activist Yves Cochet to the malleable Parisian dandy Brice Lalonde; but perhaps the two most representative figures in this current were Dominique Voynet and Alain Lipietz, the two Green leaders who played a central role in wresting control of the party from Antoine Waechter in 1993.[21] Of these two, Voynet emerged as a particularly gifted politician, a woman whose vast energies poured into her elected roles as a Green spokesperson and regional councillor, then as Minister of the Environment and of Aménagement du Territoire after 1997. She therefore lacked the time (and perhaps the inclination) to lay out her thinking systematically in a book.[22]

Not so Lipietz, whose many publications on economic and environmental issues brought him recognition not only in France but abroad as well. One book in particular, published in 1993 and translated into English as *Green Hopes*, clearly articulated the overall logic of this strain of social environmentalism. Lipietz addressed his readers in the form of an open letter:

"To a Left-wing friend still hesitating to join the Ecologists." And he went on to explain:

> Green shows very strong resemblances to Red. Both are "principles of hope" with similar origins: materialist (the starting-point is a critical knowledge of the real world), dialectical (the expectation is that the real world will give rise to its own material critique), historical ("the time has come!") and progressive. On this score, Green also shares most of the risks of Red, and reveals its flaws: there have been frequent denunciations of the "fundamentalism" of German or French Greens (as an exact analogy of "Leftism"); it is likely we will soon see condemnation of their "realism" (analogous to the old "opportunism"). Green has nevertheless one significant advantage over Red: it postdates it, by more than a century of trial and error.[23]

This "trial and error," for Lipietz, had infused into French green thought certain unshakeable convictions: that old leftist goals like the "seizure of power" or "nationalization" were counterproductive, because they only served to reinforce the already excessive ascendancy of the state; that deep and lasting changes came through long and patient struggles within civil society, and were won through the voluntary allegiance of hearts and minds, not through coercive institutional means; that no single class or group could claim a privileged role in the ongoing transformation; and that it was not capitalism per se that needed opposing, but the underlying (and much more insidious) logic of productivism.

For Lipietz, the Green party was nothing less than a vehicle for bringing together all the loose strands of progressive French politics into a single front for common action; in fact, he only joined the Green party in 1988, after spending several years trying (unsuccessfully) to create precisely such a "rainbow coalition." At the core of this new "progressive pole," he argued, lay four basic values:

> *Solidarity:* rejecting the exclusion of certain individuals, social categories, or groups of countries. *Autonomy:* being in control of the consequences (and, if possible, the conditions) of one's activities. *Ecological responsibility:* not just being "need-oriented" (we are aware of how needs can be manipulated), but sometimes limiting one's own needs, and always choosing the means to fulfil them which take into account the interests of life on our planet and the rights of future generations. *Democracy:* systematically sounding out the opinions and aspirations of every person on the range of problems concerning their existence, and equally systematically searching for a peaceful and negotiated solution to the contradictions which thus emerge between different perspectives.[24]

It only takes a brief scrutiny of the Green party's political platform, formally articulated at various electoral junctures since 1984, to find these values being consistently translated into concrete political proposals. Alongside the predictable references to sustainable development or shutting down nuclear power, for example, one finds fully two-thirds of the Greens' 1999 platform devoted to a far-reaching set of progressive social and political reforms going well beyond nature protection: reducing unemployment through job-sharing or a shorter work-week; extending equal legal rights to women, immigrants, gays, and others possessing the status of "outsiders"; creating new government bodies to make sure these equal rights became a social and economic reality; instituting proportional representation in the electoral system and broadening the right to conduct popular referenda; stepping up financial assistance and social programs for the poor and homeless; expanding the annual outlays for foreign aid to developing countries; and adopting an avowedly internationalist foreign policy that shifted France's diplomatic center of gravity to the level of the European Union, and that traded the old Gaullist rhetoric of national "gloire" for a new vision based on collective security among peoples.[25] Lipietz cheerfully admitted that this platform went much further than "environmental politics" as traditionally construed: now that the Green party had matured, broadening its vision and its electoral base, he argued, it was ready to affirm itself as a serious contender for national political power.

These, therefore, constituted the four main intellectual orientations of social environmentalism: the critique of productivism; concern about global economic disparities; a commitment to balance the urban and rural worlds; and the desire to build a new progressive pole in French politics. We must be careful, however, not to draw too sharp a line between these four currents (taken as a whole) and the agenda of the nature-centered environmentalists. Though these various lines of thought certainly remain analytically distinguishable from each other, they are by no means incompatible; indeed, many greens would most likely regard them as mutually reinforcing facets of a single vision. In practice, it was quite common for a nature-centered environmentalist to embrace many (or all) of the tenets of social environmentalism—and vice versa. To take but one example: the scientist Jean-Pierre Raffin, who taught courses in zoology and ecology at the University of Paris, served for many years as president of France Nature Environnement (the FFSPN); he joined the Greens and was elected to a seat in the European Parliament; he actively supported the position of Voynet and Lipietz within the party; he sat as an ecological specialist on various government regulatory committees; and he ardently continued his campaigns in the nature-protection societies.[26] Not everyone, of course, was capable of such breadth of range; but it was almost impossible to be a green activist without encountering this creative tension between nature-centered environmentalism and social environmentalism as a recurring theme in one's life and work.

What Is Distinctive about the French Green Visions?

In 1992, the philosopher Luc Ferry published a broadside attack against the French greens, *Le nouvel ordre écologique* ("The New Ecological Order"), in which he argued that this newly popular political grouping posed a grave danger to the future of democracy.[27] Ferry's book stirred up a major ruckus in French intellectual life: it immediately won the prestigious Medici prize, and its soft-spoken author became a fixture on talk-shows and in the nation's editorial pages (the book was translated into English in 1995). Ferry, I will now argue, completely misunderstood the greens—who they were, where they came from, what they wanted. But by addressing his elaborate attack, point by point, we can develop a better grasp of what the French greens *did* stand for, and to what extent their ideas set them apart from the greens of other nations.

As is often the case, Ferry was in fact reacting to a prior work by another philosopher: Michel Serres's *Le contrat naturel* ("The Natural Contract"), published in 1990.[28] In this book Serres argued that the tradition of social contract theory inherited from Rousseau possessed a crucial flaw: it left out those parties who could not speak for themselves, and whose interests were therefore ignored in the formulation of the social contract. The natural world— trees, rivers, weather patterns, ecosystems—stood out as perhaps the most prominent example of such a voiceless, and hence disenfranchised, party. Another such helpless party, of course, was the future generations of humans whose interests would be harmed by any irreparable damage done to the natural world by those alive today. Thus for Serres the prime task facing our generation lay in redefining our notion (and practice) of justice in such a way as to incorporate these vitally important but unrepresented "participants" in global affairs. A new *natural contract* would have to supplement the old social contract, offering an effective way to adjudicate the interests of nature through a broadened sphere of ethics and law. The result would be a new legal system in which, in principle, a forest could sue those humans who were dumping pollution into it, and seek compensation for the damages incurred (the suit would presumably be brought on the forest's behalf by a group of human trustees, in the same manner as is currently done with children or other legally incapacitated parties).[29]

As soon as it came out, Serres's book elicited strong reactions in French intellectual circles—a response whose most antagonistic undercurrents were effectively summed up in Ferry's *Le nouvel ordre écologique*. Ferry declared himself appalled by the implications of Serres's argument, explaining that he saw it as symptomatic of an entire current of contemporary thought that was rather insouciantly drifting away from the core values underpinning democratic society. For Ferry, modern liberalism rested on the uniquely human capacity for cultural self-awareness, without which any notion of moral agency, and of individual liberty, became meaningless. Human beings, he argued, were fundamentally different from the rest of nature because they could distinguish their actions according to the concepts of right and wrong; this moral faculty, in turn, laid the foundation for all the hard-won political freedoms that we have come to associate with liberal democracy. Thus, the same quality that gave us freedom also, by the same token, set humans irrevocably apart from all other creatures. Michel Serres, by deliberately blurring the line between humans and nonhumans (trees, animals, ecosystems), was in effect undermining liberalism itself, and thus opening the door for a wide array of authoritarian values and dangerous political extremism. Such a pernicious philosophical démarche could not be allowed to go unrefuted.

Ferry actually had a point. In one portion of his book he put forth a detailed and cogent argument that any attempt to stretch our current legal concepts (individual, interested party, justice, fairness, compensation) to include nonhumans could very quickly fall into all manner of contradictions and conceptual confusion. At the very least, Ferry raised important and sophisticated questions, which the proponents of "forest lawsuits" would have to address before the matter could move forward.

But, unfortunately, Ferry's passionate defense of liberalism led him to go quite a bit further. In his zeal to stamp out the threat to democratic principles, he launched what amounted to a full-scale witch-hunt, sniffing out the enemy even where, it turned out, the enemy did not exist. The name he gave to his adversary was Deep Ecology; and he spent the better part of his book trying to show that the French greens were acting like a Trojan Horse for Deep Ecology, infecting France with an ideology that amounted to a creeping moral equivalent of Nazism. His attack took the form of four basic propositions:[30]

1. *Antihumanism.* The greens subscribed to a worldview that valued the earth, or ecosystems, more highly than humans. This antihumanist stance meant that, when push came to shove, greens would choose the welfare of trees or animals over the welfare of human beings.

2. *Authoritarianism.* The greens considered the threat of environmental collapse so dire as to justify coercive and authoritarian measures; if given the

power to do so, they would suspend the rule of law and the due process of representative government in the name of saving the planet.

3. *Fascist roots.* Antihumanism and authoritarianism were not new in European political movements that drew their inspiration from the veneration of Nature: the Nazis, too, with their völkisch "Blood and Soil" slogans, had embraced a similar philosophy in the 1930s. In France, this tradition could be traced to the ruralist ideology of Marshall Pétain and the Vichy years—a tradition that the greens were bringing back to life in the seductively camouflaged guise of "protecting our country's beloved nature." The greens were therefore deeply tinged with brown—the color of Fascism.

4. *Antimodernism.* At the deepest level, the greens' *Weltanschauung* could best be understood as a visceral rejection of modernity. Not just industrialism and technology, but also the modern era's social gains of individualism, rationalism, and feminism, and the political forms of bourgeois democracy—these were what the greens really loathed, and wanted to see overturned. Their campaigns, in the end, amounted to a dangerously utopian struggle in the name of a mystical communitarianism, a reactionary "return to the primitive."

In a sense, the first of these accusations—the charge of antihumanism—was the most puzzling of Ferry's arguments. Had he leveled this charge against the Norwegian followers of the Deep Ecologist Arne Naess, or the North American proponents of a Gaia-centered "earth religion," or the tree-hugging Chipko activists who defended Indian forests and birds against loggers, one could at least understand Ferry's underlying point: these were people who *appeared* to be putting nature above man. (Whether they were truly doing so, which is highly debatable, could then become the subject of a detailed discussion.) But to attempt to portray the French greens in such a light was to miss the point entirely, for one of their most distinctive features lay precisely in their positive vision of the potential human role within nature: a complex and sophisticated vision in which the human and the nonhuman might find not only coexistence but reconciliation and mutual enrichment. Among all the world's greens, the French arguably offered one of the most unabashedly integrative conceptions of the human relationship with nature.

The sources of this relatively positive vision undoubtedly lie in the broader Gallic cultural traditions from which the French greens emerged—the distinctive "feeling for nature" in France as compared with other countries. Cultural historians have speculated that several factors may have contributed to shaping Gallic perceptions of nature.[31] At the most immediate level, France's territory, like that of other West European countries, has been undergoing intensive human intervention for thousands of years. The contrast is particularly revealing if one compares France (or its neighbors) with nations like Canada, Russia, or Australia, whose vast and remote hinterlands have experienced considerably lower levels of human impact. Thus, to speak of "nature" in France is to speak of a historical space, shaped and reshaped many times over by human hands—a boundary-blurring interplay of human and nonhuman forces on a time-scale of centuries or even millennia. The territory itself is simply tamer here, and far more humanized, than in the reaches of Upper Saskatchewan or along the Tunguska plateau.

A second factor arguably lies in France's Latin culture, as compared, for example, with the Nordic or Teutonic traditions of her northern European neighbors. Although the heritage of the rough-hewn Gauls certainly plays an important part in French myths of national identity, it is the classicist (and heavily urbanized) heritage of ancient Rome that looms especially large here. In France (and Italy) one finds little reference to anything like the German *Ur-Wald,* the primeval forest out of which the Germanic culture was supposed to have been born.[32]

Finally, of course, we must take into account the traditions associated with French Cartesianism— the long-standing penchant for abstract and a priori reasoning, both in theological matters and in the natural sciences. Unlike the British, for example, whose Enlightenment naturalists eagerly embraced empirical methods of fieldwork and whose philosophers comfortably drew inferences from common experience, the French developed a reputation early on for dry rationalism, sweeping logical systems, and a reluctance to "dirty their hands" in direct contact with the physical world. Although one would not want to push these national stereotypes too far, the broad outlines of this cultural divide nonetheless become apparent, for example, in the contrast between traditional English and French gardens: the former gladly incorporating a certain wild or untamed element, the latter meticulously arraying all flora according to strict geometric discipline.[33]

Whatever the long-term cultural causes, the results were fairly clear. In postwar France, the word "nature" possessed an exceptionally broad range of meanings: the stark wilderness of Antarctica, the sparsely inhabited forests of the Vosges, the farmed countryside of Provence, the Bois de Boulogne in Paris, the herb garden behind one's house. In one particularly exhaustive survey conducted in 1991, French citizens were asked what kinds of territorial features they associated with the word "nature." While predictably high percentages of respondents (93–99 percent) regarded forests, swamps, rivers, and mountains as part of the natural world, a surprisingly large number also answered affirmatively for relatively tame features: wheat field (88 percent);

vineyard (86 percent); herb garden (84 percent); urban park (63 percent); tree-lined avenue (56 percent). Similarly, when asked what kind of natural space they personally preferred, fully 47 percent gave first place to such tame sites as orchards, cultivated fields, and herb gardens; only 28 percent gave the top ranking to "a natural site untouched by man."[34]

What was striking about the French greens was how comfortable many of them seemed to feel with the full gamut of these meanings—from the "pure" to the "mixed," from the "wild" to the "tame." (I discuss this theme in greater detail in Part IV.) Not surprisingly, they all placed a high priority on saving the world's last remaining wildernesses, such as the Amazon rainforest or the jungles of Africa; but they also understood the word "ecology" as having a direct and positive application to the semi-humanized *paysage* of France. Antoine Waechter, for example, made it clear in his book *Dessine-moi une planète* that there could be no facile equation between "wild" and "good," "tame" and "bad." In discussing the problems of the *exode rural,* he argued forcefully that a depopulated French countryside would be a grievously degraded territory, despite its return to "wild" vegetation. Nothing made him sadder than the image of once-cultivated land, abandoned to itself:

> Forsaken and untended, the land makes its way back toward the forest ecosystem—a transition which is not bad in itself but which must not be allowed to empty a territory of its population, which has once filled it with history and culture.[35]

Needless to say, this is scarcely the hallmark of an "antihumanist" attitude!

The same mentality appeared in the writings of Bernard Charbonneau, who conceived of nature not as the radical "Other," but as a meeting-ground for the human and the primal, a meeting-ground in which both partners were deemed equally important. "There can be no marriage between humankind and nature," he wrote, "without a countryside in which rural folk practice agriculture."[36] In another revealing passage, Charbonneau derided the extremism of contemporary "back to nature" movements:

> "Organic" produce, which has become all the rage in recent years, reflects the dreams and nostalgic yearning for nature that pervades industrial society. It is a fiction arising out of the frustration of people subjected to the extreme artificiality of the contemporary world. In reaction, they project an equally distorted counter-myth, the "naturism" which purveys a vision of wilderness so chemically pure as to be in its own way unnatural.[37]

While Charbonneau certainly rejected the productivist vision—man as lord over nature—he also refused to invert this vision, by simply asserting the priority of nature over man.

What French greens like Waechter and Charbonneau advocated was better evoked by Charbonneau's word, "marriage"—two very different beings, entwining their lives over many years, giving and taking in reciprocity, and perhaps bringing forth something new, a unique and astonishing synthesis of their antipodal characteristics. To call this vision "antihumanist" would be absurd, since humans played a central role in shaping this ongoing relationship and making it work. But to call it "humanist" would also risk a misunderstanding, because its essence consisted precisely in moving beyond the ancient zero-sum game in which one side either dominated or submitted to domination. Perhaps the word "humane" would serve better, insofar as it left room for a broader meaning: a balanced and respectful relation of give-and-take between the human and the nonhuman—a relation framed by humans but taking into account the needs of both humanity and the wider earth.[38]

The second and third of Ferry's accusations against the greens—authoritarianism and Fascist roots—can be despatched quite straightforwardly. It would be hard to find, anywhere on the French political scene, a more viscerally (and indeed cantankerously) anti-authoritarian grouping than the greens. Before they formed a political party, they insisted on "biodegradable" (i.e., temporary) electoral organizations, precisely so as to avoid the formation of stable power structures that might even slightly encroach upon the prerogatives of the movement's grassroots membership. When they formed a party, Les Verts, they instituted elaborate procedures to ensure that grassroots democracy would prevail and endure in their new organization: mandatory rotation of leadership positions within the party and of elective offices held on behalf of the party; a collective leadership; open meetings with the floor available to all members; and a complex federative structure, designed to make sure that all key decisions and policies would be formulated at the grassroots level, then transmitted upward from the local chapter to the national coordinating bodies. The Greens insisted on keeping these arduous democratic procedures in place, even when they discovered that their cumbersome and constraining rules were exacting a high cost in political and organizational effectiveness. Moreover, while a handful of greens, over the years, openly discussed the possible need for politically authoritarian measures to enforce global environmental responsibility, the vast majority of greens vehemently and consistently rejected such a position; in virtually all their electoral platforms and major policy statements since 1974, they have advocated a reinforcement of democratic procedures and civil liberties in France.[39]

It remains true, to be sure, that in the 1970s a sizeable minority of French greens did accept violence against property (never against persons) as part of their overall strategy. In the campaigns against nuclear testing at Moruroa, some French Greenpeace activists regularly used techniques of civil disobedience in order to gain media coverage for their cause. More seriously, one green faction in the struggles against EDF's nuclear reactors adopted the combative stance of their anarchist comrades, and began sabotaging tractors, breaking down fences, or even carrying Molotov cocktails to demonstrations. What is striking, however, is how utterly complete the failure of this minority current proved. By the late 1970s, those who had adopted extremist tactics found that they were being clobbered by the government, that their methods alienated French public opinion, and that the majority of green activists vigorously repudiated them.

Thus, in the decades that followed, one of the distinguishing features of the French greens, as compared with those of many other nations, lay in their relative moderation, both in ideology and in concrete practice. One is hard-pressed to find in France any bitter rift like that between Realos and Fundis in Germany; the radical current of Deep Ecology found very few adherents here. If one imagines a polar spectrum, with a "maximalist" green program at one end and a "minimalist" environmental agenda at the other, it is undoubtedly true that France's greens would position themselves all along such a linear continuum; but the majority would lie somewhere near the middle, and would no doubt agree with the following assessment by Alain Lipietz:

> When Greens are asked whether they are reformists or revolutionaries, even the most "fundamentalist" among them are at a loss for a reply, quite simply because they cannot see what would be *the* point of application of an "ecologist political revolution." They are in favor of changing many things, but power as such, state power, is hardly in their sights. It would change neither work relations, nor consumer mentalities, nor relations between the sexes. As heirs of Michel Foucault and Félix Guattari rather than Marxism, they dream of a multitude of small breaks with the past, of a molecular revolution never completed. They know that being in power can get things done, help struggles along, influence relationships based on relative strengths, but also that the main thing is happening elsewhere—in changes to myriad behavior patterns.[40]

This moderation of goals—seeking "a multitude of small breaks with the past"—went hand-in-hand with moderation of means. After the 1970s, one could not find in France any sizable "direct action" organizations like Earth First! in the United States or the Chipkos in India. Most French environmentalists could best be described as "radical reformists": pursuing a far-reaching transformation, but through incremental changes in laws, values, and daily practices. Though they might wax impatient at the agonizing slowness of the process, they remained true to legal and democratic methods, and to a politics of compromise, negotiation, and the gradual winning over of hearts and minds.[41]

As for the alleged Fascist connection, the facts speak for themselves. The greens have been constant and implacable foes of France's neo-fascist organization, the National Front, opposing its policies over the years through a wide variety of measures: from organizing demonstrations against racism and xenophobia, to electoral campaigning against National Front candidates, to collecting donations of cash for anti-National Front organizations such as SOS-Racisme.[42] That the ludicrous accusation of a "green-Fascist linkage" should surface from time to time is only rendered possible by a peculiarity of French history: the tradition of right-wing ruralism that goes back to the Vichy regime, with its call for a return to the soil and to the virtues of traditional country life. Though the Vichy regime is long gone, many of the values it stood for continue to exert a strong appeal among certain segments of the French Right.[43] Indeed, in 1989, a new party appeared on the electoral scene, bearing the colorful name of "Chasse, Pêche, Nature, et Traditions" ("CPNT," or "Hunting, Fishing, Nature, Traditions"); it promptly began getting around 5 percent of the vote in national elections.[44] France has 1.5 million registered hunters, the largest number of any nation in Europe, and these men (they are an overwhelmingly male group) have formed a political movement to defend their access to fields and forests from what they see as the extremist encroachments of environmentalists and animal-rights organizations. But CPNT is more than just a hunters' lobby. It also appeals to many conservative (or downright reactionary) antimodernists among the citizenry—those who feel nostalgia for an idealized version of France's rural past. Evidently, the presence of the word "nature" in this party's name has been enough for some observers to lump the greens together with them in the same ideological boat. Whether such an accusation results from ignorance or cynical political calculation, it remains equally baseless and preposterous in either case.

Ferry's fourth accusation focused on the greens' alleged "antimodernism." "In all cases," he wrote,

> the deep ecologist is guided by a hatred of modernity, by hostility toward the present. ... The ideal of deep ecology would be a world in which lost epochs and distant horizons take precedence over the present. It is not by chance, then, that it continually hesitates between conservative romantic themes and "progressive" anticapitalist ones.[45]

Ferry was actually on to something here: the ambivalence or "hesitation" he described in the greens' attitude toward the past was a real and recurring feature in green literature and debates. He went astray, however, in thinking that the greens wanted to throw away all of modernity indiscriminately, returning to a romanticized golden age. The greens, rather, wanted to build a different *kind* of modernity, drawing selectively from both past and present to bring forth a new synthesis. From the present: human rights, democratic institutions, religious tolerance, critical reason, cosmopolitan culture and communications, and certain technologies (including quite a few high-tech machines). From the past: a smaller scale of daily social and economic life; values of neighborhood and community; a sense of rootedness in the land; a reverence for the wider earth of which humans formed an integral part.

The French greens arguably stood out among the world's environmentalists for their particularly enthusiastic embrace of modernity. Fast trains, the Internet, global communications, and labor-saving devices did not frighten them: they saw these as so many tools, to be considered carefully (as Illich had taught how to do) for their systemic costs and benefits, and to be adopted judiciously as needed. (The trick, of course, lay in vigilantly reining in these "needs," which otherwise tended to proliferate so rapidly as to become damaging and self-defeating.) Nor did contemporary cities frighten these greens: many of them loved the spontaneous and unpredictable mix of viewpoints and cultural backgrounds that only an urban setting could offer. Instead, they asked themselves how cities could be re-engineered, redesigned, so as to minimize the alienation of vast impersonal spaces and institutions, and to breathe new life into neighborhoods and historic quarters, where work and shopping and leisure could unfold on a more human scale.[46] Technological complexity did not frighten them either: they eagerly explored the science of batteries, solar receptors, and hydrogen fuel cells, knowing that these might allow a revolution in energy use; they embraced modern Western medicine, calling only for its being equally accessible to all and (like other tools) subjected to critical scrutiny for its systemic effects.[47] Even in their relation to nature, they accepted a need for science and technology to play a growing role: on the one hand, cleaner industries, sophisticated new recyclable materials, energy-efficient homes; on the other hand, a continued effort in fields like biology, climatology, or ecology to understand how best to reconfigure human activities so as to coexist constructively with nature's basic patterns and rhythms.

The key, in all these cases, lay in the *critical* and *selective* application of modernity's tools—as opposed to the blind and uncontrolled application that had prevailed since the Industrial Revolution. In their 1999 electoral platform, for example, the Greens proposed that the "precautionary principle" apply to all scientific research, particularly in those areas such as genetics where unknown risks loomed large (see the discussion in chapters 11 and 13). But they did not demand a reduction of such dangers to zero, as some of their critics have implied; for they accepted that all innovation entailed potential risks, many of which, upon judicious scrutiny, could prove worth running. And they reminded their readers:

> Here is a paradox: sometimes it is only through science itself that we can come to understand the negative effects produced by our scientifically advanced society. After all, it was scientists who taught us about the dangers of pollution, the loss of biodiversity, the degradation of ecosystems; and they were only able to sound the alarm because they had the tools to comprehend the complexity and spatio-temporal dynamics of natural phenomena! We therefore reject all forms of anti-scientific obscurantism: we refuse to abandon critical reason.[48]

Environmentalism, in the eyes of the French greens, had grown out of industrial modernity, and it made no sense in any context but that of a thoroughly modern world. The key concepts that they used—from ecosystems to global warming, from productivism to appropriate technology, from human rights to global solidarity—these were all distinctively modern concepts, indissociable from the history of the industrial era. What the greens now proposed was to take up the critical tools of modern culture and to turn them upon that modernity itself, picking and choosing which elements to retain and which to leave aside. Far from constituting a rejection of modernity, this was really a *continuation* of the modernization process, pushing ahead, through an agenda of far-reaching reform, into a new (and hopefully better) era. Thus, the French greens never abandoned the core Western ideal of historical progress; rather, they sought to redefine the underlying values and assumptions by which progress would henceforth be measured. Going backward was not an option; the only question, for the greens, was whether humankind would succeed in going forward intelligently enough to allow its own survival and that of the biosphere.

> > >

To sum up: Luc Ferry got the French greens just about 100 percent wrong. The extremist "Deep Ecologists" whom he attacked may well have existed as a small but significant strain among the greens of other nations, such as Germany, Britain, or the United States, but they were practically nonexistent in his native France. Rather, the picture that emerges from the foregoing discussion is one of a French green movement possessing four particularly pronounced features: a positive and integrative conception of the human place within nature; moderation of goals and methods, coupled with earnest adherence to the principles of democratic change; ardent anti-authoritarianism; and a critical but still enthusiastic embrace of modernity. These were of course relative qualities, which might certainly be found to varying degrees among the greens of many other nations. Nevertheless, taken together, they arguably added up to a distinctively "Gallic green" identity.

But something is still missing from this depiction of the French green ideology, namely, a concrete sense of the whole. How would all these ideas hang together, in actual practice? What might the Gallic green visions look like, translated into the real world? These are the questions we take up in the chapter that follows.

6   What Might It Actually Look Like?

The French Green Utopia: A Guided Tour

The slower you go, the more you discover the wonder of it. But if you really want to know its riches, you have to become its *inhabitant*. The most beautiful place of all is the one you inhabit, because it's here that time mingles with space to allow us to explore all its enfolded secrets, to discover its protean diversity ceaselessly renewed through the passing seasons and years. This can only happen in a place where our roots have the time to go down into the earth.
—Bernard Charbonneau, 1991[1]

Thus far we have traced the historical development of the French green movement, and laid out the broad outlines of the ideology that animated it. In this concluding chapter of Part II, I would like to put some flesh on the bare bones of this intellectual portrait, by imagining what it would be like to visit an actual incarnation of the French green ideology—a utopian society situated in the not-too-distant future, in which green ideas have been given a chance to come to full and systemic fruition.

This utopian sketch is of course my own invention—a composite drawn from the broad range of contemporary French environmentalist ideas. Although I would expect that different aspects of it would elicit objections from a variety of French greens, I have striven, in creating it, to remain faithful to the core principles underlying the greens' major publications and policy statements. If I had to point to a single document as having constituted my most important source and "blueprint," it would be the 1999 electoral platform for Les Verts;[2] but I have also drawn heavily on my own interviews with French environmentalists, and on forty years of their writings along these lines.

In putting together this imagined field trip, I have tried to steer a middle road between "realism" and "optimism"—assuming no major changes in human nature or the laws of physics, but nevertheless postulating a sweeping cultural shift of the sort that the French have actually witnessed from time to time in the course of their long history. Needless to say, the portrait that follows should not be taken too literally. It is a greatly compressed and simplified microcosm of green ideas, projected onto a manageable narrative scale: the result is, unavoidably, a stylized and impressionistic account, designed to capture the "feel" of a certain constellation of philosophical values in concrete embodiment. The real world, if it ever goes dark green, will be a vastly more complicated, contested, striated, and ambiguous place.

> > >

It comes into sight rather abruptly as you pedal your bike, huffing and puffing, over the rise, and at first glance it doesn't seem all that different. You stop by the side of road and take it in.

A French country village at mid-morning on a weekday in June, moss-covered stone roofs and medieval church steeple, surrounded by lush countryside: fields, hedgerows, lanes cutting at different angles, marked by receding lines of ancient chestnut trees and oaks. A narrow water runnel, alongside the road, is gurgling softly, its banks a tangle of watercress and ferns, its clear flow looking very cold.

This is the heart of the French ecological utopia: a village (imaginary, of course) named Vignac, around the year 2020, somewhere along the banks of the Dordogne river, in rural south-central France. But it's not what it appears. It is not a piece of France's past, a quaint vacation-spot for Dutch or British tourists seeking a break from the frenetic pace of London or Rotterdam. This is no backwater: not anymore.

Behind one of the barns of a nearby farmhouse, you see the glint of sunlight on a satellite dish. A tractor is working the field up ahead—silently: it's an electric tractor, powered by a zero-emissions hydrogen fuel cell. The only sound it makes comes from the steel cutting blades as they turn up the loam; the only exhaust it leaves behind is an invisible vapor of pure water. You look more closely: there's a man plodding behind the tractor, inspecting the furrows as he walks. And the tractor cab is empty: it's going by itself! The farmer has all his fields mapped on a program that's linked through his computer to a Global Positioning Satellite, accurate down to two centimeters: the computer is running the tractor, adjusting for variations in soil quality and density as the machine advances. The farmer looks up as you ride by, and watches you, but does not wave until you raise your hand in greeting.

You approach Vignac. The first thing you notice is the solar panels on the southwest side of all the roofs; they catch the sunlight in little striations and rainbows. The next thing you notice is the quiet. People moving to and fro, bicycles, a car here and there, one truck—but all electric, all silent. As you come closer you hear a clamor of children playing: it's recess at the elementary school.

A small round blue sign by the road says "Bienvenue à Vignac," and beneath, in smaller letters, "Commune d'Europe."

Down the main street, which is lined with tall elms, you see a fountain splashing in the main square. To the left is a long three-story stone building with a logo on it: Vignac Logiciels, known throughout the world more simply as "VL," one of the leading innovators in the global software industry. The company has more than ten thousand employees, but only three hundred work here in the administrative center. The others all work at home (all over Europe) and "telecommute" by computer for most of their daily business. VL's stock was up 14 percent last year, and all employees, from janitors to managers, receive annual stock options and profit-sharing.

Bicycles. Everywhere. Leaning against trees, parked in racks, small ones, tall ones, high-tech racers, black clunkers that look like they date from the 1940s, funny-looking three-wheeled contraptions with large wicker baskets behind the seat. (The baskets are another local specialty. Renowned for their lightness and durability, they are highly prized all over Europe.) As you make your way down the main street, a young woman on a bike whizzes out from a narrow cross-street and nearly collides with you. RingRing! She sounds off at you with her handlebar bell, and before you can even react, she's gone. You look down: you're standing in a bike lane. Quickly you retreat to the sidewalk, walking your bike along.

The bicycle is the foundation of the transportation system here. If you need to go to the next village, Ceyrac, there's a bus every hour (with a large bike rack in the back). If you need to go farther, the train is best: there's a fast minitrain every two hours to the regional hub, Aurillac. From there you can get TGV connections all over Europe: Bordeaux, Toulouse, and Lyon in about one hour, Paris in four hours, London or Brussels in just under six. But it's expensive: the government keeps prices high, both to discourage unnecessary travel, and to pay for the significant costs of soundproofing and tree-planting along the rail lines. Students are given deep discounts on all rail fares, to encourage them to visit other cities and countries; and each household is allotted a sheaf of discounted (and nontransferable) tickets once a year. A similar set of rules applies to air travel: one trip per person per year on a heavily discounted basis, with extremely high prices after that. Within the quotas, travel is cheap and easy; above the quotas, travel is a luxury that few allow themselves.

Same goes for cars. That's why there are so few on the streets here. What with the purchase tax and the energy tax and the road tax and the luxury tax, a private car lies beyond the reach of most citizens. But this does not mean that people can't move around as they wish. Apart from the dense and efficient network of public transport, there are more flexible alternatives: cheap electric taxis in the big cities, and public loan cars in smaller towns and villages. The loan cars work very simply: you punch your address into a computer and order a car. A few minutes later someone drives up to your door with a publicly owned car—usually a mid-priced, sturdy, zero-emissions Peugeot, Citroën, or Renault. The delivery-person has his bike on a rack on the back; he scans your credit card and rides off toward the car depot. You get in and drive wherever you wish, paying a low tariff based on distance and time. Insurance is included in the price. (The tariff is heavily subsidized for trips up to 100 kilometers, using funds the government gets from the energy tax, road tax, and luxury tax.) When you're done with the car, you swipe your card on the dashboard reader, lock the doors, and walk away. The car automatically radios the dispatcher that it's ready for pick-up.

The only time this loan-car system comes under stress is during bad weather, when many would prefer to ride a car than a bike. But here the public transport system rises to the occasion: a special fleet of extra buses and minivans (all electric, of course) comes into service during these periods, passing down the streets every three minutes and servicing the entire town. Local public transport is swift, dependable, and completely free. So even during foul weather the demand for loan-cars remains manageable.[3]

Now you come into the town square, still walking your bike. Trees. Steep sloping rooftops on the old surrounding buildings. A café, le Bar Sport, its tables spilling out onto the smooth cobbles of the square. Beautiful fountain, reflecting the sunlight. RingRing! An old lady barreling along on a three-wheeler swerves wildly to avoid you, then curses in local dialect as she continues off across the square. You look down: bike lane again. Meekly you make your way to one side. This is going to take some getting used to.

The stately neoclassical building across the square says "Mairie" on the front: Town Hall. People are going in and out, some in a hurry, talking on cell phones, others more leisurely, gesticulating in little groups. There's a bronze sculpture to one side of the building, a modernist design with lots of hoops and circles of different sizes. You go closer to have a look. The hoops are arranged concentrically, their angles offset like a model of the solar system's planetary orbits. Inside each metal ring you see an engraved word: "Citoyen" ("citizen") on the small central hoop, then "Vignac" on the next largest, then "Auvergne," "France," "Europe," and "Terre" on the successively larger circles. France abolished its Senate ten years ago, replacing it with a Chamber of Regions; represented in this new political body are eighteen territorial units that hark back to the time of Louis XIV, bearing names like Bretagne, Normandie, Languedoc, Auvergne, Gascogne, Savoie. The smaller *départements*, dating to French Revolutionary days, had come to be seen as artificial entities, bearing little relation to the historic and linguistic identity of France's regional cultures; they were dissolved, and their powers absorbed by the newly consolidated and invigorated regional governments. Many former functions of the central state, such as social welfare, health care, and *aménagement du territoire*, are now handled directly at the regional level as well.

If you were to ask a local resident where she feels the most allegiance, she might reply, "I am from the Auvergne, and I am a European." If pressed, she will acknowledge that she is very much French as well, but she will quickly add that her Frenchness is not as important as it used to be. What matters most now is the distinctiveness of her native region, the Auvergne, with its mountains and rivers, ancient traditions and vibrant contemporary cultural life. And of course her Europeanness, the sense of belonging to a unique heritage of literatures, values, and habits shared in common with other peoples of the continent's western reaches—the Italians, Spaniards, Dutch, Germans—even the English! "In some ways," she might tell you, "I have more in common with a Lombard woman, or a man from Salzburg, than I do with many Parisians—for the issues that confront us here in our daily lives are those of a rural and mountainous region, far removed from the concerns of those flatland city-dwellers."

But the people of Vignac—they call themselves *les Vignacois*—would laugh at the thought of being called "provincial." There is no such thing any more as "center" and "periphery"—at least not in the sense these terms used to mean. A man from Vignac gets up in the morning, skims through several electronic news sheets transmitted from editorial rooms in the regional capital of Clermont-Ferrand, from Paris or Frankfurt, from Los Angeles or Tokyo. He goes to work by computer, transacting business from continent to continent, speaking the universal language of English.[4] He listens to music beamed in from Mombasa or New Orleans, St. Petersburg or Buenos Aires.

He follows with interest the political developments in Indonesia, Sicily, or Chile. And then he comes back to the present horizon, here in Vignac, meeting a couple friends in the neighborhood café to discuss the upcoming mayoral election.

On the front of the Town Hall, carved into the marble pediment, you see the familiar slogan of the French Revolution: *Liberté, Égalité, Fraternité.* But underneath, in characters mimicking the same neoclassical style, there is a new trio of words: *Responsabilité, Identité, Solidarité.* You're just beginning to ponder these terms when a brouhaha erupts from behind the café: people arguing, angrily yelling. Sounds serious. You make your way over. Clusters of men and women, arms waving. They keep pointing at the ground: then you smile. It's a game of *boules.* One wiry old man in a beret appears to be claiming his boule is closest to the tiny target ball. A short-haired young woman taps her head: "Ça va pas, non?" ("You crazy or something?"). A paunchy fellow with a huge handlebar moustache tries to intervene, but they brush him aside. The wiry fellow gets out his string and re-measures. Tense silence. Smugly he holds up the string. The woman heads back to the throwing line, grumbling. She turns and takes aim. The others look on, intense. Her body swings, the boule flies, a long slow arc, landing with a metallic Tchac! right on the wiry man's boule, sending it flying and taking its place. Grins all round, a scowl from the wiry man. The woman tries unsuccessfully not to look triumphant.

What strikes you suddenly is the composition of these *boules* players. They're not the usual assembly of crusty village old-timers. These are young people and old, men and women. There's also a young Arab-looking man among them—Algerian perhaps. What you're seeing here is the result of the twenty-five-hour work week: people with time on their hands, time to fish, to paint, to read (and write) books, to play *boules* on a sunny weekday morning. With more people spending less time at their jobs, unemployment has come down to 2 percent nationwide, and is almost nil here in Vignac. The vast majority of workers declare themselves well satisfied with this new arrangement of their labor time, happy to trade a decline in income for the time to live richer lives. Those who prefer to work longer (and earn more) are free to do so, taking on extra jobs as they see fit. But statisticians have shown that, although the number of hours worked by each citizen has gone down 37 percent from the old forty-hour week, most people are still taking home about 80 percent of their former full-time pay. The reason for the discrepancy lies in two factors: the increased productivity of a well-rested and highly motivated workforce, and the fact that declining unemployment has allowed the government to reduce payroll taxes, which in turn has allowed businesses to pass on the tax savings to employees in the form of proportionately higher salaries.

As you turn away from the *boules* game, you spy a buffet counter inside the café. The strenuous ride into town has made you hungry: you lean your bike against a tree and head inside. Amazing display of foods, a cornucopia of fresh vegetables and salads and *terrines* and *patés* and wizened little salamis. To one side an entire section with nothing but cheeses: round, square, dry, creamy, peppery, ash-covered, goat, sheep, cow, bright white *fromage frais*, yellowed fusty-looking Rocquefort. Long fresh-smelling baguettes sticking out of baskets like floral arrangements. Small carafes of the house white, chilled and sweating. The barman beckons you to help yourself, which you gladly do, taking a full tray out to the breezeway tables under a flowering canopy of wisteria. Once you get started you find the food even more delicious than it looked.

Yet this is not surprising either, because the quality of food has become not just a question of lifestyles here in the Auvergne, but a hot political issue as well. The French have long complained about the creeping advance of "la mal-bouffe américaine" ("lousy American-style eats"), but it was only in recent years that they finally mustered the political will to break away from the underlying agro-economic system that had come to dominate their country during the *trente glorieuses*. When the change came, it was swift and drastic. The French government imposed hefty tariffs on agricultural goods imported from abroad. Then it slapped a stiff "ecological tax" on domestic agribusiness, forcing the large food producers to pay high prices for the fertilizers and chemicals they spread on their fields. The proceeds from the ecological tax went to subsidize small farmers who produced high-quality farm goods in a manner consistent with ecological sustainability. A new "transportation tax" forced food distributors to rethink the way they shipped products to market: they now had a strong incentive to encourage the local consumption of locally produced farm goods.

The result, over time, was nothing short of revolutionary. Many young persons, observing the small farmers' growing prosperity, eagerly made the move out of cities and back onto the land. The desolate legacy of the *exode rural* gradually reversed itself, as remote ghost towns slowly came back to life, the schools filling back up with children, the post office opening again, the café, the bakery, entire local economics resurrected. As the French came to re-inhabit their ancient provinces, they gradually rediscovered the meaning of the word *terroir*—that ineffable word that conveys so many things at once: a plot of farmed land, a particular micro-climate in a vineyard, the space between two crumbling stone walls tucked away in the corner of a valley, the impression of a particular stand of poplars along a ridge, a place with a history all its own, flavored by the inflections of the local patois, the names of forgotten ancestors, the comings and goings since Roman times, a familiar nuance in the taste of the water, a unique spot in one's childhood memories. All this (and more) in one term: *terroir.*

Implicit here was a slow, time-worn process, spontaneous yet cumulative, of putting down genuine local roots: to ride your bike down a lane and see the cows whose milk your children drank at breakfast; to buy a chunk of cheese and know that the person who made it went to grammar school with your mother; to drink a glass of wine and think of walks in nearby vineyards with your sweetheart twenty years ago, vineyards where the very vines that made this wine were already growing. All these things, which had once seemed like vanished characteristics of a bygone era, turned out to be perfectly compatible with technological modernity: but only with a particular *kind* of modernity, shaped and nurtured by a concrete set of political and economic choices.

The transformation did not come without a price, of course. France had to break with its free-market partners in the European Union and GATT over the imposition of agricultural tariffs. The politicians in Paris had to endure howls of protest from the powerful lobbies of agribusiness. As in the time of General de Gaulle, the French were once again accused of selfishly wrecking the delicate structures of international commerce. But in the end, it was not as hard as one might have thought. An astonishingly large number of Germans, Italians, or Danes—and many Americans as well—actually regarded the French move away from agribusiness as a sensible and even courageous act. There were many who felt that they, too, had precious *terroirs* worth protecting, in the countrysides of Bavaria, Tuscany, or California. As time went by (and after the French government agreed to compensate its trade partners for the lost agricultural exports), many other nations gradually followed suit with similar policies of their own. Eventually a new international system of agriculture began to emerge, a system in which market forces still operated, but in which social and ecological priorities played a far greater role in shaping policy.

You get up from your table, a little giddy from the wine. A man in overalls is approaching down the sidewalk on a rusty old clunker of a bike. Down the side street you see a young woman coming fast with an infant in the basket on her handlebars. They can't see each other. Looks like a sure-thing collision: you start to yell out but it's too late: they both swerve, he to the right, she to the left, and somehow miss each other. RingRing! RingRing! (Angrily, from both of them.) And they're gone.

After a strong espresso at the bar, you head back out to the square to get your bike. Time for another ride into the countryside: a visit to Vignac's famous wind farm. Down a side street, past the old church, out the medieval gates into the fields. The plots are small and multicolored, showing the signs of intensive farming: beets, carrots, lettuce, corn, kale, potatoes, mustard, lavender, cabbage. Some other kind of purple vegetable you can't identify. Suddenly an electric motorbike veers around the bend ahead of you, going much too fast: two farm kids in overalls, their hair flopping in the wind, zoom past you on their way into town. You pedal harder, half indignant at their "cheating" with electric horsepower, half wishing you had one of those mopeds yourself. Especially as you round the turn and see the steep switchbacks of the hill up ahead. Along the crest, through the trees, you can already make out the white shapes of wind turbines.

France has begun phasing out nuclear power altogether, with the goal of reducing it to zero by the year 2050. In order to do this, it has had to continue relying heavily on imported oil and natural gas (as well as domestic coal) for heating homes and generating electricity; these fossil fuels still make up a whopping 60 percent of French energy consumption today, in 2020. Try as they might, the French have only been able to bring about a ten percent decline in their nation's total energy use since the year 2000; their continuing efforts at conservation and efficiency are aimed at further reductions of 25 percent by 2050, when the last nuclear plant finally shuts down. At that point, if their projections hold good, France's "energy pie" will look something like this: 45 percent renewable energy sources (solar, wind, hydroelectric, tidal, geothermal, biomass); 25 percent natural gas; 10 percent coal; 20 percent imported oil. In total, they will be consuming roughly one-third less energy each year than they had been in 2000.[5]

This result disappoints many ecological activists, who had hoped to convert France into a "100 percent renewable-energy economy" by the mid-century. Most of them, however, had never actually sat down to do the numbers: renewable energy sources, despite their continuing technological advances, devour vast quantities of precious space. For example, to generate the same amount of electricity as a single mid-sized nuclear power plant, contemporary solar receptors would have to cover a swath of land one kilometer wide and 100 kilometers long![6] By the year 2100, therefore, as Third World energy consumption continues to grow, and world fossil fuel reserves start tapering off, the French will face a difficult choice: either to force upon themselves a truly draconian reduction of their energy consumption, or to bite the bullet and return to some type of nuclear combustion. Unless, of course, the scientific deus ex machina intervenes in the meantime, offering some revolutionary new technology for clean energy.

Machine/Symbol: The Wind Turbine

But what a strange new world the renewable energies are already creating! You come up the hill, panting from the climb, and stand in awe before the Vignac wind farm in all its vastness. All along the crest, to the hazy edge of sight, and along the neighboring ridges, and halfway down the Vallée de la Haspe below (chosen for its strong prevailing wind patterns), a dense white forest of tall fibreglass towers, their huge three-bladed rotors placidly turning in the breeze. The whole landscape seems to be crawling, everywhere at once, with a surreal, slow-motion, palpitation of white. A weird low rumbling Whoosh fills the sky: the sound of 1,700 rotors catching the valley's airstream. The sound does not seem to affect the flocks of cows that graze in the grasses below the towering shapes. This is one of the largest wind farms in France, apart from those in the Pyrenees and in the huge Atlantic and Channel offshore installations. It produces about the same output per year as a nuclear power plant or a gas-fired electric station.

The world's first known windmills were developed in Persia around 200 B.C. for grinding grain.[7] By the mid-fourteenth century the Dutch had become the world's leaders in the technology, using their famous four-bladed design to power pumps for moving water in the fields. The first wind-powered electric generator was built in 1891 by a Danish inventor named Poul de Cour, one of the pioneers of modern aerodynamics. In the late twentieth century the technology took another leap forward, after the 1973 oil shock rendered alternative energy sources more attractive. By the 1990s the Danes had taken a commanding lead, capturing fully 50 percent of the world's wind-energy market—a market that grew during that decade at the remarkable rate of 50 to 60 percent every year. Indeed, by the year 2000 fully 14 percent of Denmark's electricity was wind-generated.

Here at Vignac in 2020, the French have tacitly acknowledged the continuing commercial and technical leadership of the Danes, having adopted one of the largest Danish models for the turbines along the ridges and in the valley below. The machine, which looks appealingly simple on the outside, is actually a highly sophisticated piece of technology. Each tower is 71 meters tall, with rotors 63 meters in diameter (this puts each of the three giant blades at about 31 meters, or 101 feet, in length). The rotor revolves at between 30 and 40 rpm, turning a geared shaft that powers a generator, producing 1,500 kilowatts of electricity. A computer in the nacelle behind the rotor gathers data several times per second from wind sensors, micro-aligning the rotor assembly to keep it facing straight into the wind, continually adjusting the pitch of the blades to maximize their efficiency. At the same time the computer also monitors the quality of the electricity output, adjusting various generator functions to keep the electric flow clean and smooth.

The three-bladed turbine is not as efficient as other designs with more blades, but it has the advantage of being able to withstand the extreme weather conditions that it will encounter during its twenty years (120,000 hours) of continuous operation. (By comparison, an average automobile's useful lifespan is 5,000 hours.) The blades themselves are the end-result of many years of aerodynamic research. They curve slightly along a complex gradient to maximize their "bite" on the air all along their length; their back edges are shaped so as to minimize turbulence and noise; their tips have hydraulic vanes that instantly adjust to shifting gusts and wind conditions.

This is, in a sense, the ultimate ecological machine. It is safe, clean, quiet, reliable, and powerful. It uses a plentiful resource that will not run out. Over its lifetime it will generate 80 times more energy than it takes to build, maintain, operate, dismantle, and recycle it. It produces a kilowatt of electricity for about the same cost as a coal-fired power plant fitted with smoke-scrubbing technology—but with zero emissions, negligible heat, and zero dependence on foreign fossil fuel suppliers. Compared to other alternative energy sources, it uses the least amount of land for each unit of electricity produced: about 400 times less than solar panels, about 40,000 times less than biofuel (wood, vegetable oils, and the like). Wind turbines, moreover, do not have to be huge and imposing like these at Vignac: they come in all shapes and sizes, adaptable to all manner of needs and applications. They are ideal for many parts of the Third World, where decentralized energy production is essential to meet the needs of remote and far-flung settlements. Finally, they create jobs—both in manufacturing them and in maintaining them over the long years of their service life.

One turbine can do many things. In one year it will produce about 5 million kilowatt-hours of electrical energy—enough to meet the needs of 2,200 households. Its energy can be used directly to power electrical devices, or in chemical plants to separate hydrogen out of water by electrolysis. The hydrogen can then be used in fuel cells to power cars, trucks, or ships. Hydrogen fuel cells can also power large regional electric generators on days when there is no wind, thus keeping the electric grid flowing even when the wind farms are becalmed. The only drawback of wind energy, compared to nuclear or fossil fuel energy, lies implicit in the sheer expanse of the wind farm here at Vignac: even though it is far more efficient than solar or biofuel energy, it still requires the creation of these "fibreglass forests" covering entire mountainsides and ridges.

This, indeed, can be seen as one of the underlying ironies of an environmentally oriented society: the shift to clean, renewable energy requires the creation of vast tracts of highly artificialized land (and sea) for the extraction of energy from the natural rhythms of the earth. To walk through a wind farm, among the grazing cows and shiny white towers, under the dizzying movement of a sky filled everywhere with gyrating blades, is to walk through a bizarrely futuristic landscape, something out of science fiction, far removed indeed from the ideals of any "return to nature." And yet, when you mention this to several people in Vignac, in the café later in the day, they shrug it off: "What's the alternative?" they ask. "Besides, if you want a real forest, we have a beautiful one just two kilometers away, on the other side of the river between here and Ceyrac."

The more philosophically minded among them reflect aloud about humankind's ability to reshape the world and to adapt to the "new nature" it has created. But it's the barman, following the conversation while he rinses glasses behind the counter, who cheerfully interrupts and sums it up most concisely: "We're like the cows: we get used to it!"

> > >

Back down to the village, to visit the recycling plant—one of the most sophisticated in Europe, financed by a grant from the deep coffers of Vignac Logiciels. On the way, you see a man walking along the roadside, carrying a shotgun and a couple rabbits slung over his shoulder. Hunting, in this intensively green society? You pull over to talk to him. It turns out he's the vice-mayor, a representative of the small right-wing party known as "Chasse, Pêche, Nature, et Traditions" ("Hunting, Fishing, Nature, Traditions"). You ask to see his morning's catch, and he proudly shows you his two young hares, holding their limp heads up by the ears. Trying not to look at the bloody holes in their sides, you cast about for a question: "Is game plentiful around here?" He frowns and shakes his head. "They make it a nightmare for us," he complains. "They" means the regional government. Waving his hand in the direction of the neighboring valley, he explains that wolves and lynxes have been reintroduced into the forest of Verdolles, over the past few years, in the hope of re-establishing the full diversity of the region's ecosystem. Problem is, the new predators don't stay put within the wildlife preserves; they come out into the fields at night and catch rabbits, hedgehogs, pheasants, quail, you name it. Sometimes they wreak havoc in the local farmyards—and when a farmer shoots one of them, he gets slapped with a 5,000-Euro fine! The vice-mayor goes on for quite some time, getting worked up: the complicated seasonal restrictions, the hunting permits with their exorbitant surtax (which pays for game wardens to monitor the woodlands), the proliferating number of "protected species," the outrageous penalties for even small violations.

As politely as you can, you interrupt him, explaining that you have an appointment in the village (not technically true, but this fellow is looking like he's ready to go on for another forty-five minutes). You take off down the steep road, enjoying the wind and the turns.

Last time you were going this fast on your bike was three days ago, in Paris. Coming down the hill from Montmartre. It seems like ages. You had bought a Derain poster at the Musée d'Orsay that morning, and it fell off, in its cardboard tube, as you came down the bumpy street from the Place Pigalle. You braked as fast as you could, and a man picked it up and brought it to you. With a smile.

The Parisians still had a reputation for being rude, like New Yorkers—yet it really wasn't that way anymore. Paris had changed. With the twenty-five-hour work week, Parisians had enough time on their hands now to let go of the daily rush a bit. Not *too* much: just enough to smile and pick up a fallen package for someone.

Paris was smaller now. The population had peaked in 2003, at ten million (eight million in the suburbs, two in the central city); now it was down to five-and-a-half million (still two million in the central city). But the whole layout had changed—not dramatically, as in the time of Baron Haussmann, but subtly, profoundly. Today Paris was jokingly described by its residents as "a confederation of villages." Each historic district had its own local government with wide-ranging powers, its own public library and community cultural center, its own open-air markets, pedestrian zones, parks, and tree-lined squares where cafés overflowed onto the sidewalks. Bicycles everywhere, baby carriages, people milling about. And so few cars! The free electric buses and trams, free (and fast) *métropolitaine,* ubiquitous bike paths—coupled with the whopping Vehicle Tax that effectively tripled the cost of owning a car—had produced their effect in the space of less than five years. Seventy percent of the city's automobile owners gave up their vehicles, or kept them in free underground garages outside the city limits. The sudden absence of noise, along the Seine near Notre Dame, on a summer's evening, was downright disorienting—especially to the Parisians themselves. That background roar of traffic was simply gone, like lifting a veil of auditory grime. In its place, punctuating the quiet, one could hear human voices, the occasional bicycle bell, a dog barking, teenagers skateboarding, the sad whistle of a passing bateau-mouche, the church bells tolling Vespers in Saint-Sulpice—even birds singing! Paris was definitely still Paris: the food, the night life, the music, shops, students, artists' exhibitions, bickering intellectuals. But for someone who had been visiting (and loving) this city over many decades, it was as if the clock had suddenly turned back to the Belle Epoque. Paris had become more "itself" than ever.

Which is not to say that the Parisians—and the French more broadly—

still did not find plenty of things to complain about. They groused about high taxes and sclerotic government bureaucracies. They expressed disgust at the machinations, and periodic revelations of corruption, among politicians. They worried about street crime and drug abuse, which continued to pose serious problems, especially in the suburbs of major cities. Some accused the government of having gone much too far with this "Green Adventure," while others bitterly denounced it for not having gone far enough.

What was striking, though, was the difference in tone, compared with the France of a few decades past. One sensed a mood of hope, of cautious optimism, that had not existed before: people seemed to feel that their society was on the move, in ways that they could actually have a chance of influencing and shaping. Of all the changes that had come over this nation, this was certainly one of the most significant: the renewed sense of civic involvement, the belief that even the most intractable social and economic problems could be worked on, with a real possibility of making headway.

Your bike bumps over the cobblestones of Vignac's medieval streets as you coast back through the ancient stone gate and head for the village center. In the main square, you pause by the fountain to catch your breath and splash some cool water on your face and neck. A busload of Japanese tourists is unloading on the other side of the square, under the trees. They immediately begin standing in little rows and threesomes to take each other's pictures.

Three Arab women in Muslim veils are sitting on a shady bench near the café, their children playing a variant of hopscotch on the sidewalk. From behind their veils you hear them chatting and laughing with each other. One turns to her daughter and calls out in what must be Arabic. The daughter answers in French.

You ask a passing man how to get to the recycling plant. He explains: it's on the other side of the Dordogne river, about ten minutes' ride beyond the bridge. You thank him, then sit down again, feeling lazy. You look on as the man (a white European) continues across the square and approaches the Arab women. He stands in front of them, and they begin conversing animatedly. The children stop playing and come listen. He gesticulates, telling some kind of a story. Finally he finishes with a grand sweep of his arm, and they all burst out laughing. The women move aside, and he sits down on the bench beside them.

To heck with the recycling plant. You decide to stay here, in the sunshine by the splashing fountain, and watch the locals.

You've seen quite a few people in Vignac who look like immigrants from former French colonies. There were two grey-haired black men in the bar, wearing business suits, and several Arabs in a group of youths who walked by earlier. For all its remoteness, the Auvergne has been a leader in the national policy of "Undoing Colonialism." The policy operates at many levels: a long-term program to facilitate the assimilation of immigrants into French economic and social institutions, while encouraging them to retain their distinctive cultural traditions; a new multicultural orientation in French schools, emphasizing "respect for difference" as a core value; and a dramatic escalation of aid to developing countries, orchestrated through the European Union and United Nations. The change hasn't come easily, for certain aspects of immigrant culture—attitudes toward women, for example—provide endless sources of friction and debate. But the overall policy is there, none-theless, setting the terms for this slow, sometimes painful, sometimes astonishingly beautiful, encounter between "Frenchness" and the other cultures of the world.

A majority of French citizens now believes that "sustainable development"—while it certainly begins at home—will fail unless it takes hold globally. Hence they have accepted to tax themselves heavily, devoting fully 10 percent of GDP every year to the promotion of ecological balance and social justice throughout the world. The goal is fourfold: to reduce world population to two billion by the year 2200; to eradicate poverty and illiteracy; to adopt clean technology and agricultural practices in all nations; to move toward a "steady-state" global economy—an economy of continuing technological and commercial innovation, but of stable equilibrium in its impact on the biosphere. This arduous agenda, long derided as utopian among mainstream economists, has now received official endorsement at all levels of government; more importantly, it has apparently hit home among ordinary citizens. "Small is Beautiful"—the slogan that seemed revolutionary when E. F. Schumacher coined it in the 1970s—has become a commonplace in the mentalities of today: smaller cities and towns, smaller farms, smaller circles of daily social life—but all linked together in loose, flexible, far-flung networks. The fact that "Small" can only be coherently sought on a global scale, in a systematic effort spanning complex chains of cause and effect that reverberate throughout the planet—this has become one of the founding paradoxes of contemporary political economy.

The Arab women and the man get up from their bench, calling the children. They amble off together. The square is quiet in the afternoon light.

For no apparent reason you feel an impulse to go down by the river. You get on your bike and pedal across the square, picking up speed, letting the breeze flutter through your shirt as you enter the tree-lined main street.

One of the Japanese tourists, aiming a camera at his friends, suddenly backs out from between two elms and steps into the bike lane just ahead of you.

No time to think. You swerve hard, almost grazing the back of his feet.

Glancing over your shoulder, you glimpse his startled smile. RingRing!
The wind rushing on your face.
Life is good.

> > >

Our brief tour of Vignac is over. But we can find implicit here, in this imaginary village with its wind turbines and bicycles, some of the tough choices that faced real French citizens during the second half of the twentieth century. Vignac, in one respect, clearly represents "the road not taken." And yet this is not entirely accurate: for certain important features of this village had indeed begun to take shape, albeit in a partial and inchoate way, in the real history of France between 1960 and 2000.

The green activists and theorists of the 1970s—Gorz, Dumont, Illich, Charbonneau—were true revolutionaries. Although they eschewed violent methods of social change, they nonetheless advocated a clean break from "productivism," a total metamorphosis of industrial civilization. Yet in the end their hopes were frustrated by the remarkable staying-power of mass consumerism—the resilient ideology of the *trente glorieuses,* the eager millions happily bowing to the god of "More." Most French citizens, to be sure, found certain aspects of the greens' ideas highly appealing: they earnestly agreed that the human impact on nature needed urgent attention. Yet when the chips were down, they balked at the prospect of actually giving up their own cars, elaborate appliances, spacious homes, foreign vacations, and other pleasant appurtenances of modernity's cornucopia.

So they hedged. On the one hand, the French sincerely pushed for the widespread implementation of environmentalist practices, sometimes even making considerable sacrifices and extending their efforts well beyond the superficial level. On the other hand, they stubbornly refused to go all the way into a systematic application of green changes like those that characterized Vignac: if the costs or drawbacks seemed too drastic, they recoiled, falling back on older and more familiar patterns of behavior. The result was an enormously complex tangle of ad hoc solutions, arising each day in a thousand workplaces, homes, and public institutions: here a half-measure, there a full-blown green experiment; here a superficial and palliative effort, there a well-organized and amply funded environmentalist program.

By the year 2000, the cumulative effect of all these ad hoc changes had brought into being a social system that could no longer be dismissed, as some embittered greens tended to do, with the disdainful epithet of "écologie-spectacle," a meaningless "ecology show." It amounted to much more than that, for the whole ethos of the society had been affected: patterns of consumption, manufacturing, earning a living, leisure, travel, education.

True, the full-scale revolutionary transformation had failed to materialize: Vignac remained but a dream. Yet it was also undeniable that France had become a substantially different place, a place in which the "green factor" now played a part—whether superficial or profound—virtually everywhere.

In Part III we explore systematically the constitutive elements, and inner tensions, of this "half-revolution" and the new social order it created.

PART III

A Society Goes Light-Green

7   The Dual Nature of Light-Green

For many of us the meaning of the world depends on clear boundaries, pure categories, and the separation of nature *out there* from us, our bodies, and our work, *in here*.
—Richard White (1995)[1]

The central feature of the light-green society consisted in a two-way blurring of the boundary between the "social" and the "natural." In France between 1960 and 2000, objects and experiences associated with "Mother Nature" acquired an ever-higher priority in the scale of human values, and increasingly came to permeate the social world; at the same time, human agency increasingly penetrated and shaped the surrounding land, sky, and waters. On one side, in other words, a preoccupation with natural qualities and natural equilibrium increasingly infused the nation's economic and cultural life: from eco-friendly appliances to organic vegetables, from green tourism to nature documentaries, from recycling programs to governmental regulation of industrial effluents. On the other side, the artificialization of the territory proceeded apace, as human activities encroached ever more massively upon the territory, and as human efforts to "save" nature resulted in an intensified and systematic effort of "ecological management": research, physical intervention, monitoring, legal and economic action. To an unprecedented degree, the boundary blurred: ecological criteria set new ground rules for economic production and consumption; man-made devices, both visible and invisible, lay their increasingly pervasive touch upon the biosphere. Nature into society, society into nature: this accelerating interpenetration became the hallmark of the light-green social order.

By way of introduction and illustration, it is useful here to explore two very different machine/symbols, each oriented toward one aspect of this bidirectional blurring of boundaries.

Nature Penetrating into Society—Machine/Symbol: The *Train à Grande Vitesse*

One technological product that perfectly embodied the ambivalence of the light-green society—the heartfelt and simultaneous adherence to ideals of ecology and productivist modernity—was the TGV, or high-speed train. Like the Concorde, it was fast, sleek, "sexy"—an incarnation of French high-tech prowess; but unlike the Concorde, it was also cost-efficient, fuel-efficient, relatively nonpolluting, and accessible to a wide socioeconomic range of travelers. The French national rail company, SNCF, skillfully played on both these scales of value in promoting its signature product: "Ride the TGV," said the SNCF's billboards in effect, "and you will be Green and Ultra-Modern at the same time."[2] In this sense, the TGV was like a "green Concorde:" it epitomized the fundamental compromise at the heart of the light-green society, the pervasive overlay of environmental considerations over the Promethean ethos of the *trente glorieuses*.

The TGV holds the world speed record for trains, a whopping 515 kilometers per hour (309 m.p.h.); in everyday service it whisks passengers across the land at a cruising velocity of 360 k.p.h. (216 m.p.h.).[3] One does not have to be a technological aficionado to feel the allure of this huge, aerodynamically swept machine as it glides into one of the bustling, grimy nineteenth-century Parisian stations, its electric motors humming with their 8000 kw of power. To travel in a TGV is a rather surreal experience: the ride utterly smooth and hushed, the scenery outside rushing past as if one were crop-dusting astride a cruise missile.

Despite its celerity, the TGV boasts an impressive safety record: it has been in regular service for more than two decades, racking up ten million passenger-kilometers per year, and has not had a single fatal accident. It does, however, hold the world's record for high-speed derailment: in December 1993 a TGV doing 294 k.p.h. across the plain of Picardy hit a section of track that had given way under heavy rains. The train immediately derailed, but, amazingly, its sophisticated articulation held it together without jackknifing over the 2.3 kilometers (!) that it took to come to a stop. (No one was hurt, although in the aftermath one elderly gentleman complained, not unreasonably, of chest pain.)[4]

Unlike the Concorde, moreover, this complex engineering achievement has also proved economically successful: it has not only turned a profit on its main lines every year since it commenced operating in 1981, but has also attracted prospective buyers as far afield as South Korea and the state of Florida.[5] In 2000, the Acela, a French-designed TGV model built under license by the Canadian firm Bombardier, began serving the Washington-Boston corridor (though antiquated American infrastructure restricted the train's performance to the 100–120 m.p.h. range).[6]

The TGV was first proposed by the SNCF in the early 1960s; engineers and administrators at this venerable institution had noted the stunning growth in automobile and air travel during the 1950s, and they knew that they had to come up with a revolutionary new technology or else watch rail travel undergo a steady decline.[7] The idea for a high-speed train soon caught the eye of officials in de Gaulle's government, particularly after they saw the favorable international attention garnered by Japan's new Shinkansen "bullet train," which could reach 210 k.p.h. The French resolved to beat the Japanese and create their own world-class train.[8]

The first TGV went into service fifteen years later, in 1981, on a dedicated set of tracks that had been laid between Paris and Lyon. Its designers had opted for an all-electric power plant, partly because of the oil crisis; and they had chosen to stay with traditional steel rails, rather than experiment with magnetic levitation technology, so that the TGV could adapt seamlessly to France's existing rail network.[9] Perhaps the greatest technical innovation lay in the sharing of wheel trucks between two adjacent cars, thereby reducing the number of wheels by half, saving weight, and affording greater rigidity and structural integrity at high speeds.[10] The train was an immediate success, both as a commercial undertaking and as a way of reinventing railroads in the guise of a "new" form of mass transportation: in the decade following 1981, the number of rail travelers between Paris and Lyon nearly doubled. At the same time, automobile and airplane traffic between the two cities markedly declined, while they continued to rise unabated throughout the rest of France.[11] Granted, the results were not always this dramatic when TGV service was extended to other cities, such as Bordeaux, Strasbourg, Brussels, or through the Channel tunnel to London; nevertheless, the overall result was one of offering travelers a plausible and agreeable alternative to cars and planes, during a period when the overall volume of intercity and international travel has been steadily rising.

By and large, only two types of dissident notes have troubled the happy history of the TGV. The first of these came from social critics like Jacques El-lul, who regarded this machine as merely one more facet of the mindless acceleration of life in contemporary society,[12] or Bernard Charbonneau, who argued that the high-speed rail links would subject France's far-flung local cultures to the irresistible homogenizing pressure of the capital's dominant society and economy.[13] The other main group of TGV critics came at it from a more concrete perspective, because the new train ran literally through their backyards. During the late 1980s, citizens in the southeastern region of Provence began reading in their local newspapers that the SNCF was going to extend TGV lines down from Lyon to Marseille and Nice—the so-called TGV-Mediterranée.[14] But unlike the citizens of Picardy, Alsace, and Brittany, who were clamoring to get TGV service as quickly as possible, the Provençals rejected the widely held assumption that this machine would act as an economic growth-engine for their region. Instead, they emphasized four main points: first, the TGV would chop their cherished countryside in two, destroying or degrading the rural atmosphere of ancient vineyards and farms in a way that no amount of monetary compensation could ever make good; second, it would mainly benefit the city-dwellers of Paris, Lyon, or Marseille, since the very nature of high-speed travel meant that stations would be few and far between; third, the SNCF should spend its money upgrading local and regional rail links rather than building technological marvels; and fourth, the SNCF had never bothered to consult with local citizens, and had shown an arrogant heavy-handedness throughout the whole process of planning the new route.[15]

By 1992, this grassroots anti-TGV campaign had begun to draw sympathetic responses from all over France—and the state hastily changed its tune. The Minister of Transport opened negotiations with the Provençal activists, and issued a decree stipulating that all subsequent projects of this nature would follow much more exhaustive procedures to ensure that the public had been fully consulted and its concerns taken seriously.[16] According to the philosopher Bruno Latour, this marked a significant milestone in the history of relations between the French state and its citizens: a government long prone to act in the imperious spirit of Louis XIV was gradually beginning to accept a broader opening of democratic process in the collective definition of the public good.[17] As for the TGV-Mediterranée, the SNCF and local citizens' groups agreed by the late 1990s on a compromise solution, in which the TGV would extend to Marseille but not to Nice, and would include a long-term commitment to link the high-speed line with an upgraded network of regional trunk connections.[18]

What about French environmentalists? On balance, they accepted the

TGV—some with resignation, others with outright enthusiasm.[19] The reason was simple: compared to the jet plane or the automobile, the TGV constituted a relatively benign way to move large numbers of people.[20] The key word here was "relative," for in fact this cutting-edge technology presented a whole slew of paradoxical characteristics: a machine for the mainstream economy, unabashedly designed to meet the ever-escalating demand for travel and mobility among French citizens; and yet an energy-efficient machine, consuming far less per passenger-kilometer than the available alternatives. A machine whose electric motors polluted much less than rival modes of mass transportation; and yet a machine powered from France's vast grid of nuclear-fired generators. A machine whose rail lines sliced the countryside in half, sealed off as they were, for safety reasons, from the surrounding fields, roads, and rivers. And yet a machine whose impact on the land remained far lighter than that of a highway or an airport, both in terms of noise and of the amount of space occupied. A complex technological system, conceived, built, and operated by the central state; and yet a potent tool of decentralization, especially after new lines began directly linking provincial capitals, without going through the hub of Paris.[21] Thus, the TGV paradoxically embodied two sets of properties that were usually held to be in tension with each other, if not mutually exclusive: on the one hand, a list for the technological enthusiast, in which the key words were "growth," "progress," "high technology," "complexity," "mastery," "powerful," "faster," "more"; on the other hand, a very different list for the environmentally concerned citizen: "low-emission," "energy-efficient," "cost-effective," "safe," "low-noise," "decentralizing," "available to all," "appropriate technology."

The TGV epitomized "light-green" precisely because it allowed the French to have it both ways. From an ecological perspective, it marked a major improvement over other modes of mass transportation; at the same time, it left intact and unchallenged the existing system of expectations surrounding unlimited travel and mobility. If one recognized the large-scale, growth-oriented mass society as the likely norm for the foreseeable future; if one believed that technology was likely to play an ever-growing role in shaping Western economies; if one acknowledged that demand for transportation would only continue to increase; and if at the same time one wanted to chart the most environmentally sensible course into this future—then the TGV fit perfectly. It allowed the French to continue their headlong rush under the banners of "Progress," "Growth," "Complexity," and "More." And it allowed them to do so with the knowledge that they had taken environmental factors seriously into account, and were treading far more lightly on the land than they would have done with cars and planes.

A sleek TGV gliding through beautiful valleys, with gently sloping fields, thin woodlands, country lanes—in this recurring visual motif of the SNCF's advertisements and posters, three key features of the light-green society clearly stood out. The marriage between technology and ecological conscientiousness, the compromise between fast-paced modernity and cherished rural traditions, and above all the integration of machine and natural space into a harmonious ensemble—such was the ideology self-consciously conveyed in the imagery of modern rail travel. The "natural" had penetrated into the "social," in the sense that a quintessentially social activity—travel by train, transportation by means of a sophisticated mechanical behemoth— was being presented to French consumers as a genuinely green alternative, a way to go swiftly from here to there while enjoying and respecting the spectacle of nature. Where once the SNCF's advertisers would have wanted to portray their machine as a triumph of human ingenuity over natural constraints, now they bent over backwards to emphasize its attunement to the underlying rules and rhythms of the biosphere.

Many other machines and consumer products, to be sure, could also be said to symbolize the postwar penetration of nature into society: a smoke-stack scrubber for removing pollutants from factory effluents, a Cousteau documentary on the sea, a low-emissions automobile, an organically grown peach, a 100-percent recyclable plastic chair. But the TGV seems particularly appropriate, precisely because it was not explicitly conceived from the outset as a green technology. Rather, its environmental advantages only gradually became apparent, as more and more French citizens slowly came to think in such terms, and began demanding goods and services that met increasingly stringent ecological criteria. In this sense, the TGV incarnated the broader process of dawning ecological awareness that spread through France over several decades—a process that ultimately taught the French to see technology itself in an entirely new way.

For here, indeed, lay the enduring appeal of "light-green." If the TGV's happy marriage of machine and ecology could be applied successfully throughout society at large, then the future suddenly looked far less ominous. Technology would henceforth require redoubled scrutiny and intensive oversight; but it also offered the promise of stunningly successful solutions to the most apparently intractable environmental problems. Neither the nightmare scenario of ecological collapse, nor the equally unappealing prospect of self-abnegation and strict ecological restraints, had to become real. The *trente glorieuses* would not have to end, after all: they would surge forward indefinitely like the scenery outside the window of a TGV—a blur of material abundance and ecological balance, excellent machines and verdant nature.

Society Penetrating into Nature—Machine/Symbol: Brittany's Pointe du Raz

Technically, to speak of the Pointe du Raz as a machine is a bit of a stretch. It is a barren rocky crag jutting spectacularly into the Atlantic, at the westernmost extremity of the Breton département of Finistère (which means, literally, "the end of the earth").[22] There is not much there—just a great deal of rock, ocean, and sky—which is precisely what renders the site appealing. Tourists have been visiting the Pointe du Raz since the nineteenth century, drawn to its stark scenery, its bleak emptiness, its ever-present winds, and the feeling it gives of standing on the prow of a ship, one of the outermost tips of the Eurasian landmass projecting into the vastness of the Atlantic.

Five hotels were built around 1900 in the immediate hinterland of the site, to accommodate well-heeled visitors who came in summer to clamber up and down the cliffs and enjoy the bracing breeze.[23] Then, in World War II, the German army built huge concrete bunkers here, with cannons pointing out to sea; when the Wehrmacht soldiers retreated, they burned all the hotels to the ground, thereby erasing a good deal of the human presence on the promontory. During the postwar economic boom, however, the tourists began to return, prompting local developers in 1962 to rebuild a variety of hotels, shops, and other amenities along the cliffside.

And here the problem began. The number of tourists slowly crept upward with each passing year, swelling into the hundreds of thousands annually by the mid-1980s. With the regional economy faltering, local mayors and town councils were only too happy to encourage this trend: they advertised the Pointe du Raz far and wide, and obtained its official designation as a "Grand Site National." The tourist numbers rose accordingly, ultimately pushing 800,000 per year—as many visitors as the entire Vanoise National Park, a territory larger by three orders of magnitude—and the result, not surprisingly, was traffic jams, litter, overcrowded restaurants and hotels, not to mention a severe degradation of the fragile lichens and succulents that held the promontory's meager soil in place.

In 1989, the local government teamed up with a national body, the Conservatoire du Littoral, to address the crisis. The Conservatoire had been created in 1975, under the auspices of the Ministry of the Environment, with the mission of purchasing endangered or ecologically remarkable stretches of coastline so that they might be protected for future generations to enjoy; despite its rather niggardly budget, it had succeeded by the 1990s in bringing under its tutelage a total of 13 percent of France's 6,000 kilometers of coastal lands.[24] Together, the representatives of the Finistère council and the Conservatoire worked up a plan with a twofold aim: restoring the Pointe du

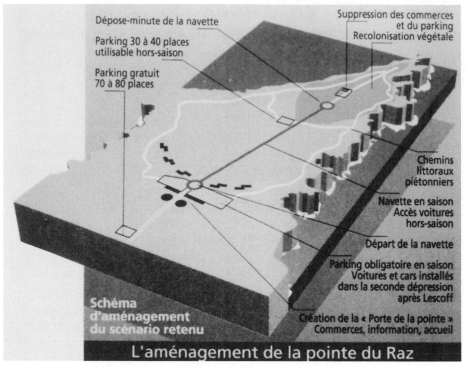

Dépose-minute de la navette

Parking 30 à 40 places
utilisable hors-saison

Parking gratuit
70 à 80 places

Suppression des commerces
et du parking
Recolonisation végétale

Chemins
littoraux
piétonniers

Navette en saison
Accès voitures
hors-saison

Départ de la navette

Parking obligatoire en saison
Voitures et cars installés
dans la seconde dépression
après Lescoff

Schéma
d'aménagement
du scénario retenu

Création de la « Porte de la pointe »
Commerces, information, accueil

L'aménagement de la pointe du Raz

Figure 6. The *aménagement* of a natural site: The Pointe du Raz in Brittany. (Courtesy of Institut Français de L'Environnement and BET "Campanile cités conseil.")

Raz to its original ecological condition, while nonetheless finding a way to manage more effectively the site's annual torrent of visitors.

The result was both ingenious and thought-provoking (see figure 6).[25] A professional governing board was created, to coordinate restoration efforts and manage the site in the future. The board's first project was to eliminate, so far as possible, all traces of human presence on the promontory, razing the existing hotels and concession stands and dynamiting the wartime bunkers. Next, they transplanted shrubs and tufts of hardy grass from nearby cliffs, and re-established the battered vegetation, using a new technique that consisted in spraying a mixture of water and fertile seeds through a high-pressure hose. Then they refurbished the access trails, demarcating them carefully with signs to channel the flow of passers-by. Finally, they built a brand-new complex of parking lots, restaurants, boutiques and a visitor center 1.5 kilometers from the park entrance, linking them to the cliffside footpaths with a continuous minibus service. An elaborate website, Pointe-du-raz.com, allowed people to learn about the promontory and nearby tourist amenities electronically.

But a thorny question remained: amid all the sophisticated restoration efforts and seamless managerial practices, what had become of the Pointe du Raz? The dilemma was hard to resolve: on the one hand, the park's governing board wanted to encourage people to visit this remarkable site, experience its bleak beauty, learn from its wilderness displays, and contribute to the region's tourism. On the other hand, since the site's attractiveness consisted precisely in its desolate, wind-swept wildness, what would be left of these qualities when hundreds and thousands of persons every day were crawling all over its craggy surface like colorful ants on an anthill? In the end, would it turn out that the very designation of this location as a "site protégé" had contributed, paradoxically, to the avalanche of human attention that spelled its undoing as a wild place?

At one level, of course, to think of the Pointe du Raz as a kind of machine is ridiculous. A machine, according to most dictionaries, is a man-made device designed to fulfil some specific purpose, like an eggbeater or a car. Long before humans existed, the Pointe du Raz was already a cliff projecting into the ocean; and given the scale of geological time, it is quite reasonable to imagine this rock formation far outlasting human civilization. To assimilate such an entity, created by nonhuman forces and existing for eons outside the realm of human purposes, into the same category as an eggbeater or an automobile seems simply nonsensical.

Nevertheless, the comparison with the household machine is illuminating, for the Pointe du Raz no longer stands on its own, but has been incorporated into the complex web of meanings and manipulations that constitute human society. It has been altered physically, several times over—with the most pervasive and systematic intervention arguably being the recent efforts at "restoration." It has been given legal standing, with detailed statutes defining its social value and setting parameters for what may and may not take place within its boundaries. It has been equipped with parking lots, trails, and other social amenities. It has been studied by scientists, who have laid out the broad outlines of its geological and ecological constitution, and who have made this knowledge available through the displays at the visitor center and in books. It has been integrated into the regional economy, a true "heavyweight" in the annual budget of the tourism industry. It possesses its own governing body, which meets regularly and takes action on its behalf. It even exists in cyberspace, and sports a "dotcom" on its name. In the pregnant language of French public policy, it has been thoroughly "aménagé"—which means, literally, to "transform something so as to render it more useful, more enjoyable."[26]

Overall, it does not seem unreasonable to say that the Pointe du Raz has been intelligently and tastefully managed: it is pleasing, for example, to think that this site has not been given over to real estate developers—as might have happened on the Côte d'Azur, where randomly metastasizing formations of high-rise apartments have engulfed long stretches of what was once a spectacularly scenic coastline. You can still go to this barren Breton promontory, on any given day, and feel the wind biting your face, admire the ocean waves crashing below, experience the sweep of the sky above. Nevertheless, the comparison with the eggbeater cannot help but linger in the mind: to what extent has this site been taken up into the human world and partially remade into a kind of instrument—a reliable instrument of physical and cultural gratification for 800,000 visitors, a powerful instrument of profits and livelihood for the people who live nearby?

The tourists come from far and wide; they stay in local hotels; drive to the visitor center; peruse the exhibits and boutiques; ride the minibus to the promontory; hike the trails, taking in the view; return to the minibus; get in their cars and go home. It is tempting to think of this orchestrated ensemble of practices as a smooth-running system, akin to an assembly-line, processing visitors at the remarkable rate of two to three thousand per day, giving them a certain type of experience—a set of impressions and emotions that they may or may not have anticipated beforehand. In this sense, it may not be too farfetched to view this site through the metaphor of the *cyborg*: the kind of crossover entity that the literary theorist Donna Haraway sees proliferating in our technologically expansive world, part organism, part machine.[27] From this perspective, the Pointe du Raz is neither natural nor artificial, but *both at the same time:* a large, multifaceted ensemble of objects and living creatures, comprising organic raw materials and man-made alterations, tangible and intangible features, fauna and flora, human bodies and human practices—an inescapably hybrid entity suspended between the aimless materiality of nature and the teleological world of human purposes. And one of those purposes, of course, consists precisely in optimizing the daily interaction between large numbers of people and something ineffable called "Mother Nature."

If a cement factory, a commuter suburb, or a golf resort had been situated at the Pointe du Raz, it would of course be a straightforward matter in such a case to speak about the penetration of the "social" into the "natural." This kind of penetration asserts a fairly blatant form of human mastery over the land: the all-too-familiar process of artificialization that has been gathering momentum since the Industrial Revolution and accelerating since World War II. What renders the Pointe du Raz particularly interesting is the fact that, in this case, human beings did their best to avoid this kind of artificialization: they laboriously erased the traces of their species' previous activities along the cliffside, and took great pains to keep major man-made structures at a distance. And yet, in the end, even this exceedingly thoughtful and circumspect series of actions could not help but add up to a particular type of "aménagement"—the transformation that "renders something more useful, more enjoyable."

Whether or not one finds the metaphor of the cyborg illuminating in the case of the Pointe du Raz, the dilemma implicit here cuts to the core of the human relationship with nature in the era of the light-green society. It boils down to a deceptively simple question: can wildness and large numbers of humans coexist in the same space? As we explore this issue in Part IV, we will need to take into account both of the modes through which the "social" tends to penetrate the "natural": the gross artificialization that occurs when humans, paying little heed to nature's needs, establish their dwellings and businesses in a piece of the territory; and the more subtle, ambiguous shift in qualities that occurs when humans, keen to protect and restore "wild" nature, bring their most sensitive, well-intentioned touch to the land.

8 Greening the Mainstream Consumer

Ironic Twists of a Partial Revolution

AUTARKY. We are one girl and three guys, living in a hut in the Cévennes. We'd like some fun chicks to come join us. We plan to live by farming and herding. A whole lot of other things may well be imagined. Spoiled brats need not apply. Write us before coming for a visit.
—Ad in Paris newspaper, *Libération,* 1969[1]

Surface Change and Deep Change

Let us begin by making a detailed distinction between two levels of economic and cultural change—the superficial and the profound. One finds an excellent example of the first of these almost every time one enters a hotel room, anywhere in the industrialized world: the little sign hung near the towel rack, proclaiming the hotel owner's fervent adherence to green ideals, and urging the hotel guest to consider re-using his or her towels rather than having them washed each day anew. That this practice saves a great deal of soap, water, energy, and pollution—especially when adopted in hundreds of thousands of establishments throughout the world—is undeniable. It costs the hotel guest only a minimal amount of sacrifice, it saves the hotel owner an appreciable sum of money over time, and it slices a fraction off the hotel's negative impact on the environment: everybody wins, everybody emerges feeling a little more virtuous. Yet I classify this as "superficial change" precisely because it costs everybody so little and exerts such a proportionately minuscule effect. Though certainly laudable, it alters by only a very small percentage the total burden placed on the environment by the overall *system* of business and leisure travel in today's world. That system, as a whole, remains unchallenged and unaffected by this intelligent micro-adjustment. The change scratches the surface.

Not so with our second example: the "profound change" implicit in sustainable agriculture. A farmer who abandons chemical fertilizers and pesticides, making the move to environmentally oriented cultivation, must (in most cases) retool his entire operation from top to bottom. Seed strains, ploughing patterns, erosion control, farm implements, seasonal cultivation cycles, watering practices, pest-control techniques, storage facilities, marketing strategies, distribution timetables—everything must be rethought, marking the transition from one set of goals ("maximize output") to another ("maximize output within stringent ecological constraints"). This transformation requires considerable time, money, and effort; and like any venture into relatively uncharted territory, it entails risks. From an economic point of view, the newly green farm may not be able to compete with its neighbors if they continue to use chemical-intensive methods of cultivation; its initial success may well depend on a combination of stable demand from consumers and fiscal and financial incentives from government. Sustainable agriculture, in other words, constitutes a truly alternative *system* of farming—a system that can only function effectively if it forms part of a broader cultural and economic transformation. I call this "profound change," therefore, because it requires leaving behind the entirety of an "old world"—with all its associated practices, habits, techniques, values, and assumptions—and bringing forth something that is in all these respects qualitatively different and new.

What kinds of factors led the French to shy away from "profound change"—from the full-fledged green social order embodied in our imaginary village of Vignac? What led them, instead, to move toward the complex amalgam of half-measures and compromises that constituted the light-green society? One way to approach this issue is by briefly comparing the green movement with twentieth-century socialism—that other widely influential mass-movement calling for radical and systemic change.[2] Any ideology that aims at sweeping socioeconomic transformation arguably faces an inherent tension between moderation and radicalism. Already at the turn of the twentieth century, the European Left had its own *Realos* (realists, compromisers) and *Fundis* (fundamentalists, ideologues)—Eduard Bernstein and Jean Jaurès preaching gradual reform on one side, Rosa Luxembourg, Jules Guesde, and V. I. Lenin issuing the call to arms on the other.[3] In some parts of the world, such as Russia and China, twentieth-century socialism evolved under desperate circumstances of extreme suffering and repression; this decisively influenced the worldwide balance between moderates and radicals, ultimately resulting in the emergence of a hardline current with a huge mass following, implacably committed to violent change.

With the green movement, by contrast, no such development ever occurred. Green activists, try as they might, never succeeded in persuading a large percentage of the population that an imminent ecological collapse loomed over their heads; the types of extreme hardships and deadly dangers that had fueled the mass-radicalizing tendencies of twentieth-century socialism simply did not appear in the industrialized world during the first four decades of environmentalist agitation.[4] Instead, the alarums that the greens could plausibly use as incentives for mobilization fell into two broad categories: catastrophic long-term threats projected into an unknown future, decades or even centuries away; and more precise and modest threats in the present, such as oil spills or disappearing species. Both of these could and did become grounds for concerted civic action; but neither was dire enough in its immediate implications to justify, in the eyes of most citizens, the draconian changes and sacrifices that the full-blown green vision would have entailed.

The result, by the early 2000s, was a phenomenon that bore greater similarities to the piecemeal, incremental transformation wrought by Europe's trade unions and moderate social-democratic parties than to the sudden, sweeping changes provoked by communist revolutions. Some green activists were understandably disappointed by the twists and turns of this frustratingly slow transformative process—just as many ardent socialists of the twentieth century had been dismayed at the extraordinary malleability and resilience of capitalist society and culture. But in the end, the light-green society defied easy categorization under the black-and-white headings of "victory" or "defeat." The kind of change it embodied was neither merely superficial nor rigorously profound, but a messy tangle of elements drawn from both. In some cases, the implementation of green reforms entailed real sacrifices, and produced equally real environmental gains; in other cases the impact of green ideals remained mere window-dressing. Hence the deliberately contradictory term in the title of this chapter: "partial revolution." How can a revolution be partial or unfinished, if it is truly a revolution, and not just a casual or ephemeral shift? Yet what other word but "revolution" can describe a set of changes aimed at achieving, as their end-result, a complete break from the past, a radical and systemic transformation? Here is the paradox that stubbornly recurs throughout the chapters that follow. In essence, the impact of environmentalism on postwar France might best be described as a gradual and disorderly movement *toward* revolutionary goals—an uneven tectonic shift, far-reaching in some of its implications, yet persistently marginal and limited in other key domains.

Back to Nature

The craving runs deep in civilized women and men for something that lies beyond, or beneath, civilization. Pastoral poetry in the classical world, the celebration of "the picturesque" in seventeenth-century Italy, the French aristocracy's flirtation with rustic pleasures, the explosion of Romantic sensibilities in Europe and the New World—all these cultural currents, in their diverse ways, played upon the human encounter with the nonhuman world of wild plants, creatures, and places. Horace, in his Epistles, addressed the following words to his city-dwelling friend Fuscus: "I praise the lovely country's brooks, its groves and moss-grown rocks. You may drive out Nature with a pitchfork, yet she will ever hurry back, and ere you know it, will burst through your foolish contempt in triumph."[5] Well before the Romantics, the eighteenth-century English poet William Cowper noted the pathos of urban dwellers assiduously tending their tiny house plants in broken pots and shards:

> Are they not all proofs
> That man immured in cities, still retains
> His inborn inextinguishable thirst
> Of rural scenes, compensating this loss
> By supplemental shifts, the best he may?
>
> . . . .
>
> And they that never pass their brick-wall bounds
> To range the fields and treat their lungs with air
> Yet feel the burning instinct; over-head
> Suspend their crazy boxes, planted thick,
> And watered duly. There the pitcher stands
> A fragment, and the spoutless teapot there;
> Sad witnesses how close-pent man regrets
> The country, with what order he contrives
> A peep at nature, when he can no more.[6]

In the aftermath of 1968, many French youths played out this age-old fantasy, for the most part blissfully unaware that they were following in the muddy footsteps of countless generations before them: they quit Paris and hitch-hiked into the boondocks, looking for Nature.[7]

Their story easily invites caricature and derision, for they were a motley assortment of individuals, their misadventures proportionately variegated and colorful. Yet, at another level, they also command respect, both for the idealism with which they set forth, and for the courage with which they shucked off the trappings of their upbringing and recklessly tested the outer limits of human sociability and of nature's rules. Disaffected schoolteachers, laid-off factory hands, philosophy students, social workers, clerks and sales-people bored with city routines—they banded together and formed communes, pooling their meager savings to buy broken-down farmhouses or barns in the semi-deserted reaches of France's most inaccessible countryside. In the wooded valleys of the Cévennes or along the bleak, windswept plateaus of the Lozère they raised goats, stitched leather goods, planted subsistence gardens, and settled in for the long haul. Some of them nearly starved, or froze, in their first hard winter. Some of them quarreled violently and went home, embittered. But others toughed it out, determined to play a role as forerunners of a new kind of civilization: a more open, spontaneous way of being together with other people, a closer and more authentic relationship with their physical surroundings.

Not surprisingly, France's real *paysans* did not have much truck with these disheveled, guitar-playing newcomers. Those who were not scandalized by the newcomers' rather casual attitude toward monogamy were likely to be put off by their patronizing outlook on rural culture: in one case, the newly transplanted Parisians invited all the neighboring farmers and their families, and put on a rigorously avant-garde play by Mayakovsky in one of the barns![8] (One cannot help but imagine the eloquent eyebrows of the grizzled local *pépères* as they traded impressions the following day in the village café.)

In the end, this "neo-ruralist" phenomenon proved ephemeral, marking the first half of the 1970s, with perhaps several thousand communes springing up throughout France, then gradually disappearing one by one. Out of a national population of sixty million, this hardly amounted to a statistically significant social current: snickering Parisians referred to the rural communards as "margi-bouseurs" ("marginal dung-mongers").[9] And yet, in retrospect, the *margi-bouseurs* mattered. They mattered because, while most citizens would not have dreamed of actually *doing* such a thing, they nonetheless understood and appreciated what these free spirits had been seeking. In the words of one pair of young sociologists who visited many communes in the mid-1970s and interviewed their inhabitants:

> Who, today, between two subway trains, does not dream of living in the coun-
> tryside? Who does not dream of finding, far from the frenetic urban scene, that
> simple way of life, in harmony with nature, that the peasants are supposed to
> have lived? Nostalgia for a village in which everyone knew everyone else, nos-
> talgia for a kind of work in which you could see and touch the product that
> you made, nostalgia for those fundamental kinds of knowledge (today buried
> or unappreciated) that allowed one to get a handle on one's world, nostalgia for
> a wisdom that gave man a place within nature.[10]

While most French citizens balked at the idea of jettisoning careers, homes,
and comfortable urban lifestyles in the name of a problematic adventure in
the countryside, they nonetheless resonated with the notion that their lives
had become too hurried, artificial, and confining. Although they had only a
vague inkling of what was missing, they felt a nagging sense of having drifted
out of touch with something ineffable but important—something that the
word "nature" still powerfully evoked in their imaginations. The result was
one of the most far-reaching and enduring shifts in patterns of consumption
of the postwar era: the move toward "natural" products and lifestyles.

Eco-consumerism: The Overflowing Cornucopia of "Less Is More"

The first distinction we need to make here is between "natural" products
and "environmentally friendly" products—for the two categories, while inti-
mately connected with each other, are by no means coextensive. For example, an "organic" dietary supplement of bee pollen might be packaged in
ozone-destroying styrofoam; conversely, some biodegradable soaps, composed of complex chemical mixtures, are anything but "natural." Nevertheless, both these categories reflect the same underlying idea, which had in fact
been given its clearest embodiment by the *margi-bouseurs,* and which now
proliferated (in diluted form) throughout the consumer economy: the idea of
voluntary simplicity, concisely captured in the slogan, "less is more."

In the case of "natural" products, this idea reflected a desire to fill one's
life with objects and experiences that offered escape from the highly artificialized atmosphere of urban modernity: "less" meant a lower degree of
man-made complexity, a slower pace, a renewed closeness to primordial
biological processes. In the case of "environmentally friendly" products,
the idea of "less" reflected a desire to tread lightly on the earth: it meant seeking a lower degree of human intrusiveness into the flows of energy and matter that made up the biosphere. In both cases, a highly idealized image of
nature prevailed—a nature imbued with its own extremely complex meta-

equilibrium, which had established itself over the course of eons, and which greedy humans had lost sight of and were now dangerously disrupting. The ideology of "less is more," if earnestly and systematically applied, was supposed to restore the lost balance, both for humans in their perceived quality of life, and for nature in its return to a robust and healthy condition.

The entry of this ideology into concrete practice can be thought of as falling into five broad "lifestyle" categories: the body, the home, transportation, leisure, and culture. In all these areas one finds similar processes at work, as the twin values of the "natural" and the "environmentally friendly" gradually entered common currency after the early 1970s.

1. The Body

Foods, medicines, and health practices were arguably the first to reflect this emerging shift in *mentalités*. As early as 1964, an organization named "Nature et Progrès" began offering French shoppers organic produce and other health products touting the dual benefits of greater purity and greater respect for the environment.[11] But it was not until the 1980s that this kind of product began attracting the attention of mainstream consumers, as the media began reporting with growing frequency on the troubling health-related effects of a food industry that relied heavily on chemical additives ranging from hormones and fertilizers to coloring dyes and preservatives. The first large supermarket chain to take note of these trends and capitalize upon them was Monoprix, whose 280 stores throughout France took the initiative in the late 1980s to launch a comprehensive "natural" product line, offering its customers everything from biodegradable soaps to health foods to new forms of recyclable packaging. "It was a stunning success," noted Joseph de Pirey, a Monoprix manager—to the point that other supermarkets, fearful of losing market share, quickly followed suit by cobbling together their own "green aisles" of offerings.[12] In the realm of fashion and clothing, a parallel development was reflected in the huge popularity enjoyed in France by such international companies as the Body Shop, with its "natural cosmetics" specialties, and Patagonia, with its line of "eco-textiles."[13]

Nevertheless, the overall impact of this shift in consumption patterns remained limited. By the late 1990s, only 0.5 percent of French farms were dedicated to "l'agriculture biologique," or organic methods of cultivation (though, to be sure, this small number was growing at the remarkable rate of 9 percent per year).[14] In two surveys conducted in 1998, only 11 percent of shoppers reported regularly buying organic produce; moreover, among those who did so, 66 percent cited health concerns as their primary reason, while only 10 percent cited the fact that such products were grown in a manner that respected the environment.[15] At a broader level, while 60 percent of French shoppers declared themselves more likely to buy a consumer item if it could plausibly claim a superior degree of eco-friendliness, their willingness to buy such a "green product" dropped off sharply if the price rose more than 10 percent above that of conventional products.[16]

The cultivation, distribution, and consumption of food in France remained, by the year 2000, an overwhelmingly "productivist" affair. Despite all efforts to halt or reverse the rural exodus, irresistible economic pressures continued to drain the French countryside, with farmers declining from 13 percent of France's workforce in 1970 to a mere 4 percent in 1996; meanwhile, the average size of farms continued to grow, as those who remained on the land were forced to adopt the methods of agribusiness, under the triple banner of capital, machinery, and chemicals.[17] The bulldozing of ancient patchwork plots into vast, Nebraska-esque fields proceeded apace; zoologists pointed to the loss of hedgerows, water channels, swamps, copses, and meadows, which had once provided havens for a plethora of animals and birds, as the prime cause of an accelerating crisis in the populations of France's endangered species.[18] Both the French government and the European Union enacted policies to slow these processes (or at least bring them under control), but they appeared to have little effect: fertilizer use remained as high as ever throughout the 1990s; the use of pesticides, fungicides, and herbicides increased by an average of 20 percent between the mid-1980s and mid-1990s; the surface of irrigated land tripled between 1970 and 1995; runoff from farms posed an increasingly serious problem, polluting the water supply of some five million citizens.[19] A major reform of the European agricultural policy, passed in 1992, offered some hope of addressing these troubling trends; but the new regulatory bodies that resulted were only beginning to function as the century drew to a close. Thus, for all the passionate rhetoric about cherished peasants and ecological values that animated the public sphere during the 1980s and 1990s, the hard fact remained that France, by the year 2000, had gone a long way toward Americanizing its rural world. If French citizens were truly serious about rejecting the "American model," they would have to undertake a far more trenchant (indeed, revolutionary) set of changes in the century to come.

2. The Home

In French households, the "green turn" took almost as many forms as there were gadgets and gizmos being used there. With the price of domestic tapwater steadily rising, many families traded in their inefficient dishwashers and washing-machines for new models that did the same job while consuming less electricity and half as much water. Detergents without phosphates offered the promise of reducing pollution; "smart" appliances saved energy; a wide variety of products came in lighter packaging, thereby cutting the volume of garbage; "green" batteries reduced the amount of heavy metals in landfills. On the streetcorners of virtually all French cities, starting in the 1980s, recycling bins began appearing; roughly half of all households began sorting and recycling their cans, bottles, paper, and cardboard on a regular basis.[20] By 1997, 22 percent of all household containers and packaging were being recycled; and the amount was rising every year.[21]

This was the good news. The bad news was that, in the aggregate, the society of the *trente glorieuses* continued inexorably to do what it was explicitly designed to do: it consumed more energy and raw materials, and produced more garbage and effluents, with every passing year. For all the environmental education campaigns and recycling programs, which became steadily more widespread and sophisticated over the years, the total amount of garbage produced annually by the French tripled between 1979 and 1996.[22] The figures for household energy use are equally striking: between 1960 and the oil shock of 1973, annual energy consumption increased by 240 percent. Then, after the population had dramatically taken cognizance of energy issues—at which point one might expect to see a flattening or even reduction in energy use—annual consumption nonetheless continued to gallop ever upward: from 1973 to 1996, it increased again by 144 percent![23] Official projections for the year 2020 offered three potential trajectories of energy use: a further rise of 40 percent, if contemporary market trends continued; a rise of 30 percent, if existing plans for energy savings were successfully implemented during the intervening years; and a rise of 13 percent if a much more drastic program of energy savings were imposed on the population. Government planners and private-sector economists, after conducting exhaustive analyses of past consumption patterns, election results, and consumer surveys, concluded that the French citizenry would simply not stand for the kind of major upheaval that an actual *reduction* in energy use would require.[24]

In the case of garbage, however, one needs to take into account the important qualitative shift that had occurred: for much of the 170 million tons of garbage produced in 1979 had gone into unfiltered incinerators or unprotected landfills, while the 627 million tons of garbage produced in 1996 was subject to a far more rigorous array of environmental controls. Overall, the destructive impact on the environment was demonstrably lower in 1996, despite the greater volume of trash: for France had by then equipped itself with procedures for safely processing a large portion of its industrial, agricultural, and household wastes. Clean incinerators (many of them co-generating electricity as they burned garbage), leak-resistant landfills, the systematic sorting and reclaiming of many kinds of metals, plastics, and wood fibers; the composting of organic matter for fertilizers—all these strategies were being adopted, on an increasingly intensive scale, as the 1990s drew to a close.[25]

The overall picture was a mixed one, therefore. A majority of French households were doing their best to conduct their daily affairs in an environmentally responsible way; and as a result, the most glaring forms of pollution, such as open dumps on the outskirts of towns, had been done away with. Nevertheless, French society continued each year to consume more energy than the year before, and the treatment of solid wastes amounted to a *relative* improvement (compared with the heedless trashing of the 1950s) rather than an actual reduction in the aggregate use and discarding of raw materials.

3. Transportation

French car manufacturers began vying with each other in the 1970s to offer models that polluted less while getting better gas mileage; in the 1980s they began introducing automobiles whose components could be recycled to increasing degrees. Sometimes their efforts to portray themselves as defenders of the environment bordered on the comical, as in the case of Michelin's alleged "green tire"—so named because it generated less friction and hence offered marginally improved energy efficiency.[26] In the case of Peugeot, a major campaign of "green image-making" became necessary in the 1980s after its CEO, Jacques Calvet, gained notoriety for his no-holds-barred (and ultimately unsuccessful) battle against the introduction of catalytic converters.[27] Nevertheless, by the 1990s, the average car rolling off French assembly lines emitted one-tenth the amount of noxious gases and particles that the vehicles of the 1970s had done. Similar kinds of progress had been made in the technology of trucks, buses, and civilian aircraft as well. The result was a steady decline, on an order between 8 percent and 18 percent, in the total amounts of pollutants released annually into the air by French vehicles between the 1980s and 1990s (though the concentrations in cities continued to reach dangerous levels).[28] The one significant exception was carbon dioxide, which rose by 9 percent during the period 1990–1995 alone—a result of the fact that this greenhouse gas could not be captured by catalytic converters.[29]

But this modestly rosy picture should not mislead us, for in reality the transportation sector deserved to be unambiguously counted as one of the most refractory and "un-green" areas of the light-green society. The reason is simple: the French, like their counterparts in other industrial nations, indulged a love affair with the automobile that apparently grew in passion and reckless abandon with every year that went by. They bought more cars per family; drove farther and more frequently; took fewer buses and trains; went faster in bigger cars; resisted the transition to lead-free gasoline; walked and rode bicycles less; scoffed at car-pooling; became outraged at gasoline taxes; and clamored for ever more highways (which they promptly got). What was more, this attitude applied to other modes of transport as well: over the years, the French shipped more freight by truck and plane and less by the relatively eco-friendly train. For passenger travel, they took fewer trains and switched over (in droves) to the relatively fuel-guzzling, noisy, and polluting jet plane—even for relatively short domestic trips. Smog in the cities, traffic jams, deadly accidents, proliferating asphalt, noise, parking headaches, crowded airports, hair-raising duels with eighteen-wheelers on the lanes and byways—nothing deterred them.[30]

Government policy in this area was understandably timid, given the public's ferocious attachment to the "right to drive." Apart from periodically tightening the laws on vehicle emissions, and ordering government agencies to buy low-emission cars and trucks, the state's only recourse was a (fruitless) campaign to promote public transport by bus and rail.[31] (Although the TGV continued to enjoy great popularity, its positive impact could not overcome the aggregate decline in train travel.) In 1995, the French government and EDF signed an agreement with France's major car manufacturers to promote research on zero-emission vehicles, with a tentative goal of placing 100,000 electric cars on the roads of France by the year 2000.[32] The Atlantic coastal town of La Rochelle (famous as a Huguenot bastion in the wars of religion) successfully bid to serve as an experimental site for three hundred electric Peugeots and Citroëns, with quick-charging "filling stations" strategically placed throughout the city limits by EDF.[33] Though the experiment appeared promising, and the citizens of La Rochelle waxed enthusiastic about their innovative (and generously subsidized) cars and scooters, only 1,500 such automobiles were being bought nationwide per year in the late 1990s—98 percent of them by government agencies![34] A new and more stringent law on air pollution, passed by the Assemblée Nationale in 1999, offered renewed hope to the "electric enthusiasts"—but the time when France's 25 million cars would plug in rather than "fill 'er up" was clearly not around the corner.[35]

4. Leisure

To feel like a *margi-bouseur*—but only for ten days a year—this became the ambition of increasing numbers of well-heeled and well-educated French city-dwellers during the 1980s and 1990s.[36] For the most part, the

French masses remained impervious to this yearning, continuing to spend their weekends and vacations at the familiar crowded sites, frequenting the beaches (and boutiques) of the Riviera in summer, the ski-slopes (and boutiques) of Chamonix in winter. But for a sizeable and rapidly growing minority of the citizenry, the traditional "tourism industry," with its chicken-farm approach, came to seem unsatisfactory as a source of release and replenishment from the rigors of urban life. They began looking elsewhere, to a kind of excursion that came to be known as *tourisme vert,* or green tourism.

Tourism experts made a distinction between the "soft" and "hard" versions of *tourisme vert.*[37] Practitioners of the soft version tended to go in search of a closer contact with nature: they took up hiking, sailing, backpacking; they explored national parks; they rented cottages in the countryside. One of their favorite pastimes was to visit the new (and burgeoning) network of *gîtes ruraux,* or rural hostels—typically a working farm in which the enterprising owner had set up a few bedrooms in the house or barn to rent out to city folk, with breakfast included, and the experience of unadorned rural life as the main attraction. "Hard" green tourism, by contrast, sought not so much communion with nature as excitement and extreme sports in a natural milieu: it comprised such activities as parasailing, whitewater kayaking, rock climbing, and scuba diving, but also more environmentally destructive activities such as mountain biking and ATV trekking.

Statistics on green tourism revealed a steady increase between the mid-1980s and mid-1990s: by a factor of 100 percent for the rural hostels, 71 percent for visitors to national parks, 320 percent for rock-climbing, and 400 percent for kayaking. The most spectacular increase was in mountain bikes, which went from 1,000 in 1984 to 800,000 in 1990 to 6,000,000 in 1996 (though this number needs to be tempered by the fact that, by the mid-1990s, such bikes had become trendy, and a large number of their owners never dreamed of venturing off the asphalt). Overall, between 1964 and 1994, the proportion of tourists who visited the French coastlines or mountains, as opposed to other more urban destinations, increased by 42 percent.[38]

From an environmentalist's perspective, of course, this did not necessarily add up to good news. Certain parks and ecological reserves, following the pattern experienced by Yellowstone or Yosemite in the U.S., faced such an onslaught of eager Nature-seekers that they had to begin restricting the influx of visitors. The Vanoise National Park in the southwestern Alps, for example, which had been saved from Monsieur Schnebelen's ski resort in 1969, faced a new threat starting in the 1980s: the overweening attentions of 800,000 wilderness-craving sightseers per year. The only solution was to divide the park into two concentric spaces: a central zone with severe restrictions on human access of any sort, and a peripheral zone, open to such low-impact activities as hiking or bird-watching. (See the discussion in chapter 14.)

Apart from these kinds of quandaries, moreover, the broader fact remained that France, at the turn of the year 2000, was the number one tourist destination in the world: 73 million arrivals from abroad, 1.3 billion visitor-nights spent on its territory per year, the tourist sector adding up to 10 percent of GDP.[39] The sheer weight of all these visitors could not help but exert a substantial impact on the nation's environment: for example, roughly one quarter of all travel within the national territory could be linked directly to tourism and vacations. To take a more specific example: in the Alps' remote Val d'Isère, whose year-round population was a modest 1,729, the influx for ski vacations during the winter months swelled the population well above 300,000—with an impact on water usage, trash collection, sewage treatment, road traffic, and other infrastructures that unavoidably strained local resources to the breaking-point.[40] Along the Mediterranean coast, the growth of the tourism industry between 1984 and 1994 brought about an increase of 66 percent in water usage, 61 percent in the volume of garbage, and 106 percent in the amount of urbanized land. On the other hand, the locals' concern to maintain an attractive aquatic environment, so as to keep the tourists coming, undoubtedly contributed to the steady rise in coastal water quality achieved along the Mediterranean during the same period—a jump from 70 percent to 90 percent of all bathing spots meeting the tough European Union guidelines.[41]

Le tourisme vert, therefore, exerted a small but not negligible impact on the juggernaut of French tourism—when it did not take the form of mountain bikers ripping turf off remote hillsides. Overall, it reflected a heightened sensitivity toward nature among France's urban population, a growing desire to encounter the rural world on its own terms. On the other hand, the proportions of this phenomenon should not be exaggerated: in 1997, the number of visitors to all of France's national parks totaled some 5.5 million; during the same year, the number who visited Mickey at Euro-Disney, outside Paris, was 11.7 million.[42]

5. Culture

It was a journalist, Jean Carlier, who first took up the defense of the Vanoise National Park in the 1960s; since that era, the press (of both Left and Right) has proved one of the most stalwart promoters of environmental causes in French civil society. By the end of the 1970s, most major French newspapers had developed a regular rubric on environmental issues, with specialized journalists to investigate and report on the subject; by the end of the 1980s, this was true not only of all major daily papers and weekly news magazines, but of the televised news media as well.[43] A survey of print news media conducted in 1996 showed a total of 1,394 articles devoted to environmental issues for that year, with the highest percentages in the categories of "nature" (21 percent), air and water pollution (13 percent), nuclear safety (13 percent), and transportation (12 percent).[44] French television, having started with Cousteau's pioneering films in the 1950s, offered its viewers a steadily growing array of documentaries on topics of nature and environmental protection—with the viewing public continually clamoring for more.[45]

The French educational system was slower to change, however. From the 1940s through the mid-1970s, the textbooks used in French high schools, in the fields of geography and natural science, offered young citizens a blandly predictable representation of nature: it was a national resource to be "valorisée" (exploited), an endless repository of potential prosperity.[46] Only in the late 1970s, after the environmental movement had been making headlines for about a decade, did this image start (very timidly) to change: some natural science textbooks now began including brief sections on pollution and other forms of environmental degradation.[47] The evolution was even slower in the instruction of geography—a required subject for all French students—in which explicit environmental themes only began entering into currency toward the end of the 1980s.[48] By the early 1990s, however, the green trend had clearly affirmed itself, as most geography textbooks no longer relegated "the environment" to a separate heading, but reformulated and reoriented their entire table of contents, weaving environmental issues into the discussion of virtually every aspect of the French territory: the land, demography, regional diversity, commerce, transport, energy, agriculture, and the European Union.[49]

During the 1990s, moreover, students in French secondary and high schools were offered a growing array of hands-on experiences with environmental issues outside the traditional classroom. A nationwide network of educators and volunteers from France's nature-protection societies, known as the Réseau Ecole et Nature, helped to coordinate field trips and lectures for hundreds of schools each year.[50] In 1995, the Ministry of Education gave its blessing (and indirect financial backing) to these kinds of activities; it also formally stipulated that all students should take at least one course on environmental topics during their high school years.[51]

The impact made by these kinds of gradual and highly dispersed cultural agencies is notoriously hard to assess. On balance, it is probably fair to say that the news media acted like a locomotive of cultural change, since they intervened early on, and often played a decisive role in publicizing the ideas and activities of environmental pressure groups. The educational system, by contrast, was more like a caboose, following the lead given by other sectors of civil society, and reflecting the "green turn" only after a notable time lag had elapsed. However, judging from the relatively sophisticated environmental education being offered to French boys and girls by the mid-1990s, it is possible that these roles will be reversed in the decades to come, and that French schools will become the more powerful formative agency in the development and dissemination of green ideas.[52]

Eco-labels and "Eco-Friendliness"

Not surprisingly, the success enjoyed by firms like Monoprix, with their comprehensive green product lines, rapidly spawned imitators by the dozens, as marketing executives in one industry after another scurried during the early 1990s to establish the requisite credentials of "greener than thou." The result, in stores and supermarkets throughout France (and across Western Europe), was a mess: side by side on a single shelf the bemused consumer could find several items, comparable in quality and price, each professing to be far and away the most eco-friendly of its kind—with "scientific" evidence to prove it. Many unscrupulous firms, unwilling or unable to go through the expense of retooling their product lines, simply repackaged their existing items in a green wrapper, and unabashedly joined the cacophonous chorus of Gaia lovers.[53]

In order to address this problem, consumer organizations and environmental groups began pushing for the establishment of a standardized, and credible, "green stamp of approval" that would allow consumers to distinguish between eco-product and eco-*poseur.* In this area the worldwide pioneers had been the West Germans, who in 1977 had established precisely such a label, known as the *Blauer Engel,* or Blue Angel (the name being derived not from the 1930 Marlene Dietrich film but from the United Nations environmental logo, which bore the characteristic UN color of blue).[54] In France, the effort to create a similar eco-label bogged down through most of the 1980s in bickering over standards and procedures; finally, in 1991, the French version of the Blue Angel emerged, under the less poetic name of "NF Environnement"—where "NF" stood for "Norme Française," the official government designation for quality and safety in consumer products.[55]

Many consumers, however, continued to hold two false beliefs about eco-labels. First, they thought that the quality of "eco-friendliness" was something objective and straightforward: if you pour this paint thinner into a creek, it kills lots of fish; if you do the same with that paint thinner, the fish stay alive; end of story. In reality, it turned out that assessing the environmental impact of a product through its entire life cycle—from cradle to grave, as the experts put it—was not only difficult and costly, but often yielded inconclusive or controversial results. Scientists disagreed over the extremely complex evaluations they were asked to make, from the acceptable levels of a chemical in a landfill or natural habitat, to the impacts of extracting and transporting materials, to the byproducts of the production process, to the requirements for safe usage and disposal. At every stage of the assessment process, far-reaching assumptions had to be made, often based on very limited information; the result, in many cases, was a confusing tangle of data, highly technical in nature, pointing to ambiguous or contradictory recommendations. A classic example of such an inconclusive environmental-impact analysis was that of the "diaper wars" that raged in Britain and the U.S. during the early 1990s, over the relative advantages and disadvantages of disposable diapers as compared with washable diapers: in the end, both sides in the debate marshaled impressive scientific evidence; both sides accused the other of bias in favor of their own commercial backers; both sides claimed victory; and the consumer was left with a Solomonic choice of whether to fill the landfills with disposables or fill the rivers with detergents.[56] "Eco-evaluation," it turned out, was a far from straightforward matter.

The second popular misconception about eco-labels concerned the concept of "eco-friendliness" itself. Many consumers assumed that "green" products had been so designated because they exerted a neutral, or even beneficial, impact on the environment. Yet if the scientists and environmental experts did agree on anything, it was on one uncomfortable point: there was practically no such thing, in the end, as a truly eco-friendly consumer product.[57] Nearly every consumer article, in one way or another, at some point in its life cycle, detracted from or adversely affected the earth's natural environment. A paint thinner that killed no fish when poured into a creek, for example, might only be producible by using the bark of a rare tree, or by adopting a chemical process that released terrible toxins into the air at the factory stage of the product cycle. Even the most seemingly benign and simple items, like an unpainted wooden toy or a "natural" textile, only very rarely made it through the complex life-cycle of manufacture, packaging, transportation, distribution, marketing, selling, use, and disposal, without exerting at least a modest negative impact at one or more points along the way.

Here was where the concept of "eco-friendliness" led most people astray. In a modern consumer economy, the real question behind eco-labels nearly always consisted in ascertaining which articles were the *least harmful*—which ones, in other words, possessed product cycles that caused the lowest (or most easily reversible) levels of disruption to the underlying processes of the biosphere. Realistically, all that an environmentally conscious consumer could hope for was to limit the damage as much as possible, focusing one's choices systematically on the lesser of the many available evils.[58] Whether this rather grim situation could fit under the concept of "eco-friendliness" depended on how loosely one defined the term.

> > >

"Imagine," André Gorz had written back in 1974,

> imagine the production of practically indestructible materials, of apparel last-ing for years, of simple machines which are easy to repair and capable of func-tioning for a century or more. . . . Imagine that the major industries, centrally planned, produced only that which was required to meet the basic needs of the population: four or five styles of durable shoes and clothing, three or four models of sturdy and adaptable vehicles, plus everything needed to provide the collective services and facilities. . . . Would we still be eager to join the traf-fic jams on the freeways if there were comfortable, collective transport to rec-reation areas, bicycles and motorbikes readily available when required, an extensive network of mass transit for urban and suburban areas? . . . Each neighborhood, each town, would have public workshops equipped with a complete range of tools, machines, and raw materials, where the citizens could produce for themselves, outside the market economy. . . . Would we still really require all of our individual equipment which lies idle much of the time?

And he concluded: "It is possible to be happier with less affluence."[59]

A great irony of the light-green society lay in the fact that many French cit-izens apparently liked Gorz's idea, or other ideas along similar lines: they found such visions appealing, they daydreamed about such a down-to-earth and environmentally aware lifestyle, and they even tried to put these ideals into practice as they went about their daily lives. In the stores, at their jobs, in their readings, even in their vacations, they opted more and more for ob-jects and experiences that drew their inspiration from the ideals of voluntary simplicity and natural equilibrium. And yet, in the end, these ideals did not result in a retreat from the consumer mentality of the 1950s—far from it. The consumer economy continued to offer its ever-shifting, ever-expanding cornucopia of goods and services; and the "green turn," instead of *replacing* that economy with a slimmed-down, minimalist array of products, merely *added* a new theme to the plethora of choices available.

Gorz and the radical environmentalists of the 1970s had envisioned a folksy community market whose rough-hewn shelves would feature an austere selection of plain, sustainable goods. What they got, instead, was a dazzling new aisle of attractive green offerings, amid the sprawling neon-lit abundance of the largest supermarket in history.

9 The Environmentalization of the State

We went as far as we could, into the heart of the forest—and what we found was the State.

—Rural communard, mid-1970s[1]

Anti-statism, More Government

Like the greens of other nations, the French environmentalists of the 1970s heaped scorn on the governing institutions of the nation-state. "We are victims of a centralizing bureaucratic state that is subjecting us to internal colonialism!"—so ran an environmentalist leaflet handed out among demonstrating farmers and students on the remote Larzac plateau in 1973, during a pivotal struggle with the French army over rural land use.[2] "The nation-state," affirmed the greens' electoral platform of 1981,

> was born out of a desire to fit all people into the same mold, to crush their cultural differences, to reign over them and constrain them rather than to stimulate or persuade them. There is a profound parallel between the aggression of industry against nature and the aggression of the state against local communities.[3]

Too big, too centralized, too rigid and peremptory in its power; not responsive enough, not effective enough, not sufficiently connected to the real needs of real people: the state was both too much and too little at the same time.

This attitude stemmed from many sources. For the more left-oriented greens (like Gorz), the state was ultimately a tool of narrow capitalist interests; for the libertarian/anarchist types (like Dumont), it seemed a dangerous concentration of power in the hands of an entrenched elite; for the nature-protection advocates (like Waechter), it was a hulking institutional embodiment of the productivist ideology, frustratingly resistant to their proposals for reform; for the champions of *terroirs* and local regeneration (like Charbonneau), it behaved like an octopus whose bureaucratic tentacles were slowly choking the life out of the provinces. For all these reasons, the greens placed the banner of anti-statism at the very forefront of their cause, and (as we have seen in chapters 4 and 5) insisted on structuring their own political movement along rigorously decentralized and nonhierarchical lines. The state, they believed, was not only going to prove unhelpful in addressing the earth's pressing environmental problems; the state was itself a key part of those problems. How to go about dismantling the prevalent system of governance, and what kinds of institutions (if any) to put in its place, were naturally the subject of endless debate; but the underlying principle of anti-statism became a leitmotif of the new movement.

Three decades later the outcome was, to say the least, ironic. The French state had gradually transformed itself into a colossal green Leviathan, its politicians and bureaucrats propounding environmental laws and decrees and regulations and guidelines even faster than the body politic could absorb them. By the 1990s, according to one scholar, the French legal system had come to include more than one thousand specialized laws on the environment—not to mention eighty-three ordinances and regulations at the level of the European Union and three hundred international treaties.[4] The French government was one of the first in the world to create a separate Ministry of the Environment, and by the year 2000 this ministry was flanked by several dozen potent agencies charged with overseeing specific sectors such as energy consumption, zoning, or waste management.

The resulting tangle of overlapping bureaucratic and legal bailiwicks prompted one group of French scholars to publish a three-hundred-page guide for environmental activists, showing how to negotiate the many levels of governmental power at which environmental decisions were made, ranging from international treaties down to the local municipality.[5] The guidebook was itself a revealing document: although intended as a helpful and empowering "roadmap" for grassroots action, it bristled with so many forbidding acronyms, legal flow-charts, intricate official procedures, and arcane bureaucratic structures that it must have wilted the initiative of even the most wizened and tenacious green militants. Suppose, for example, that one had a problem with garbage. The plethora of laws on the subject were overseen by the Ministry of the Environment, but the day-to-day business was handled by the ADEME, or Agency for the Environment and the Management of Energy, which in 1991 absorbed the ANRED, or National Agency for the Recycling and Elimination of Wastes. If the waste was nontoxic one's starting-point would be the local mayor's office, which operated under guidelines stipulated by FNADE, the National Federation on Wastes and the Environment; if the waste was recyclable one would call upon either Eco-Emballages or Adelphe, the two para-statal organizations responsible for collecting and treating recyclable materials; if the waste was of medical origin one would contact Cyclamed, which specialized in handling bio-hazardous materials; if the waste came from a farm one would consult the Ministry of Agriculture's Directorate of Rural Development and Structures; if the waste came from a factory one would phone the FEDEREC, or Federation for Industrial Recycling and Environmental Management, along with the Ministry of Industry's DEPPR-SEI, or Directorate for Water and the Prevention of Pollution and Risks—Industrial Environment Service; if the waste needed to be transported far away one would first have to consult the IRT-CERNE, or Institute for Research on Transportation—Center for Evaluation and Research on Pollution; if the waste was located near a national or regional park one would naturally contact not only the nearest Regional Environmental Directorate (DIREN) but also the Ministry of Agriculture's Directorate for Rural Space and Forests.[6] The list went on—for three hundred pages. Thirty years of green activism had resulted in more, not less, government.

How did this happen? The French case illustrates a fundamental philosophical dilemma that applies more broadly to environmental movements throughout the world. When it comes to building a greener future, the available pathways of action boil down to two basic approaches: on the one hand, self-imposed changes undertaken voluntarily by individuals, businesses, or social groups; and on the other hand, changes imposed upon society through the institutions of government. Clearly, most citizens would prefer to have the option of imposing new environmental rules on themselves, on their own cities and businesses, rather than having those rules decreed willy-nilly from outside. But such voluntary actions, by themselves, are notoriously uneven in results: not everyone will choose to participate, those who do participate are unlikely to do so in a uniform manner, and some participants will no doubt fail to follow their own self-imposed guidelines. Hence the inevitability of having to turn, at some point, to a higher and universally recognized authority.

For the environmentalists, there was no getting around this difficult conundrum: who but the state could protect such ethereal public goods as air and water, which belong to everyone and to no one? Who but the state could set nationwide environmental goals and safety standards? Who but the state possessed the resources to monitor the vast territory in order to ensure compliance? And (last but not least) who but the state possessed the requisite powers to impose sanctions on rule-breakers? Environmental problems, intricately enmeshed in all levels of contemporary society's functioning, ultimately led straight back to Thomas Hobbes: whether the greens liked it or not, tackling problems of this scope and complexity required a central agency for arbitration, coordination, and enforcement.[7] "We will continue to need the state," admitted Antoine Waechter in 1990, "to act as a counterbalance for the immense power of big industry and big finance, to ensure that the laws are respected by corporations, and to provide a focal point for concerted international action."[8] The result, by the 1990s, was a phenomenon that one sociologist, Florian Charvolin, summed up with the ungainly but effective phrase, "the environmentalization of the state."[9]

The Layer Cake of Green Governance: Six Levels, Three Modes

If one looks at the rhetoric used by the environmental activists of the 1970s, it becomes clear that many of them had an oversimplified and excessively Manichaean understanding of the relation between citizens, nature, and government. The main actors in their morality play consisted of industrialists and the central state on one side, hell-bent on the pursuit of productivist profit-making; while on the other side lay the common citizens and local governments, bravely but fruitlessly seeking to prevent the despoliation of nature.[10] As the years went by, and green activists increasingly took a hand in policymaking—both as elected officials and as negotiators representing the nature protection societies—this picture not surprisingly became progressively more complicated. Green activists learned that local governments could pander just as shamelessly to business interests as the national deputies in Paris; they observed that when it came to making tangible sacrifices in the name of ecology, common citizens could be just as selfish and short-sighted as the captains of industry; they found that government officials were often men and women of good faith, doing their best to negotiate workable solutions amid a tug-of-war of conflicting (and equally legitimate) interests; they confronted the labyrinthine technical nature of most environmental problems—the sheer complexity, for example, of a phenomenon like air pollution, with its multiplicity of sources and even greater multiplicity of stake-holding actors and constituencies.

Above all, they discovered that environmental action was rarely as simple as passing a law and seeing to its swift enforcement: they learned that, in most cases, the initial conceptual framing of an "environmental problem" was itself just as political as the compromises and deals that led to the drafting of legislation; and that the successful implementation of a new law depended not just on an edict from Paris, but on budgets, the competition among bureaucracies, the overlapping claims of different agencies, the existence of viable mechanisms for monitoring and enforcement.[11] Precisely because the environment was itself a "total" phenomenon, affecting virtually all aspects of people's lives, tackling one of its problems often meant nothing less than engaging its implications across an equally "total" range of society's economic institutions and governmental structures.

By the year 2000, environmental governance in France comprised six levels of power: municipality, département, region, nation-state, European Union, and international bodies like the United Nations. At most of these levels, the tools available to policymakers were threefold: laws or treaties, taxes, and subsidies.

1. Municipality

France in the 1990s possessed some 36,000 municipal governments—more than all the other states of the European Union put together.[12] Local notables, jealous of their prerogatives, stubbornly resisted the integration of the nation's micro-polities into mid-sized territorial units comparable to those in other countries; despite generous incentives from Paris, only about 1,000 communities moved to fuse their identities into larger, more efficient local structures. The result, from an environmentalist's perspective, was a serious problem, because local municipalities in France were responsible for a wide range of basic services: garbage collection and treatment, water distribution, upkeep of parks and green spaces, and noise control. Since the complexity and sophistication of waste treatment methods steadily increased over time, the costs rapidly outpaced local resources; and although some municipalities did federate themselves into consortia for such purposes, the fragmentary nature of France's municipal governments remained a key obstacle to the modernization of the nation's waste management systems.[13]

2. Département

This layer of government, which dates back to French Revolutionary days (and which the Greens would like to see abolished), had the responsibility of managing the larger parks and "sensitive natural spaces" that lay outside municipal jurisdictions. It also played a role in organizing and harmonizing the water-treatment policy of the municipalities.[14]

3. Region

France's twenty-two regional governments were given new and expanded powers during the early 1980s, and by the 1990s were providing several kinds of environmental services. They oversaw the management of rivers, from flood control projects to irrigation policy; they monitored levels of agricultural pollution, such as the penetration of pesticides and fertilizers into aquifers, and punished offending farms; they operated special treatment plants for handling dangerous forms of industrial waste.[15] In addition, they were responsible for managing France's thirty-eight Parcs Naturels Régionaux—a series of mixed rural and semi-natural spaces whose protective statute was considerably less stringent than that of the National Parks, but whose total surface area was about twenty times larger, comprising about 11 percent of the French territory.[16]

4. Nation-state

Despite the greens' wishes to the contrary, the central government in Paris remained the pivotal level of power in French environmental governance. The Ministry of the Environment, as well as the environmental departments of the Ministries of Industry, Agriculture, Education, and Transportation, all played decisive roles in setting environmental policy. Together, they controlled about 40 percent of the French state's environmental budget.[17] Another 48 percent went to the National Water Agencies responsible for managing France's aquifers and water treatment plants; nine such agencies existed in the year 2000, divided according to the natural watersheds of the territory. The remaining 12 percent of the annual budget was divided among a plethora of specialized administrative bodies of the French state, the most important of which were (in decreasing budgetary rank): the ADEME (Agency for the Environment and Management of Energy); the National Office on Hunting; the High Council on Fishing; ANDRA (National Agency for Treatment of Radioactive Wastes); and INERIS (National Institute for Management of Industrial Hazards). All five of the government ministries named above (and most of the specialized agencies) not only financed their own operations, but also contributed crucial funds to the regional, departmental, and municipal bodies that handled environmental matters. Finally, it was in the Assemblée Nationale that France's fundamental environmental legislation was framed, and often through the central state's representatives—most notably the prefects and the higher courts—that this legislation was enforced.[18]

5. European Union

The unification of European nations into a supranational entity has been proceeding by fits and starts ever since the early 1950s; in the 1980s and 1990s the process advanced dramatically, with a new series of policies branching out from the economic sphere and embracing social, political, and even military matters. One of the first environmental programs at the European level was a rather meek antipollution drive launched in 1973; but it was not until the Single European Act of 1986 that environmental protection became the object of explicit supranational legislation.[19] By the year 2000, the European Commission—Europe's executive body—had created a specialized Directorate-General for the Environment, charged with overseeing the implementation of some eighty-three pieces of supranational legislation that bound all fifteen of the Union's member states (another seventy such laws were in the pipeline).[20] These laws ranged over the entire gamut of environmental issues, from the establishment of maximum thresholds for atmospheric pollution to the creation of international networks of wildlife refuges.[21] In addition, the European Union had a small environmental fund, known as the Life Programme, which supported wildlife conservation efforts and ecological pilot projects in member nations.[22] Finally, the European Environmental Agency, created in 1993, acted as a clearinghouse for environmental research and statistics from the fifteen member states, providing scientists and policymakers with an invaluable comparative database.[23] France, as a founding member of the EU, found itself increasingly forced to take into account the supranational dimension of its own domestic policies: one French agency estimated that, if the European Court ruled against France on various environmental cases pending against it during the late 1990s, the fines could add up to more than four million francs per day (about $230 million per year)—equal to 6 percent of the total French environmental budget.[24]

6. International Treaties

France has played a key role in launching and sponsoring international environmental agencies, from the creation of the International Union for the Conservation of Nature in 1948 to that of the Global Environment Facility (a specialized fund administered by the World Bank) in 1991.[25] It also has been highly active on the diplomatic front, signing literally hundreds of multilateral treaties and accords on behalf of environmental protection—from the Ramsar Convention of 1971, aimed at the protection of the world's wetlands, to the Kyoto Protocol of 1997, regulating the emission of greenhouse gases.[26] As a key member of the UN, moreover, France played a role in shaping the policies of the United Nations environmental bureau, UNEP, as it did with the environmental departments of the World Bank and other global agencies like the Food and Agriculture Organization.

> > >

At most of these levels of governance, policymakers disposed of three major types of instruments to implement their environmental agendas. The most direct method, of course, was simply to pass a law (or sign a treaty) banning certain types of practices, such as the dumping of garbage along roadsides, or the use of CFC's in aerosol sprays. While this approach worked well for many kinds of applications, it also required a cumbersome and expensive apparatus for monitoring and enforcement. A more indirect approach lay in fiscal policy: to levy special taxes on environmentally undesirable practices, such as the emission of certain chemicals from factory smokestacks—thereby giving an industrial firm the option of continuing to pollute (but at a cost) or altering its procedures (with the cost of the alteration at least partially offset by the avoidance of a tax penalty).[27] Apart from creating strong incentives for cleaner industrial practices, this approach also had the added bonus of raising substantial tax revenues that could in turn be allocated to other green programs. The French (like other Europeans) were reluctant to adopt a widely used North American variant of this approach, namely, the trading of "pollution rights"—a system whereby government allocated a fixed quantity of allowable emissions for each industry, but permitted individual firms to buy and sell these "pollution credits" among themselves. This system, while granting a high degree of flexibility to industry, was regarded by many Europeans as insufficiently stringent, and as leaving too much leeway to grossly polluting factories.[28] Finally, a third instrument lay in subsidies, either in the form of tax breaks or government grants, to encourage businesses or municipalities to embark on costly environmental programs. The French made ample use of this approach, often phasing in new environmental regulations over many years, while softening the blow with a concomitant schedule of subsidies to offset the initial financial impact of the change. Some environmental experts complained that this policy went too far, in many cases amounting to a coddling of industry at taxpayers' expense.[29]

Key State Actors, Key Legal Turning-Points
1. The Ministry of the Environment (1971)

As we saw in chapter 4, the creation of this new ministry, while an important innovation, did not mean that a fully formed and autonomous bureaucratic actor had suddenly appeared, shoulder-to-shoulder, amid the ranks of high-level government fiefdoms. On the contrary, it took form as a relatively rachitic branch of government, cobbled together from a bewilderingly disparate array of existing programs, agencies, and state functions.[30] Its mandate was as yet unclear, its budget minuscule—a mere 0.3 percent of the total state expenditures for that year.[31]

During the decades that followed, the new ministry's budget shrank even further, until it stabilized in the 1990s at about 0.1 percent of state expenditures.[32] What was perhaps even more problematic, according to scholars who have studied the ministry's history, was the isolation of this fledgling institution, and its lack of effective bureaucratic instruments for monitoring and enforcing the policies it was supposed to implement.[33] When the ministry's officials needed scientific data, they had to call their colleagues at Agriculture or Industry; when they needed to establish links with local governments, they had to go through DATAR, the territorial management agency, or other bureaucratic channels; when they wanted to prosecute polluters, they had to call on the prefects, or borrow the services of experts from the Ecole des Mines.[34] As Prime Minister Michel Rocard was to admit in his memoirs, "France has proved incapable of creating, within its governmental structures, a Ministry of the Environment having the attributes of an adult."[35]

Nevertheless, the creation of this ministry made an important difference. At one level, it meant that, in the minds of French citizens, "the environment" would henceforth be more readily conceived as a unitary issue, having a priority comparable to the other great sectors of public policy, such as health, education, or defense. At a more concrete level, the presence of this ministry stimulated the other branches of government to beef up their own "environmental departments"—for fear of losing them to the upstart newcomer. As a result, the ministries of Agriculture, Education, Industry, and Transportation all underwent a fairly rapid "greening" during the 1970s, propelled by the bureaucratic imperative of integrating ecological governance into their own ministerial specialties.[36] The Ministry of Transportation, for example, began actively promoting train travel, seeking to resist the tidal wave of consumer enthusiasm for cars and planes. Last but not least, the Ministry of the Environment became a rallying-point for active lobbying by greens and the nature protection societies, giving them an "insider's platform" from which to influence government policy: from the shepherding of laws through parliament to the creation of new agencies like the ADEME or ANDRA. In all these ways, the ministry's wide-ranging influence was certainly much greater than its picayune budget would lead one to expect.

2. The "Nature Law" of 1976

One of the most glaring deficiencies that Robert Poujade observed when he became the first Minister of the Environment in 1971 was the obsolescence of existing legislation for the protection of nature: the main law in force dated back to 1930 (!), and was oriented more toward safeguarding artistic monuments than natural sites. Both Poujade and his successors therefore put a high priority on drafting a new and comprehensive law that would not only bring France up to date, but would pave the way for subsequent additions and refinements over the years. The result, promulgated under the decidedly self-effacing name, "Law 76-629," did all that and more.[37] Basing itself on the general principle that "the protection of natural spaces and species is in the public interest," it extended protection not only to animals and plants themselves, but more importantly, to the habitats in which they flourished.[38] Henceforth, therefore—as with the spotted owl or snail darter in the U.S.— an endangered species could provide the legal basis for declaring a marsh, a forest, or a mountainside off limits to development. To give teeth to this provision, the law also mandated that every new construction project on French territory, whether public or private, would have to file an environmental-impact study prior to the start of work—the first such requirement in any European nation.[39] It also gave the nature-protection societies an unprecedented right to sue, on behalf of the general public, any state-owned or private enterprise that violated environmental regulations.[40] Finally, the law opened the way for a series of supplemental legislative acts, promulgated over the decade that followed, setting forth in detail how specific aspects of the environment were to be managed: coastlines, forests, mountains, wild birds, wetlands, mammals, rare plants, and so on. It added up, in the words of one Minister of the Environment, Michel d'Ornano, to a "quiet revolution."[41]

Nevertheless, like most revolutions, this one, too, had its failings. Several scholars have faulted the 1976 law as a kind of "jurisprudence by engineers": a vast accumulation of ten thousand very precise technical prohibitions, lacking an overall vision or mission to tie them together.[42] Worse still, these critics argue, the French state failed to provide the administrative and budgetary means for the new law to be effectively implemented: no dedicated body of investigators, no special "eco-police," no coordinating agency to ensure that violators of the law would be brought to justice. The sobering result, according to one survey conducted in 1988, was that "95 percent of environmental pollution crimes either escaped observation or went unpunished."[43]

Even when a polluter was caught red-handed, according to the scholar Pierre Lascoumes, the justice system left a great deal to be desired: he cites the example of a chemical firm named Protex, which manufactured textile additives and advanced plastics in the countryside near the city of Tours.[44] Starting in the early 1970s, the region's industrial-safety inspectors began finding serious problems with Protex's facilities and procedures. Over a period of fifteen years, they issued nine separate warnings and official orders to the firm, threatening it with fines and ultimately with closure if it continued to violate the law. But the company's directors knew that Protex was practically untouchable, because of the considerable employment and revenues it brought to the local economy. So they continued to flout the law: during the early 1980s, fourteen more incidents of environmental pollution and hazardous procedures were officially registered by the frustrated, but apparently powerless, local authorities. Finally, in the spring of 1988, the regional government initiated procedures to close the defiant factory down; on June 8, before the measures could take effect, a fire broke out in the Protex storage depot. Undermanned, ill-equipped, poorly organized, the factory's night watch failed to control the fire, while neglecting to call the fire department. The conflagration engulfed the entire complex, and when firefighters finally managed to put it out, they inadvertently flushed huge quantities of toxic chemicals into the adjoining river, a tributary of the Loire. Aquatic wildlife was wiped out over a large area, while the city of Tours had its water supply cut off for five days. Four years later, after lengthy judicial proceedings, the factory's directors were given suspended jail sentences, and fined the relatively modest sum of $20,000.

What the Protex case revealed, according to Lascoumes, was a multilayered set of problems: a glaring absence of any independent and well-funded state agency charged with implementing environmental law and ensuring compliance; and an inherently flawed personnel system in which the same technicians who served as paid consultants to industrial firms often ended up—after a quick change of hats—serving as government inspectors and as judicial experts on behalf of environmental prosecutions.[45] More broadly, Lascoumes charged, the widely held image of a strong, centralized French state became profoundly misleading when it came to environmental law: for in the name of decentralization, and in the absence of a forceful Ministry of the Environment, the actual implementation of environmental regulations in daily practice often devolved into the most blatant wheeling-and-dealing on the local or regional level. The 1976 law left open the possibility of "adjustments" for special local situations, and this loophole resulted, more often than not, in the subjection of national norms and technical criteria to the vagaries of local politics: a "parallellogram of forces" among business interests, local politicians, environmental technicians, and nature-protection advocates, resulting in compromises that all-too-often defied rationality.[46]

One result—and a telling one—was the extraordinary variation that existed in legal thresholds for pollutants from one locality to another. To take but one example, the case of lead-based toxins in public landfills: as of the year 1990, in the town of Argences, the maximum allowable threshold was 0.05 milligrams per liter; in the town of Bellegarde it was 0.1 mg/liter; in the town of Vaivre it was 0.5 mg/liter—an overall variation of a factor of ten![47] The possibilities were twofold: either the citizens of Argences were being overzealous, and subjecting themselves to the high costs of producing "excessively pure" waste; or (more likely) the citizens of Vaivre were exposing themselves, because of a political deal, to a higher dose of lead than was good for them. In Lascoumes's view, curtailing this "politics of compromise" on environmental issues needed to constitute a high priority for green advocates in the first decade of the new millennium.[48]

3. The National Plan for the Environment (1990)

During the 1980s, environmentalists became increasingly aware of the wide-ranging problems we have just described; and in 1988, when the newly designated prime minister Michel Rocard appointed Brice Lalonde as Minister of the Environment, the greens saw their chance: they pushed for a sweeping *aggiornamento*—a systematic strengthening of French environmental policy and the ways it was implemented. Enthusiastically backed by both Lalonde and Rocard, the "Plan National pour l'Environnement" was accordingly drafted by the Ministry of the Environment and passed by the Assemblée Nationale in 1990.[49] It comprised three main reforms: the creation of twenty-two regional environmental directorates (DIREN), under the control of the Ministry of the Environment; a pledge to increase the environmental budget by 8 percent per year throughout the 1990s; and the consolidation of the state's plethora of environmental agencies into a more streamlined and effective bureaucracy. In addition, the new plan also set ambitious goals for the year 2000, establishing targets for a wide range of environmental thresholds ranging from greenhouse gases to air and water quality.

The balance sheet ten years later was, not surprisingly, mixed. Environmental budgets grew during the 1990s by an annual average of 3 percent rather than 8 percent. Some of the targeted thresholds, such as those for CFC and CO_2 emissions, were met on time, while others, like those for agricultural pollution and noise abatement, were missed by a wide margin.[50] Several new state agencies, most notably the ADEME (for energy management), and the INERIS (for handling major industrial hazards), successfully consolidated the congeries of existing bodies into potent and far more effective national actors. Another new creation, the Institut Français de l'Environnement (IFEN), while relatively small in budgetary terms, began playing an important role as a collector and disseminator of environmental statistics and scientific studies.[51]

Arguably the most important innovation, however, lay in the DIREN—

the twenty-two regional environmental directorates.[52] Conceived as a means of fortifying the Ministry of the Environment, by giving it territorial arms and legs with which to follow its various projects through to completion, these agencies ultimately embodied a combination between two types of state power, the "vertical" and the "horizontal." On the one hand, they were designed to transmit into the provinces the decisions of a central Parisian ministry—a "vertical" form of authority, flowing down the hierarchy from the Ministry at the Avénue de Ségur to its outlying bodies. On the other hand, they were also given the "horizontal" mission of working with a wide array of other state and private-sector actors, serving as a coordinating agency for environmental policy at the local level; in this capacity, the DIREN would have an "inter-ministerial" role, ensuring that municipal governments, prefectures, and the local branches of the ministries of Industry, Agriculture, or Transportation were not functioning at cross-purposes.

On paper, this idea looked excellent. On the ground, however, several factors undermined the DIREN from the start. First and foremost, they were chronically underfunded and understaffed: each regional body had between thirty and forty employees, who had to cover the full range of environmental topics—rare wildflowers to industrial waste, agricultural pesticides to highway expansion—out of a single small office. The fourfold mission of the DIREN included: to ensure that existing laws were being enforced; to conduct scientific studies and environmental impact reports, disseminating the results to the public; to launch new initiatives, from environmental pilot projects to the creation of "green jobs"; to participate in any planning processes, undertaken at any level of government, that might have an impact on their regional territory. "Thirty job lines to do all these things in four départements at the same time—it's just ridiculous," complained one harried official.[53]

The other ministries, moreover, were less than thrilled at the prospect of having their own jealously guarded prerogatives wrenched away from them, and they lobbied successfully to keep their own local branches in place, rather than handing over functions to the Ministry of the Environment. The end-result was that the DIREN had to fit in *alongside* the myriad local branches and agencies, rather than replacing some of them and consolidating them into a more streamlined system. Thus, instead of hacking back the thicket of green governance, the creation of the DIREN added yet another variety of briars to the existing tangle.

Having said this, however, one should not overlook the positive effects of this administrative reform. First, it contributed concretely to the power and credibility of the Ministry of the Environment, substantially increasing its field of effective action. Second, the transversal coordinating function served by the DIREN had been badly needed, and resulted in a relative clarification and fortification of environmental action at the local level. Finally, the DIREN provided a vital and continuous link between Parisian center and regional periphery—between the "global" and the "local," in the words of one participant—where before these two levels had often failed to mesh effectively.[54] Compared to the situation in the mid-1980s, therefore, the overall impact of the National Plan for the Environment could still be construed as a considerable improvement—even though it undoubtedly fell short of the high hopes pinned on it by its creators.

4. The "Barnier Law" of 1995

Michel Barnier was an exemplar of that *rara avis*, the green Gaullist. For the most part, the moderate Right in France has aligned itself over the years with business interests, and with the "productivist" philosophy that they championed. Though right-wingers from Jacques Chirac on the center Right to Jean-Marie Le Pen on the extreme Right have all taken up green rhetoric with considerable verve, they have not, by and large, played a significant role as initiators and promoters of environmentalist causes. One important exception was Georges Pompidou, who created the Ministry of the Environment; another was Michel Barnier.

Barnier began representing the Haute Savoie as a Gaullist (RPR) deputy in the Assemblée Nationale in 1978, and served several times on the staff of the Ministry of the Environment.[55] In 1990 he published a book, *The Environmentalist Challenge,* that must have raised the hackles of a good many of his right-wing political associates: in one chapter, he questioned the rationality of France's nuclear-electric wager, urging that the EDF program be phased out in favor of a vastly enhanced commitment to renewable energy sources; in another chapter, entitled "Growth isn't Everything," he questioned the whole mentality of the *trente glorieuses,* advocating an economic and political agenda that sounded closer in some ways to that of the moderate Greens than to that of his fellow Gaullists.[56] When the RPR leader Edouard Balladur became prime minister in 1993, therefore, he offered this political black sheep (green sheep?) the Ministry of the Environment—a post which Barnier accepted and held until 1995.

In February 1995 Barnier succeeded in getting a path-breaking law passed through parliament, revising and strengthening key provisions of the 1976 nature-protection law. The Barnier Law, as it came to be known, affirmed four basic ideas as the axiological foundations of French environmental jurisprudence:

A. The precautionary principle, which dictated that, in the absence of scientific certainty, French laws should be based on the best available estimates of potential risks of environmental damage, and should require public officials to take all necessary steps to avert such risks before they materialized.

B. The principle of preventive action, which dictated that French laws should aim at avoiding environmental damage at the source, rather than attempting to repair such damage after it had already occurred.

C. The "polluter pays" principle, according to which all measures of prevention or correction of a given type of pollution must be financed by the parties responsible for that pollution.

D. The principle of participation, whereby citizens possessed the right to obtain all available information regarding environmental conditions, including the presence of environmental hazards.[57]

These ideas were not, in themselves, particularly innovative, since they had already been partially enshrined in the Maastricht Treaty of the European Union, and in the Rio Declaration of 1992. Nevertheless, they marked a conceptual shift in French environmental law—a transition from a rather rigid jurisprudence based on thousands of highly precise and technical prohibitions, to a more flexible and enforceable jurisprudence based on broad principles, to be applied and interpreted on an ad hoc basis by judges, lawyers, and policymakers.[58] The new law was also far more proactive in its approach than the previous set of statutes, emphasizing prevention rather than restoration, and seeking to involve citizens more directly in environmental protection. Finally—and this was particularly striking for legislation drafted by a member of a "pro-business" party like the RPR—the new law placed the burden of responsibility squarely on the shoulders of polluters; under this new legal regime, such travesties as the Protex affair would be much less likely to occur.

5. The European Union's Treaty of Amsterdam (1997)

What the Barnier Law had done for French jurisprudence, the Treaty of Amsterdam did for European supranational legislation. Already, in the Single European Act of 1986 and Maastricht Treaty of 1992 (through which the legal outlines of the present EU were laid out), environmental protection had been adopted as one of the new polity's fundamental objectives, on a par with such goals as promoting economic integration, social welfare, and human rights.[59] The 1997 Treaty of Amsterdam, however, took this commitment to a new level: it amended Title I of the founding treaty, enshrining the concept of sustainable development at the core of the Union's economic policy; and it mandated that "environmental protection requirements must be integrated into the definition and implementation of other Community policies."[60]

Together, these two moves added up to a significant conceptual shift: they cast aside the old notion of "the environment" as a separate thematic domain, like agricultural or foreign policy, and replaced it with a conception of the environment as forming an integral part of *every single aspect* of Community action. Foreign affairs, public health, finance, commerce, agriculture—all these areas were now seen as intrinsically possessing environmental components, and as requiring the integration of "sustainable development" into their daily governance. If the Amsterdam Treaty worked as intended, therefore, the various EU bureaucracies would no longer be allowed to address environmental issues in a haphazard way, tacking a few green paragraphs onto their agendas as a sort of coda; rather, the environmental impact of any given policy would henceforth form a central part of that policy's initial framing and subsequent implementation.

In 1998, the European Commission showed that it was taking this new philosophy seriously: it ordered revisions in the Common Agricultural Policy, making community subsidies contingent on compliance with environmental regulations; required that all nations applying for EU membership demonstrate a strong commitment to environmental protection; mandated environmental impact reports on all Community projects costing over $45 million; freed new funds for environmental assistance to needy nations; beefed up the environmental component of regional planning; and initiated a program for meeting the greenhouse gas threshold undertaken at Kyoto for the year 2008.[61]

For the French, this "upping of the ante" at the European level became a potent stimulus to further action. According to Jacques Theys (one of the co-authors of the National Plan for the Environment),

> Europe is gradually imposing on us a [more rigorous] system of environmental management based on fixed norms and across-the-board thresholds—a system rather far removed from our own traditional approach, with its emphasis on negotiation and compromise.[62]

In many cases, moreover, when French environmentalists found themselves stymied at the local or national level, they could increasingly turn to European laws and courts for support. To cite but one representative case: throughout the 1980s, a group of French activists fought a losing battle to save a large wetland known as the Marais Poitevin, along the Atlantic coast near La Rochelle, from local agribusiness interests that were pumping water out of this delicate swampland to irrigate wheat fields.[63] The Marais Poitevin had been officially designated as a Regional Nature Reserve, and the greens clearly had the law on their side when they argued that this kind of irrigation was manifestly illegal. Nevertheless, because of the farmers' strong political connections, the pumping continued; the local and regional governments did nothing to stop it; and the wetland continued to deteriorate. Finally, in 1989, the exasperated activists sued the French state in the European Court of Justice, arguing that by neglecting to protect this endangered site, the national government was violating its own laws as well as those of the EU. The judicial proceedings dragged on for another ten years (!); meanwhile, in 1998, the Minister of the Environment, Dominique Voynet, effectively took the side of the activists by ordering a comprehensive survey of the wetland and its history, which was forwarded to the European Court as additional evidence.

Finally, in November 1999, the Luxembourg high court issued its verdict: it condemned the French government, ordered it to pay all legal costs, and demanded that it rectify the situation as quickly as possible. This kind of humiliating international condemnation arguably exerted an even more potent effect than monetary fines (which might still be levied if the French failed to comply); and the French government responded shortly thereafter by appointing a special inter-ministerial commissioner to try to reach a negotiated solution between activists and wheat farmers.[64] As of the early 2000s, the fate of the Marais Poitevin remained uncertain, but the efficacy of playing the "European card" appeared undeniable. Europe, it turned out, could provide an excellent point of leverage from which common citizens (armed, to be sure, with an extraordinary amount of perseverance) could challenge local and national political forces far greater than their own.

6. Absorbing DATAR into the Ministry of the Environment (1997)

The unprecedented alliance between Greens and Socialists in the legislative elections of 1997 yielded sweet fruits for both parties: the prime ministership for the Socialist Lionel Jospin, six parliamentary seats and the Ministry of the Environment for the Greens (see chapter 4). Jospin decided to launch a rather bold experiment: the DATAR (Agency for Aménagement du Territoire) which had traditionally been housed in the Commissariat au Plan or the Ministry of Transportation, would instead be melded into a bigger and more powerful Ministry of the Environment (see chapter 2 on the creation of DATAR).[65] To some, this move seemed foolhardy: for DATAR and the greens had long been poles apart—the former busily funding highways, airports, power lines, and new industrial plants in the provinces, the latter tugging more often than not in the opposite direction. It seemed like a shotgun wedding between productivism and environmentalism, and many in both camps expected the relationship to wind up quickly in divorce.

But in the end Jospin's gamble paid off—a result attributable, in large measure, to his choice of Dominique Voynet as head of the new ministry. Voynet proved a quick study, passing deftly from the easy-going egalitarian banter and wool sweaters of the Green Party headquarters to the stiff formality, footmen in livery, and political hardball of a government ministry. During her first few months in office, she made several important tactical errors, embarrassing herself or losing bureaucratic battles—but she learned from each mistake, and freely admitted as much in her press conferences.[66] The French public, unused to such candor, and impressed by her no-nonsense pursuit of her ministerial agenda, soon accorded her a place as one of the most popular and respected ministers in Jospin's government—a sort of Gallic Petra Kelly.

Voynet and her team moved swiftly.[67] Within her first weeks in office she persuaded Jospin's government to close down the notorious reactor at Creys-Malville; to terminate the Rhine-Rhone canal project; to cease construction of another controversial nuclear plant at Carnet; and to set up a more sophisticated (and expensive) system for radioactive waste disposal. Representing France at the Kyoto summit in December 1997, she galvanized European opposition to the foot-dragging policy adopted on greenhouse gases by the U.S. delegation—opposition which finally helped prod the U.S. to take a more moderate stance.[68] Back at home, she fought hard in the corridors of power for a larger ministerial budget, and secured a 30 percent increase between 1997 and 2000; during the same period, she raised state funding for the nature-protection societies by 80 percent. In 1999 she presided over the creation of France's first true "eco-tax"—the General Tax on Polluting Activities (TGAP)—which far surpassed the existing fiscal system in penalizing polluters and rewarding environmentally sound enterprises.[69]

Arguably the most important achievement of her first three years, however, was the "Voynet Law" adopted by the Assemblée Nationale in January 1999—a "Law on the *Aménagement* and Sustainable Development of the Territory" (LOADDT).[70] From the start, Voynet had considered the administrative fusion of DATAR and Environment as much more than just a bureaucratic victory: she interpreted it as a sign that the dominance of the productivist worldview was no longer unchallengeable, and that the time was ripe to launch a gradual, incremental reorientation of France's territorial policy around the principle of sustainable development. Her new law translated this idea into practice. In the domain of transportation, it reversed the priority that had predominated throughout the *trente glorieuses*: rather than promoting the creation of ever more highways and airports, it emphasized "a better use of existing road and rail networks, and the limitation of greenhouse gas emissions."[71] At the same time, it provided resources for a major overhaul and upgrade of public transport, with an emphasis on rail. In the domain of agriculture, it put the highest priority on rolling back erosion and pollution, finding alternatives to chemical pesticides and fertilizers, and giving incentives to farmers to help with the upkeep of the landscape. In the domain of energy policy, it provided new resources for encouraging energy conservation among both citizens and businesses; and it funded new research on renewable energy sources.

Needless to say, the mere passing of such a progressive law did not mean that car owners, agribusiness, and energy consumers—not to mention the SNCF, Ministry of Agriculture, and EDF—would suddenly become green converts. What was significant, rather, was the fact that such a law could be passed at all, in the face of substantial opposition and behind-the-scenes obstructionism from precisely such constituencies. On the one hand, Voynet had clearly done her homework, assiduously preparing the political ground: "The key," she later told a nature-protection meeting, "is to make sure, before you make your move, that you have the balance of forces solidly aligned in your favor."[72] On the other hand, no amount of skillful cajoling and advance preparation would have sufficed, if the concepts she was proposing had not sufficiently penetrated into the mainstream to be seen as desirable and practical. After three decades of green activism, the idea of sustainable development—pursued in a gradualist, level-headed manner—evidently sounded attractive enough to a sufficient number of French citizens (and parliamentarians) to cobble together a winning coalition.

> > >

By the year 2000, the "environmentalization" of the state was well advanced. It had begun with President Pompidou's relatively simple goals—educating the French about the need to protect their nation's rivers, birds, and natural spaces, while establishing a modest governmental body to oversee such efforts over the decades to come. From here the process took on a momentum of its own: the Minister of the Environment immediately realized that he lacked the legal instruments for doing his job, and set into motion the drafting of the 1976 nature-protection law; this law, in turn, proved inadequate because no arm of government existed to implement and enforce its provisions effectively. And this in turn led to the major institutional innovations of the 1990s, starting with the reforms triggered by the National Plan for the Environment and culminating in the comprehensive "Voynet Law" of 1999. "The process strikes me as irreversible," noted Dominique Voynet in an April 2000 speech:

The old "ministry of nature" has metamorphosed into "the house of sustainable development." . . . What was once a rather marginal government agency—a sort of "itching powder" of public affairs—has now become a major branch of government, wielding substantial powers.[73]

Ecological constraints had come to constitute part of the very fabric of French law and public policy.

10 Industrialists as Ecologists

Not only can we *reconcile* the environment and economic growth, we can turn the environment into a *catalyst* of economic growth.
—Bernard Collomb, CEO of Lafarge-Coppée Corporation, 1992[1]

Factories and Big Business: New Constraints, New Strategies

Captains of industry, in the eyes of the early environmentalists, ranked high in the pantheon of "ungreen" forces. The virulent campaigns by Peugeot against catalytic converters, or by Rhône-Poulenc against phosphate-free detergents, were only the most obvious and highly publicized examples.[2] Behind the scenes—most greens suspected—the industrialists could be found busily lobbying to block environmental legislation and weaken green governance: although they were admittedly not the only ones responsible for the evils of rampant productivism, they could generally be counted on to fight a stubborn rear-guard action against all efforts to transform the French economy along environmentalist lines.

By and large—especially during the 1970s and early 1980s—this picture was not far off the mark.[3] Most industrial leaders and professional economists assumed that environmental retooling would weigh heavily on France's business enterprises, raising costs, dragging down productivity, and seriously undermining competitiveness in global markets. Accordingly, they did their utmost to play down environmental threats, and to thwart or at least postpone the adoption of environmental measures; when all else failed, they raised the perpetual specter of factory closings and unemployment. "Force us to go green," they said in effect, "and you will be greening yourselves right out of a job."

Nevertheless, in the end, the greens had to confront yet another major paradox here: for it was the industrial sector of the French economy that made the quickest and most profound turnaround in its behavior vis-à-vis the environment.[4] Far more than private citizens, retail stores, farmers, or local governments (where the transformation came piecemeal and slowly if at all), the factories and large-scale business enterprises of France swung round into alignment with green ideas during the 1990s, and took substantive steps to improve their environmental performance. By the year 2000, the smoke-belching factories of another era had given way—with a few notable exceptions—to a strictly controlled and much cleaner mode of production: large industrial firms arguably constituted one of the preeminent green success stories of the late twentieth century.

> > >

At least four causal factors played a role in pushing this transformation along. First and foremost, of course, were the new laws and regulations continually being passed at the national and supranational levels—laws restricting the release of chemicals and waste products into the environment, laws laying down increasingly strict penalties for polluters, but also significant subsidies and tax-breaks for companies willing to undertake a serious environmental restructuring of their operations. Second, and perhaps equally important, was the role played by public opinion: for under the keen scrutiny of the nature-protection societies and environmental specialists in the mass media, no company could long afford the public-relations debacle of appearing openly as a foe of environmental protection. For example, after Peugeot's CEO, Jacques Calvet, launched a well-publicized campaign against catalytic converters in the early 1980s, the company had to spend vast sums over much of the next decade to reverse its negative image in the public eye.[5] A third factor lay in the high cost of pollution cleanup procedures—a budgetary item that grew steadily in importance, as the "polluter pays" principle made its way into French legislative and administrative practice (culminating in the promulgation of the Barnier Law in 1995). Finally, many companies learned that adopting cleaner technologies in their production process actually saved them money in the long run: the initial cost of setting up new machines and procedures was often outweighed by the savings in energy and resources that they entailed over the years.[6]

The results were not long in coming. In 1997, an environmental report by the prestigious international body, the OECD (Organization for Economic Cooperation and Development) singled out the French industrial sector as one of the nation's most impressive areas of green progress. Both when compared with France's European neighbors, and when compared with the other sectors of the French domestic economy such as agriculture and transportation (which got flunking grades), large industrial firms emerged as the most successful exemplars of environmental retooling.[7]

The bottom line: between 1974 and 1995, French industrial emissions declined by 323 percent for organic wastes and 207 percent for toxic wastes.[8] Between 1981 and 1994, while overall industrial production grew by 14 percent, water use by industrial firms declined 21 percent, and energy use declined 2 percent—reflecting a steady increase in efficiency and conservation. (This achievement becomes all the more impressive when one recalls that, during the same years, total national consumption of energy was more than doubling.) By the 1990s, 25 percent of the metals used in manufacturing came from France's recycling plants; 70 percent of all lead was used and re-used in this manner. Nearly all major factories had their own purification systems for chemical effluents; many also treated their own hazardous wastes, under the regular surveillance of the ADEME (Agency for Environment and Energy Management) and the local DRIRE (Regional Directorate for Industry, Research, and Environment). By the late 1990s, such infamous cases as the Protex Affair—with its Keystone Kops combination of weak regulation, recidivist violations, and lax enforcement—had clearly become a thing of the past.

In general, large firms made this transition more smoothly than small ones: to a minor regional company with a few dozen employees, installing a sophisticated smokestack scrubber or overhauling a drainage system could mean nothing less than bankruptcy. For this reason, France's regional governments began putting money aside in the 1990s to help small and middle-sized firms finance major environmental changes.[9] Overall, French industrial enterprises in the 1990s were allocating between 3 and 5 percent of their investment budgets for environmental protection; two-thirds of this sum went for major retooling, such as the installation of filtration systems; the remainder went to cleanups, recycling, and risk prevention.[10] The sum was growing by an average of 5 percent per year.[11]

ISO-14000 and Eco-Audit: The Case of an Industrial Pioneer

In 1993, the Nicoll Company, a leading French plastics manufacturer with one thousand employees and four factories in the lush countryside of

Anjou, decided to launch an environmental overhaul of its operations.[12] Partly this decision flowed from the general policy of its parent company, the Etex Group, which possessed a vigorous and proactive environmental directorate of its own; and partly the decision stemmed from straightforward cost-benefit logic. On the one hand, implementing an environmental retrofit would no doubt cost a considerable sum up front. On the other hand, it would yield four potentially significant benefits.

1. *Cutting expenses.* Preliminary in-house studies showed that Nicoll stood to gain considerably more than it lost from environmental retooling, because of cumulative energy and resource savings, as well as tax benefits, over the years to come.

2. *Reducing environmental liability.* With the emergence of the "polluter pays" principle, many firms faced huge and unexpected expenses for cleaning up their manufacturing procedures and factory sites. Insurers, bankers, and stockholders were increasingly taking this risk factor into account in assessing a company for possible investment. Therefore, adopting a systematic policy of prevention and risk management would allow far greater control over this environmental wild card.

3. *Corporate image.* During the 1990s, opinion polls among the general public, as well as among business leaders, all indicated a major growth in sensitivity to environmental "good citizenship."[13] Even for a fairly specialized company like Nicoll, whose products were generally not sold directly in retail, the significance of being perceived as an environmentally responsible firm could yield intangible but important goodwill dividends in its local region, among its suppliers and customers, and among its own employees as well.

4. *Preparedness for future legislation.* With environmental regulations steadily escalating in their severity and comprehensiveness, a well-managed company needed to know its own potential weak spots for the middle-term and long-term future. Conducting an environmental self-study would allow Nicoll to anticipate future laws that pertained to its products and manufacturing processes, thus allowing it to start preparing for such regulatory changes well in advance.

For all these reasons, Nicoll's leadership decided to apply simultaneously for two distinct types of official environmental certification, the ISO-14000 and Eco audit.[14] Both these certification systems were just being launched in the mid-1990s—the former under the auspices of the International Standards Organization in Geneva, the latter under the tutelage of the European Union. The ISO-14000 and Eco-audit were somewhat similar to the eco-label, except that in this case it was an entire company, not a particular prod-

uct, that constituted the object of evaluation. Companies seeking certification had to establish a formal "Environmental Management System"
(EMS)—a comprehensive set of procedures for integrating environmental
factors into the design, manufacture, and marketing of their industrial products. The ISO-14000 and Eco-audit were similar in underlying goals and
philosophy: companies applied voluntarily, conducted their own self-study,
implemented an EMS, and then called for inspection and certification. The
main difference was that the ISO-14000 only required reinspections every
three years, whereas the European Union's Eco-audit placed the bar higher,
requiring annual inspections, as well as annual publication and public dissemination of a comprehensive environmental impact report.[15]

For Nicoll, this meant that the year 1994 was spent conducting an exhaustive environmental self-study. Seventy of the company's divisional managers made systematic assessments in their particular sectors—from calling
in the local fire department to evaluate emergency evacuation procedures, to
inspecting the factory's vast network of underground drainage pipes; from
measuring chemical outflows in smokestacks to testing soil quality. In the
end, they produced a comprehensive plan—the EMS—in which they
pledged:

- to increase energy efficiency in their plants, starting with a new
  heating system;
- to increase the use of recycled materials by 25 percent over three
  years;
- to install a water-purification system on two of their discharge
  pipelines;
- to install scrubbers on several smokestacks;
- to commence cleanup on the soil of a polluted field discovered
  during the self-study;
- to assign personnel on a permanent basis for environmental
  monitoring and follow-up;
- to train all their personnel more systematically about environmental
  impacts of their work;
- to set up a regular forum for cooperation with neighboring factories
  on environmental protection in the Anjou region;
- to pursue a general policy aiming at continual environmental
  improvements, based on an ongoing process of self-monitoring and
  setting ever-higher standards;
- to create an ongoing research program for finding ways to improve
  their products' environmental life-cycles, "from cradle to grave."

Following a series of inspections in 1995, Nicoll accordingly became the first company in France to obtain certification under both the ISO and EU standards.[16] One needs to exercise caution, however, in making generalizations from this particular case—for only a very small proportion of France's industrial enterprises went as far as Nicoll. As of the year 2000, only 640 French firms had received the ISO 14000 certification, and an even more paltry 37 firms had passed the EU's Eco-audit—out of a national total of approximately 500,000 enterprises![17] The vast majority of companies remained satisfied to toe the regulatory line—meeting the minimum legal requirements for their particular industries, and leaving the eco-pioneering to others.

Nevertheless, a real sea-change was undeniably taking place. "The remarkable thing," wrote a representative of the French Environmental Institute (IFEN) in 1999, "is that large-scale industry has begun to integrate environmental concepts into the very core of the manufacturing process: the design and conception of products, the training of personnel, the domains of marketing and advertising."[18] More and more companies, while stopping short of launching a full-scale EMS, were nonetheless allocating resources and assigning personnel to monitor environmental performance and to follow up on the environmental dimension of their business. While this process was undoubtedly still in its early stages, its overall trajectory, from an environmentalist's perspective, could not but be regarded as promising.

The New Eco-Professions: Expansion in the Tertiary Sector

One of the best measures of the greening of industry lay in the rapid proliferation of "eco-professionals" during the 1990s—the army of specialized environmental technicians, consultants, inventors, engineers, biologists, and chemists who became increasingly indispensable to public and private enterprises as they grappled with environmental management or retooling. "Times change," wrote one business researcher in 1991:

> The environment, once perceived as an economic constraining factor, today offers a real opening for firms that know how to stay one step ahead of the public's shifting desires. It's a dream opportunity for the more innovative and far-sighted businesses to make great money.[19]

The European Union defined eco-industries in 1994 as "all those enterprises whose primary purpose is to produce goods and services oriented toward measuring, limiting, or reversing the harm done to the environment by human beings."[20] Thus broadly defined, this part of the French (and European) economy constituted one of the most salient "boom sectors" of the late twentieth century, growing at about 10 percent per year in the late 1980s and early 1990s, then slowing somewhat but still cruising ahead at 4 percent growth rates in the late 1990s.[21] In 1994, French eco-industries were grossing about $20 billion per year—a figure that placed this sector between pharmaceuticals and computers in the domestic economic ranking; French firms weighed in second only to the Germans in the European market for such goods and services. Some 280,000 persons were employed in this domain—about 1.2 percent of the French working population—and the number of jobs was growing steadily by 2 percent per year. Most significantly, perhaps, in a land where unemployment was considered Public Enemy Number One, the jobs generated by eco-industries amounted to fully 14 percent of all new positions created—the second-largest growth sector behind social services. One 1998 guidebook, oriented toward high school and college graduates, bore the title, *Environmental Professions: Earning a Living by Protecting Living Things;* it described 150 different careers, from forester to meteorologist, from pollution inspector to recycling plant operator—and in most of these lines of work it offered the promise of plentiful job openings and competitive salaries.[22]

Eco-professions fell into three thematic areas: pollution control, nature protection, and environmental research. The first of these, which included the huge sectors of water treatment and trash management, absorbed three-quarters of all environmental expenditures; it was dominated by two giant conglomerates, Générale des Eaux (part of the Vivendi group) and Lyonnaise des Eaux.[23] These two venerable old firms, whose roots went back to the nineteenth century, not only divided between themselves the French market for fresh water supply, but also branched out into virtually every aspect of environmental engineering, from purification to recycling. At the other end of the size spectrum, a plethora of small and middling eco-companies also competed furiously with each other, selling specialized items such as high-performance filters or measuring devices, or offering technical services in green management and the preparation of environmental impact reports.[24]

The second category, nature protection, included rangers and wildlife experts, park administrators, agronomists, and oceanographers—comprising 13 percent of France's 280,000 environmental jobs. Compared with careers in the burgeoning sector of pollution control, these professions were not very well paid: a forty-one-year-old ranger with scientific training and thirteen years' experience was earning $20,880 in 1998—but the position had the considerable advantage of offering a life in the outdoors.[25] Finally, a third aspect of the eco-professions consisted in basic research on environmental technologies—the quest for new and cleaner modes of production, the ongoing search for innovative ways to purify contaminated soil, to restore a natural habitat, to recycle chemicals more effectively. By its very nature, this was a highly variegated and interdisciplinary field, dispersed among institutions large and small, public and private: fully 60 percent of such research was carried out by the private sector, in the laboratories of eco-industries. As of 1994, the French were spending about $300 million, or 1 percent of their annual science budget, on this type of research; the funding for such studies grew by 20 percent between 1983 and 1993.[26]

> > >

To an old-timer green activist—someone who had discovered environmentalism during the 1970s and had fought for green ideals through the three decades that followed—the panorama of France's industrial economy in the year 2000 must have seemed fraught with paradox. The ideology of economic growth continued to dominate public discourse; but greens were now part of the government, and played a significant role in shaping that discourse. Productivism was alive and well, in all sectors of French society, but many of the products themselves, and the ways they were made and used, were increasingly subject to effective ecological constraints. French citizens still believed in something called progress, but most of them now reflexively included environmental features in their definition of this word. Factories and industrial sites—the billowing smokestacks of yesteryear—were spending millions to clean up their operations, and the government was following close on their heels, wielding both carrot and stick. Though many French greens might still cling to an old concept, zero economic growth, others were now using a more recent term, "sustainable development." To many young people, the word "environment" now meant something more than just protecting nature—it meant jobs, in one of the most rapidly expanding sectors of the contemporary economy. Green ideas, once predicated on zero growth, had themselves become a significant economic growth factor.

11 Elusive Sustainability

A Territorial Balance Sheet

Two hundred years ago, almost everywhere, human beings were comparatively few, poor, and at the mercy of the forces of nature; and two hundred years from now, we expect, almost everywhere they will be numerous, rich, and in control of the forces of nature.
—Herman Kahn et al., 1976 (Critique of *The Limits to Growth*)[1]

In the foregoing chapters we have focused on the gradual process by which ecological factors and the value of "the natural" came to weigh more and more heavily in the myriad activities of French society, from production to consumption, from work to leisure, from laws and institutions to the more ethereal *mentalités*. Now, in this concluding chapter of Part III, it is time to reverse our perspective, and to ask: What has this all meant, in practice, for the land and water and sky of France? What kinds of environmental results has the light-green society been able to deliver?

The State of the French Territory: An Ecocentric Perspective

That France is a beautiful country to visit is common knowledge (or should be); what is often less well known is the extraordinary variety of natural sceneries that one can find within its borders. In the Alps and Pyrenees, craggy snow-covered peaks of relatively young mountain ranges still being carved and eroded by glaciers; expansive flatlands in the north-central plains, crisscrossed by thin rivers; desolate marshlands surrounding the Rhône and Loire deltas—the Camargue, where half-wild horses still run, and the lush greenery of the Atlantic wetlands; the forest of the Landes, one of the most extensive in Europe, an expanse of tall pines covering one million hectares; high dunelands west of Bordeaux, stretching three hundred kilometers along the wind-swept Atlantic; the rolling countryside of Brittany, austere and deserted behind its rocky coastline; dense oak forests in the Vosges and Jura, dotted by waterfalls and cataracts; the gorges of the Tarn, where the river has carved a tortuous path through the bleak Cévennes mountains; the spectacular red-dirt formations of eastern Provence; the strange volcanic cones, or *puys,* projecting like steep tumuli from the horizon of the Auvergne.[2]

By any standard, it adds up to a remarkable richness of landscapes, particularly for a mid-sized nation situated in the heart of Europe's temperate zone. And all of it is steeped in history. For ten thousand years or more, this territory has been the object of intensifying human activities: by the late twentieth century, someone seeking a primal wilderness, relatively unmarked by human agency, must look elsewhere.[3] Even as early as 7000 B.C., the vast deciduous forest that covered most of Europe was already being worked at by Mesolithic peoples, using fire to enlarge the meadows where edible plants and wildlife abounded.[4] From this point on, the reach of human shaping and manipulating steadily increased: agriculture, the domestication of animals, the growth of stable settlements, the invention of new technologies for intensified irrigation or cultivation, the resultant rise of population. It would be a mistake to think of this process as a straight, linear expansion: during the fourteenth and fifteenth centuries, for example, with the ravages of the bubonic plague taking a huge toll on human numbers, the trees made a swift recovery, spreading back into the abandoned fields.[5] But the overall thrust of change was nonetheless clear: by the eighteenth century, although roughly 15 percent of France was still being described in royal documents as uninhabited woodland, the extent of the primeval forest had fallen to zero.[6]

This does not mean, however, that human intervention has always necessarily gone hand-in-hand with a degradation of the territory's natural attributes. Especially since World War II, some parts of France have actually regained a relatively pristine quality lost centuries ago; and in many parts of the nation, by the year 2000, ambitious efforts at protection and restoration were under way. No univocal narrative—either of degradation or of amelioration—will do justice to the complexity of what has been taking place "on the ground" over the past half-century.

The Land

As of 1997, the French territory, which covered 55 million hectares (about three-quarters the size of Texas) comprised 56 percent agricultural land, 28 percent woodlands and forests, 8 percent protected natural spaces, and 8 percent human habitations and infrastructures.[7] This was not as far removed as one might expect from the United States, which had 45 percent agricultural land and 30 percent forests, though very different from a nation like Sweden, which had 68 percent forest and only 7 percent agricultural land.[8]

France's farmlands ranged from the vast monocultural wheatfields of the northwest to the widely dispersed patchwork plots of traditional family farms. One of the most important transformations of the postwar era consisted in *remembrement*—the government-sponsored consolidation of tiny plots into larger units amenable to the use of mechanized farm implements. Though this process, pursued systematically after the 1950s, indeed raised productivity considerably, ecological scientists realized during the 1990s that the bulldozing of hedgerows and stone walls had taken a huge toll on a wide variety of animals that made their homes around the edges of fields— from birds to rodents, from insects to amphibians. A second government-sponsored program had aimed at the drainage of marshes and swamps to increase arable land—and this too had caused a swift degradation of wildlife habitats, impinging particularly hard on fish, aquatic reptiles, and migratory birds. In both these cases, therefore, environmental activists began pushing (with some success) for a revised agricultural policy that took into account the precious resource of "fringe lands" formerly dismissed as valueless.[9]

Agriculture, according to an OECD study conducted in 1997, remained one of the weak spots of French environmental policy: it continued to rely on aggressive chemical-intensive methods that did real damage to both the soil and the underlying aquifers.[10] Erosion constituted a serious problem wherever wheat and vineyards were grown; and agronomists pointed to wide expanses of land whose nutritive quality had been sapped by systematic overuse. Soil experts also worried about a growing trend among farmers: the widespread use of nutrient-rich muck from sewage-treatment plants as a fertilizer. Though it killed two birds with one stone—getting rid of organic wastes by using them to nitrify the fields—this practice was thought to be introducing dangerously high levels of heavy metals into the soil.[11]

No "old-growth" forests survived in France at all, and many areas classified as woodlands amounted to little more than vast tree-farms, assiduously monitored and tended by the professionals of the timber industry. One major trend of the postwar decades came as a side-effect of mechanized farming: with 90 percent of small farmers gradually abandoning the land and switch-

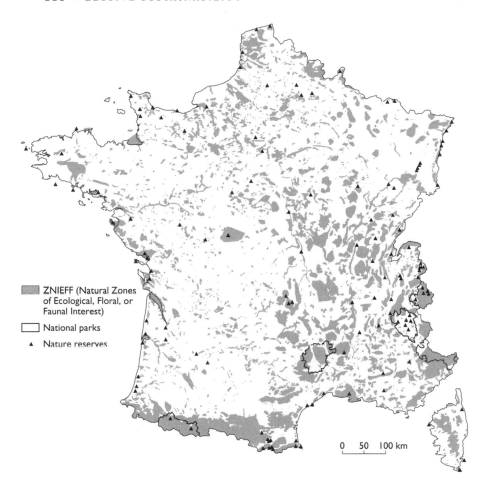

Figure 7. Three official categories of protected natural spaces in France: Zones of ecological, floral, or faunal interest (Znieff); national parks; nature reserves. (Courtesy of Institut Français de L'Environnement and Muséum National d'Histoire Naturelle.)

ing to new professions, large areas of France were reverting to a state known as *friche agricole*—abandoned fields and pastures, slowly reentering the natural cycle of spontaneous regrowth, from bushes and saplings on up. The Ministry of Agriculture estimated this trend as affecting some 72,000 hectares per year, thereby adding about one percent to existing woodlands every two years.[12]

The 8 percent of French land that qualified as "protected natural spaces" broke down into several subcategories.[13] About a quarter of these areas—

two percent of the national territory—remained close to a pristine natural state, with severe statutes enforcing a "hands-off" policy from surrounding human activities; these areas included the inner zones of France's seven national parks, and about 230 smaller nature reserves scattered throughout the country (see fig. 7).[14] The remainder of the protected spaces allowed a higher degree of human activities within them, such as fishing or hiking—but regulated these activities strictly, with an eye to protecting animal habitats and the natural character of the site. Finally, a third and distinctive grouping was comprised by the thirty-three Parcs Naturels Régionaux, whose mixture of woodlands, fields, villages, country lanes, meadows, and farms placed them in a category of their own. These parks, which covered another 11 percent of the national territory (distinct from the 8 percent that comprised "protected natural spaces"), possessed considerably looser regulatory statutes commensurate with the wide range of activities they embraced.

All but a few of these natural spaces had come under formal legal protection for the first time between 1960 and 2000–a direct result of rising environmental awareness. In addition, the overall area covered by such protective statutes continued to grow by an average of 10 percent per year—more slowly for the national parks and nature reserves, more swiftly for the mixed zones like the Parcs Naturels Régionaux.[15] Though French environmentalists would understandably have liked to see the pace further quickened, France was clearly no longer playing "catch up" in this domain, as it had been during the 1960s; by the year 2000, its basic statistics on national parks and nature preserves compared respectably with those of any other European nation.[16] (As of that year, only 3 percent of the world's total land surface was set aside for nature conservation; in the United States, the figure was the same as for France: 8 percent.)[17]

A final 8 percent of the territory was covered by human contrivances: dwellings (4 percent), factories, shops, and offices (1.4 percent), roads, airports, and rail lines (2.5 percent).[18] This heavily artificialized environment was growing by about one percent (40,000 hectares) per year, almost always at the expense of agricultural land. Between 1960 and 1997, for example, France's highways grew an average of 140 percent per year, passing from 170 to 8,940 total kilometers; TGV lines and high-tension wires sliced across the land, their networks steadily becoming denser; suburban malls, dwellings, and parking lots spread rapidly around the outskirts of most cities and major transport hubs. For all the fuss about aménagement du territoire during the 1970s and 1980s, it was only in the 1990s that these kinds of large-scale infrastructures and unchecked urban growth became subject to stricter and more systematic controls.

Water and Sky

During the late 1990s, many French citizens were cheered by a widely trumpeted piece of good news about their aquatic environment: over the preceding twenty years, the nation's beaches and lakeside swimming spots had steadily become cleaner; the number of sites meeting stringent E.U. water-purity criteria had passed from 65 percent to 91 percent.[19] But before they could savor the news, another official study spoiled the fun: scientists at the National Marine Research Institute (Ifremer) announced, after several years of surveying marine habitats, that the Mediterranean seabed off the French coast was littered with an estimated 300 million pieces of garbage.[20]

This decidedly mixed set of impressions sets the tone for any overview of French aquatic ecosystems. France's 6,000 kilometers of coastline constituted a key target for real estate developers both during and after the *trente glorieuses,* as economic prosperity fueled a boom in seasonal tourism and led large numbers of citizens to seek secondary residences by the sea. Between 1975 and 1990, the total area occupied by houses and apartments along the seacoasts grew by 15 percent—despite increasingly stringent regulations governing such construction.[21] In some regions, such as Corsica and the Languedoc-Roussillon, the growth rate reached as high as 30 percent. But urban growth did not constitute the only threat to marine ecosystems: between 1964 and 1996, for example, the number of pleasure boats increased tenfold, leading to serious problems of water and noise pollution, as well as forcing the construction of dozens of new port facilities.[22]

Countering this wave of growth was far from easy, given the immense commercial stakes involved. Perhaps the most effective protective instrument was the Conservatoire du Littoral, a state-run agency whose mission was to purchase notable natural habitats along the waterways and coastlines, thereby shielding them from the pressures of development. Once purchased by the Conservatoire, a piece of land could never be sold again, and had to remain open to public use (along strict ecological principles). Between its creation in 1975 and the year 2000, the Conservatoire bought up 13 percent of French shorelines in this fashion: its long-term goal was to raise the total to a full third of all coastal lands by 2050.[23]

France's freshwater habitats faced similar pressures, but from a different quarter: agriculture. Particularly in the northwestern sections of the country, where large-scale mechanized farming was prevalent, the aquifers and watercourses showed signs of pollution by nitrates and pesticides. Eutrophication—the overgrowth of algae and other plants due to pollution by organic nutrients—became a serious problem in these regions, as runoff from heavily fertilized fields made its way into rivers and lakes.[24] At the same time, the wetland habitats that provided crucial foci of wildlife preservation were slowly but steadily declining; a National Wetlands Observatory was created in 1995 to monitor their condition and to make recommendations for their systematic protection.[25]

Air pollution, for its part, began making headlines for the first time in the late 1990s, as ozone concentrations in several cities reached dangerous levels, forcing mayors to restrict automobile traffic for days at a time. Up until this point, most French citizens had remained blissfully oblivious to the problem, because of their nation's fortunate location at the western edge of the continent, where prevailing winds came in from the Atlantic rather than from the heavily industrialized zones to the north and east. Thus, sulfur dioxide, acid rain, and low-level atmospheric ozone all constituted relatively minor environmental issues in France, compared with Scandinavia, Germany, or the nations of eastern Europe.[26]

Along with the rest of the European Union, France had been adopting progressively more stringent restrictions on air pollution over the years, subjecting both the industrial and the transportation sectors to tight regulation. The result was a steady decline in the major forms of emissions prevalent during the 1960s: hydrocarbons, sulfur dioxide, lead, and CFCs. One notable exception, of course, lay in greenhouse gases, such as carbon dioxide, which could not be "converted" by catalytic converters or "scrubbed" by smokestack scrubbers: emissions of these kinds of gases continued inexorably to creep upward (one to 4 percent per year), reflecting the seemingly irresistible growth in French energy consumption.[27]

Fauna and Flora

In 1992 a pack of Italian wolves crossed the Alps from Piedmont's Parco Naturale delle Alpi Marittime and settled in France.[28] (Some wags speculated that they were among the first European residents to take advantage of the Maastricht Treaty's relaxation of border restrictions.) The wolf had been wiped out in France early in the twentieth century, but had managed to survive in the remote mountain passes of the Abruzzi, southeast of Rome. (How the creatures got from the Abruzzi to the Piedmontese mountains, across five hundred kilometers of a densely populated modern nation, remained something of a mystery.) On the French side, now, the wolves discovered an appealing new home in the Parc National du Mercantour, where they were not only legally protected from hunters, but found plenty of animals to feed upon. By 1996, the French population of *Canis lupus* had grown to approximately twenty individuals, divided into four packs.

Unfortunately, they had also developed a taste for lamb. Some three hundred old-style shepherds still made a living along the fringes of the Mercantour, raising flocks of sheep and goats, and producing highly prized traditional cheeses from the milk. About fifty of these flocks became regular targets for the wolves. The confrontation quickly escalated, as the shepherds fought back with rifles and strychnine, then found themselves the objects of police action and widespread eco-vituperation. Like the bitter episode of "Logger vs. Spotted Owl" in the U.S., the conflict quickly polarized French public opinion: wolf against shepherd, Nature against Civilization. The Minister of the Environment, Dominique Voynet, personally intervened, seeking to broker a compromise: state-funded compensation for the shepherds, specially trained dogs to ward off the predators, reconciliation meetings between shepherds and environmentalists.[29] Defenders of the wolf found themselves continually frustrated by the horrific imagery that surrounded this species in popular mythology. Although zoologists and environmentalists did their best to educate the public about the wolves' real nature, portraying them as timid, doglike creatures who only wanted to be left in peace, many French citizens nonetheless persisted in envisioning them as cunning and rapacious killers. As of the year 2001, the struggle went on: "When all the lambs are gone, those wolves will begin eating humans!" cried one wrought-up shepherd. "If only they'd start with the imbeciles, . . . " muttered a green activist.[30]

Wolves were not the only species to stage a comeback after years of near-extinction or absence from the territory. Lynxes, once hunted to extinction in France, were reintroduced into the Swiss Jura mountains in 1985, and eventually made their way back across the border; under a new statute of stringent protection, their numbers grew to approximately twenty individuals by the late 1990s.[31] Vultures, the last of which had been shot as recently as the 1940s, were reintroduced into the Cévennes in the 1970s, and quickly began flourishing once again. Unfortunately, not all such efforts resulted in success: the Pyrenean brown bear, whose population still numbered around seventy individuals in the 1950s, had dwindled to seven by the late 1990s.[32] Local environmentalists launched a widely publicized campaign to save the reclusive animal—affectionately dubbed "Lou Moussu" in Pyrenean dialect ("Le Monsieur," or "The Gentleman")—even resorting to the last-ditch introduction of two Slovenian brown bears in 1996; but the pressure of a steadily shrinking habitat was apparently proving irresistible, and the bears continued to die off.[33]

As the new millennium began, the list of severely endangered animal species in France comprised 9 mammals, 22 birds, 2 reptiles, 3 amphibians, 3 fish, and 77 insects.[34] France still possessed the richest variety of bird populations in Europe—278 native species—and played a key role in continental migration patterns. Between the 1970s and late 1990s, only one type of bird, the arctic tern, ceased to frequent its former French habitats (a series of islets off the Breton coast); during the same period, six new species established themselves on the territory (only one of these through human intro-

duction).[35] The list of endangered plant species comprised 97 varieties ranging from trees to flowers and grasses; nine species were known to have become extinct during the twentieth century, out of a total number of some
4,800 domestic varieties. In 1988, France established a network of six National Botanical Conservatories (funded through the Ministry of the Environment), whose mission was to study, protect, and if necessary cultivate and
reintroduce endangered plant species throughout the French territory.[36]

Both the French government and the E.U. took increasingly vigorous
steps in the late 1980s and 1990s to protect threatened plants and animals.
In 1992 the E.U. launched "Natura 2000"—an ambitious conservation program linking the national parks and nature reserves of fifteen countries in a
continent-spanning wildlife network.[37] The major innovation here lay in
the official recognition that ecological challenges, just like the flights of
migratory birds or the drift of air pollution, passed freely across national
boundaries, and that effective measures of nature protection could only
be undertaken on a commensurately continental scale. Though this pathbreaking international structure was not scheduled to enter full-fledged
operation until 2004, the bureaucratic and legal steps for creating it were
already well under way in all fifteen E.U. member-states by the year 2000.
Two existing environmental decrees from Brussels—the "Birds" directive of
1979 and "Habitats" directive of 1992—provided the legal basis for Natura
2000, requiring member-states to submit an inventory of special protected
zones within their territories that would together make up the new continental network. France, as the European Union's largest nation, submitted in
1998 a list of 1,028 sites covering 5.7 percent of its territory for the "Habitats" directive; its list for the "Birds" directive comprised 115 sites covering
1.5 percent of its territory.[38] Dominique Voynet, in an April 2000 speech before the members of France Nature Environnement, singled out Natura 2000
as the one of the most important juridical instruments for nature protection
to affect the French territory in decades. "This European text," she said, "allows us at last to go beyond the *pointillisme* of individual reserves, parks, and
other local biotopes, and shift our perspective to the higher level of entire
ecological systems, taken in all their global complexity."[39]

> > >

What are we to conclude, then, from this brief overview? First, environmentalism has clearly made a huge difference for the French territory—putting
the brakes on many dangerous forms of pollution, and spurring a vigorous
and systematic effort of nature protection. Had the trajectory of the 1950s
continued unabated, France today would be a grievously disfigured country,
with large parts of its land simply unliveable. Instead, the French have shown
that they can recognize an emergent problem and move relatively swiftly to

address it—despite the sometimes considerable costs and exertions that this shift has entailed. Not only have the French avoided the catastrophic degradation of their country's environment, they have actually restored and strengthened many important ecosystems throughout the land.

Having said this, however, it is equally clear that the French territory remains far from a state of perfect health. Agriculture continues to pollute and pillage the soil; coastlines feel the pressure of urbanization; highways and power lines bite ever more deeply into the countryside; waterways and aquifers cloud over with the byproducts of chemical runoff; greenhouse gases waft into the skies; retreating wetlands or mountain habitats leave some plants and animals with no place to live. Overall, one gets the impression of a territory in which the worst excesses of industrial modernity have been effectively curbed, but in which many destructive forces remain active—on a subtler, and hence more insidious, level. In the words of Jacques Theys, a co-author of the *Plan National pour l'Environnement,*

> Our main concern during the past half-century has been to bring the environmental "flux" under control—pollution emissions, exhaustion of resources. Over the next century the challenge will consist more in undoing the damage we've already done: a much more aggressive effort to prevent irreversible harm before it happens, a systematic campaign to restore and rehabilitate degraded resource stocks and natural habitats.[40]

The Anthropocentric Perspective: Is the Light-Green Society Sustainable as a Habitat for Humans?

On the surface of it, the concept of sustainable development sounds simple enough: will we be able to keep our civilization going over the long haul? Will we end up exhausting our biospheric resources, or not? Will we drown in a sea of our own effluents, or not?

It turns out, however, that answering these kinds of questions is anything but straightforward. One Australian scholar actually sat down and counted how many distinct definitions of "sustainable development" he could find in the writings of environmentalists, economists, and philosophers: he came up with more than sixty![41] Arguably the most famous (and intuitively graspable) of these was given in 1987 by the Brundtland Report of the United Nations: "meeting the needs of the present without compromising the ability of future generations to meet their own needs."[42]

The key problem here, of course, resides in the word "future." By its very nature, the concept of sustainable development traces dotted lines into a distant tomorrow: long-term projections of economic performance, far-reaching trajectories of estimated natural resource use—and the truth is that humans have generally proved remarkably bad at such prognostication. What will future generations consider to be their "needs," and under what constellation of constraints will they be forced to meet them? The wildly sanguine forecast offered by Herman Kahn on the first page of this chapter was like a gauntlet deliberately thrown in the face of the Club of Rome and its experts—the "prophets of doom," as Kahn liked to call them. "Catastrophists" and "Cornucopians," they were dubbed by one exasperated British environmentalist in the 1980s, Stephen Cotgrove, as he sought to make sense of these two schools of thought and their ridiculously divergent predictions.[43]

Three distinct categories of human ignorance come into play here.[44] First, we do not know enough about the dynamics of most ecosystems to be able to forecast where and how they might break down: too many variables, not enough information. Second, we cannot predict what the wild card of technological innovation will bring: limitless clean energy or cataclysmic bio-engineered epidemics or none of the above? Third, we haven't the slightest idea what humans themselves will be up to during the coming century: warring or making friends, greedier or more modest, alienated from nature or ecologically deep?

Even if—for the sake of argument—one uncritically accepts the grim predictions of the 1972 Club of Rome report, and decides wholeheartedly to follow a prescription for "zero economic growth," it remains far from clear what this latter concept would require in practice. Would it mean freezing all producing and consuming at their 1972 levels? Would it entail, as Ernest Schumacher insisted, scaling back to a much smaller and more modest form of civilization? Would it necessitate calling a halt to most forms of technological innovation? Anyone addressing such questions runs into the same recurring problem: the fact that humans, for all their scientific data and computer models, actually do not know very much. They carry on much of their earthly activity under the numinous sign of "Clueless."

The German philosopher Hans Jonas proposed an ingenious way out of this epistemological impasse in 1979, with his book *The Imperative of Responsibility*, in which he set forth a concept that came to be known as "the precautionary principle." For Jonas, the increasingly profound dangers associated with technological innovations required a commensurate self-restraint on the part of the humans who developed them. In the case of certain very powerful technologies (such as genetic engineering, for example), the fact that we could not be absolutely sure whether they would someday prove harmful should not stop us from aggressively reevaluating their development in the present. With the stakes so frightfully high, Jonas maintained, it was morally necessary to err on the side of caution: in some cases, this might well necessitate abandoning (or at least postponing) certain promising lines of research and technological innovation.[45] Better to have missed out on a few promising new inventions through an excess of caution, he argued, than to be obliterated by one of our own creations because we proved unable to rein in our curiosity and ambition at a sufficiently early stage.

Jonas's idea, which understandably provoked heated debate in scientific and philosophical circles, ultimately proved widely persuasive. It became particularly useful in setting environmental policy, because it provided a handle for dealing with the inherent uncertainty that pervaded the prognostications of ecological science. Such uncertainty, according to the precautionary principle, should not stop government agencies from making the best "educated guess" they could about future trends, and designing their legislation accordingly. One hundred fifty nations formally applied this principle to their environmental policies through the United Nations Rio Declaration of 1992:

> Principle 15: In order to protect the environment, the precautionary approach shall be widely applied by States according to their capabilities. Where there are threats of serious or irreversible damage, lack of full scientific certainty shall not be used as a reason for postponing cost-effective measures to prevent environmental degradation.[46]

This precautionary principle (formalized in French jurisprudence through the Barnier Law of 1995) was not always easy to implement in practice, but at least it provided a fairly straightforward set of guidelines: even where high levels of controversy clouded an environmental decision, policymakers should make the best judgment that contemporary knowledge allowed, and take appropriate action without delay.[47]

> > >

In the spirit of this rather tenuous "management of unknowns," we can now hazard a few educated guesses of our own. Is the French society of the year 2000 compatible with basic principles of sustainable development? Almost certainly not.

First, it makes little sense to speak of a national society as being "sustainable," in separation from the broader global context. Even though the French have only a limited say in determining the environmental course charted by humanity as a whole, it will undoubtedly be their fate either to sink or to stay afloat alongside all the other passengers on the planetary boat. So long as vast portions of the earth, and of the human species, live under conditions of exploding population and wretched poverty—leading to an accelerating degradation of global ecological systems—it will matter little whether the French have put their own national house in order: the collapse of the ozone layer, or global warming, or various other planetary debacles, would catch up with them in the end.[48] In this sense, the long-term survival of the French, like that of other relatively prosperous peoples, is inextricably tied to that of the Third World.

By and large, the French record on this global front has been quite strong. France has signed onto virtually all the major international environmental treaties and accords, and has done a good job of living up to its pledges; in many cases, French diplomats and environmentalists have taken a leading role in bringing such international agreements into existence.[49] France currently ranks second in the world (after Japan) in the total cash amount of foreign aid it dispenses for Third World development each year; the French foreign aid budget constitutes 0.55 percent of GNP—twice as high a percentage as Japan's, and five times as high as that of the United States.[50] Most environmental experts agree that the world's rich countries are doing far too little to address systematically the environmental (and human) catastrophe taking place in the southern hemisphere of the globe. If every wealthy nation followed France's bold lead in this domain, there is no doubt that the chances of a favorable outcome would be considerably improved.

What about France's performance within its own territory? The basic requirements of sustainable development fall under two main headings, both marked by the concept of *dynamic equilibrium:* on the one hand, the need not to use resources more quickly than they can be replenished, and on the other, the need not to produce harmful effluents faster than they can be neutralized by a healthy biosphere.[51] By most reasonable measures, contemporary French society flunks both these tests.

Environmental economists love to talk about energy consumption, because it is easily quantifiable, and because it can in some ways be used to sum up, in a single all-encompassing variable, the behavior of entire social systems. "All is energy," goes the (rather nerdy) motto.[52] And the news on the French energy front is not good. Despite the considerable success of new technologies in raising the efficiency of all sorts of machines during the past half-century, the overall pattern remains unmistakable: more oil, more electricity, more cars, more planes, more appliances, more needs. Energy consumption has risen steadily and massively—about 350 percent between 1960 and 1997–and is projected to continue to rise for the foreseeable future by as much as one percent to three percent per year.[53] France's "energy pie" in 1997 looked like this: about 41 percent oil, 29 percent nuclear-generated electricity, 13 percent natural gas, 6 percent coal, 3 percent electricity cogenerated from trash incineration, and 8 percent renewable sources (hydroelectric, wind, solar, biomass, etc.).[54] Three quarters of the renewable energy came from hydroelectric dams.

Even the most pusillanimous of forecasters could scarcely refrain from pronouncing a trenchant negative judgment on the "sustainability" of this scenario. Energy consumption rising, 92 percent of energy coming from nonrenewable sources, insufficient conservation measures: the only positive note here, ironically, lies in the fact that France's heavy wager on nuclear power (29 percent of total energy consumption) places it in a comparatively favorable position for controlling greenhouse gas emissions (since nuclear generators produce negligible amounts of these gases). To an environmentally concerned French citizen, the thought that many other countries are doing even worse (first in line: the cretinously gas-guzzling United States) affords scant consolation.

Some French natural resources, such as wood, are actually in fine shape. French foresters estimate that the nation's woodlands have increased in size since the 1960s, by about 0.6 percent per year; the trees, by and large, are in reasonably good health, and are being replaced as quickly as they are harvested.[55] But this appears to be rather the exception than the rule: a more common pattern is the one established in the domain of food production. French farms continue to evolve in the direction of heavy mechanization, high productivity, and chemical-intensive methods of cultivation: erosion, polluted aquifers, tainted drinking water, and deteriorating soil quality now form part of the litany of worries facing the nation's countryside. Though modest agricultural reforms are under way, they have not altered the basic trajectory of French farming into a world of agribusiness in which long-term environmental balance constitutes a relatively low priority. As for the nation's fisheries, according to government studies, they are being "chronically and systematically" overexploited; stocks of many important species are diminishing at an alarming rate, and so far most policies aimed at reversing this trend have resulted in complete failure.[56]

On the other side of the sustainability equation lies the production of harmful effluents. Here, French society has made major progress since the 1960s, cutting back on a wide range of pollutants and actually eliminating some of them altogether. Nevertheless, certain persistent weak spots remain, the most salient being greenhouse gases and agricultural chemicals, not to mention the unique category of radioactive wastes. Government policy in this latter domain has amounted to little more than a decision to store these "megatoxins" in deep underground vaults, letting them accumulate over the years, while waiting for a safe and cost-effective method of treating them to be discovered. This constitutes, by any standard, a rather remarkable way to deal with a major industrial hazard: it might be likened (somewhat loosely) to someone who refuses to stop smoking cigarettes, in the confident expectation that modern medicine will someday find a cure for lung cancer. While scientific experts can easily be found on both sides of the nuclear debate—some arguing that present storage methods are safe for the long haul, others contending that they are dangerous and irresponsible—the current policy amounts at best to postponing the resolution of a serious environmental problem, leaving it to future generations to figure out how to fix it.[57] Almost by definition, this runs counter to the very essence of sustainability.

The production and treatment of trash by French society in the early 2000s continues to offer an emblematic portrait of the "civilization of More." Despite valiant efforts at recycling and important positive strides in resource conservation, the total volume of trash rose by 370 percent between the late 1970s and mid-1990s. True, the overall "flow of garbage" was much cleaner and more environmentally safe in 1996 than in 1979, because of major advances in the technologies of incineration and disposal. But a simple fact remained undeniable: the sheer volume of material resources passing through French production and consumption had more than tripled in 17 years; more than two-thirds of these resources were not being recycled or replenished.[58]

Here, therefore, we come to the "bottom line" of French society's sustainability. Despite the significant degree of greening that has taken place in the mentalities and economic practices of French citizens over the past forty years, their country in the early 2000s is still borrowing from the future in order to live richly in the present. In a wide variety of ways, the French are using resources more quickly than they can be replenished, and producing effluents faster than they can be absorbed. To be sure, the past few decades have witnessed a rapidly accelerating institutionalization of environmentalist ideas—in government, economic practice, the educational system—indeed, in all the rich complexity of France's social and cultural life. But there is no denying the dauntingly long road that still lies ahead, before anything remotely resembling a sustainable equilibrium could be achieved.

> > >

In 1971, Robert Poujade had presided over a Ministry of the Environment whose mission was to restrain the worst excesses of industrial society, fending off chemical dumps or pleading with citizens not to toss their trash into the nearest ravine. Most French men and women, in the 1970s, still identified "the environment" with certain tangible and highly personalized aspects of their surroundings: the creek behind one's house, the mountain meadow where one went for family picnics. Protecting these kinds of natural spaces seemed a worthy goal for civic action; but once people felt that this purpose was being accomplished, they were satisfied.

As the decades went by, however, the picture steadily became more complicated.[59] Saving a creek, it turned out, meant more than just stopping the local paper mill from dumping chemicals: it also meant paying attention to zoning restrictions, fish migration patterns, wild bird habitats, air quality. It meant working with a bewilderingly varied array of actors, public and private, domestic and foreign, economic, social, and cultural. The multidimensional nature of environmental problems—their inherently interconnected and imbricated character—increasingly forced people to think more broadly, to redefine the problems themselves, taking into account ever-wider and more labyrinthine contexts. Soon it was not just creeks and meadows, but society itself, and "the quality of life," that became objects of critical scrutiny—patterns of consumption, the blind forces of a global market, the types of products being made, the types of needs being fostered.

Thus, Dominique Voynet found herself presiding over a very different mission than the one that had faced Poujade. Although the defense of natural spaces remained a central priority in the year 2000, "protecting the environment" now connoted much more as well: it meant actively shaping and channeling the way people interacted with the whole territory. Rather than "intervention"—a relatively punctual and circumscribed concept—environmentalists and policymakers now spoke in terms of continuous monitoring, assessment, and administration. In French, the recurring phrases were "gestion du territoire," "gestion de l'environnement," "gestion des ressources"—the key term being, of course, "gestion" (management), with its connotations of supervising, organizing, regulating. Not surprisingly, such "gestion" comprised far more than the activities of any single social constituency or government agency. Farming, manufacturing, transportation, tourism, taxation, fishing and forestry, air and water quality, consumer products, recycling, flood control, national parks, chemical effluents, biotechnologies, noise abatement, regional planning—in all these domains the eyes and hands of environmental experts and government officials now ranged over the land, incessantly scrutinizing, adjusting, tweaking, groping for control.

In Poujade's time, the "social" and the "natural" had still been perceived by most French men and women as worlds apart. The environment had seemed to them like something "out there"—a domain separate from the way they earned a living and went about their daily lives, a distinctive sphere of natural spaces and creatures, threatened by human encroachments, and worthy of protection.

In a mere thirty years' time, the qualitative shift was notable. By the year 2000, the environment connoted something that went beyond "out there" or "in here"—it seemed everywhere at once, a "total" factor closely interwoven with all aspects of social and economic life. Refrigerator and ozone hole, automobile and global warming, ham sandwich and polluted countryside, wooden table and disappearing jungles—"the environment" continuously linked the human and nonhuman worlds in a bidirectional relationship that could no longer be escaped or ignored.

In Part IV we explore the broader significance of this "blurred" social order: the place of human beings within the fragile web of ecological constraints they had so dramatically come to recognize; the place of nature in an increasingly technological world.

PART IV

The Future of Nature in a Light-Green World

LONG-TERM GLOBAL IMPLICATIONS

12 The Light-Green Horizon

The time of the finite world has begun.
—Paul Valéry, 1931[1]

Broader Implications of the French Story

It will not have escaped the reader's attention that the phenomena described in the first three parts of this book could also be observed taking place in the broader world, well beyond the boundaries of France. Certainly, the French case had its own peculiarities, its own fascinating quirks; but, seen from a global perspective, some version of the transformation we have explored appears to have swept through virtually all the industrial democracies. My underlying hypothesis in Part IV, therefore, is that the emergence of the light-green society constitutes a general characteristic of the second half of the twentieth century, discernible (with significant variations) throughout the democratic portions of the industrialized world.

A rigorous demonstration of this hypothesis would require that the same kind of detailed analysis undertaken in this book be applied, one by one, to several dozen nations. Needless to say, such a gargantuan project goes well beyond the scope of the present work. I will content myself, therefore, with laying out some of the suggestive ways in which the specific case we have studied affords plausible grounds for making this broader, more generalized inference: that the concept of the light-green society constitutes an illuminating paradigm not just for France but for many other kindred nations as well.

As we saw in Parts I and II, the genesis of the light-green society was rooted in two primary factors: rapid technological and economic modernization, and the growing environmentalist response that this modernization provoked. Without a doubt, the French experience of this process possessed several distinctive features. France industrialized later than some nations, such as Britain and Germany, and earlier than others, such as Italy and Spain; its struggle for modernization in the decades after 1945, strongly conditioned by its harrowing defeat in the world war, bore more than the usual measure of angst about national autonomy and soul-searching about national identity. The French made unstinting use of their state apparatus in propelling and channeling the modernization process—considerably more than the United States, considerably less than the Soviet Union, about the same as West Germany or Sweden (albeit in different forms). The French, moreover, proved particularly attached to the practices and meanings of a peasant society: they had to pry their hands loose from that mode of farming, finger by finger, wincing with pain. All these national particularities are summed up by the tangible figures of the nuclear reactor, the Concorde, and the peasant village, which have recurred like leitmotifs through our narrative.

But these important peculiarities should not distract us from an equally salient fact, namely, that French society, seen from a broader comparative perspective, did *not* follow a unique or strikingly special path into technological modernity (no matter how ardently some French citizens might have wanted to believe this). Taken as a whole, the majority of the social, economic, and technological changes that this nation experienced during the postwar years were in fact *shared,* in large measure, by her European neighbors and (to varying degrees) by her fellow democracies throughout the world. This was true not only of the modernization process, as it swept through farms and factories, homes and halls of government; it applied to the rise of ecology as well.

Consider the following impressionistic list of features, all of which have typically formed part of the characteristic "signature" of social and economic modernity in democratic polities: the emergence of a consumer economy, hell-bent on building homes and offices and filling them with appliances, gadgets, and accouterments; the decline of agriculture as a major sector of the national economy; the importance (real and perceived) of technology as an economic growth factor; an increasingly tight web of connections to the global economy, through imports, exports, and multinational corporations; the link between technological prowess and military rank; the proliferation of transportation and communication technologies; the steep rise in energy consumption; the institutionalization of the welfare state; the alternation of moderate left and moderate right in political power; an independent judicial system; a competitive array of uncensored mass media; fairly stable population levels; high levels of literacy and education; low infant mortality; and the enfranchisement and rising empowerment of women. These kinds of features all manifested themselves in France during the past century or so, many of them advancing with particular swiftness after 1945; but they are not, of course, exclusively French. On the contrary, they merely underscore the extent to which the French case—despite its colorful peculiarities—partook of the same broad constellation of shifts and adjustments that was emerging throughout large swaths of the world. The modernization of France was certainly tinged by the presence of important idiosyncratic elements, but in its larger outlines it followed a more general and ubiquitous pattern.

Much the same can be said for the rise of green awareness and influence: in France as in other countries, it passed through the particular lens of national history and culture, but ultimately it remained clearly identifiable as the expression of a broader pattern. The rapid economic growth of the twentieth century did not *automatically* beget green movements. Rather, as we have seen, certain key elements had to come together, under specific propitious conditions: a scientific establishment capable of recognizing the emerging stresses on the environment; a public sphere free and open enough to allow for the dissemination of information and for the gathering of concerned individuals into effective associations and political forces; a dissident counterculture sufficiently potent and widespread to challenge the social and economic status quo; a population prosperous and well educated enough to resonate with the green message and give it a central role in public life; a competitive political system, in which persuasive new ideas could make headway and become part of the electoral mainstream; a civic and legal establishment sufficiently malleable, and open to democratic pressures, to permit the steady infiltration of new priorities into public policy and institutions; a responsive and flexible economic system in which shifting consumer choices could rapidly transmit new values into the processes of manufacturing and marketing. All these features (to name just the main ones) formed part of the particular historical constellation that rendered the light-green society thinkable and achievable: this constellation began emerging in France after 1960, but it was also simultaneously manifesting itself in the United

States, Canada, Germany, Britain, Sweden, New Zealand, and a dozen other countries. After a certain time lag had elapsed, moreover, the contagion spread to other similarly structured and similarly sensitized societies: Italy, Spain, Japan, Mexico, Korea, India, and others.

Here too, to be sure, the French greens soon exhibited their own significant particularities: a relatively tamer and more humanized conception of nature, going hand-in-hand with a strong affection for rural traditions; an ingrained resistance to the siren songs of Deep Ecology; a willingness to give critical but serious consideration to high-tech solutions; a classic French flair for schismatic bickering and infighting; a strong network of fiercely independent grassroots organizations; a national parliament rendered inaccessible to fringe parties by carefully crafted electoral rules; an exceptionally forbidding milieu for antinuclear activism. But these national traits, for all their indubitable importance, should not be allowed to obscure the fundamental continuities and similarities between the French greens and their counterparts in other countries. Their ideological origins, the goals for which they fought, their methods and organizational patterns, their social and electoral constituencies, the opponents they encountered, the problems they faced (both internally and externally)—these all formed part of a larger cross-national pattern, within which the French case fit squarely and solidly.[2]

This mix of national particularities and international commonalities means that the greening of the industrial democracies—even as it developed along parallel lines—looks intriguingly different in each individual case: the United States has an EPA (Environmental Protection Agency) and no Ministry of the Environment; Germany has a huge antinuclear movement and France has EDF; Australia has the immense Outback and France has the Pointe du Raz. The list of such contrasts could go on indefinitely, and its importance should certainly not be underestimated. The point here, however, is to underscore the equally important way in which the case of France seems to form part of a broader structural transformation—a shift in the way the peoples of all these countries were framing their place within nature.

If, for example, we survey the cultural and economic landscape of the relatively diverse democracies just mentioned above (United States, Australia, Germany), we immediately recognize *in all three of them* the central paradoxical features associated in this study with the light-green society: the presence of a vibrant and influential green movement, side-by-side with a tenacious popular faith in economic growth and technological progress; a consumer economy that incorporates many elements of ecological thinking, while continuing to offer shoppers an explosively proliferating gamut of products and services; widespread practices of recycling and other forms of nature conservation, coexisting with rampant increases in energy consumption, the volume of trash, and the use of cars and planes; environmentalist ideas playing a regular role in political discourse, but then very often taking a back seat to other priorities; the systematic institutionalization of environmental protection within the laws and the apparatus of government, while at the same time key green initiatives languish for lack of funding or support; the business world scrambling to incorporate ecological measures into everyday practices of production and selling, while still focusing primarily on short-term competitiveness and the bottom line.

All these features have had their own distinctive history within each nation, of course. The environmentalists of one country might focus ruefully on their nation's relative "backwardness" in the legal sphere, while the greens of another country might point an accusatory finger at their country's political establishment, still colluding more cozily than they would like with big business. The variations are bound to be many and important; but, nevertheless, the overall constellation of these features should prove easily recognizable to any attentive American, Australian, or German. As we look around us, we cannot help but observe that these paradoxical qualities have come to form part of the "givenness" of our everyday social world; and as we travel abroad within this subset of the world's nations, we are likely to find that the similarities from country to country are simply too striking to ignore.

What this suggests, therefore, is an underlying pattern experienced to varying degrees by the peoples of virtually all the industrial democracies during the second half of the twentieth century. It suggests that those peoples, faced with a tough choice between technological modernity and a green vision of the future, did roughly what the French did: they hedged, and in effect chose both. Through a long, incremental process of improvisation and give-and-take, they pieced together a new kind of social order—an increasingly pervasive overlay of ecological ideas and environmental constraints upon the growth-driven, consumer-oriented system inherited from mid-century. In short: it suggests that they each launched their own versions of the light-green society.

Humans and Nature on a Shrinking Earth

If the foregoing hypothesis is valid, and the case of France can be read as the local expression of a much broader phenomenon, then we immediately confront a new set of questions: what are the implications of the light-green social order, if its features are played out on a scale that embraces not just one nation, but large portions of planet Earth as a whole? If the pattern exhibited in France (or some cognate version of that pattern) gradually came to be writ large on a global canvas, where would such a transformation leave us? What would a "light-green world" look like? What would it feel like to live in?

We arrive, with these questions, at the culminating phase of this book: the task of evaluating the light-green society, from the most basic and generalized perspective, as a human and ecological totality—as one mode (among many possible ones) of establishing a human place within the natural world. This is, of necessity, a speculative task, one that entails standing back from the story we have told and surveying it at a relatively large scale, tracing past patterns and envisioning potential future trajectories over long units of time. It is also a broadly philosophical task, requiring us to pose fundamental questions about how humans fit into and derive meaning from their natural surroundings—and how they might do so in a light-green future.

My aim here, in other words, is to go considerably beyond the scope of the discussion in Parts I, II, and III, posing questions that take us outside the frame-of-reference of a single European country and the late twentieth century. The issues that interest me in Part IV are the more basic (and viscerally gripping) ones that have lain implicit, for the most part, in our discussion thus far: What are we in the process of doing to our terrestrial home? What shape will the human relationship with nature take over the next century? How much of a say do we have in determining how that relationship develops?

The core issue here can be summed up by the image of the "shrinking planet"—the sense that a rapidly rising human population, with its accelerating technological powers, has made the Earth feel like a much smaller place than ever before. This phenomenon considerably predates the twentieth century: it arguably has its roots in the Industrial Revolution, or even earlier, in the seafaring exploration that opened up large parts of the world to European colonization. By the early decades of the twentieth century, an alert observer like the poet Paul Valéry was already taking stock of it:

> The era of empty landscapes, of open territories, of places belonging to no one, thus the era of free expansion, has ended. Nowhere can you find a rock that doesn't have someone's flag stuck into it; no more blank spaces on the map; no clear expanse lying beyond customs barriers and laws; not a single remote tribe whose daily affairs do not generate dossiers in the far-away office of some scribbling humanist. *The time of the finite world has begun.*[3]

Valéry made this observation in 1931: he died fourteen years later, just as the Second World War was ending, and as the harsh light over Hiroshima was rendering his intuition about a "finite world" more painfully accurate than ever. The revolutionary destructiveness of nuclear weapons soon brought home to large numbers of postwar citizens a simple fact that proved crucial to the subsequent development of environmentalist awareness: the fact that humans now possessed the technological capacity to incinerate themselves, and the entire planet, whenever they wished.

The psychological implications of this development are hard to overstate. Throughout much of recorded history, nature had been perceived as the vast domain within which the human world resided—Mother Nature, the all-encompassing substrate, the primal order from which we all came. And yet, in the decades following World War II, this millennial relationship appeared to undergo a dramatic change—a reversal of the age-old power ratio, in which master and servant traded positions. After Hiroshima, it was not so clear anymore where the power lay. From time to time, an earthquake or a hurricane obliterated some hapless settlement, and the world's pundits began somberly admonishing their fellow humans to beware of hubris, to remember that Mother Nature still held our lives in her hands. But as the decades went by it became increasingly clear that industrial civilization had itself become something of a hurricane, its impact leaving nothing untouched, from the atmosphere up above to the aquifers down below. It began to dawn on more and more people that, if Mother Nature held our lives in her hands, we also held *her* life in *our* hands! An ancient set of power relations appeared to be shifting under our feet—a shift that did not come quickly or evenly, but that will no doubt remain one of the most salient features of our time.

Paul Valéry was not alone in feeling a deep-seated claustrophobia as he contemplated this epochal shift: indeed, it was arguably in North America, where large swaths of territory had remained relatively untouched well into the twentieth century, that the sense of loss hit hardest. In the late 1980s, an American journalist named Bill McKibben, writing in *The New Yorker* magazine, voiced Valéry's lament in even starker terms. By century's end, according to McKibben, even the most remote areas of the globe had come to feel the effects of the technological activities undertaken by our insatiably restless, ambitious species. Even in the vast northern forests, even in the depths of the Antarctic, nature had been decisively altered by human technology—either directly, through human intervention, or indirectly, through its side-effects. No territory on the planet, for example, escaped the depletion of the ozone layer, or the creeping rise of CO_2 emissions—both of these phenomena being measurable side-effects of human activity. And in this sense, McKibben felt, we had lost something. We could no longer tell ourselves that *somewhere*, we knew not where, a truly untouched, pristine corner of wilderness still survived. Every place had now been touched in one way or another by human artifice. We had witnessed nothing less than the end of wild nature.[4]

Whether or not one accepts this kind of starkly framed argument (we take it up in detail in chapter 14), it does get us right to the heart of the matter. One way of understanding the rise of environmentalism, in the decades after 1960, is precisely as a response to this dawning awareness, this gnawing (and increasingly urgent) sense of loss. Not just in France, but throughout the world, the fervent defenders of nature sought to tackle head-on the phenomenon of the "shrinking planet," reorienting industrial civilization toward a radically new equilibrium between the natural and the artificial. Wild nature, they hoped, could still be saved; the human world of artifice could still be beaten back, or at least held at bay; somehow a lasting balance could still be struck.

And yet, as we have seen in the foregoing chapters, such a balance proved elusive (to say the least), and the outcome by the year 2000 was something much more ambiguous: the complex tangle of half-measures and hybrids that made up the light-green society. This new social order gradually absorbed a significant portion of the environmentalists' message, incorporating many of their reforms into its daily functioning; but it remained, as much as ever, a society profoundly committed to economic growth, the consumerist cornucopia, and massively accelerating technological intervention in the material world.

Here, therefore, lies the crux of the matter: how would the advent of a global light-green era affect the phenomenon of the "shrinking Earth?" What becomes of wild nature, in a world increasingly permeated by human devices and activities? Can the deep paradox at the heart of the light-green society—the attempted fusion between technological modernity and ecological values—ever result in a coherent planetary equilibrium between these two polar extremes? These are the broad philosophical issues we explore in Part IV, taking contemporary France as our point of departure, but posing our questions with an eye to the global *longue durée*. Our discussion will focus on four analytically distinct groups of questions, each taken up in turn in the chapters that follow:

1. *Artificialization.* What exactly are people like Valéry and McKibben referring to when they speak of the "finite world," the artificialization of the planet? What is the basic scope and character of this phenomenon?

2. *Wild nature.* Is it true, as McKibben argues, that the concept itself of "pristine" nature has become an anachronism, a thing of the past? What does the word "wilderness" mean in today's increasingly technological world?

3. *The blurring of the social and the natural.* In a light-green future, what relationship seems likely to emerge between nature and artifice, between the wild and the tame? How much leeway exists for human agency and choice, in the shaping of that relationship?

4. *Cosmic nature.* With the gradual advance of space exploration, will human beings come to encounter another kind of "natural environment" beyond Valéry's "finite world"—among the surrounding planets and stars? In a light-green era, might it be possible for outer space to begin functioning in human culture as an extension of the terrestrial wilderness?

13 Artificialization and Its Discontents

The idea is that of the earth not only becoming covered by myriads of grains of thought, but becoming enclosed in a single thinking envelope so as to form, functionally, no more than a single vast grain of thought on the sidereal scale.
—Pierre Teilhard de Chardin (1955)[1]

This is what we mean by eco-power: this thoroughgoing application of scientific knowledge and technological capabilities, through the lens of political power, over all living systems.
Pierre Lascoumes (1994)[2]

The Rising Tide of Artifice

One of the defining features of human civilization, as it has evolved in the past two hundred years, might be summed up as the accelerating "anthropization" of the planet, the emerging power to touch, pick up and put down, shape or transform, just about anything we please. This process has two facets: a quantitative dimension and a qualitative dimension. The quantitative dimension runs roughly parallel to the exponential increase in such indices as human population or human energy consumption. On this subject, the graph in figure 8, showing human population growth, speaks more eloquently than words.[3] Even by this crudest of measures—sheer numbers of us, with all our needs, projects, and behaviors—the impression of extremely

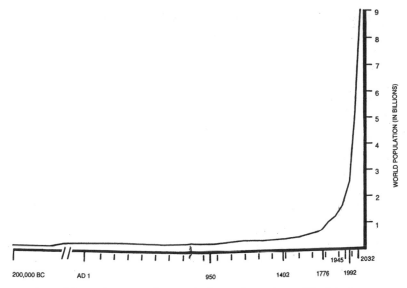

Figure 8. World population trends over the *longue durée*. (From "Earth in the Balance" by Al Gore. Copyright © 1992 by Senator Al Gore. Reprinted by permission of Houghton Mifflin Company. All right reserved.).

rapid quantitative expansion is simply inescapable. Nearly every measure that geographers and demographers can muster points in the same direction, showing the myriad activities of our species spilling over the territory—and into the skies and waters—almost faster than any one of us can really grasp.[4]

A recent book by the historian J. R. McNeill, *Something New Under the Sun*, offers a global *tour d'horizon* of this phenomenon, analyzing in systematic detail the growing human impact on the material world. It makes for breathtaking (and depressing) reading. A fourteen-fold increase in global economic activity, a sixteen-fold increase in energy use, a forty-fold increase in industrial output, a quintupling of irrigated acreage, a seventeen-fold increase in carbon dioxide emissions, a thirty-five-fold increase in marine fish catch—such is the nature of the quantitative "bottom line" for the twentieth century.[5] "The human race," writes McNeill,

> without intending anything of the sort, has undertaken a gigantic, uncontrolled experiment on the earth. In time, I think, this will appear as the most important aspect of twentieth-century history, more so than World War II, the communist enterprise, the rise of mass literacy, the spread of democracy, or the growing emancipation of women. . . .
>
> In natural systems as in human affairs, there are thresholds and so-called nonlinear effects. . . . Water temperature in the tropical Atlantic can grow

warmer and warmer without generating any hurricanes. But once that water passes 26 degrees Celsius, it begins to promote hurricanes: a threshold passed, a switch thrown, simply by an incremental increase. The environmental history of the twentieth century is different from that of time past not merely because ecological changes were greater and faster, but also because increased intensities threw some switches. For example, incremental increases in fishing effort brought total collapse in some oceanic fisheries. The cumulation of many increased intensities may throw some grand switches, producing very basic changes on the earth. No one knows, and no one will know until it starts to happen—if then.[6]

Mining the seabed, building roads, pipelines, and power-transmission lines, damming rivers, drilling into the earth's depths, densely criss-crossing the sky with air travel routes, filling the lower reaches of space with satellites, cramming the airwaves with data bits, dragging nets across vast ocean fisheries, unleashing urban sprawl in the deserts: even though the world is large, the sheer number and range of our activities are increasing their pressure, rapidly and tremendously, with every passing year.

As for the qualitative dimension of the artificialization process, it too is best described in the language of exponential curves. The variety of machines, the capabilities of technology, the number of scientists, the number of patents, the proliferation of newly discovered (and newly created) entities ranging from cloned sheep to subatomic particles—once again, the trend is one of accelerating expansion in human abilities to reshape organic and inorganic matter in fundamental ways.[7] One of the most vivid exemplars of this qualitative dimension lies in the development of genetically modified organisms—virtually science fiction only a few decades ago, and today pouring out of the laboratories, through the farms of agribusiness, into our kitchens and stomachs. Genetic technology ratchets the meaning of artificialization to a new level: it means reaching with our devices into the innermost constitution of a living thing, and reconfiguring its internal life-processes according to our needs and purposes. A brief survey of recent trends in French biotechnology can provide us with a useful (and broadly representative) glimpse into the issues raised by this rapidly developing scientific field.

Machine/Symbol: Biotechnologies

Humans have been altering plants and animals with great gusto for thousands of years, using a variety of crossbreeding and selection methods: the results have sometimes proved rather disconcerting (bonsai tree, dachshund) but have generally remained uncontroversial until recently. Then, in the 1990s, as genetics research took advantage of high-speed computers and new splicing methods, the topic reached a watershed. Scientists revealed in 1998 that they had succeeded in creating a "fishberry," taking an antifreeze gene from the Arctic flounder and inserting it into the DNA of strawberries, thereby rendering the new breed of fruit frost-resistant.[8] This was not, to put it mildly, something that you could have gotten a fish and a strawberry to do in the old-fashioned way. Announcements like these, coupled with the appearance of a cloned sheep named Dolly on the front pages of newspapers in 1997, stirred up a wave of controversy that shows no signs of abating.

Europeans have generally reacted with considerably more alarm to these scientific developments than Americans; within Europe, the populations marked by the most negative perception of genetic manipulation tend to be those of Austria, Sweden, Norway, and Germany, while the Italians, Spaniards, Greeks, and Portuguese seem much readier to embrace the new technology.[9] France lies squarely in the statistical middle, with about 40 percent of the population believing that biotechnologies will ultimately prove beneficial, and about 20 percent of the population holding that they are dangerous and should be stopped. (Researchers have speculated that the "North-South" difference in these results can be at least partly explained by correlating it with the higher level of publicly available information on biotechnologies that circulates in the northern nations.)[10]

Apart from the more spectacular cases like the fishberry or Dolly the sheep, which have predictably garnered the most attention, the development of biotechnologies has been quietly advancing along several fronts—particularly in the domain of agricultural crops. A strain of corn created by the firm Novartis, for example, incorporates a gene from the bacterium *Bacillus thurengiensis*, which renders it toxic to certain insect pests; the bug-resistant corn is now widely grown in both the United States and Europe.[11] Monsanto, for its part, offers farmers a strain of rapeseed (no pun intended) that has been rendered genetically resistant to the company's premier herbicide, Roundup; when the two products are used together, the rapeseed flourishes and all the weeds around it disappear as if by magic.[12] Both the Novartis corn and the Monsanto rapeseed are present in food items currently being sold on both sides of the Atlantic.

Approximately 85 percent of the research being done in France on transgenic species focuses on plants; the animal kingdom is being approached more gingerly.[13] Still, the developments that came over the horizon in the 1990s include the treatment and prevention of disease in farm animals by means of recombinant proteins; the creation of genetically identical laboratory animals for use in biomedical experiments; the selection and/or enhancement of desirable traits in farm animals; and the creation of transgenic pigs whose organs could one day be used as transplants in humans (without the risk of immune-system complications).[14]

Given the potentially enormous market for these kinds of genetically modified organisms, it is not surprising that both the private and public sectors have invested heavily in biotechnological research. In 1986, the French government created a small agency, the Commission on Biomolecular Engineering, to oversee research in this domain and to grant permits for the experimental cultivation of transgenic crops: in the first decade of its existence, its caseload grew more than tenfold.[15] In 1998, France became the first country in Europe to approve the commercial cultivation of a transgenic plant (Novartis corn).

French environmentalists, while stopping short of advocating an outright ban on all biotechnologies, have raised three major concerns about them.[16] First, they worry about "genetic pollution"—for example, the unintended cross-breeding of transgenic plants, through airborne fertilization or other forms of spontaneous pollination, across the boundaries of their original fields and into the population of wild plants. If this were to happen, for instance, with a herbicide-proof rapeseed, then farmers might someday face an onslaught from a new generation of "super-weeds." A second area of concern lies in the potential loss of biodiversity, as farmers worldwide concentrate their production on an increasingly narrow gamut of transgenic species, abandoning thousands of old-fashioned animal breeds and plant seed strains that simply cannot compete with their high-performing cousins. Finally, the environmentalists worry about an escalating commercialization of living things, as firms invest millions in the development of various forms of transgenic plant and animal life, and then (understandably) seek to defend their investments through a vigorous application of patents and other forms of property rights.

Since dealing with these kinds of intractable but crucial issues will take time, many environmentalists advocate a moratorium on biotechnologies, arguing that the precautionary principle was incorporated into French law precisely to handle this type of controversial, cutting-edge scientific field. They also advocate greater transparency in the way the state's Commission on Biomolecular Engineering reaches its decisions; more substantial opportunities for common citizens and environmental associations to have a say in policymaking; and a nationwide labeling system for food items, requiring all products coming from transgenic sources to be readily identifiable as such.[17]

In June 1998 the French government showed that it was paying attention.

Acting under the auspices of a special parliamentary commission, it invited a group of fourteen citizens (all of them nonscientists, and selected by an independent opinion-polling agency) to participate in a two-day seminar on genetically modified organisms. This "citizens' conference" was widely followed and commented upon in the media, as scientists and environmentalists presented the pros and cons of the subject in considerable detail. In the end the participants were asked to reach practical conclusions: they voted against the idea of a moratorium, but strongly urged the government to establish a food labeling system.[18]

Through biotechnology, human artifice moves to a new level: from the relatively superficial manipulation and reshaping of natural objects, to the creation of new forms of life itself. Holding a fishberry and a regular strawberry in the palm of one's hand (or even popping them into one's mouth), one would quite possibly fail to tell them apart; but the difference is still there, profound and unsettling. Not only does the fishberry scramble the identities of two very different kinds of organism; it undermines, perhaps irreparably, the conceptual boundary between what is made and what is given, the designed and the spontaneous, artifact and creature. Inside this small red fruit, a triangle of blurred relations now resides: man-animal-plant, a taste of things to come.

La Gestion du Vivant: The "Management of All Living Things"

In France, as in the rest of the industrialized world, reactions to the accelerating process of artificialization have ranged widely—from enthusiasm to despair. Let us consider two extreme cases.

In 1955, shortly after the death of the French Jesuit priest and paleontologist Pierre Teilhard de Chardin, his followers published a book he had been working on for nearly twenty years, *The Phenomenon of Man.* Teilhard had been regarded by his superiors in the Catholic hierarchy as a dangerously outlandish thinker: he had been forced to give up his teaching position at the Catholic Institute in Paris, and then was "exiled" for two decades to the remote deserts of western China, where he worked on archaeological digs and wrote down (but obediently refrained from publishing) his ongoing reflections on cosmology.[19]

His book created a sensation when it first came out, because it offered a highly original synthesis of Western scientific and religious worldviews, centered around the concept of evolution. For Teilhard, the history of the universe could best be rendered intelligible as a single, teleological story: the progression of matter through ever-higher stages of complexity and creative order, culminating in the appearance of the human species on earth. Here, with humankind, the cosmic movement leaped to a new level, into the realm of ideas—or, in Teilhard's words, from the material level of the biosphere to the spiritual level of the "noosphere." The noospheric progression continued upward through human history, with the rise of ever more complex forms of civilization, until—at some unspecified future moment—it too would reach its culminating moment of ripeness. The destiny of the human species, as Teilhard saw it, was to saturate the earth thoroughly with its intelligence, thereby counteracting the universe's downward slide of entropy: this tiny planet, which had once been nothing but a habitat, would one day come under the total grasp of human technology and understanding. At that moment—the Omega point, he called it—the world would end, as the inner purpose of the cosmic adventure flowered forth in the final union of the physical and the spiritual, of Man and God.

Teilhard's synthesis, for all its originality, was not without echoes in the works of other thinkers. In some respects, for example, it bore a striking similarity to Hegel's depiction of history as the upward march of Spirit toward an equally symphonic apotheosis.[20] Nevertheless, to a reader of the early twenty-first century, it could not help but seem rather poignantly dated: its brash optimism, totalizing narrative, and easy subordination of the biosphere to human ends, were likely to strike a dissonant chord. To attain complete mental and physical domination over the material world before shedding it like an old skin: far from embodying a utopian hope, this might even be construed as an unwittingly (but none the less profoundly) dystopian vision.

Such would undoubtedly be the judgment of one scholar, Pierre Lascoumes, a sociologist who has written extensively about the assimilation of environmentalist ideas in French society, and whose response to artificialization stands at the opposite extreme from Teilhard's.[21] Following closely on the theoretical work of Michel Foucault, Lascoumes reads modern French history as a story of institutions and normative practices closing in ever more tightly around individuals, controlling their lives in ever more sophisticated and inescapable ways. The nineteenth-century prisons and asylums described by Foucault, the twentieth-century welfare state with its pervasive forms of social control—these are only steps on the way to an even more tightly meshed social order, which Lascoumes calls "eco-power." The picture he paints is reminiscent of Orwell's *1984* or Huxley's *Brave New World*, but without the crude features of blatant dictatorship: in the more subtle (and insidious) embrace of eco-power, humans are simply doing what they do best, namely, imposing rational order and predictability on every aspect of their material and social surroundings. "In this system," Lascoumes writes, we still find the imperative that Foucault described—that of *optimizing life* through various mechanisms of knowing, surveillance, and regulation—but now this imperative is extended beyond human society, and encompasses all living things. . . . Biological and ecological norms are now integrated into political decisions and public policy, making their way into the politics of *aménagement,* industrialization, agriculture, public health, scientific research, and so on. . . . This is what we mean by eco-power: this thoroughgoing application of scientific knowledge and technological capabilities, through the lens of political power, over all living systems.[22]

For Lascoumes, the nightmarish possibility implicit in an "ecologically organized" society lies in the extension of human control over the entire biosphere—*la gestion du vivant,* or "the management of all living things."

Teilhard and Lascoumes are actually painting rather similar pictures—the one as utopia, the other as dystopia. Are these pictures realistic? Do their forecasts of total human mastery seem even remotely plausible? We would probably do better to think of them not as literal scenarios of a likely future, but rather as illuminating one of the more powerful propensities of technological modernity: the ability to inject ever-deepening levels of machine-like order into the physical and social world.

Traveling in an airplane at cruising altitude from continent to continent, one still invariably passes today over vast stretches of land that seem utterly uninhabited. These wide open spaces may not be "pure" wilderness, but they certainly dwarf the puny marks made on them by humans. Seen from this elevated perspective, all the worries about anthropization or total human mastery seem not only farfetched but rather overwrought. They smack simultaneously of paranoia and of arrogance—a sort of homocentric hubris. The paleontologist Stephen Jay Gould has addressed this topic with his characteristic panache:

We are virtually powerless over the earth at our planet's own geological time scale. All the megatonnage in our nuclear arsenals yield but one ten-thousandth the power of the asteroid that might have triggered the Cretaceous mass extinction. Yet the earth survived that larger shock and, in wiping out dinosaurs, paved the road for the evolution of large mammals, including humans. We fear global warming, yet even the most radical model yields an earth far cooler than many happy and prosperous times of a prehuman past. We can surely destroy ourselves, and take many other species with us, but we can barely dent bacterial diversity and will surely not remove many million species of insects and mites. On geological scales, our planet will take good care of itself and let time clear the impact of any human malfeasance.[23]

Gould takes pains to emphasize that this argument should not be interpreted as a license to rape and pillage the earth to our heart's content; he goes on to advocate an ambitious environmentalist agenda. But his point is a broader one: we should not lose sight of our relative puniness and ephemerality. The natural world operates according to rules of its own. It may not seem infinitely resilient from our own particular perspective, but the fact remains that its expanses will always contain us, and its rules will always set the outer limits on our action. Ultimately, it will abide, while we flicker and vanish.

Gould's perspective offers a useful corrective to the technocentric vision of thinkers like Teilhard and Lascoumes. But Gould may also turn out to be simply wrong. He wrote his essay in 1990; and in the years that have elapsed since then, scientists have begun talking about yet another dimension of technological development—the field of nanotechnology, whose potentialities might make nuclear weapons, global warming, and genetic engineering seem like relative child's play. We are still in the highly speculative phase of this nascent field of research, which is based on the notion of building microscopic robots—very simple, virus-sized, self-replicating machines—that could be programmed to perform a wide variety of tasks, from chewing up all the cholesterol buildup in a person's arteries to assembling together into complex structures such as chairs or buildings.[24] The key to these machines is that humans would not have to make them all: we, the creators, would simply manufacture the first few hundred, and then the machines would multiply by themselves. We get them started, and they take it from there—in goal-oriented swarms of millions and billions.

Some scientists have voiced concerns that this kind of self-replicating micromachine, if it ever got out of control, might become like the magically proliferating waters in the story of the Sorcerer's Apprentice, or like the Ice Nine in Kurt Vonnegut's novel *Cat's Cradle*: a molecular mass that simply grows, exponentially, until it consumes or engulfs most of the matter on the planet. According to one scientist, Bill Joy (a co-founder of Sun Microsystems), this particular danger has now progressed far enough away from science fiction, and close enough to reality, to be taken seriously:

> Among the cognoscenti of nanotechnology, this threat has become known as the "gray goo problem." Though masses of uncontrolled replicators need not be gray or gooey, the term "gray goo" emphasizes that replicators able to obliterate life might be less inspiring than a single species of crabgrass. The gray goo threat makes one thing perfectly clear: we cannot afford certain kinds of accidents with replicating assemblers. Gray goo would surely be a depressing ending to our human adventure on Earth, far worse than mere fire or ice, and one that could stem from a simple laboratory accident. Oops.[25]

This particular technology—replicating microassemblers—may or may not become a reality. The underlying point, however, is that Gould may have seriously underestimated the emerging power of human artifice, as it evolves over the next fifty to one hundred years. He speaks confidently about the lopsided relationship between human time and geological time, human power and the earth's power, as if these were fixed at the level of 1990. But the grey goo problem makes it clear that this lopsidedness might yet rapidly shift, in favor of technology.

No one can predict, of course, whether humanity will indeed make the leap into a world populated by these kinds of truly revolutionary machines. Still, it appears foolhardy to dismiss the unmistakable trend of human technological development, over the past two centuries, as something insignificant. Human powers are on the rise, and the rate of their growth is accelerating; we simply do not know where this will leave us a hundred years hence. That should be more than enough for us to take seriously the question of planetary-scale anthropization: more and more people, more and more technology, more and more varieties of human intervention in the biosphere—all this taking place within a finite and constant amount of territory.

The light-green social order does not offer much comfort in this regard. Predicated on the continued and unabated application of technological inventiveness to addressing ever-wider arrays of needs and desires, the light-green model does not repudiate machines and human intervention, but merely calls for a more critical and judicious application of them. And so the basic question remains: what becomes of wild nature in such a world?

14 The Enduring Mirage of Wilderness

Philosophies of Nature for a Technologically Intensive Age

There is nothing natural about the concept of wilderness.
—William Cronon, 1996[1]

Consider the following thought-experiment offered by the Australian philosopher Robert Elliot: let us imagine a large lake with two good-sized islands in it.[2] One island has an old-growth forest untouched since time immemorial. The other has an equally magnificent forest on it, but we know from historians that this forest was chopped down two hundred and fifty years ago, and that the island was then purchased (two hundred years ago) by new owners who meticulously replanted the forest and restored it over several generations to a condition very close to its former beauty. From one perspective, the two islands might today seem virtually indistinguishable. But in the estimation of some observers (Elliot included), the mere fact that, as we cast our gaze over the second island, we *know* that its forest has been replanted, cannot help but diminish its value considerably. As we look up at a particularly large and beautiful tree there, we cannot help but recall that somebody put it there: that person not only chose what type of tree to plant, but also (whether consciously or not) made a series of decisions about where to plant. Thus, an element of human design has been introduced, *volens nolens.* Restored nature, Elliot argues, does not have the same value as original nature, in exactly the same way as a superb, virtually indistinguishable copy of a Van Gogh does not have the same value as the genuine article.

The philosophical issue at stake here seems likely to become increasingly important as the twenty-first century unfolds. What exactly is it about the world's wild places that we value so highly? Why does one natural site elicit our veneration and awe, while another place, seemingly just as beautiful, seemingly just as deeply permeated by natural beings and processes, nonetheless strikes many of us as possessing a lesser value?

In a light-green world—a global society marked by the uneasy marriage of technology and ecology—these kinds of questions will demand the attention of both citizens and policymakers more forcefully than ever. With man-made devices extending an ever-more powerful reach over the earth, the question of how to handle "wild nature" must inevitably arise with growing frequency and urgency. How to adjudicate between society's needs and nature's needs? Which tracts of land merit special protection, and why? Does any piece of territory ever deserve to be completely "written off" as an ecological loss? Might an environmentalist effort to restore a natural site unwittingly mar that site beyond redemption—simply because, ipso facto, any human intervention unavoidably injects artifice into the land it affects? These are among the thornier philosophical issues that environmentalists are already confronting today. In a light-green future, a new generation of decision-makers will face such questions even more pressingly, as they struggle to manage the increasingly tight interaction between the human and the nonhuman, on a planet that will no doubt seem smaller than ever.

If Not the Dualism of Nature and Culture, then What?

When Bill McKibben declared, in his 1989 series of influential *New Yorker* articles, that we had witnessed "the end of nature," he was not of course arguing that humans had reached Teilhard's Omega Point, the total transfiguration of the material world by intelligent design. His position was more modest: we humans had irreparably altered the *meaning* of the material world, simply by touching it everywhere. "An idea, a relationship," he argued,

> can go extinct, just like an animal or a plant. The idea in this case is *nature,* the separate and wild province, the world apart from man to which he adapted, under whose rules he was born and died. . . . We have not ended rainfall or sunlight . . . but the *meaning* of the wind, the sun, the rain—of nature—has already changed.[3]

Not surprisingly, McKibben's argument drew fire from many quarters. Two of his most eloquent critics, the environmental historians Donald Worster and William Cronon, converged on the same basic point in his reasoning: they argued that McKibben's conception of nature was a straw man.[4] It rested on an extreme duality between the human and the not-human, a stark bipolar opposition between primeval wilderness and the artifice of civilized society. Like matter and antimatter, these two could not come into contact without instantly precipitating a violent reaction, in which one side, the human side, engulfed and transformed the other. The minute I blaze even the thinnest of trails into a primeval forest, according to McKibben's view, I change that forest into something tamer, less than what it was. It is now a place where artifice exists.

For Worster and Cronon, this constituted an unreasonable and counterproductive way to think about nature, because it left no room for human beings to engage their material surroundings in a constructive manner. As long as nature is seen as the radical "Other," as a space so qualitatively separate from me that I cannot enter it without somehow violating its pristine and primal character, this does not allow me much leeway for interacting with it. I either leave it completely alone, and it continues to be pure nature; or I reach out and touch it, but it immediately becomes something less than it was, marred by the human contact. And once this deep qualitative damage has occurred, what is the use of further efforts at protection? In the judgment of Worster and Cronon, the twenty-first century's environmental movements needed a more flexible set of concepts, a vision of nature that constructively accommodated the vast range of human interactions with the realm of the nonhuman.

In recent years, growing numbers of thinkers have come to think along these lines, questioning the idea of nature as a domain utterly separate from the human world. For convenience, I will refer to these thinkers as the "hybridity school" (even though they have not been working together and are certainly not in cahoots): they would include writers like Bruno Latour and Michel Serres in France, Claus Emmeche in Denmark, Donna Haraway, William Cronon, and Richard White in the U.S—and many others.[5] Despite their differences, all these thinkers have been exploring the border zones where things flow together—the confluence, within a single entity or system, of characteristics that traditionally have been thought of as belonging to qualitatively separate domains: animal and man, man and machine, plant and animal, organic and inorganic, nature and culture. In various ways, they are interested in subverting these age-old dualisms—particularly the one between nature and culture.

One particularly vivid example of this kind of thinking is Richard White's portrayal of the Columbia River as an "organic machine": by the late twentieth century, he argues, this mighty river has become like a cyborg, part natural, part artifact—a strange coalescence of dams, salmon, water, energy, work, politics, Indians, storms, radioactive elements, and money. Nature or culture? The only reasonable answer, for White, is "both!"[6]

An equally striking example is offered by the literary scholar Katherine Hayles, who is fascinated by the simulated reality that cybernetics researchers have created inside their computers, using sophisticated logic and programs to populate their virtual ecosystems with complex entities exhibiting a wide variety of behaviors and characteristics. The result, according to Hayles, is a world unto itself, an electronic territory that often takes its creators genuinely by surprise: sudden catastrophic shifts, unexpected new creatures arising and passing away, bizarre and unforeseen properties emerging—indeed, all the kinds of spontaneous and apparently self-organizing change that one might expect to find in a nonsimulated ecosystem. Inside the machine, a marked quality of "otherness" manifests itself: a world of beings evolving according to their own rules, and no longer directly tied to human control. Isn't this, asks Hayles, the mark of a certain kind of "wildness," in a cognate sense to what we mean when we unexpectedly encounter a wild animal crossing the path ahead of us in a forest meadow? And she concludes: "The world as we experience it is neither wholly apart from the human nor wholly of it, neither completely natural nor completely artificial. This is as true of walking through a rain forest as it is of cruising a virtual habitat that exists in the computer."[7]

For many of these "hybridity thinkers," the rejection of the nature-culture dualism reflects a clear underlying purpose: to reintegrate humans constructively into their physical surroundings. William Cronon's lucid articulation of this aim is worth quoting at length:

> [We need to] abandon the dualism that sees the tree in the garden as artificial—completely fallen and unnatural—and the tree in the wilderness as natural—completely pristine and wild. Both trees in some ultimate sense are wild; both in a practical sense now depend on our management and care. We are responsible for both, even though we can claim credit for neither. Our challenge is to stop thinking of such things according to a set of bipolar moral scales in which the human and the non-human, the unnatural and the natural, the fallen and the unfallen, serve as our conceptual map for understanding and valuing the world. Instead, we need to embrace the full continuum of a natural landscape that is also cultural, in which the city, the suburb, the pastoral, and

the wild each has its proper place, which we permit ourselves to celebrate without needlessly denigrating the others.[8]

On the one hand, therefore, we encounter openly dualistic thinkers like Robert Elliot, with his trenchant distinction between "authentic" wilderness and "fake" (restored) wilderness, or Bill McKibben, with his growing sense of claustrophobia as he looks around him and sees an increasingly artificialized planet. On the other hand we find the hybridity thinkers, fervently seeking a way to bind humans both in body and in heart to the totality of the physical world, in the hope of rendering possible a constructive and responsible co-existence between the human and the nonhuman.

As one steps back from this implicit debate, one cannot help but get a sense that both sides are hitting on something important and true. Mc-Kibben, for all the lack of nuance in his dualistic vision, nonetheless seems to be on to something when he says that we are losing an aspect of our planetary home that is both irreplaceable and infinitely precious. Who, in today's world of rampant and proliferating technological powers, can confidently say that there is no danger of our reducing most of the earth to a vast sea of human artifice? Even if we reject McKibben's excessively purist vision of wilderness, can we really avoid sharing his creeping feeling of dismay at the direction our civilization has taken—a future in which our heavy footprints will lie, to varying degrees, almost everywhere?

Thinkers like Hayles, Cronon, and White, of course, would be among the first to decry this grim prospect: but they argue that the best way to avoid such an outcome is to resist the reification of "pure wilderness" that characterizes the dualists' thinking, for this kind of rigidly polarized framework will only demoralize and paralyze us. Only by conceiving the human place within nature as a more nuanced continuum—city, suburb, pastoral, wild—can we offer ourselves (and our offspring) a positive and enduring place within the unfolding biosphere. Paradoxically, for these thinkers, it is only by embracing our own hybrid nature—and the fundamental hybridity of the physical environment we inhabit—that we can hope to conserve those aspects of the nonhuman world that we rightly treasure.

The issues at stake in this debate can be clarified somewhat if we look more closely at the concepts themselves of "hybridity" and "wilderness."

The Case for Hybridity: A World of Intertwinings

A recent book by the French philosopher of science, Bruno Latour, provides a good starting point. In his *Politiques de la nature* (1999), Latour proposes an ambitious reshuffling of major epistemological and metaphysical traditions that come down to us all the way from the time of Plato.[9] The Western tradition, in Latour's view, has tended to divide the world according to the following types of dualistic constructs:

A	B
Nature	Culture
Object	Subject
Fact	Value
Science	Politics

The concepts on the left have traditionally been regarded as pertaining to the "real world," from which any authoritative knowledge must ultimately be derived; the problem is that this world is mute, and its truths have to be interpreted and spoken by humans. The entities on the right, by contrast, are far from mute: they constitute the loquacious realm of human knowing, valuing, and feeling. The problem here, under column B, is that this world remains epistemologically handicapped by the inherently perspectival nature of its activity, and is consequently lost in an unresolvable cacophony of competing visions, opinions, and interpretations. The Western tradition, in other words, posits a world divided in two: nature (on the left) and human cultures (on the right), leaving us nothing but the unpalatable choice between a static and definitive (but mute) truth on one side, and a shapeless flux of (loquacious) relativism on the other.[10]

As a way out of this trap, Latour proposes that we reshuffle the properties of columns A and B, redefining their relationships as part of a single, two-phase process:[11]

Phase 1: The "power of taking into account." In this phase, which might be described as the moment of "opening," Latour situates inquiry, exploring, curiosity, and questioning—the gathering of new information, the challenging of old constructs.

Phase 2: The "power of ordering." In this phase, which might be described as the moment of "provisional closure," Latour situates the making of value judgments, the taking of decisions, the setting of policy, the institutionalization of ideas and theories.

The key to this two-phase process is that it *never ends,* perpetually iterating through its two phases of opening and closure over and over again; and that *everyone participates* at both stages, representing every kind of knowing and acting: scientists, politicians, economists, moral philosophers, citizens in general.[12] In Latour's view, we should stop talking about nature as a numinous, authoritative presence "out there," to which we turn for definitive illumination. What we have, instead, is an ongoing, perpetually unfinished process of opening and provisional closure, in which the human and the nonhuman are continually flowing together, creating and re-creating the same underlying qualitative realm: the realm of natural-cultural hybrids.

What practical implications follow from this philosophical shift? If nature does not exist as something fundamentally separate from us, if the world is filled with nothing but an infinite variety of hybrids, part-natural, part-cultural, then do we risk losing the sense of nature as something worth preserving? On the contrary: the very opposite may be the paradoxical result. It is precisely when we think of nature as a pure essence, totally separate from the human, that the earth tends to take on the "fallen" aspect of McKibben's lost wilderness—the tragic condition of a pristine landscape already irretrievably marred by human action. But when we construe the world's lands, waters, and skies as so many points of confluence between the human and the nonhuman—commingling nature and artifice in countless gradations and intertwinings—then the door is left open for a much wider, more constructive range of interactions. It is only then that we can begin to make serious distinctions, placing one hybrid beside another and making comparisons between their separate constellations of qualities.

This is particularly true for a country like France, where humans have been refashioning the physical environment for millennia. In such a land, McKibben's Manichaean vision offers no guidance at all: by his definition of nature, the whole French territory is just one big tame garden. Latour's concept of hybridity, on the other hand, allows an immense variety of contrasts and juxtapositions to come to light—some subtle or intangible, others stark and vividly striking. For not all hybrids are created equal.

Let us consider three concrete cases within the French territory, comparing the different ways in which the natural and the artificial come together in constituting their hybrid character: the forest of the Landes, the wetland of Poitou, and the Vanoise National Park. These three sites can be thought of as representing a broad spectrum, ranging from one extreme—nature thoroughly permeated by human agency (the Landes forest)—to nature at the other extreme, the Vanoise park, which remains about as close to primordial wilderness as any other place in metropolitan France.

The forest of the Landes, south of Bordeaux, is a fascinating place: artifice folded within artifice.[13] In the early years of the nineteenth century, there was not a tree in sight here—nothing but dunes, bogs, and trackless fens; then, at mid-century, Emperor Louis Napoleon decided to launch a major tree-planting campaign, concentrating on pinewoods, which for both economic and aesthetic reasons were highly favored at the time.[14] Today, one hundred and fifty years later, it is the biggest pine forest in Western Europe, covering one million hectares. Largely under private ownership, it is regularly harvested for wood, and intensively micromanaged: modeled on computers, traversed by logging roads and drainage ditches, surveyed by satellites, inspected by foresters and pruned assiduously, cleared continually of undergrowth, sprayed with pesticides from helicopters, and then finally clearcut and replanted.[15] This vast forest is just as much an "organic machine" as Richard White's Columbia River: a confluence of nature and artifice in which neither one nor the other has complete control, and in which both continually complicate each other's lives.

Our second point of reference, about halfway across the artificiality spectrum, is the *marais Poitevin,* or wetland of Poitou.[16] Situated on the Atlantic coast near La Rochelle, this swamp is a tangle of large and small waterways, lush vegetation, and myriad forms of aquatic life that have earned it the nickname, "Green Venice." Since the Middle Ages, the 97,000 hectares of swampland have also provided a livelihood to local peasants, who have farmed its highly fertile fringe areas, and also made a living by hunting and fishing the brackish backchannels of this verdant labyrinth, paddling about in small wooden flatboats. Though the peasants have dug ditches and built small levees here and there over the centuries, their relationship might best be described as one of symbiosis with the rhythms of the swamp: the rise and fall of tidal waters, the slow evolution of meandering freshwater channels. Unfortunately, the *marais Poitevin* has been shrinking in recent years because large-scale irrigation in the surrounding farmlands has dramatically altered the flow of the underlying aquifer; and environmentalists are currently campaigning to save it. This is where the wetland stands today: slowly retreating, embattled, but still there, a liminal space in which the human and the nonhuman have intertwined for centuries.

Our final point of reference is the National Park of the Vanoise, situated high in the Alps.[17] Created in 1963, it covers 57,000 hectares, and is divided into two zones: a central zone, comprising the most remote crags and glaciers where a rare species of mountain goat makes its habitat; and a larger peripheral zone, embracing several valleys inhabited by hardy peasants ekeing out a living as their ancestors have done since time immemorial. Restrictions on human activity in the central zone are very severe, amounting to a philosophy of minimizing human contact and allowing nature to take its course with as little disruption as possible. The rules are more flexible in the peripheral zone, allowing camping, hiking, and other low-impact activities along specially designated nature trails.

Forest of the Landes, wetland of Poitou, Vanoise park: if these are all hybrids arising out of the same matrix of intertwined nature and culture, it nonetheless remains true that they partake of these two polar qualities in very different ways. As with the air and gasoline in an automobile engine, it is the mixture that makes all the difference. In the Landes, the concept of human stewardship over the land has been given an unabashedly aggressive and homocentric interpretation: nature resides there, to be sure, but it needs all the help it can get, or else it will produce stunted trees, fewer trees, ugly trees, useless trees, dead trees.[18] Nature, for the Landes foresters, tends to make a bit of a mess of things; it needs guidance, channeling, supervision, in order to produce its full bounty. Stewardship, in this context, is akin to gardening or even farming. As the website for one of the Landes forestry companies puts it, "L'homme, architecte de la nature"—"Man, the architect of nature."[19]

The situation is quite different for the environmentalists who are trying to save the *marais Poitevin*. Here, stewardship means defense against a destabilizing set of changes coming from outside the ecosystem. Within the marshland, the human role is simply to live in symbiosis with the other creatures that reside there, adapting oneself to the prevailing rhythms of the place. Over the centuries humans have indeed left a mark, but that mark has remained much smaller in scale and scope than the basic nonhuman forces that made the wetland what it is. So we have here two scales of hybridity clashing with each other, in what is perhaps the classic environmentalist drama: outside the swamp, the surrounding hybrids of agribusiness, with their powerful water-pumps, are marshaling natural and economic forces on a titanic scale; and these forces threaten the very existence of those delicate hybrids that constitute the wetland ecosystem. Stewardship, in this context, consists in an effort to build a barrier between these two domains of the nature-culture continuum, swamp and wheat field, so that one will be prevented from engulfing the other. Of course, if the environmentalists succeed in creating such a barrier, then that barrier itself can also be thought of as one more natural/artificial hybrid: a device assembled out of legal, physical, economic, scientific, biological, and cultural elements, with the sole purpose of keeping two other types of hybrids apart.

In the Vanoise park, by contrast, the notion of hybridity might seem to require some stretching, for the park's central zone appears as a completely uninhabited, untouched, and hence "natural" space. It might almost satisfy Bill McKibben. But it turns out that even in the most inaccessible reaches of the central zone, scientists and rangers have discovered traces of past human activity: stylized drawings on cave walls, reminiscent of the imagery used by Australian aborigines; caches of stone tools; ancient paths cut into the rockface along the mountain passes. All these artifacts testify to a human presence that has left a slight but unmistakable mark over at least 10,000 years.[20] One could also point to the inevitable blurring of boundaries that occurs as animals and plants (and air and water) pass into the park and out of the park

from the surrounding regions, where human activity is far more pronounced.

But the notion of hybridity here extends even deeper: for the Vanoise itself
is a legal space, and it is only this fact, abstract and invisible (but very real
nonetheless), that prevents these mountain passes from being drastically altered by the avid hands of ski developers. Do the chamois and wildflowers
know, or care, that humans have drawn a line around this terrain and given it
a precise legal status? Probably not. But this status in itself affects the territory
in at least two ways: it staves off human interventions that would otherwise
have intruded upon it; and it profoundly alters the character of the terrain in
the eyes of humans themselves, who now see it in association with all the
conceptual and emotional baggage that goes along with the term, "national
park." Words like "protected," "wilderness," "national heritage," "famous
site," "historic landmark," all give the land an aura that it would not otherwise have possessed. Here, then, the concept of stewardship waxes paradoxical: it boils down to the artifice of holding artifice at bay. A piece of the
territory is seen as possessing intrinsic value, and its distinctiveness lies precisely in its relative isolation from the human world. The best steward, in this
context, is the one who does nothing, and who aggressively prevents others
from doing anything either—a man-made force field to shield the land from
man-made forces.

Forest of the Landes, wetland of Poitou, Vanoise park: when we construe
these spaces as three varieties of natural/artificial hybrids, the concept of artificialization immediately becomes more transparent and manageable. We
no longer have to worry that *even the smallest amount* of human agency will
ipso facto turn the wilderness into a "fallen" space or "mere" garden—for
that fear, it turns out, was based on an excessively rigid dualism. What we
have, instead, is a spectrum of countless shades and gradations, marking out
the different types of combination with which the human and the nonhuman
can come together: on one side, hybrids like the Landes forest possessing a
heavy component of artificial shaping; on the other side, hybrids like the
Vanoise with a much lighter human touch.

The Case for Dualism: Wilderness as the Irreducible Other

At this point, however, a set of thorny questions arises: do we feel comfortable creating a world in which the Landes forest becomes the norm, and
in which spaces like the Vanoise are nothing but rare museum-like islands in
a sea of intensive human agency? Why do we assign such a high value to sites
like the Vanoise in the first place? What makes them worth preserving? Why
should one hybrid be more precious to us than another?

These questions, it turns out, are hard to answer from the perspective of "hybridity" alone. If we say that the Vanoise is given special protected status because it possesses a higher degree of wildness, then this merely brings us back again to our original question: what exactly is it about the world's wild places that we value so highly? It is tempting, at first glance, to answer this by seeking some kind of "essence" or "core meaning" in the wilderness; but this ultimately proves to be a fruitless approach. Even the most cursory look at broad historical studies like Max Oelschlaeger's *The Idea of Wilderness,* or Clarence Glacken's *Traces on the Rhodian Shore,* makes it clear that it would be a grave mistake to posit any overarching, trans-historical meaning for a term like "wilderness"—for it is undoubtedly one of the most protean constructs in human culture.[21] Virtually every society in history has confronted some version of this idea in its many guises and forms: as geographic environment, as biological foundation, as a source of food, as land to be occupied, as the territory of myth and imagination, as untamed frontier, as literary or artistic landscape, as an object of scientific inquiry, as the raw material for techno-logical manipulation, as an ecological order requiring human stewardship, as a space of leisure, as a sacred locus of spiritual replenishment.

Leaving aside, therefore, the futile search for any "core meaning" of wilderness, we can nonetheless shed light on this concept by looking (much more modestly) for certain recurring or common elements among the im-mense diversity of its manifestations. One such recurrent theme, particularly suggestive for our present purposes, has been described by the historian William Cronon as the motif of the "flight from history":

> Seen as the original garden, [the wilderness] is a place outside of time, from which human beings had to be ejected before the fallen world of history could properly begin. Seen as the frontier, it is a savage world at the dawn of civiliza-tion, whose transformation represents the very beginning of the [American] national historical epic. Seen as the bold landscape of frontier heroism, it is the place of youth and childhood, into which men escape by abandoning their pasts and entering a world of freedom where the constraints of civilization fade into memory. Seen as the sacred sublime, it is the home of a God who tran-scends history by standing as the One who remains untouched and un-changed by time's arrow. . . . Wilderness fulfills the old romantic project of secularizing Judeo-Christian values so as to make a new cathedral not in some petty human building but in God's own creation, Nature itself.[22]

What is striking here is that a great many people, hailing from a wide variety of societies ranging across time and space, have apparently hit again and again upon the same persistent theme—the experience of wilderness as a "flight from history," a transcendence, a place that takes us beyond the human world. What we have here is not the same thing as a "universal meaning": for many non-Western cultures (and quite a few individuals within the West) might find this notion of the "flight from history" rather strange and baffling. Rather, we are encountering here an intriguing pattern, identifiable within a significant *subset* of the meanings of wilderness: certainly not an "essence" at the level of content, but something more akin to a recurring formal property. I will refer to this particular way of perceiving the wilderness—the tendency to construe it as a "flight from history"—as the sensibility of transcendence.

Cronon's metaphor of the cathedral assumes particular significance in this respect. A cathedral is more than just an ordinary building, because it is regarded as a place *in* the world that also gestures powerfully *beyond* the world. It exists simultaneously in two different planes of reality, and acts as a sort of window between them.

Something similar might be said for the concept of wilderness. For that heterogenous portion of humanity attuned to the sensibility of transcendence, the wilderness appears to possess one irreducible quality: as with a cathedral, it is a space that points beyond itself, to something outside itself. It is a place where one goes with the expectation of coming face to face with a certain kind of radical otherness—the nonhuman, in all its overwhelming strangeness and wondrousness. Seen in this way, a wild place is more than just a place: it is also an invitation to apprehend something beyond the dimension of the here and now. In this sense, a crucial formal quality underlying the concept of wilderness might be described as the logical inverse of self-reference: it is a quality of *other*-reference, where this *otherness* is an intuition of a world beyond the human, a realm larger than the human, a level of reality outside our ken but whose presence many persons feel very strongly nonetheless.

This formal property of the idea of wilderness, which might be called the lure of otherness, cannot help but rest on paradox. The philosopher Ludwig Wittgenstein offered one of the most eloquent descriptions of this type of slippery, contradictory quality in his famous Ethics Lecture of 1929. He was trying to describe to his audience the difficulty of speaking about religious experience, or about the deep grounding of ethical values, in ordinary language:

> I believe the best way of describing [this experience] is to say that when I have it I wonder at the existence of the world. And I am then inclined to use such phrases as "How extraordinary that anything should exist" or "How extraordinary that the world should exist." ... I see now that these nonsensical expressions

were not nonsensical because I had not yet found the correct expressions, but that their nonsensicality was their very essence. For all I wanted to do with them was just to go beyond the world and that is to say beyond significant language. My whole tendency and, I believe, the tendency of all men who ever tried to write or talk Ethics or Religion was to run against the boundaries of language. This running against the walls of our cage is perfectly, absolutely hopeless. Ethics so far as it springs from the desire to say something about the ultimate meaning of life, the absolute good, the absolutely valuable, can be no science. What it says does not add to our knowledge in any sense. But it is a document of a tendency in the human mind which I personally cannot help respecting deeply and I would not for my life ridicule it.[23]

This quality of "running against the boundaries of the human world," of reaching out toward the Radically Other, is similar, in a sense, to what Wordsworth encountered one day at the Simplon Pass in the Alps; to what John Muir celebrated, arms outstretched, gazing into the sky above El Capitan; to what Cousteau beheld in the silent blue depths of a coral grotto: certainly not one and the same experience, but rather the vibrant impact of a specific family of meanings, a recurring type of liminal gesture. These individuals, like so many others before and after, came *through the wilderness to the edge of their world* and caught a glimpse—a fleeting, life-changing intimation—of something on the other side. In this sense, for a significant portion of humanity scattered across space and time, Wittgenstein's expression serves rather well: to go into wilderness is to run against the walls of our cage.

Cronon is quite right, then, to insist that the experiencing of wilderness is a fundamentally human, and social, phenomenon. It happens in history, and its occurrence can be traced from epoch to epoch, from lifetime to lifetime, like any other historical fact. It forms part of our human cultural heritage, part of our hybrid world. *And yet, and yet:* it is also something else. The underlying formal gesture that recurs in many of its myriad meanings lies in the fact that, from a place within our hybrid world, it points toward a world that is not hybrid, but radically, purely other. That other world—by whatever name it may go—has been described in the notebooks and poems, the songs and incantations, the paintings and carvings made by countless individuals scattered through the whole range of human cultures. Among the testimonials passed on to us, certain themes recur: that other world was not made by humans; it lies outside human control; it existed before human beings did, and will probably continue to exist long after we are gone; it remains mysterious to us, and fills us with awe and wonder; yet it also attracts us irresistibly, because we feel deeply linked to it; it is powerful, in the ultimate sense of the term. We do not really know how we know these things about it; but we experience the knowledge with a rare kind of immediacy and authenticity—an intensity similar to religious experience. As Wittgenstein wisely observes, we cannot say much about it beyond this simple acknowledgment that it exists: all we can do is sense its presence, and take comfort in the fact that many other humans, all over the world and throughout history, appear to have shared a similar intimation of that presence.

Herein lies the irreducible otherness embedded within the concept of wilderness, like an arrow pointing in an arc, up and out of a circle. Take away this stubborn duality, this ever-recurrent tension between two qualitatively distinct realms—the human, and the world beyond the human—and the iridescent bubble of its meaning instantly pops and vanishes. The special quality of wilderness lies in the fact that it is simultaneously a hybrid and also something else, grounded in a "beyond" that only pure dualism can render into language.

From Wilderness to Wildness: A Paradoxical Synthesis

We are left, therefore, with a bit of a quandary: for Cronon is certainly persuasive when he insists that our respect for nature needs to encompass far more than "pure wilderness," and that a fixation on pristine, far-away territories has too often blinded us to the equally important glimpses of natural value that beckon in the orchards, streetsides, and gardens of our everyday lives. But McKibben, I have argued, is equally persuasive when he maintains that a key feature of wilderness lies in something radically separate from the human, a quality absolutely and irremediably beyond our grasp. Nature as environment, nature as wilderness: we need a conceptual scheme that preserves the integrity of both categories, embracing the hybridity of the former and the dualism of the latter—if such a thing is possible.

One way of resolving this problem, perhaps, lies in the distinction between wilderness and *wildness*. The concept of wilderness (especially as used by McKibben) tends to trap us in a static and reified notion of "privileged spaces": wilderness remains intact until the moment of human touch, and then, once breached, it is gone forever. The concept of wildness, by contrast, is much more resilient and flexible, because it refers to a quality that can exist in varying degrees. It can increase or diminish over time, as we mean for example when we speak of allowing a formerly farmed field to "grow wild." It can apply to animals or places—and even in some ways to humans themselves. In the present context, to speak of shades and gradations of wildness in different pieces of territory is simply to say that some places are more conducive than others for taking us to the edge of our cage.

Strolling through the forest of the Landes, for example, we can certainly still find many aspects of wild nature. But we have to look hard: we bend down, and note the insects that have made a home under a fallen branch, despite the pesticides sprayed from helicopters. Peering into the trees, we see that a pair of storks have made their nest in the upper reaches of the tallest pine. One tree has grown a strangely twisted pattern in its trunk, heedless of the foresters' assiduous efforts to keep it straight. Everywhere we look, the irruption of spontaneous, unbidden processes manifests itself, reminding us that human control can never be total, and that the nonhuman presence is an active one, even beneath the surface of all this intensive human arranging and ordering.

Nevertheless, this is still a very different experience from the one that presses itself upon us as we stand atop a crag in the high Vanoise. We don't have to look for nonhuman otherness here: it comes to us whether we like it or not, and seizes us, and lifts us away. The sky, the clouds, the receding crests of mountains all the way to the jagged horizon, the valley far below reduced to a delicate miniature landscape, the wind whistling in our ears: an order broader than ourselves, an inhuman scale of time and perspective and inscrutable forces at play, simply compels our attention and takes us with it. Wildness lives here in great strength; we are but ephemeral visitors.

This distinction among different gradations of wildness helps us address our original question about the special value of the Vanoise, as compared with the forest of the Landes. We tend to assign a high value to those hybrids that embody wildness in a particularly intense, original, or striking way: they are like spontaneously occurring "cathedrals" that we encounter within the territory, whose uniqueness and potency we hold commensurately in reverence.[24] Since these kinds of places are rare (and becoming rarer), their value tends to become even greater with the passing of time. The Landes forest is a hybrid whose modest component of wildness speaks softly, from subtle hiding-places; the Vanoise is a hybrid whose much heavier degree of wildness grabs us by the scruff of the neck and hurls us into another world.

The conceptual scheme implicit here remains open to the full range of meanings associated with the word "nature." On the one hand, we can think of all the entities in our world as an infinitely variegated continuum of natural-cultural hybrids, intertwining the human and the nonhuman in countless combinations and nuances. On the other hand, we can simultaneously remain attuned to one particular quality of the nonhuman, as it confronts us to varying degrees in the hybrids around us: the quality of wildness, with its insistent tug on our spiritual innards, gesturing toward an ineffable (but immeasurably potent) otherness.

We are admittedly, in this conceptual framework, having our cake and eating it too: hybridity and dualism in the same bite. The key lies in the way we have defined the term "wildness"—as a quality that *beckons toward* a realm of pure otherness, but that does so from here on earth, while combining promiscuously with the creatures and places of this world in an infinite number of ways and degrees. We thereby avoid the pitfalls of trying to instantiate that pure otherness in an impossibly pristine wilderness à la McKibben; but we also avoid the equally pernicious pitfall of banishing all irreducible otherness from the world altogether. By thinking of wildness as a variable quality rather than as a fixed place or thing, we give ourselves the requisite flexibility to encounter nature as hybridity and as duality at the same time.

On one final point here, then, we must part company with Cronon's formulation of hybridity. "The tree in the garden," he maintains,

> is in reality no less other, no less worthy of our wonder and respect, than the tree in an ancient forest that has never known an ax or a saw—even though the tree in the forest reflects a more intricate web of ecological relationships. The tree in the garden could easily have sprung from the same seed as the tree in the forest, and we can claim only its location and perhaps its form as our own. Both trees stand apart from us; both share our common world. The special power of the tree in the wilderness is to remind us of this fact. It can teach us to recognize the wildness we did not see in the tree we planted in our own backyard.[25]

It appears that Cronon, in his (laudable) desire to elicit an egalitarian sense of reverence for all forms of natural life, has felt compelled here to minimize the difference between garden tree and wild tree almost to the vanishing point. But if one truly accepted this line of argument, then on what grounds could one defend a stand of old-growth redwoods against the lust of real estate developers planning to chop them down and build condos in their place? The developers could plausibly claim that the new saplings they intended to plant would be "no less other, no less worthy of our wonder and respect." Making distinctions among different gradations of wildness, and among the degrees of natural value that go with them, constitutes an essential aspect not only of understanding nature, but also of protecting it.

The problem in Cronon's argument here appears to lie in a confusion about sources of value. Both the garden tree and the wild tree may possess high value in our estimation; but they do so for very different reasons that reflect their very different natures. The garden tree is like an old companion: we fondly remember the day we planted it, cradling its tender roots in our hands; today it gives neighborhood children a place to climb and play; it bends patiently to our will, as we trim it to keep it off the roof; its changing form interweaves with the accumulated memories of a family growing and living side-by-side with it; and last but not least, it reminds us, through its own partial wildness, of a different order of things, within which our own suburban garden forms but a tiny part. All these factors can, and should, elicit in us a profound sense of respect.

But this should not prevent us from distinguishing our beloved tree from the much stranger, more intensely nonhuman presence of the old giant we encounter in the forest, sprouted long before our city had even been founded, and weathering its endless round of seasons in relative isolation from human affairs. This wild tree is likely to evoke in us a quite different range of thoughts and feelings from the familiar tree in the garden: a sense of awe commensurate precisely with the very *otherness* that it so powerfully embodies.

Both trees certainly deserve our respect; but we should not make the mistake of thinking that they do so for identical reasons. Fortunately, however, this elision of the distinction between garden tree and wild tree remains entirely unnecessary. The conceptual framework we have just proposed is perfectly compatible with Cronon's quest for a revalorization of the more common forms of nature that confront us in our everyday lives: backyard plants, farmed fields, logged forests, suburban greenways, dammed rivers. These kinds of overtly humanized spaces, symbolized by the idea of the Garden, need not bear the stigma of "fallen" nature; nor need they be seen as utterly lacking in the fertile tension of wildness. They are expressions, rather, of the paradoxical coexistence of hybridity and duality—of the comfortably familiar and the astonishingly other—within our world.

15   The Shifting Landscape of Tame and Wild

> There they go, proliferating, these newspaper articles describing the entangled hybrids of science, politics, economics, law, religion, technology, fiction All of culture and all of nature are to be found here, continually stirred round and round in the same pot, day after day.
> —Bruno Latour, 1991[1]

In the foregoing chapters we have described the rising tide of artifice, the galloping "anthropization" of the Earth; and we have analyzed two basic strains of meaning evoked by the concept of wilderness in this intensively technological age: nature as dualism, nature as hybridity. Now, therefore, we are better placed to make a final assessment of the light-green society, and of the boundary-blurring process that constitutes its cardinal quality. How does such a "blurred" world look and feel, and in what ways does its advent change our lives? Amid this uneasy confluence of ecology and technological modernity, what relationship emerges between the wild and the tame?

Nature Penetrating into Society: Emerging Connectedness
Let us begin with the penetration of the natural into the social—the blurring that occurs when supposedly "cultural" or "social" elements are forced to open up and integrate within themselves the features and processes of the nonhuman world.

A particularly illuminating description of this process is conveyed in the following passage by the historian Richard White:

> I type at a keyboard. On this clear June day I can see the Olympic Mountains in the distance. . . . [But] I cannot see my labor as separate from the mountains, and I know that my labor is not truly disembodied. The lights on this screen need electricity, and this particular electricity comes from dams on the Skagit or Columbia. These dams kill fish; they alter the rivers that come from the Rockies, Cascades, and Olympics. The electricity they produce depends on the great seasonal cycles of the planet: on falling snow, melting waters, flowing rivers. In the end, these electrical pulses will take tangible form on paper from trees. Nature, altered and changed, is in this room. But this is masked. I type. I kill nothing. I touch no living thing. I seem to alter nothing but the screen. If I don't think about it, I can seem benign, the mountains separate and safe from me. But, of course, the natural world has changed and continues to change to allow me to sit here. My separation is an illusion.[2]

This type of dawning realization—in which one suddenly perceives the underlying connectedness between things that one had previously thought of as separate—proved to be a hallmark of the light-green society.

But this was not all, for the changes came from even deeper than a mere shift in perspective (important as that shift might be). The change also affected the actual design, manufacture, and use of nearly all the tangible objects that humans took up in their daily lives. It changed not only how people perceived those objects, but in most cases altered the objects themselves: what they were made of, how they were put together, how they were put to use, how they were disposed of when worn out. The transformation, in other words, was both profoundly cultural and fist-poundingly concrete at the same time.

Our narrative in Part III explored this process in considerable detail. In the light-green society, a consumer product like a radio battery, for example, suddenly came to be seen not only as a delightfully convenient way to carry energy around, but also as a potentially nasty little packet of heavy metals that would leach out of the landfills into the aquifers and thus eventually make their way back into our own bodies. The perception of this social product changed: but this shift was soon followed by a concomitant change in the product itself. New, "green" batteries appeared, whose key feature consisted in providing electricity without incurring the associated risk of chemical toxicity. This was precisely what it meant for the realm of nature to "invade" the domain of society: a "social" object now incorporated, in its basic design, an invisible but very real connection with the territory and its aquifers. Or, if we prefer to reverse the perspective: the integrity of a "natural" space—underground rivers and porous rock strata—now became a tangible factor in the engineering and use of a common household product.

The connection that had once been hidden now came out into the open: one held a green battery in one's hand, and one was grasping not just an isolated metal cylinder, but a whole chain of causes and effects cascading off through time and space around oneself, binding this object seamlessly with its surroundings. Social product on one side, natural space on the other—what had once been framed as a qualitative chasm now took on the character of a fluid continuum: natural materials coalescing, through human agency, into manufactured objects; manufactured objects unraveling, through use and decay, and dispersing once again into the territory. In the light-green society, more and more citizens gradually acquired the habit of thinking in this startling new way, factoring the entirety of a product's life-cycle into its identity; and the result was that they either abandoned the product entirely (as in the case of CFC's) or modified its design so that it fit less destructively into the web of physical and biological relationships of which it formed a part.

To be sure, in talking about products like a green battery, the distinction between the social and the natural could still be sustained: but only as a rather self-conscious abstraction, a deliberate mental effort that entailed identifying specific analytical qualities and holding them apart. The underlying object itself—the green battery—remained from the outset a symbiosis of the two. The product's "fit" with the biosphere now formed part of its essence: no such thing as a green battery could exist except as a device designed to do two things at once, namely, fulfil a utilitarian purpose *and* avoid the pollution of the aquifers. In the era before the light-green society, these kinds of considerations had either been ignored, or had remained largely unexplored or unarticulated. Now they came to the forefront: a battery became an object that existed simultaneously in two realms, meeting human needs and nature's needs as a matter of equal priority—with this duality lying at the core of its very definition.

If this process of reconceptualizing, redesigning, and retooling had only taken place in the case of a few consumer products, such as batteries and aerosol sprays, then the impact might not have added up to much. But in fact, as we have seen, it swept through every nook and cranny of the social world. What people ate, what they threw away, how they got around, how they organized their homes, where they went for vacations, how they earned a living, the laws they lived by, the products they made and the ways they made them, their political ideologies, their governing institutions, their visions of progress and the future—all these domains were unmasked (to use

White's expression), torn loose from their state of illusory isolation, and rein-scribed within the broader matrix of their "natural" preconditions and reper-cussions. All of them underwent the same type of reappraisal and (in many cases) restructuring, facing the same core set of questions: What demands does this object (or this practice) place on the biosphere? How does it use natural resources? How does its life-cycle impinge on the environment? How sustainable is this?

To begin thinking in this way, and to reorganize one's society in this way, is to have experienced a kind of "invasion" by nature. It is a benign invasion, to be sure, and it has been brought about entirely by social agencies, as hu-mans reevaluate their place within the physical world. But its repercussions—as with any invasion—cannot help but prove far-reaching. Everywhere one looks, henceforth, the everyday objects and habits of one's life ripple off into widening circles of causes and effects, linking them to the larger orders of the biosphere: long-lost origins, future ramifications, reverberations coming in and going out, enveloping unfamiliar places and strange creatures.

Put gas in your car, for example, and you cannot help but know that you are pouring part of the subterranean fluids of a far-off desert, fluids finite in quantity, fluids derived from the bodies of plants and animals that lived and died eons ago, and which in turn derived their life-substance from the sun. You know that this fluid was pierced by giant drills and then pumped out of the sand by men and machines, leaving an unmistakable imprint on the earth's surface. You know that this fluid, as it burns in your car's engine, will turn into gases that float up to the sky, contributing to the alteration of cli-mate and vegetation everywhere. You would prefer, perhaps, not to think of all these things, and to proceed simply and serenely about your errands. But this becomes difficult, because large portions of the surrounding culture and economy have now been reconfigured in such a way as to remind you of what you are really doing. You live in a civilization that increasingly con-spires, in large and small ways, to reconnect you with nature.

If you really want to, of course, you can still suppress this awareness: that is always an option. But you have to choose to do so, actively ignoring this quality of connectedness, of embeddedness in the biosphere, that your cul-ture has gradually begun to incorporate. This is the direction in which the light-green society is taking you.

Society Penetrating into Nature: Ambiguous Control

On the other side of the light-green society, we find the penetration of the social into the natural—the blurring that occurs when supposedly "wild" or "nonhuman" elements are forced to open up and integrate within themselves the features and qualities of the human realm. At the heart of this process lies the phenomenon of artificialization, the increasingly potent human effort to control more and more aspects of the material world.

But this control, it turns out, is itself ambiguous: as with the tuning of a musical instrument, *too much* can be just as bad as *not enough*. On one side we have *Breakdown:* the impression of a global civilization skidding out of control. Overpopulation, resource depletion, disrupted natural equilibrium, strange epidemics, unmanageable complexity, unforeseen side-effects piling up—humanity, like a car without a driver, hurtling ever-faster on a high plateau surrounded by cliffs and the abyss.

On the other side we have *Gridwork:* the impression of a global civilization ensnaring itself (and the physical world) in too much control. Satellites watching from above, wildernesses shrinking to protected islands, scientists unlocking the genome, information technologies penetrating the home, the body, the economy, the state, gently enfolding the earth in a dense blanket of Cartesian coordinates—a mesh of human agency growing finer and finer, seeding artifice everywhere, leaving less and less room for the spontaneous, for things unchanneled and untamed.[3]

Out of control, too much control.

Both these nightmares, Breakdown and Gridwork, start from the plain, factual observation of the accelerating increase in humanity's ability to intervene in the material world. The first scenario, Breakdown, posits the existence of an underlying natural order of things, which humanity, with its growing powers, seems in danger of fatally disrupting. The second scenario, Gridwork, posits a deep human need for freely evolving, unruly, nonhuman forces in the world: it expresses a fear that humanity, with its growing powers, might inject so much machine-like homogeneity and predictability into the planet as to rob it of the very qualities that make it satisfying as a place of dwelling. How seriously should we take these two bleak visions? To what extent does the light-green society contain the latent potentials for their realization?

Most environmentalists—and, judging from opinion polls, a significant percentage of the world's citizens—would argue that the danger of Breakdown is all too real. If efforts to stem the growth of human population continue to prove as futile as they have done to date; if the wretched poverty in which three-quarters of humanity festers should continue to prove as intractable as it has done thus far; if the citizens of rich nations continue to resist the imposition of more stringent controls on their resource consumption and effluent-spewing—in short, if current patterns persist, without a significant change, then the odds of avoiding Breakdown in the long run do not look particularly good.

But the story told in this book does not necessarily point to such a grim conclusion: the case of France leaves the future more open, more intriguingly unresolved, than that. On the one hand, we were forced to conclude that the French light-green society, as it stood in the year 2000, remained quite far from achieving meaningful levels of sustainability. While the worst excesses of the 1960s—open landfills, smoke-belching factories, and the like—were effectively confronted and neutralized, and while many natural sites throughout France were successfully brought under protection, the nation's overall pattern of production and consumption remained far-removed from a mode that could reasonably be regarded as sustainable over the long haul.

On the other hand, however, the French case also gives some plausible grounds for hope. When one thinks back to the prevailing *mentalités* and economic reality of 1965–the world in which Rachel Carson and Roger Heim first sounded their alarms—and compares this with the myriad environmentalist institutions and practices that characterize the light-green social order of the year 2000, the contrast is remarkable. This transition took thirty-five years: what would have seemed like a utopian reverie in the 1960s has now become a massive, complex, and very real part of contemporary French society.

The danger of Breakdown, therefore, continues to loom ominously on the horizon; but it does not loom like a hurricane, bearing down on humankind with a force that lies entirely outside our control. Rather, it looms more like a difficult test or challenge that lies ahead, an approaching crisis that we can reasonably hope to confront with success—*if* we apply ourselves vigorously and intelligently, with a willingness to make the necessary changes and sacrifices.

That "if," of course, is a big one.

> > >

What about the image of Gridwork? Let us assume, for the sake of argument, that none of the worst-case scenarios depicted earlier will actually become a reality over the coming decades: neither genetically programmed biosphere nor noospheric fusion, neither Breakdown nor gray goo. Let us hazard the optimistic assumption, in other words, that human beings will behave relatively reasonably, and do their level best (by and large) to act responsibly with respect to each other and the planet. Can they come to grips successfully with the accelerating process of artificialization?

The answer suggested by the foregoing chapters is a rather disconcerting one: even if humankind succeeds in averting Breakdown, through a rigorous greening of its attitudes and behaviors over the coming century, this may not in itself prove sufficient to slow the trend toward artificialization. Only a specific *kind* of greening—a fairly draconian kind—can realistically offer the hope of achieving this.

Consider the following two scenarios, which I will label respectively as Eco-Management and Eco-Restraint. Both of these take today's light-green society as their starting-point, and both assume a continued trajectory of deepening environmental awareness and steady increases in the measures taken for environmental protection. Both of these assume, in other words, that humankind succeeds in reaching a plateau of sustainable development at some point in the coming century.

Where they differ, however, is in their underlying attitudes toward nature. Eco-Management emphasizes the concept of control: it rests on the premise that avoiding an environmental catastrophe will require ever-more stringent forms of human supervision and regulation over the interaction between civilization and the biosphere. Eco-Restraint, by contrast, emphasizes the concept of selectively relinquishing control. Even though it entails many of the same tangible environmental measures as Eco-Management, its overall approach is to reduce human intervention systematically, and to the greatest degree possible.

Eco-Management, in effect, incarnates the light-green society, as it might foreseeably develop in the early decades of the twenty-first century. Given the trends that we have identified in the present book, the following three-way mix appears as a rather optimistic (but still plausible) depiction of what would lie ahead under this model: some reckless exploitation of nature (gradually decreasing as the years go by); some proactive and conscientious stewardship (gradually increasing as the years go by); and some full-scale conservation of wild tracts (holding steady, or perhaps increasing, as the years go by).

Nevertheless, even this optimistic projection of the future still entails a steady, ineluctable increase in the process of artificialization. Why? Because, apart from the protected islands of relatively wild nature established here and there throughout the world, most of the rest of the planet, according to this scenario, cannot help but enter increasingly into daily interaction with human beings. Those interactions may be direct or indirect, blatant or subtle, violent or gentle: but increase they must.

Perhaps the best way to envision the scenario of Eco-Management concretely is by returning to the concept of a broad continuum of natural-artificial hybrids—cities and suburbs at one end, then farmed countryside, artificial lakes, and dammed rivers; then parks, seasides, and logged forests, free-flowing rivers and old-growth forests; and finally, at the other end, remote and legally protected wild territories far from any roads or settlements. If we hold this continuum in our minds, then the process of artificialization simply means that, as human population and the reach of technology continue their growth, all these diverse kinds of spaces will tend to rub up against the human more often, and in more intensive ways.

In places like cities, this may not make much difference, for the human presence there is already hovering at a high level. At the other extreme, if humans are legally prevented from gaining access to certain spots (as with the Vanoise), then there too the passage of time may not bring much change. But it is in all the wide range and variety lying between these two extremes that the real change is likely to occur: like a Doppler shift of electromagnetic wavelengths, one is likely to see a gradual movement of these middling hybrids away from the wild and toward the pole of artifice. On the farms: more machines, subtler forms of fertilization and pest control, sophisticated methods of erosion containment, new breeds of plants and animals, complex systems of automation. In the suburbs: rapid and carefully planned growth, incorporating many green belts and scenic watercourses. In the mountains: roads and rail lines studiously integrated into the landscape, leisure resorts subjected to rigorous ecological regulation, forests logged in ways that maximize biodiversity and conservation. On the rivers: hydroelectric dams equipped with elaborate bypass channels for fish, with the health of aquatic wildlife carefully monitored and managed. In the skies: a dense grid of air routes, designed to handle seamlessly the traffic of a thousand varieties of aircraft large and small, their pullulating movement always visible up there. In the oceans: huge fisheries overseen by international law, patrolled by anti-poaching police, monitored by satellites and underwater observation stations, culled each season by semi-automated fleets.

This scenario remains far indeed from Lascoumes's nightmare of "total control." In such an ecologically managed, post-industrial world, the space for spontaneous, unpredictable, or uncontrollable events would remain enormous. In some ways, as the "gray goo" problem suggests, that space might even increase, through the unintended and unforeseen effects of various human enterprises great and small. But overall, in the daily life of humanity's interaction with the natural world, the quality of *relative freedom from human intervention* that we associate with wildness (as one of its essential features) would inevitably become scarcer than it is today. Wildness would retreat and shrink all around us because, in all the wide variety of territories described above, human beings would be busily doing what comes naturally to them: injecting their own ideas of order into their surroundings, studying and forecasting, adjusting and manipulating, guiding and channeling, restraining and encouraging, nurturing and eradicating—fine-tuning the flux of the biosphere to fit their goals and norms. Even if we were to make the additional highly optimistic assumption that human population could be stabilized at some point in the next century—say, at the current level of six billion—those seething billions would still dispose of unprecedented (and rapidly increasing) capabilities and powers. The breadth and depth of human intervention would go on steadily growing.

The underlying point here is that, as we saw in the case of the Pointe du Raz in chapter 7, even the most well-intentioned efforts at coexisting respectfully with natural spaces can easily lead to the paradoxes of *aménagement*. Ultimately, if large numbers of humans wish to interact with a relatively wild space—even with an attitude of the utmost care and reverence—then the unavoidable conundrums begin: How should they get there? Where should they stay? Where do they eat? How many of them should be allowed into the site at a time? Should they be allowed to go wherever they wish, or should their paths through the territory be regularized and controlled? None of these problems arises if only one or two people are visiting the site; it only becomes an issue when the numbers rise into the hundreds and thousands. The pressure of two or four shoes on a moss-covered forest floor is entirely bearable; an attentive pair of hikers can pass through and scarcely leave a trace. But the pressure of 25,000 shoes (even reverently tiptoeing) unavoidably becomes a steamrolling juggernaut: it destroys, at least partially, that which it came to admire.

At this point, under the worldview of Eco-Management, someone perforce has to come forward and say, "You may step here and here, but not over there. Please stay on the paths. Please do not touch the tree bark: it is wearing thin from too many hands. Keep your voices down, or you won't be able to appreciate the sounds of the forest. If you need to go to the bathroom, please use the portable johns over there."

This is a reasonable, respectful way to handle a natural space when great numbers of people will be passing through it. It preserves a good deal of the wildness that resides there. But visiting such a space in this fashion cannot help but be very different from plunging (alone, or with one or two friends) into the undergrowth of a pathless, overgrown forest in which no person has ventured for a long time. The highly frequented wild space, whether we like it or not, has been subtly but significantly Doppler-shifted toward artifice. Like the Pointe du Raz, it has been thoughtfully *aménagé*: gently regulated and controlled, becoming a site in which people will henceforth encounter nature through the mediation of a loosely scripted and orchestrated set of procedures and institutions.

Not all territories in this future world would face these kinds of pressures, of course. The planet is large, and it would still remain a highly diverse place, full of many elements and gradations of wild and spontaneous nature. But the overall trend would be unmistakable: humans increasingly moving through land and water and sky, wielding ever more powerful technologies, rearranging the world as one does with a lovingly tended garden.

This is the distressing conclusion toward which our argument leads: even with the most responsible attitude, even with the most ecologically sophisticated practices of territorial management, *we cannot stop the wildness from slowly leaching out of our world.* If we want to be truly effective in braking the process of artificialization, we will have to try something else.

The French Green leader, Antoine Waechter, offers a hint of where this "something else" might lie:

> It is vain to think that nature can be cooped up in "wildlife preserves": it has to be protected everywhere, throughout the land, in all its varying degrees of freedom. Those havens of spontaneous biological life that still survive in Europe have to be declared inviolable: rivers, wild gorges, our highest peaks, our ancient forests. But beyond those havens, on the whole territory, our farmers and foresters must ask themselves every day, as they go about their work, how they can allow the highest degree of biological diversity to flourish on their land. The peasants of a bygone era, before the arrival of tractors, managed to bring forth a countryside that teemed with life, even richer in plants and animals than the vast forest they had cut back to make way for their patchwork of fields and pastures. Accepting the wild: this means allowing life enough breathing-room to develop according to its own powers, without human interference, right alongside our human species.[4]

I refer to the attitude described by Waechter as Eco-Restraint: to coexist with a plant or animal, but not to interfere with its flourishing or suffering, its movements or habits; to know that one has the power to do something, but to refrain from doing it; to learn how to stay away, watch from a distance, let things be.

This, it turns out, is a profoundly difficult thing for a human being to achieve. We are rather deeply wired, most of us, to form concepts about our surroundings, and then to take action, making tangible adjustments in the reality that confronts us out there, until it conforms more closely with our ideas. We are inveterate interferers. And yet, it seems, this is precisely the habit we would have to unlearn, if we wanted to have a chance of stemming the rising tide of artificialization. We would have to learn how to be comfortable with holding back, standing clear, refraining. The opposite of intervention. The opposite of control.

A natural world approached through the ethos of Eco-Restraint would no doubt manifest a similar type of continuum to the one we described in the case of Eco-Management; but it would also have to be qualitatively different. At one extreme, humans would have to become much more comfortable than they are today with fencing off large tracts of territory and barring human presence from them altogether: some parts of the land (and ice and sky and water) would simply have to be declared off limits. But in all the wide variety of other kinds of spaces and territories, the underlying questions posed by Waechter would have to take a high priority: How can I allow the greatest degree of biodiversity to flourish in this space? How can I leave as much breathing-room as possible for nature to take its own course here? Insofar as I *must* intervene, how can I reduce my impact to an absolute minimum?

This attitude, Waechter emphasizes, does not just apply to the relatively pristine, remote places on our earth. It applies down the entire gamut of hybrids, right into our own backyards. On the farms: launching a systematic effort not only to avoid pesticides and herbicides, but also to leave room for a wide variety of uncultivated places—hedgerows, copses, swampy depressions, all those kinds of liminal areas in which fauna and flora can make a home and do their own thing. In the suburbs: enacting a similar philosophy, based on the creation of many interstitial spaces that no one interferes with, and that are allowed to grow according to local patterns of spontaneous seeding or natural animal and insect migration. Around the cities: creating industrial zones in which manufacturing activities are concentrated, and forbidding the establishment of new industrial sites and real estate developments. In the mountains: closing down some roads, and confining traffic to a few main arteries; building fewer recreational resorts, and lumping them together in large parks; restricting access to wilderness areas; finding substitutes for wood, and reducing the amount of logging. On the rivers and coastlines: setting aside many watercourses, large and small, to be allowed to run free; resisting the impulse to build dams; restricting human access to large stretches of beachfront. In the skies: channeling air traffic along specific corridors; learning to forego unnecessary travel; banning air traffic over large areas of the land. In the oceans: cutting back sharply on fishing; finding alternative foods; confining what fishing remains to certain delimited areas.

This impressionistic sketch makes it clear that the ethos of Eco-Restraint remains very far indeed from contemporary social and cultural reality. In virtually every one of the different types of territory just mentioned, some kind of sacrifice, self-imposed limit, higher cost, or act of relinquishment, would be required of human beings. Yet that is where the choice will ultimately lie. If humankind decides at some point to put the brakes on artificialization, or perhaps even to begin to reverse it, then these are the lines along which it will have to move. Nothing less will do the job.

16   A Cosmic Wilderness?

Cousteau's Grandchildren Swim the Rings of Saturn

Well, I dreamed I saw the silver space ships flying
In the yellow haze of the sun,
There were children crying and colors flying
All around the chosen ones.
All in a dream, all in a dream, the loading had begun.
They were flying Mother Nature's silver seed
To a new home in the sun.
Flying Mother Nature's silver seed to a new home.
—Neil Young, "After the Goldrush" (1970)[1]

There remains, of course, one rather drastic way to seek an escape from artifice—to run up against the outer boundaries of
our human world—and that is to leave behind the home planet
altogether. If the Earth is irretrievably finite, the sky is not: what
about outer space? Might it be that, in the century to come,
some of the roles played in human culture by wilderness will
come to be complemented, or extended, by the surrounding
planets and stars? Can our species find another dimension of
wildness out there, a partial outlet from the threat of earthly artificialization?

To an ardent green activist, the idea of looking for a new
wilderness in outer space might sound downright blasphemous.

It carries ominous overtones of defeatism and resignation, of writing off the home planet as a territory already spoiled, of running away from a problem rather than seeking to face it. This is probably why the notion of an extraterrestrial nature gets relatively short shrift in green circles.[2] Nevertheless, the idea is an intriguing one—and one that seems likely to press itself with growing forcefulness upon the citizenry of tomorrow, as the science and technology of space exploration make their faltering, groping progress during the decades to come. What will be the relationship between the nature that resides here on the crust of this small celestial body, and the nature that lies beyond? Whether this question makes environmentalists uncomfortable or not, it seems likely to fall under that category of issues—like the ethics of genetic engineering—that technological modernity simply compels a reluctant humankind to confront. A light-green future may well present humankind, *volens nolens,* with the unprecedented problems and promises of an "extraterrestrial ecology."

> > >

In France, much as in other industrialized nations, the main literature on space exploration has tended to appear as something quite separate from environmentalist writings.[3] Government planners, technology boosters, iconoclastic economists looking at long-term trends, readers of science fiction, futurologists—these form the main constituency from which the literature on outer space emanates. Among scientists, it is the physicists, engineers, and chemists, rather than the zoologists or ecological experts, who tend to be the ones asking most of the questions about the future of humanity's interaction with the stars.[4]

To be sure, many contemporary ecological scientists eagerly make use of high-altitude photographs and global climatic data rendered uniquely available through the potent medium of artificial satellites.[5] In a similar way, most historians of environmentalism would no doubt acknowledge that a fundamental threshold was crossed, in the evolution of popular attitudes toward the environment, when the earth's inhabitants got their first look at their blue planet as seen from the perspective of the moon.[6] In both these senses, the rise of environmentalism has indeed been closely linked to the rising fortunes of space exploration. But this is precisely the point: environmentalists have tended to remain profoundly earth-centric in their concerns, paying attention to space travel only insofar as it directly contributes to an understanding of terrestrial ecological systems.[7] When the astronauts' gaze shifted outward, away from earth, the environmentalists' attention immediately waned. Space stations, interstellar travel, colonization of neighboring planets—these concepts almost never appeared within the green agenda (whether in a positive or a negative light).[8]

This blind spot probably stems from two main causes. First, environmentalists evidently feared that space exploration would divert humankind's energies from the more urgent task of striking a balance in its relationship with earthly nature. Visions of space colonies, in this sense, would only distract people and nurture false hopes about a technological escape from terrestrial problems.[9] A subtler but perhaps equally important reason for the environmentalists' disaffection has been the prevailing language and imagery used by the promoters of space travel—a brash discourse of technological enthusiasm and unbridled optimism that would understandably grate on the ears of many green activists. One should not underestimate the influence exerted in this domain by critics of technology like Lewis Mumford and Jacques Ellul, not only in France, but among environmentalists worldwide.

Nevertheless, the question stubbornly remains: Might it someday be possible for outer space to function in human culture as an extension of the terrestrial wilderness? In addressing this issue, the case of France proves quite illuminating, for this nation has arguably rivaled the United States, Germany, and Russia in its enthusiastic and sustained pursuit of aeronautics and space exploration—both in the pioneering efforts of nineteenth-century visionaries, and even more vigorously since World War II. If we analyze the contemporary French scientific and commercial literature surrounding space programs—in practice, this means the Ariane rocket series and the European Space Agency (in which the French play a leading role)—we find that it falls roughly under three main headings, which can be labeled as Mystery, Money, and Power. In all three of these areas, the profound and recurrent parallels between the imagery of outer space and the imagery of earthly wilderness are simply too striking to ignore.

Under the heading of Mystery, we can situate all those writings whose genealogy goes back to Jules Verne's 1865 classic, *From the Earth to the Moon,* and to the lesser-known work by Camille Flammarion, *The Last Days of the World,* published in 1894.[10] Already in these pioneering works of French science fiction, we find outer space taking on the attributes that so captured the imagination of the post-World War II era: space as the realm of tangible infinity, a domain coming before the human and vastly greater than the human, pristine in its radical otherness, a place for adventure and heroism precisely because it lies beyond human control. As one French official with the European Space Agency recently put it: "Freeing oneself from gravity, exploring the universe: humankind is on the threshold of realizing its most ancient and mythic desires."[11] That this imagery of adventure in a boundless, primordial, uncharted realm closely echoes the classic literature of wilderness exploration hardly needs underscoring.[12]

Under the second heading, that of Money, we find a great deal of contemporary French literature about space programs. After an initial period of Gaullist pride and lavish spending for the early space conquests of the 1960s, French taxpayers in the 1980s and '90s wanted above all to know what they were getting in return for their investment.[13] Thus, most of the official pamphlets and press statements issued by the French offices of the European Space Agency in recent years have carefully avoided any reference to adventure and heroism, and have cleaved to a soberly practical line. Advanced telecommunications, mining of extraterrestrial resources, creating new materials and life forms in zero-gravity labs, harvesting energy from the surrounding galaxy—all these possibilities recur (somewhat breathlessly) in the mix of scientific and commercial literature that has emerged.[14]

An environmentalist reading this commercial space literature would be intrigued to find two opposed tendencies implicit here. On the one hand, space appears as a realm in which many traditional ecological constraints can be happily shrugged off: virtually endless abundance of many resources that are scarce on earth; no fear of thermal pollution; energy on a scale that easily satisfies even the greediest of civilizations; boundless voids into which we can nonchalantly throw our earthly trash, lobbing it off on graceful fifty million year trajectories toward other galaxies (or simply chucking it into the Sun).[15]

On the other hand, one also finds a very different subtext in the commercial literature, a recurrent theme that might be dubbed "space ecology."[16] It turns out that the near-orbital regions immediately surrounding the earth form a sphere that is already densely polluted with man-made debris—debris threatening to collide with today's space vehicles as they go about their business, a veritable minefield of Sputniks and Landsats and Telstars and thousands of careening bits of paraphernalia from the early Cold War. Therefore, we are told, we need to pay close attention to how we use space, respecting it as an environment like any other, and enacting a new and rigorous set of laws to protect it.[17] What we find here, then, is a discourse that closely parallels the "wise use" approach to earthly wilderness areas: nature is there for the taking, rich and plentiful; but we need to exercise restraint in appropriating it, taking into consideration the needs (and profits) of future generations.[18]

Finally we have the space of Power, military space.[19] Once again, two sharply opposed tendencies characterize the literature: on the one hand, a vision of space as *the* pivotal strategic arena for the next century, the domain that a nation (or alliance of nations) must control, if it is not to lie at the mercy of others.[20] On the other hand, we find space presented as a region that should at all costs be kept free of militarization: space as the common heritage of humankind, to be shared equitably by all comers, like a boundless Antarctica in the sky.[21] Both these visions recur throughout the French official and semiofficial literature: space as beacon of cooperation, space as the latest high-stakes prize in the long story of human competition.[22] Like the New World of America in the eighteenth century, like Africa in the nineteenth, space appears as a huge, unclaimed frontier zone in which the games of power and diplomacy must play themselves out.

Mystery, Money, and Power: outer space as primal, awe-inspiring, unpredictable, untouched by human hands, overwhelmingly vast, a potential trove of resources to be tapped, a region to be protected from man-made pollution, a strategic frontier area that as yet belongs to no one. All these features form a highly suggestive area of convergence or conceptual overlap between the wild nature of earth and the extraterrestrial nature beyond: one could be describing, with these kinds of adjectives, the North American West of the eighteenth century, or the Amazon rainforest of the twentieth century, with scarcely a modification or adjustment!

What kinds of factors, then, might prevent humankind from straightforwardly embracing extraterrestrial nature as a new dimension of wilderness for the twenty-first century? Here we confront two basic sets of questions, both of them inevitably speculative. First: insofar as wilderness has meaning for us, to what extent does it have to be grounded in biological life? In other words, does wilderness have to be green? To what extent can it consist of the more narrowly physical and chemical processes that predominate among the stars, planets, and nebulae?[23] For all we know, earthly biological life may be unique in the universe. Does it stretch the word "wild" beyond recognition to speak of a lunar landscape as a wilderness? How about the fiery surface of the sun? How about the intergalactic void, light-years removed from anything solid, a mind-bogglingly vast emptiness holding nothing but background radiation from the Big Bang and an occasional neutrino zinging by?

A second group of questions has to do with the human place in such an utterly alien domain. For the sake of argument, let us suppose for a moment that the greater cosmos indeed constitutes a kind of wilderness. Does the need for space suits and expensive rockets place an insurmountable barrier between us and this wild realm? Is the "natural" quality of extraterrestrial wilderness spoiled by the fact that we cannot simply open the door and go out for a stroll there, the way we do with a desert or a forest? If we cannot hold it in our hands, feel its breath on our face, so to speak, but have to approach it through the mediation of complex technologies, does this diminish its meaning for us? Or, to the contrary, will space suits and rockets one day assume a role analogous to that of scuba suits and ocean ships, opening the way, as they did for Jacques Cousteau and his aquatic friends, to the enjoyment of new natural realms?[24] Will our great-grandchildren, without giving it a second thought, slake their thirst for contact with Mother Nature by going camping in the asteroid belt, or floating among the rings of Saturn?[25]

If Cousteau's example offers any insight here, it is that the concept of wilderness easily stretches and reconfigures itself to adapt to novel circumstances. When the young Cousteau, standing on the dockside at Toulon, looked toward land, he saw a territory already well charted, buzzing with human activity; in essence, he saw Paul Valéry's *monde fini*, the "finite world." But when he turned and looked out at the Mediterranean, he saw more than just a blue-green surface of shifting waves: he envisioned another realm in another dimension, below, beyond. The only question was how to get there. Today, thanks in large part to Cousteau's efforts, few people would find difficulty in thinking of a coral reef, or an undersea kelp forest, as an integral facet of the earth's wilderness. The capacities of our knowledge, imagination, and affection have simply pushed outward a bit, encompassing new creatures, new formations.[26]

Perhaps something similar will happen with extraterrestrial nature, as the coming century takes shape. Perhaps the frames of reference will simply shift under our feet: forest fire, stellar fire; prairie wind, solar wind; clouds as white forms on light blue, clouds as multicolored nebulae on deep black; stars as points of light, stars as worlds; space as a piece of territory, space as utter emptiness; up and down as cardinal directions, up and down as anachronisms, replaced by new arcs of movement; moon as familiar earthly companion, moons as diverse and exotic orbitals; sky as envelope of air, sky as portal to the infinite.

The key, from an environmentalist's point of view, will of course lie in the way these new dimensions of wilderness are integrated—or fail to be integrated—with their more familiar terrestrial counterparts. But embracing the stars need not necessarily imply turning our backs on the Earth. When Cousteau launched his pioneering campaigns to save the world's coral reefs, this did not noticeably detract from ongoing environmentalist struggles to protect forests or mountain ecosystems: on the contrary, Cousteau's efforts arguably heightened the public's sensitivity to green issues along the whole broad range of natural spaces and territories, on land and sea alike. In a similar fashion, perhaps, the gradual inclusion of outer space within the reach of human affections, if it takes place during the coming century, might conceivably go hand-in-hand with a deepening appreciation of good old earth. The two worlds, "above" and "below," might benefit together, in the same concomitant opening of moral horizons. In the end, the basic ecological challenge would no doubt remain the same as ever: keeping balance in the evolving relationship between the wild and the tame, as these fertile opposites continue to contrast and commingle in ever-new ways.

Conclusion

I pondered all these things, and how men fight and lose the battle, and the thing they fought for comes about in spite of their defeat, and when it comes turns out not to be what they meant, and other men have to fight for what they meant under another name.

—William Morris, *The Dream of John Ball* (1903)[1]

The Age of Ecology Arrives (But it is not what anyone expected)

French society, in the period between 1960 and 2000, called into question and profoundly modified many key features of the industrial age, making a somewhat groping entry into a new era. Perhaps the most striking characteristic of this transformation lies in a recurring gap between intentions and outcomes—between the changes that people thought they were undertaking, and the results that actually took shape. In this sense, one of the defining emotions associated with this transitional process might, in retrospect, prove to be that of astonishment.

The paradoxes underlying our story have piled up, one after another. Environmentalists wanted to undo the culture of consumerism and replace it with a more restrained economic system: their ideas made a significant impact, and the result was a further expansion of consumerism, now offering a plethora of green products alongside the traditional items of its cornucopia. Green activists hoped to dismantle or at least curtail the cumbersome, overbearing institutions of the central state: French citizens enthusiastically agreed, and the result was a steady proliferation of new laws, administered by a rapidly expanding array of new governmental authorities and institutions. The greens identified Big Industry, with its smoke-belching factories and powerful political connections, as the quintessential Goliath that they, David-like, would have to engage in an unrelenting battle for economic restructuring; in the end, it was the industrial sector that most nimbly and efficiently made the leap into a greener mode of production, far outstripping the changes undertaken by all other social constituencies. Environmentalists campaigned tirelessly on behalf of a new definition of progress, in which the old, linear model of perpetual economic growth would give way to a new, cyclical model based on steady-state equilibrium; by the year 2000, one of the few real growth sectors of the French economy lay precisely in the "eco-professions" and "eco-industries"—the burgeoning assortment of firms that specialized in pollution control and other forms of green expertise.

Arguably the most important paradox of all, however, lay implicit in the core environmentalist notion of "saving" nature from the onslaught of technological modernity. This vision rested on a conception of nature and human culture as sharply distinct entities, confronting each other either as antagonists (in the past and present) or—hopefully, in some greener future—as complementary opposites. And yet, what gradually happened, as environmentalist ideas won converts and came to be institutionalized over several decades, was a concomitant erosion of this age-old boundary. Nature and culture, in the light-green society, inexorably blurred into each other, rendering the traditional distinction between them increasingly hard to maintain. Irony, indeed: it was the advent of environmentalism—the widely popular idea of saving nature—that helped explode the old conception of nature itself.

The light-green society was never anyone's blueprint or ideal goal: it was the outcome of ten thousand forces, some blind, some intentional, interacting and jostling and evolving over time. But we should not conclude from this that the light-green society was merely an impersonal historical product, disconnected from human agency. For we have also seen, in the preceding chapters, a long struggle grounded in tenacious hope, and in the stand taken by individuals on behalf of a moral vision—a struggle in which choices mattered, and values, in the end, made a difference. The results were imperfect, often bearing only a partial resemblance to the original aims: but they added up, over four decades, to a transformation that repositioned human beings in relation to the natural world.

Overall, the pattern was unmistakable: France's economy and culture grew steadily greener over the last four decades of the twentieth century. Perhaps the best way to think of the light-green society, in fact, is precisely as a *transitional state,* moving from one cluster of assumptions and practices toward another. To be sure, we must exercise caution in framing the issue in this manner: for nothing gives us any assurance that the coming decades will follow a teleological process, carrying France like a boat on a river, toward some preordained goal. Nothing allows us to be certain that the passage of time will bring a continued deepening of the shade of green that characterizes French society. Nevertheless, the trend so far offers reasonable grounds for hope: if the French continue to push forward along the path they have followed thus far, then it is at least plausible to imagine a future era in which the term "light green" will no longer fit, and some other metaphor will be required to capture the new constellation of relations between human beings, their myriad devices, and the biosphere.

To say more than this would be fatuous. A pessimist could argue that the French have already made all the easiest changes, and that the greening process will bog down as the population faces the more drastic and painful sacrifices required by true sustainability. An optimist could just as easily argue something quite different: that the French have successfully gotten past a very difficult initial phase, and that a generation raised and educated within the transformed *mentalités* and practices of the light-green society will prove all the more amenable to tackling the arduous challenges that lie ahead. We must leave it to Cousteau's great-grandchildren to tell us, someday, who turned out closer to the truth.

A Planet of *Paysage?*

One of the more disturbing conclusions reached in the foregoing chapters lies implicit in the image of the "managed earth"—a future world in which the rising tide of artifice slowly but inexorably penetrates nearly every corner, leaving less and less room for the spontaneous play of nature's wild creatures and uncontrolled forces. Even when we adopt relatively optimistic assumptions for the coming century, positing a steady rise in environmentalist awareness and mobilization, we find that the structural implications of the light-green society remain unforgiving: the planetary ratio between the wild and the tame continues unavoidably to tilt toward the latter. Like King Midas, our species appears to be cursed with a transformative touch: whether we like it or not, whether we intend it or not, we cannot help but surround ourselves with an increasingly domesticated planetary garden. Only a truly draconian program of ecological restraint—highly unlikely, at least under contemporary political realities—could offer a chance of turning things a different way.

If this is true, then one intriguing upshot is that contemporary France—a mid-sized European nation with an ancient history of human habitation—may actually offer a more representative glimpse into the global future than, say, the United States, Australia, Brazil, the Congo, or Russia. Barring extreme scenarios like a catastrophic collapse of global ecosystems, or a drastic greening of human society, the planet a century from now is likely to be a considerably tamer place than it is today: it has a higher probability of looking like today's densely populated Western European landscape than like the immense expanses of those other nations, with their large wilderness areas. Though it may be disconcerting to admit it, a country like France, with its territory embodying the relatively tame end of the spectrum of natural-artificial hybrids—a country with few surviving wildernesses and a great variety of partially humanized *paysage*—may turn out closer to the shape of things to come.

France's territory is one of the most diverse in Western Europe, spanning just about every kind of temperate environment, from snow-covered crags to lowland prairies, from vast forests to desolate ocean shores. Nevertheless, the most common image of nature among the French, not surprisingly, tends to be one of rolling fields, punctuated by small woodlands and lines of trees, a cold clear brook here, a hedgerow there—with perhaps a country lane or a medieval village off to one side. The French, as we have seen, wax ferocious when it comes to defending this kind of scenery—their ancestral countryside, with which they deeply and passionately identify. In this domain, they have many interesting possibilities to offer the rest of us, especially those of us in the Anglo-Saxon world. They can provide insight into building a fruitful relationship with the kind of nature that we are unfamiliar with, precisely because of our tendency to equate "real" nature with pristine wilderness: the French can help us to become comfortable, as they have done, with nature as lived and partially transformed countryside. What kinds of feelings do you grow up with, when you grow up surrounded by a natural world that is already semi-humanized, teeming with natural-artificial composites and crossovers of all sorts and shapes? What do words like "ecology" and "environmental protection" come to mean in such a context? These are questions that the French have become relatively good at answering, because this is in fact one of the defining features of their home turf.

Antoine Waechter, for example, devoted an entire chapter in his book *Dessine-moi une planète* to the theme "Accepter le sauvage"—accepting the wild. Yet he made it clear that he was not merely referring to inaccessible parks like the high Vanoise: he meant every spot in the territory in which biological life presented itself. An ecological attitude, in a country like France, meant valuing the whole tremendous gamut of sites in which the human and the nonhuman coexisted side-by-side; above all, it meant taking care to give as much breathing-room as possible to the territory's partially wild creatures and ecosystems, resisting the impulse of control or mastery, and allowing them to flourish unchanneled and unbidden, in all their diversity. "Our civilization," he wrote, "needs to make the transition from exploitation of nature to a true symbiosis with it—an ongoing relationship beneficial to both partners."[2]

To draw this kind of lesson from the case of postwar France is by no means to imply that we should relent in our dogged efforts to protect the wilder and more remote stretches of territory that have survived on earth into our era—*au contraire!* We should move especially aggressively to defend such spaces, precisely because we know that, *even in a light-green future,* many of those spaces will inexorably lose a great deal of their wildness unless we take preventive action soon. Having said this, however, we can also take away a more general precept from the first four decades of the greening of France. We can learn to appreciate wildness wherever it exists, in whatever degree, in whatever startling hybrid form it assumes; we can learn how to practice the delicate art of eco-restraint, in all those territories (vast and growing swaths) in which human activity has become a part of the daily life of the land. Building a constructive and respectful relationship with this kind of partially wild nature—the physical world that surrounds most of us—can serve as a potent complement to our ongoing efforts to protect wildernesses wherever they may still be found.

NOTES

INTRODUCTION

1. André Gorz, "Two Kinds of Ecology," *Le Sauvage* (April 1974), reprinted in André Gorz, *Ecology as Politics* (Boston: South End Press, 1980), 3.

2. Ernest Callenbach, *Ecotopia* (New York: Bantam, 1975).

3. Max Oelschlaeger, *The Idea of Wilderness: From Prehistory to the Age of Ecology* (New Haven: Yale University Press, 1991).

4. Emmanuel Le Roy Ladurie, *Montaillou: The Promised Land of Error,* trans. by Barbara Bray (New York: George Braziller, 1978).

5. Interview with François Pharabod, the head of the team that built Thémis, Paris (July 1, 1993). For a technical profile of Thémis see J. Hillairet, "Thémis, La Centrale Solaire," *Entropie* 18, no. 103 (1982): 6–10. See also Michel Grenon, *La Pomme nucléaire et l'orange solaire* (Paris: Robert Laffont, 1978).

6. See Alexandre Herléa, ed., *L'Energie solaire en France* (Paris: CTHS, 1995); Alain Liébard, Cédric Philibert, and Michel Rodot, *Du Neuf sous le soleil* (Paris: Calmann-Lévy/Systèmes Solaires, 1991).

7. David Roditi and André Joffre, *Tecsol: Equipement Solaire Thermique en Europe* (Brussels: Commission des Communautés Européennes, 1992), 59–60.

8. See the discussion in chapter 4.

9. I should make it clear that, although I wrote an undergraduate thesis on Hegel twenty years ago, this dialectical logic underlying my argument in no way reflects an effort to "apply" Hegel's ideas to postwar French history. On the contrary, this dialectical structure emerged late in the project's life, after I had completed my research and had already written the first part of the book. I use it because it appears to fit the unfolding of the historical events rather nicely, and not because it mirrors the thinking of a great (albeit thoroughly out-of-fashion) philosopher.

CHAPTER ONE

1. Frédéric Joliot-Curie, quoted in Robert Gilpin, *France in the Age of the Scientific State* (Princeton: Princeton University Press, 1968), 151.

2. Charles de Gaulle, quoted in Gilpin, 39.

3. The French government's chief scientist in charge of emergency public health measures went so far as to tell the French people in a press conference on May 2, 1986 (six days after the reactor meltdown in the Ukraine): "I personally am ready to go and stand, without protection, a few kilometers away from the Chernobyl reactor, just to show you how small the danger is." Ten days later the same official admitted the government had deceived the people of France, deliberately concealing the fact that the radioactive cloud from Chernobyl had passed over significant parts of French territory. Jerôme Strazzulla and Jean-Claude Zerbib, *Tchernobyl* (Paris: La Documentation Française, 1991).

4. Jolyon Howorth, "HiroChirac and the French Nuclear Testing Conundrum: A Testing Time for the Pursuit of Grandeur," *French Politics and Society* 13, no. 3 (Summer 1995): 10.

5. "Going Green," *The Economist* 322, no. 7748 (February 29, 1992). As an example of this perception among academics, here is a typical quotation, taken from an otherwise solid comparative work by the political scientist Russell Dalton: "The French [environmental] movement probably represents the nadir of institution building [compared with other European nations]. With the possible exception of the FFSPN, the French movement has been unable to develop a strong infrastructure for environmental action; the French bird society and World Wildlife Fund are the smallest in Europe, and French ecology groups are equally weak. . . . The relative weakness of the French movement stands out as a dramatic exception to the overall advance of environmentalism in Europe. . . . One can trace the disarray among French environmentalists to organizational problems within the movement itself, the government's hostility toward environmental groups, and the public's general aversion to group-structured political activities." What Dalton is inexplicably discounting here is precisely the most important grass-roots environmentalist organization in France, namely, France Nature Environnement—the French Federation of Societies for the Protection of Nature (FNE/FFSPN), whose membership of 850,000 is (according to Dalton's own statistics) larger than those of the British and German grass-roots environmentalist associations combined! Russell J. Dalton, *The Green Rainbow: Environmental Groups in Western Europe* (New Haven: Yale University Press, 1994), 91.

6. Marlise Simons, "Paris Can No Longer Hide a Dirty Secret: Pollution," *International Herald Tribune* (July 15–16, 1995), 2.

7. Jean Fourastié, *Les trente glorieuses* (Paris: Fayard, 1979); for statistics see Jean-Pierre Rioux, *La France de la Quatrième République,* vol. 1 (Paris: Seuil, 1980), chaps. 5 and 11, and vol. 2 (Paris: Seuil, 1983), chap. 5; and Serge Bernstein, *La France de l'expansion* (Paris: Seuil, 1989), chaps. 5 and 6.

8. Stanley Hoffmann, "Paradoxes of the French Political Community," in Stanley Hoffmann, ed., *In Search of France* (Cambridge, Mass.: Harvard University Press, 1963), 1–117.

9. Claude Bourdet, *L'aventure incertaine: De la résistance à la restauration* (Paris: Stock, 1975).

10. Jean-Jacques Carré, Paul Dubois, Edmond Malinvaud, *French Economic Growth,* trans. John P. Hatfield (Stanford: Stanford University Press, 1975); Charles P. Kindleberger, *Economic Growth in France and Britain, 1851–1950* (New York: Simon and Schuster, 1964); Charles P. Kindleberger, "The Postwar Resurgence of the French

Economy," in Stanley Hoffmann, ed., *In Search of France,* 118–58; and Fourastié, *Les trente glorieuses.*

11. Jean-Pierre Rioux, *La France de la Quatrième République,* 2:175.

12. See Kindleberger, *Economic Growth in France and Britain.*

13. Stanley Hoffmann, "Paradoxes of the French Political Community."

14. Richard F. Kuisel, *Capitalism and the State in Modern France: Renovation and Economic Management in the Twentieth Century* (Cambridge: Cambridge University Press, 1981), x.

15. Herrick Chapman, *State Capitalism and Working-Class Radicalism in the French Aircraft Industry* (Berkeley: University of California Press, 1991); Spencer R. Weart, *Scientists in Power* (Cambridge, Mass.: Harvard University Press, 1979).

16. Interview with Alain Beltran (Paris, January 1993).

17. Jean-Baptiste Duroselle, "Changes in French Foreign Policy Since 1945," in Stanley Hoffmann, ed., *In Search of France,* 331–32.

18. Fritz Stern, *The Politics of Cultural Despair: A Study in the Rise of the Germanic Ideology* (New York: Doubleday, 1961); Richard D. Alexander, *Darwinism and Human Affairs* (Seattle: University of Washington Press, 1979); Bernard Semmel, *Imperialism and Social Reform* (London: Allen and Unwin, 1968); Linda L. Clark, *Social Darwinism in France* (University, Ala.: University of Alabama Press, 1984).

19. Jean-Marc Brissaud, *Eléments pour une nouvelle politique etrangère* (Pau: Front National, Université d'été, September 1985), 38, 43; Harvey G. Simmons, *The French National Front* (Boulder: Westview, 1996); Jonathan Marcus, *The National Front and French Politics* (Houndmills, England: Macmillan, 1995); Françoise Gaspard, *A Small City in France,* trans. Arthur Goldhammer (Cambridge, Mass.: Harvard University Press, 1995).

20. See Michael Bess, *Realism, Utopia, and the Mushroom Cloud: Four Activist Intellectuals and their Strategies for Peace, 1945–1989* (Chicago: University of Chicago Press, 1993), 16–25, 34–40. The term "rayonnement," translated as "radiance," plays a central role in Gabrielle Hecht's study of postwar French technology policy, *The Radiance of France* (Cambridge, Mass.: MIT Press, 1998).

21. Zeev Sternhell, "Paul Déroulède and the Origins of Modern French Nationalism," in John C. Cairns, ed., *Contemporary France. Illusion, Conflict, and Regeneration* (New York: New Viewpoints, 1978), chap. 1; Stanley Hoffmann, "The Nation: What For? Vicissitudes of French Nationalism, 1871–1973," in *Decline or Renewal: France Since the 1930s* (New York: Viking, 1974), chap. 13.

22. Claude Digeon, *La crise allemande de la pensée française, 1870–1914* (Paris: PUF, 1959); Allan Mitchell, *Victors and Vanquished: The German Influence on Army and Church in France after 1870* (Chapel Hill: University of North Carolina Press, 1984).

23. Walter A. McDougall, *France's Rhineland Diplomacy, 1914–1924* (Princeton: Princeton University Press, 1978).

24. Koenraad W. Swart, *The Sense of Decadence in Nineteenth-Century France* (The Hague: Nijhoff, 1964).

25. Theodore Zeldin, *France, 1848–1945,* vol. 2, *Intellect, Taste, and Anxiety* (Oxford: Clarendon Press, 1977), chap. 19 ("Birth and Death").

26. On the Communists and national independence, see Richard F. Kuisel, *Seducing the French: The Dilemma of Americanization* (Berkeley: University of California Press, 1993), chaps. 2–4; on the Gaullists see chaps. 6 and 7.

27. I derive the main thrust of my argument here from the excellent discussions provided in Kuisel, *Capitalism and the State in Modern France;* Gilpin, *France in the Age of the Scientific State;* and Hecht, *The Radiance of France.*

28. On French images of America, see Richard Kuisel, *Seducing the French.* On the presumed Arab threat, see Horst Mendershausen, *Coping with the Oil Crisis: French and German Experiences* (Baltimore: John Hopkins University Press, 1976); and Harvey B. Feigenbaum, *The Politics of Public Enterprise: Oil and the French State* (Princeton: Princeton University Press, 1985). On French perceptions of a "Japanese challenge," see for instance Jean-Jacques Salomon, *Le gaulois, le cow-boy, et le samouraï: La politique française de la technologie* (Paris: Economica, 1986); and Guy Faure, "Le M.I.T.I., ou la politique à longue terme," *Revue française de gestion* (numéro spécial, "Le Japon mode ou modèle?"), nos. 27–28 (Sept.–Oct. 1980).

29. Thomas P. Hughes, *American Genesis: A Century of Invention and Technological Enthusiasm, 1870–1970* (New York: Viking, 1989).

30. Institut Français d'Opinion Publique [hereafter IFOP], *Les mutations idéologiques en France au cours des cinquante dernières années vues à travers les sondages de l'IFOP* (Paris: IFOP, 1991). See also the early chapters of Elie Cohen, *Le Colbertisme "high-tech"* (Paris: Hachette, 1992).

31. Hughes, *American Genesis,* 443.

32. Hecht, *The Radiance of France,* chaps. 1, 4, 7; Kuisel, *Seducing the French;* Irwin Wall, *The United States and the Making of Postwar France, 1945–1954* (Cambridge: Cambridge University Press, 1991); Tony Judt, *Past Imperfect: French Intellectuals, 1944–1956* (Berkeley: University of California Press, 1992), chap. 10.

33. Paul Gagnon, "*La Vie Future:* Some French Responses to the Technological Society," *Journal of European Studies* 6 (1976): 172–89; see also Hecht, *Radiance of France,* chap. 6.

34. Kuisel, *Seducing the French,* chap. 6; Jean Lacouture, *De Gaulle: The Ruler, 1945–1970,* trans. Alan Sheridan (New York: Norton, 1993), chap. 28.

35. Jean Baudrillard, *La société de consommation: Ses mythes, ses structures* (Paris: Denoël, 1970); Jean-Pierre Rioux, "Vive la consommation," *L'Histoire* 102 (July–August 1987): 90–100; Paul Yonnet, *Jeux, modes, et masses: La société française et le moderne, 1945–1985* (Paris: Gallimard, 1985); Eugen Weber, *Peasants into Frenchmen* (Stanford: Stanford University Press, 1976); Susan Carol Rogers, *Shaping Modern Times in Rural France* (Princeton: Princeton University Press, 1991).

36. Raymond Aron, *Progress and Disillusion: The Dialectics of Modern Society* (New York: Praeger, 1968), 214.

37. Cohen, *Le Colbertisme "high-tech,"* 96–100. The political scientist Robert Gilpin identified here one of the central paradoxes of postwar French technology policy. The language of the politicians and technocrats hinged on national autonomy, yet most French policymakers reluctantly admitted that France, by itself, simply lacked the resources to compete successfully with the mega-economies of Japan and the United States. Only a common European effort, a pooling of national resources among the many members of the EEC (or European Union, as it came to be known) could hope to redress the balance; but if French efforts were thus dissolved into a supranational venture, what would become of national autonomy, of the specifically *French* freedom of movement to which the Gallic leaders so ardently aspired? It was, according to Elie Cohen, a conundrum that remained unresolved in the 1990s as

much as it had been in the 1960s. See Gilpin, *France in the Age of the Scientific State,* chap. 12; and Hecht, *Radiance of France,* chap. 1.

38. Walter A. McDougall, *The Heavens and the Earth* (New York: Basic Books, 1985).

39. See Gilpin; John Zysman, *Political Strategies for Industrial Order: State, Market, and Industry in France* (Berkeley: University of California Press, 1977); Philip G. Cerny and Martin A. Schain, eds., *French Politics and Public Policy* (New York: St. Martin's, 1980); Kuisel, *Capitalism and the State in Modern France;* Robert L. Frost, "Mechanical Dreams: Democracy and Technological Discourse in Twentieth-Century France," in Langdon Winner, ed., *Democracy in a Technological Society* (Dordrecht, The Netherlands: Kluwer, 1992). In French, see Jean-Jacques Salomon, *Le gaulois, le cow-boy, et le samourai;* Patrick Cohendet and André Lebeau, *Choix stratégiques et grands programmes civils* (Paris: Economica, 1987); and Philippe Braillard and Alain Demant, *Eureka et l'Europe technologique* (Brussels: Axes\Bruylant, 1991).

40. Zysman, *Political Strategies for Industrial Order,* chap. 3; and Cohen, *Le Colbertisme "high-tech."*

41. Antoine de Saint-Exupéry, *Wind, Sand, and Stars,* trans. Lewis Galantière (London: Heinemann, 1939); Stacy Schiff, *Saint-Exupéry* (New York: Knopf, 1994).

42. Paul Denarié, *L'aventure de Concorde* (Paris: Presses Noires, 1969); André Turcat, *Concorde: Essais et batailles* (Paris: Stock, 1977).

43. "Nouveau Programme Français: La Super-Caravelle," *Informations Aéronautiques,* supplément no. 64 to no. 502 (Dec. 14, 1961), 1–2.

44. Denarie, *L'aventure de Concorde,* chaps. 2–4; Turcat, *Concorde: Essais et batailles,* chaps. 1–3.

45. Elliott J. Feldman, *Concorde and Dissent: Explaining High Technology Project Failures in Britain and France* (Cambridge: Cambridge University Press, 1985), 88–90. I rely heavily on Feldman's study throughout my own account that follows.

46. Feldman, *Concorde and Dissent,* 86.

47. Turcat, 94.

48. Feldman, chaps. 4, 5.

49. For an especially embittered account of the Americans' alleged machinations, see Turcat.

50. Feldman, 107–11.

51. Cover story, "Concorde Assassiné par les Américains?" *Paris-Match,* no. 1234 (Dec. 30, 1972).

52. Feldman, 104–108.

53. Andrew Wilson, *The Concorde Fiasco* (Harmondsworth: Penguin, 1973).

54. Institut Français d'Opinion Publique, "L'Avion Concorde," *Sondages* nos. 3 and 4 (1975), 86–93.

55. Jean-Jacques Servan-Schreiber, quoted in "La prodigieuse histoire de Concorde," *France-Soir* (March 6–7, 1977).

56. Daniel Todd and Jamie Simpson, *The World Aircraft Industry* (London: Croom Helm, 1986), chap. 7.

57. "Le seul rival: Le Tupolev 144 'Concordsky,'" *La Dépêche du Midi* (March 2, 1989); Turcat, chap. 18.

58. "Concorde: Toujours mieux," *Le Figaro* (Aug. 12, 1985); "Concorde, déja vingt ans et toujours vingt ans d'avance," *La Dépêche du Midi* (March 2, 1989); "Con-

corde: Dix ans de liaison Paris-New York," *Le Figaro* (Nov. 21, 1987). For a discussion of the French Communists' support for the Concorde, see Feldman, chap. 4.

59. Rosemary Wakeman, "The Concorde as Metaphor," in *Modernizing the Provincial City: Toulouse, 1945–1975* (Cambridge, Mass.: Harvard University Press, 1997), 199–205.

60. Spencer R. Weart, *Scientists in Power* (Cambridge, Mass.: Harvard University Press, 1979).

61. Richard Rhodes, *The Making of the Atomic Bomb* (New York: Simon and Schuster, 1986).

62. Hecht, *The Radiance of France.*

63. Lawrence Scheinman, *Atomic Energy Policy in France under the Fourth Republic* (Princeton: Princeton University Press, 1965); Wolf Mendl, *Deterrence and Persuasion: French Nuclear Armament in the Context of National Policy, 1945–1969* (New York: Praeger, 1970); and Michael Harrison, *The Reluctant Ally: France and Atlantic Security* (Baltimore: Johns Hopkins Press, 1981). In French: Charles Ailleret, *L'aventure atomique française* (Paris: Grasset, 1968); Philippe Simonnot, *Les nucléocrates* (Grenoble: Presses Universitaires de Grenoble, 1978); Francis Fagnani and Alexandre Nicolon, eds., *Nucléopolis: Matériaux pour l'analyse d'une société nucléaire* (Grenoble: Presses Universitaires de Grenoble, 1979); Daniel Dollfuss, *La force de frappe* (Paris: Julliard, 1960); Alfred Fabre-Luce, *L'Or et la Bombe* (Paris: Calmann-Lévy, 1968); Gen. Pierre Gallois, *Le renoncement: De la France défendue à l'Europe protégée* (Paris: Plon, 1977); Alexandre Sanguinetti, *La France et l'arme atomique* (Paris: Julliard, 1964); Maurice Bertrand, *Pour une doctrine militaire française* (Paris: Gallimard, 1965); Gen. André Beaufre, *L'OTAN et l'Europe* (Paris: Calmann-Lévy, 1966); Raymond Aron, *Le grand débat: Initiation à la stratégie atomique* (Paris: Calmann-Lévy, 1963) [translated into English as *The Great Debate* (New York: Doubleday, 1965)].

64. See Weart, *Scientists in Power,* 262–66; and Hecht, *Radiance of France,* chap. 2.

65. On de Gaulle's role see Philip H. Gordon, *A Certain Idea of France: French Security Policy and the Gaullist Legacy* (Princeton: Princeton University Press, 1993), chap. 2; and Mendl, *Deterrence and Persuasion.*

66. Stephen A. Kocs, *Autonomy or Power? The Franco-German Relationship and Europe's Strategic Choices, 1955–1995* (Westport, Conn.: Praeger, 1995), 85.

67. Gordon, *A Certain Idea of France,* chap. 1.

68. On the more recent history and theory of the French nuclear weapons program, see Edward A. Kolodziej, "French Nuclear Policy: Adapting the Gaullist Legacy to the Post-Cold War World," in Michael J. Mazarr and Alexander T. Lennon, eds., *Toward a Nuclear Peace: The Future of Nuclear Weapons* (New York: St. Martin's, 1994); David S. Yost, *France's Deterrent Posture and Security in Europe,* Adelphi Papers no. 194 (London: International Institute for Strategic Studies, 1984); David S. Yost, "Nuclear Debates in France," *Survival* 36, no. 4 (Winter 1994–95): 113–39; Theodore Robert Posner, *Current French Security Policy: The Gaullist Legacy* (New York: Greenwood Press, 1991); Robert Aldrich and John Connell, eds., *France in World Politics* (London: Routledge, 1989); Philippe G. Le Prestre, ed., *French Security Policy in a Disarming World: Domestic Challenges and International Constraints* (Boulder: Rienner, 1989); Robbin F. Laird, ed., *French Security Policy: From Independence to Interdependence* (Boulder: Westview, 1986).

69. Richard C. Eichenberg, *Public Opinion and National Security in Western Europe*

(Ithaca: Cornell University Press, 1989), 93; Gregory Flynn and Hans Rattinger, eds., *The Public and Atlantic Defense* (London: Rowman and Allanheld, 1985), chap. 3; Institut Français d'Opinion Publique, *Les mutations idéologiques en France.*

70. Eichenberg, *Public Opinion,* 93.

71. Renata Fritsch-Bournazel, "France: Attachment to a Non-Binding Relationship," in Flynn and Rattinger, eds., *The Public and Atlantic Defense,* 82.

72. David Hanley, "The Parties and the Nuclear Consensus," in Jolyon Howorth and Patricia Chilton, eds., *Defence and Dissent in Contemporary France* (London: Croom Helm, 1984), 82–89.

73. Raymond E. Burrell, *The French Communist Party, Nuclear Weapons, and National Defense: Issues of the 1978 Election Campaign* (Washington: U.S. Government Printing Office, 1979); Diana Johnstone, *The Politics of Euromissiles: Europe's Role in America's World* (London: Verso, 1984), chap. 3.

74. Jolyon Howorth, "Defence and the Mitterrand Government," in Howorth and Chilton, eds., *Defence and Dissent in Contemporary France,* chap. 4; Gordon, *A Certain Idea of France,* chap. 5.

75. Claude Bourdet, "The Rebirth of a Peace Movement," in Howorth and Chilton, chap. 7.

76. Christian Mellon, "Peace Organizations in France Today," in Howorth and Chilton, chap. 8.

77. For an example of this "fake consensus" line of argument, see Posner, *Current French Security Policy,* 134.

78. See the exhaustive comparative compilation of such opinions in Eichenberg, *Public Opinion.*

79. Eichenberg, 124–25.

80. Charles de Gaulle, quoted in Charles G. Cogan, *Charles de Gaulle: A Brief Biography with Documents* (New York: St. Martin's, 1996), 129.

81. Rocard, quoted in Stephen Henningham, *France and the South Pacific* (Honolulu: University of Hawaii Press, 1992), 166.

82. Although one often finds the atoll's name misspelled as "Mururoa," the correct spelling, and the one used by Polynesians, is "Moruroa."

83. Roger Faligot and Pascal Krop, *La Piscine. The French Secret Service since 1944,* trans. W. D. Halls (London: Basil Blackwell, 1989); Douglas Porch, *The French Secret Services: From the Dreyfus Affair to the Gulf War* (New York: Farrar, Straus, and Giroux, 1995).

84. Another nearby atoll, Fangataufa, would also be used by the French for their nuclear tests.

85. Henningham, *France and the South Pacific;* and Jean Chesneaux and Nic Maclellan, *La France dans le Pacifique: De Bougainville à Moruroa* (Paris: La Découverte, 1992).

86. Michael King, *Death of the Rainbow Warrior* (Harmondsworth: Penguin, 1986), 229; and Robin Morgan and Brian Whitaker, *Rainbow Warrior: The French Attempt to Sink Greenpeace* (London: Arrow, 1986).

87. Paul Wapner, "In Defense of Banner Hangers: The Dark Green Politics of Greenpeace," in Bron Taylor, ed., *Ecological Resistance Movements: The Global Emergence of Radical and Popular Environmentalism* (Albany: State University of New York Press, 1995); Robert Hunter, *The Greenpeace Chronicle* (New York: Picador, 1982);

Philippe Lequenne, *Dans les coulisses de Greenpeace* (Paris: L'Harmattan, 1997); Olivier Vermont, *La face cachée de Greenpeace* (Paris: Albin Michel, 1997).

88. Chesneaux and Maclellan, *La France dans le Pacifique,* 114.

89. King, *Death of the Rainbow Warrior,* chap. 3.

90. King, chap. 4.

91. "Fabius accable Hernu et Lacoste," *Le Figaro* (Sept. 26, 1985), 1.

92. Hernu finally admitted, two years later, that he had indeed played the key role of which he stood accused: *"Rainbow Warrior* is an action of State that I conducted," he told a journalist working for *Le Nouvel Observateur* in 1987. Bertrand le Gendre, "Quand M. Hernu niait le sabotage," *Le Monde* (Nov. 5, 1987).

93. Sondage Figaro-SOFRES, *Le Figaro* (Sept. 26, 1985).

94. Sondage IPSOS-Le Matin, quoted in Chesneaux and Maclellan, 116.

95. Olivier Chevrillon, "Pouvoir: Silence, on flotte," *Le Point* 680 (Sept. 30, 1985), 69.

96. Sondage Figaro-SOFRES, *Le Figaro* (Sept. 26, 1985).

97. Brendan Prendiville, *Environmental Politics in France* (Boulder: Westview, 1994), 37–38.

98. R.C., "Greenpeace-France se saborde," *Le Monde* (Dec. 15, 1987), 15.

99. See the Greenpeace website at: http://www.greenpeace.fr/.

CHAPTER TWO

1. Fernand Braudel, *The Identity of France,* trans. Siân Reynolds (New York: Harper Collins, 1990), 2:674–75. After consulting the original French text, I have slightly modified the translation of the first sentence.

2. Fernand Braudel, *The Mediterranean and the Mediterranean World in the Age of Philip II,* trans. Siân Reynolds (New York: Harper and Row, 1972 [first French ed. 1949]), 2:757.

3. Braudel, *The Identity of France,* 2:677. After consulting the original French text, I have modified the translation of the sentence beginning, "I do not think it is right. . . ."

4. Daniel Tacet, *Un monde sans paysans* (Paris: Hachette, 1992); Jean-Marie Pesez and Emmanuel Le Roy Ladurie, "The Deserted Villages of France: An Overview," in Robert Forster and Orest Ranum, eds., *Rural Society in France* (Baltimore: Johns Hopkins University Press, 1977); Pierre Alphandéry, Pierre Bitoun, and Yves Dupont, *Les champs du départ* (Paris: La Découverte, 1989); Pierre Estienne, *Terres d'abandon? La population des montagnes françaises: hier, aujourd'hui, demain* (Clermont-Ferrand: Institut d'Etudes du Massif Central, 1988); Henri Mendras, *The Vanishing Peasant,* trans. Jean Lerner (Cambridge, Mass.: MIT Press, 1970). For an example of a novel that reached a huge audience in the early 1990s by playing directly upon the theme of nostalgia for the "lost world" of peasant culture, see Frédérique Hébrard, *Le château des oliviers* (Paris: Flammarion, 1993). For a work that calls into question the alleged tendency for modernization to destroy age-old rural traditions, see Susan Carol Rogers, *Shaping Modern Times in Rural France* (Princeton: Princeton University Press, 1991).

5. Sally Sokoloff, "Rural Change and Farming Politics: A Terminal Peasantry," in Philip G. Cerny and Martin A. Schain, eds., *French Politics and Public Policy* (New York: St. Martin's, 1980); and Michel Gervais, Marcel Jollivet, and Yves Tavernier, *La fin de la France paysanne: Depuis 1914,* vol. 4 of Georges Duby and Armand Wallon,

eds., *Histoire de la France rurale* (Paris: Seuil, 1977), 120–77, 242–68, 354–82, 597–674. For an overview of these modernization programs in their broader political context, see Jean-Pierre Rioux, *La France de la Quatrième République,* 2 vols. (Paris: Seuil, 1980, 1983).

6. See the statistics in Rioux, 2:170; and in Philippe Lebreton, *La nature en crise* (Paris: Sang de la Terre, 1988), 158.

7. Lebreton, 157.

8. See Gervais et al., *La fin de la France paysanne,* 111–19.

9. Priscilla de Roo and Jean-Paul Laborie, eds., *Atlas de l'aménagement du territoir* (Paris: DATAR/La Documentation Française, 1988), part 1 ("Espace Rural"). See also the pamphlet compiled by the Confédération Paysanne, *L'Agriculture paysanne* (Paris: Confédération Paysanne, 1990).

10. Tacet, *Un monde sans paysans.* See also Jacques Baudry and Anne-Sophie Acx, eds., *Ecologie et friche dans les paysages agricoles* (Paris: Ministère de l'Environnement, 1993).

11. Tacet, 11.

12. Mendras, *The Vanishing Peasant,* 228.

13. See the discussion in chapters 5 and 6.

14. Maurice Failevic, *Le cheval vapeur* (Antenne 2/S.F.P., 1980 [16mm., 97 mins.]). This is one among several hundred films on French agriculture, nature, and rural life held by the cinémathèque of the Ministry of Agriculture in Paris; access to these films is open to all researchers. For a listing see Ministère de l'Agriculture et de la Forêt, *Catalogue de films* (1990). See also the special issues of the journal *Ciném-Action,* "Cinémas Paysans" (no. 16 [1982]), and "Cinéma et monde rural" (no. 36 [1986]).

15. Georges Rouquier, *Farrebique* (L'Ecran Français, Films Etienne Lallier, 1947 [16mm., 90 mins.]).

16. Michel Duvigneau, "Les communautés villageoises de Maurice Failevic," *CinémAction* 36 (1986): 124–28.

17. Pierre Estienne, *Terres d'abandon? La population des montagnes françaises: hier, aujourd'hui, demain* (Clermont-Ferrand: Institut d'Etudes du Massif Central, 1988).

18. John Ardagh, *France Today* (London: Penguin, 1995), 231–40.

19. Alphandéry, Bitoun, and Dupont, *Les champs du départ,* chap. 8.

20. Gervais et al., *La fin de la France paysanne,* 480–553, 613–73.

21. René Colson, *Un paysan face à l'avenir rural* (Paris: Epi, 1976); Michel Debatisse, *La révolution silencieuse* (Paris: Calmann-Lévy, 1963).

22. Sally Sokoloff, "Rural Change and Farming Politics," 510–37.

23. De Roo and Laborie, eds., *Atlas de l'aménagement du territoir,* parts 1 and 6.

24. Jean Ferrat, "La montagne" (Paris: Productions Gérard Meys, 1964), in *Jean Ferrat: 20 Chansons* (Paris: Sacem/Temey, 1980)

25. Nicole Mathieu, "La notion de rural et les rapports ville-campagne en France: Des années cinquante aux années quatre-vingts," in *Economie Rurale* 187 (May–June 1990), 35–41.

26. Commissariat Général du Plan, *France rurale: Un nouveau contrat* (Paris: Documentation Française, 1993); Jacques Chérèque, ed., *Une nouvelle étape pour l'aménagement du territoire* (Paris: Documentation Française, 1990); Jean-Yves Capul, ed., *L'Etat de la décentralisation* (Paris: Documentation Française, 1992).

27. Braudel, *The Identity of France,* vol. 2, chap. 6.

28. Hoffmann, "Paradoxes of the French Political Community," in Stanley Hoffmann, ed., *In Search of France* (Cambridge, Mass.: Harvard University Press, 1963), 1–117.

29. Armand Frémont, "La terre," in Pierre Nora, ed., *Les lieux de mémoire* (Paris: Gallimard, 1992), 2:20.

30. Jean-François Gravier, *Paris et le désert français* (Paris: Le Portulan, 1947).

31. Rosemary Wakeman, *Modernizing the Provincial City: Toulouse, 1945–1975* (Cambridge, Mass.: Harvard University Press, 1997); Serge Berstein, *La France de l'expansion* (Paris: Seuil, 1989), 168.

32. Philippe Pinchemel, *France: A Geographic, Social, and Economic Survey,* trans. Dorothy Elkins with T. H. Elkins (Cambridge: Cambridge University Press, 1987); Xavier de Planhol, *Géographie historique de la France* (Paris: Fayard, 1988); Charles Debbasch and Jean-Marie Pontier, *La société française* (Paris: Dalloz, 1989); Christopher Flockton and Eleonore Kofman, *France* (London: PCP, 1989); Hilary P. M. Winchester, *Contemporary France* (Harlow: Longman, 1993).

33. Jean-Pierre Rioux, *La France de la Quatrième République,* 2:204.

34. Henry Rousso, ed., *De Monnet à Massé* (Paris: Editions du Centre National de la Recherche Scientifique, 1986); Richard F. Kuisel, *Capitalism and the State in Modern France: Renovation and Economic Management in the Twentieth Century* (Cambridge: Cambridge University Press, 1981).

35. Carré, Dubois, and Malinvaud, *French Economic Growth,* chap. 14.

36. De Roo and Laborie, part 4, "Communications."

37. Flockton and Kofman, *France,* chap. 4; Chérèque, ed., *Une nouvelle étape pour l'aménagement du territoire.*

38. Capul, ed., *L'Etat de la décentralisation.*

39. For a useful overview see Flockton and Kofman, *France.*

40. Antonio Jimenez-Blanco, "Bref point de vue de la doctrine espagnole," in Capul, ed., *L'Etat de la décentralisation,* 102.

CHAPTER THREE

1. Louis Napoleon, quoted in Tamara L. Whited, *Forests and Peasant Politics in Modern France* (New Haven: Yale University Press, 2000), 58.

2. Andrée Corvol, *L'Homme aux bois* (Paris: Fayard, 1987), iv.

3. Alain Corbin, *The Lure of the Sea: The Discovery of the Seaside in the Western World, 1750–1840,* trans. Jocelyn Phelps (Berkeley: University of California Press, 1994).

4. Simon Schama, *Landscape and Memory* (New York: Knopf, 1995), 546–60. See also Nicholas Green, *The Spectacle of Nature: Landscape and Bourgeois Culture in Nineteenth-Century France* (Manchester: Manchester University Press, 1990).

5. Veronique Puvilland, *Cent ans de publicité industrielle* (Paris: Editions L'Usine Nouvelle, 1991). A fine collection of these kinds of images is kept in the Centre de Documentation, Musée de la Publicité (Union des Arts Décoratifs), in Paris.

6. Clarence J. Glacken, *Traces on the Rhodian Shore: Nature and Culture in Western Thought from Ancient Times to the End of the Eighteenth Century* (Berkeley: University of California Press, 1967), 129–30.

7. See for example David Abram, *The Spell of the Sensuous* (New York: Vintage Books, 1996).

8. This definition is a composite derived from many sources. Among the most prominent: Donald Worster, *Nature's Economy: A History of Ecological Ideas,* 2d ed. (Cambridge: Cambridge University Press, 1994); Carolyn Merchant, *Radical Ecology* (New York: Routledge, 1992); Roderick Nash, *The Rights of Nature: A History of Environmental Ethics* (Madison: University of Wisconsin Press, 1989); Max Oelschlaeger, *The Idea of Wilderness: From Prehistory to the Age of Ecology* (New Haven: Yale University Press, 1991); Jean-Paul Deléage, *Histoire de l'écologie* (Paris: La Découverte, 1991); Pascal Acot, *Histoire de l'écologie* (Paris: PUF, 1988); Guillaume Sainteny, *Les Verts* (Paris: PUF, 1991); Dominique Simonnet, *L'Ecologisme,* second ed. (Paris: PUF, 1982).

9. A useful complement to this chronological perspective is provided in Richard Grove's *Green Imperialism: Colonial Expansion, Tropical Island Edens and the Origins of Environmentalism, 1600–1860* (Cambridge: Cambridge University Press, 1995). Grove argues that historians have underestimated the importance, for the history of environmental thought, of the encounter that took place in the colonial context between European naturalists and the exotic cultures that they had been sent to study and help administer. In the tropical islands of Dutch, British, and French colonies, according to Grove, we find the first instances of Europeans systematically taking stock of the damage being done by deforestation and intensive cultivation, and insisting as a result on strong measures of preservation and conservation. Though these measures were not always implemented, he contends, they nonetheless constituted the earliest exemplars of an environmentalist mentality at work. The problem with this fascinating thesis is that Grove tries to push it too far, claiming that these colonial scientists are the true progenitors of twentieth-century eco-activism—a claim that ultimately fails to persuade because he cannot show any real link of continuity between these men and the green movements of the present. The chasm is simply too great between the mass politics of an information age, animated by visions of ozone holes and global warming, and the relatively isolated (and soon forgotten) work of these pioneering colonial officials. Nevertheless, what Grove does show is that, in the small-scale context of a tropical island, the concepts of finitude and interconnectedness more readily made themselves apparent, and hence allowed these early scientists to foreshadow most intriguingly the conceptual tools of an era still far in the future.

10. Robert E. Ricklefs, *Ecology,* 3d ed. (New York: W. H. Freeman, 1990); Worster, *Nature's Economy;* Jean-Paul Deléage, *Histoire de l'écologie;* Pascal Acot, *Histoire de l'écologie.*

11. Giulio Barsanti, *La mappa della vita: Teorie della natura e teorie dell'uomo in Francia, 1750–1850* (Naples: Guida, 1983); Jacques Roger, *The Life Sciences in Eighteenth-Century French Thought* (Stanford: Stanford University Press, 1997).

12. Toby A. Appel, *The Cuvier-Geoffroy Debate: French Biology in the Decades Before Darwin* (New York: Oxford University Press, 1987).

13. See Michael Osborne, *Nature, the Exotic, and the Science of French Colonialism* (Bloomington: Indiana University Press, 1994), an excellent study from which I derive much of my present account. See also Jean-Pierre Raffin, "De l'écologie scientifique à l'écologie politique," and Serge Moscovici, "La polymérisation de l'écologie,"

both in Marc Abélès, ed., *Le défi écologiste* (Paris: L'Harmattan, 1993). See also Jean Carlier, "De la Nouvelle Héloise à René Dumont," and Alain Ravenau, "Quelques mythes fondateurs," in Thierry Grillet and Daniel Le Conte Des Floris, eds., *Les natures du vert* (Paris: Autrement, 1986).

14. Osborne, chap. 1.

15. Corvol, *L'Homme aux bois,* 10–13.

16. Schama, *Landscape and Memory,* 175.

17. Whited, *Forests and Peasant Politics in Modern France;* Bernard Kalaora and Antoine Savoye, "La protection des régions de montagne au XIXe siècle: Forestiers sociaux contre forestiers étatistes," in A. Cadoret, ed., *Protection de la nature: Histoire et idéologie: De la nature à l'environnement* (Paris: L'Harmattan, 1985); Corvol, *L'Homme aux bois;* Louis Badré, *Histoire de la forêt française* (Paris: Arthaud, 1983); Pierre Bazire and Jean Gadant, *La forêt en France* (Paris: Documentation Française, 1991).

18. Jean-Pierre Raffin and Georges Ricou, "Le lien entre les scientifiques et les associations de protection de la nature: Approche historique," in A. Cadoret, ed., *Protection de la nature,* 61–62.

19. Raymond Dominick, *The Environmental Movement in Germany* (Indiana: Indiana University Press, 1993), 41.

20. Worster, *Nature's Economy,* 269.

21. See Meyer Abrams, *Natural Supernaturalism: Tradition and Revolution in Romantic Literature* (New York: Norton, 1973); Oelschlaeger, *The Idea of Wilderness,* chaps. 4 and 5; Jean-Paul Deléage, *Histoire de l'écologie,* 33–56.

22. See Chris J. Magoc, *Yellowstone: The Creation and Selling of an American Landscape, 1870–1903* (Albuquerque: University of New Mexico Press, 1999).

23. For a fascinating discussion of nineteenth-century French apprehensions of landscape, see Nicholas Green, *The Spectacle of Nature;* see also Pascal Guillot, "Données historiques de l'environnement et perspectives d'avenir" (unpublished manuscript, Université des Sciences et Techniques de Lille, 1988), 30–37.

24. Guillot, 26.

25. Philip Shabecoff, *A Fierce Green Fire: The American Environmental Movement* (New York: Hill and Wang, 1993), chap. 9.

26. Raffin and Ricou, "Le lien entre les scientifiques," 64–65.

27. Green, *The Spectacle of Nature,* 76–127.

28. Jean-Claude Chamboredon, "La naturalisation de la campagne," in Cadoret, *Protection de la nature,* 138–52.

29. Kalaora and Savoye, "La protection des régions de montagne au XIXe siècle: Forestiers sociaux contre forestiers étatistes," in Cadoret, *Protection de la nature,* 8–12.

30. Acot, *Histoire de l'écologie,* 224.

31. Guillot, 29.

32. Jean-Pierre Raffin, "De l'écologie scientifique à l'écologie politique," in Abélès, *Le défi écologiste,* 28–29.

33. A. Gruvel, *Deuxième Congrès International pour la Protection de la Nature: Procès-verbaux, rapports, et voeux* (Paris: Société d'Editions, 1932), 548.

34. Robert Elliott, *Faking Nature: The Ethics of Environmental Restoration* (New York: Routledge, 1997).

35. Osborne, *Nature, the Exotic, and the Science of French Colonialism,* 59–61.

36. Guillot, 141–42; see also the IUCN website at http://www.iucn.org/.

37. Roger Heim, *Destruction et protection de la nature* (Paris: Armand Colin, 1952).

38. Rae Goodell, *The Visible Scientists* (Boston: Little, Brown, 1975), 39–40.

39. Richard Munson, *Cousteau: The Captain and his World* (New York: Morrow, 1989).

40. Jacques-Yves Cousteau, "Water is an Embracing Medium," *Calypso Log* 12, no. 2, English-language edition (June 1985): 24.

41. Jacques-Yves Cousteau, "Mes premiers soixante-quinze ans," *Calypso Log* 37, French edition (June 1985): 4–11.

42. Munson, 235–36.

CHAPTER FOUR

1. Maxime Le Forestier, "Comme un arbre" (Paris: Polydor, 1972).

2. I conducted interviews with a wide variety of French green activists, most of them in Paris, between 1993 and 1999. This version of the "dead fish" anecdote is a simplified composite of various accounts with which I was presented during my interviews.

3. I. G. Simmons, *Interpreting Nature: Cultural Constructions of the Environment* (London: Routledge, 1993); Catherine Larrère and Raphaël Larrère, *Du bon usage de la nature: Pour une philosophie de l'environnement* (Paris: Aubier, 1997), 23–56.

4. Rae Goodell, *The Visible Scientists* (Boston: Little, Brown, 1975), 39–40.

5. Philippe Lebreton, quoted in Florian Charvolin, "L'invention de l'environnement en France (1960–1971): Les pratiques documentaires d'agrégation à l'origine du Ministère de la protection de la nature et de l'environnement." Dissertation in political science, Université Pierre Mendès-France de Grenoble and Ecole Nationale Supérieure des Mines de Paris [Centre de Sociologie de l'Innovation], 1993), 184.

6. Jean Dorst, *Avant que nature meure* (Paris: Delachaux et Niestlé, 1965).

7. Arthur Marwick, *The Sixties* (New York: Oxford University Press, 1998).

8. Keith A. Reader, ed., *The May 1968 Events in France: Reproductions and Interpretations* (New York: St. Martin's, 1993); David Caute, *The Year of the Barricades: A Journey Through 1968* (New York: Harper and Row, 1988); and Todd Gitlin, *The Sixties: Years of Hope, Days of Rage* (New York: Bantam, 1987).

9. Walter Lewino, *L'Imagination au pouvoir* (Paris: Eric Losfeld, 1968); Alain Schnapp and Pierre Vidal-Naquet, *The French Student Uprising, November 1967– June 1968: An Analytical Record*, trans. Maria Jolas (Boston: Beacon, 1971).

10. Alain Buhler, *Petit dictionnaire de la révolution étudiante* (Paris: Didier, 1968), 45–46.

11. The writings of Daniel Cohn-Bendit, the French student leader in 1968, constitute another key source from which any direct reference to environmental issues remains strikingly absent. In his *Obsolete Communism: The Left-wing Alternative,* published in 1968, one finds abundant references to alienation and bureaucracy, Trotskyism and Gaullism, authoritarianism and capitalism—but virtually nothing on the environment. This fact is all the more notable given the future role of Cohn-Bendit in the late 1990s as a political leader of the French green movement. See also the analyses offered in D. L. Hanley and A. P. Kerr, eds., *May '68: Coming of Age* (London: Macmillan, 1989); Laurent Joffrin, *Mai 68* (Paris: Seuil, 1988); Adrien Dansette, *Mai 1968* (Paris: Plon, 1971); and Alain Touraine, *The May Movement*, trans. Leonard F. X. Mayhew (New York: Random House, 1971).

12. Brice Lalonde, *Sur la vague verte* (Paris: Laffont, 1981), chap. 8.

13. Daniel Boy, "Les écologistes en France," *French Politics and Society* 10, no. 3 (Summer 1992): 1–25; Jean-Luc Bennahmias and Agnès Roche, *Des verts de toutes les couleurs: Histoire et sociologie du mouvement écolo* (Paris: Albin Michel, 1992); Guillaume Sainteny, *Les Verts* (Paris: PUF, 1991), 13–25; Tad Shull, "The Ecologists in the Regional Elections: Strategies Behind the Split," *French Politics and Society*, vol. 10, no. 2 (Spring 1992): 13–19; and Raymond Pronier and Vincent Jacques le Seigneur, *Génération Verte: Les écologistes en politique* (Paris: La Renaissance, 1992).

14. Reader, *The May 1968 Events in France*; Neill Nugent and David Lowe, *The Left in France* (New York: St. Martin's, 1982); Philip G. Cerny, ed., *Social Movements and Protest in France* (New York: St. Martin's, 1982); James F. Hollifield and George Ross, eds., *Searching for the New France* (New York: Routledge, 1991), especially chaps. 4, 7, 9.

15. Jane Jenson, "From *Baba Cool* to a *Vote Utile*: The Trajectory of the French *Verts*," *French Politics and Society* 7, no. 4 (Fall 1989): 1–15; Jack Hayward, "Dissentient France: The Counter Political Culture," in Cerny, 1–16; and Tony Chafer, "The Anti-Nuclear Movement and the Rise of Political Ecology," in Cerny, 202–20.

16. Dominique Simonnet, *L'Ecologisme*, 2d ed., (Paris: PUF, 1982); Jean-Paul Deléage, *Histoire de l'écologie* (Paris: La Découverte, 1991); Pascal Acot, *Histoire de l'écologie* (Paris: PUF, 1988); Christian Brodhag, *Objectif terre: Les Verts, de l'écologie à la politique* (Paris: Félin, 1990); Antoine Waechter, *Dessine-moi une planète* (Paris: Albin Michel, 1990); Fabrice Nicolino, *Le tour de France d'un écologiste* (Paris: Seuil, 1993); André Gorz, *Ecology as Politics*, trans. Patsy Vigderman and Jonathan Cloud (Boston: South End Press, 1980).

17. See the special edition of the popular magazine *Paris Match*, "Spécial Marée Noire: Les Bretons se mobilisent devant le fléau qui vient de la mer" (April 22, 1967). See also the parliamentary debates reported in *Journal Officiel*, no. 24 (April 26, 1967); and François de Beaulieu, *Les dents du progrès: La marée noire* (Paris: Le Sycomore, 1978).

18. Jean Carlier, *Vanoise: Victoire pour demain* (Paris: Calmann-Lévy, 1972); see also the website at www.parks.it/parco.nazionale.gran.paradiso/.

19. Carlier, 146.

20. Georges Pompidou, *Entretiens et discours, 1968–1974* (Paris: Flammarion, 1984); Florian Charvolin, "L'invention de l'environnement en France."

21. Robert Poujade, *Le ministère de l'impossible* (Paris: Calmann-Lévy, 1975), chap. 2. Subsequent books by holders of this office include: Brice Lalonde, *Sur la vague verte* (Paris: Laffont, 1981); Ségolène Royal, *Pays, paysans, paysages: La réconciliation est-elle possible?* (Paris: Laffont, 1993); and Michel Barnier, *Le défi écologique: Chacun pour tous* (Paris: Hachette, 1991). For a balance sheet of the ministry's activities, see Philippe Lebreton, *La nature en crise* (Paris: Sang de la Terre, 1988), chaps. 5, 7, 8.

22. Poujade, 25.

23. Poujade, 26.

24. Charvolin, chaps. 4 and 5.

25. Poujade, 27.

26. A brief history of the Club of Rome is given at the following website: http://www.cacor.ca/corhis.html.

27. Donella H. Meadows et al., *The Limits to Growth: A Report for the Club of Rome's Project on the Predicament of Mankind* (New York: Universe Books, 1972); Eduard Pestel, *Beyond the Limits to Growth* (New York: Universe Books, 1989).

28. For information on the UN's biosphere reserves, see the website at www.unesco.org/mab/.

29. Philip Shabecoff, *A Fierce Green Fire: The American Environmental Movement* (New York: Hill and Wang, 1993); Pascal Guillot, "Données historiques de l'environnement et perspectives d'avenir" (unpublished manuscript, Université des Sciences et Techniques de Lille, 1988), 112–14.

30. No comparative history of the environmental movement in major industrial nations has yet, to my knowledge, been written. Anna Bramwell, *Ecology in the Twentieth Century: A History* (New Haven: Yale University Press, 1989) constitutes an unconvincing effort in that general direction. For international comparisons, therefore, one is left to scholarly monographs on each separate nation, along with scholarly comparative works on "new social movements" that include articles on environmental activism. See Sara Parkin, *Green Parties: An International Guide* (London: Heretic Books, 1989); Russell J. Dalton, *The Green Rainbow: Environmental Groups in Western Europe* (New Haven: Yale University Press, 1994); and Ferdinand Müller-Rommel, "Green Parties and Alternative Lists Under Cross-National Perspective," in F. Müller-Rommel, ed., *New Politics in Western Europe* (Boulder: Westview Press, 1989). For monographs on other nations see Fred Singleton, ed., *Environmental Problems in the Soviet Union and Eastern Europe* (Boulder, Colo.: Lynne Reinner, 1987); Vaclav Smil, *The Bad Earth: Environmental Degradation in China* (New York: M. E. Sharpe, 1984); Mario Diani, *The Green Connection: Structures of Environmental Action in Italy* (Edinburgh: Edinburgh University Press, 1994); Raymond Dominick, *The Environmental Movement in Germany* (Indiana: Indiana University Press, 1993); Werner Hülsberg, *The German Greens*, trans. Gus Fagan (London: Verso, 1988); Herbert Kitschelt, *The Logics of Party Formation: Ecological Politics in Belgium and West Germany* (Ithaca, N.Y.: Cornell University Press, 1989); Philip Lowe and Jane Goyder, *Environmental Groups in Politics* (London: Allen and Unwin, 1983); Victor Scheffer, *The Shaping of Environmentalism in America* (Seattle: University of Washington Press, 1991).

31. For overviews of the French environmental movement's history, see Daniel Boy, Vincent Jacques le Seigneur, and Agnès Roche, *L'Ecologie au pouvoir* (Paris: Presses de Sciences Po, 1995); Florence Faucher, *Les habits verts de la politique* (Paris: Presses de Sciences Po, 1999); Jean Jacob, *Histoire de l'écologie politique: Comment la gauche a redécouvert la nature* (Paris: Albin Michel, 1999); Jean-Luc Bennahmias and Agnès Roche, *Des Verts de toutes les couleurs;* Sainteny, *Les Verts;* Simonnet, *L'Ecologisme;* Pronier and Jacques le Seigneur, *Génération Verte.*

32. Pronier and Jacques le Seigneur, chap. 7; Lalonde, *Sur la vague verte.*

33. Pierre Aguesse, *Clefs pour l'écologie* (Paris: Séghers, 1971); Marcel Clébant, *Croisade pour la mer* (Paris: Fayard, 1972); Barry Commoner, *Quelle terre laisserons-nous à nos enfants?* (Paris: Seuil, 1969); Pierre George, *L'Environnement* (Paris: PUF, 1971); Philippe Saint-Marc, *Socialisation de la nature* (Paris: Stock, 1975); Jacques Vernier, *La bataille de l'environnement* (Paris: Laffont, 1971); Serge Moscovici, *La société contre nature* (Paris: Union Générale d'Editions, 1972); René Dumont, *L'Utopie ou la mort* (Paris: Seuil, 1974); Prof. Mollo-Mollo [Philippe Lebreton], *L'Energie, c'est vous* (Paris: Stock, 1974); Ivan Illich, *Energie et équité* (Paris: Seuil, 1973) and *La convivialité*

(Paris: Seuil, 1974); Jean Baudrillard, *La société de consommation* (Paris: Gallimard, 1974); René Dubos, *Nous n'avons qu'une terre* (Paris: Denoël, 1972).

34. These films are all available at the cinémathèque of the Ministère de l'Agriculture in Paris; for a complete listing see Ministère de l'Agriculture et de la Forêt, *Catalogue de films* (1990).

35. Institut Français d'Opinion Publique [hereafter IFOP], *Les mutations idéologiques en France,* 20.

36. *Sondages* (1972, no. 3), 120.

37. IFOP, *Les mutations idéologiques,* 186.

38. Ronald Inglehart, *Culture Shift in Advanced Industrial Society* (Princeton: Princeton University Press, 1990).

39. Inglehart, *Culture Shift,* chap. 11.

40. Pronier and Jacques le Seigneur, chaps. 1–3. Among the most germane of Reiser's works for the topic of environmentalism are *On vit une époque formidable, La vie au grand air, On est passé à côté du bonheur,* and *Gros dégueulasse* (all published in Paris by Albin Michel).

41. James Jasper, *Nuclear Politics: Energy and the State in the United States, Sweden, and France* (Princeton: Princeton University Press, 1990), 149–54.

42. Pronier and Jacques le Seigneur, 37.

43. Dumont, *L'Utopie ou la mort;* Jean-Paul Besset, *René Dumont: Une vie saisie par l'écologie* (Paris: Stock, 1992); Brice Lalonde, Serge Moscovici, René Dumont, and Jean-Pierre Ribes, *Pourquoi les écologistes font-ils de la politique?* (Paris: Seuil, 1978).

44. Pronier and Jacques le Seigneur, 48.

45. Bennahmias and Roche, *Des Verts de toutes les couleurs,* 35–61.

46. W. B. Yeats, "The Second Coming," in *The Collected Poems of W. B. Yeats* (London: Macmillan, 1965), 211.

47. James Jasper, *Nuclear Politics;* Jean-Claude Debeir, Jean-Paul Deléage, and Daniel Hémery, *In the Servitude of Power: Energy and Civilization through the Ages,* trans. John Barzman (London: Zed, 1991); Dorothy Nelkin and Michael Pollak, *The Atom Besieged: Extraparliamentary Dissent in France and Germany* (Cambridge: MIT Press, 1981).

48. Spencer R. Weart, *Scientists in Power* (Cambridge, Mass.: Harvard University Press, 1979), chaps. 17 and 18; Gabrielle Hecht, *The Radiance of France,* chap. 2.

49. Quoted in Debeir et al., *In the Servitude of Power,* 193.

50. Hecht, *Radiance of France,* chaps. 2 and 3; Jean-François Picard, Alain Beltran, and Martine Bungener, *Histoire(s) de l'EDF: Comment se sont prises les décisions de 1946 à nos jours* (Paris: Dunod, 1985); and Robert L. Frost, *Alternating Currents: Nationalized Power in France, 1946–1970* (Ithaca: Cornell University Press, 1991).

51. Horst Mendershausen, *Coping with the Oil Crisis: French and German Experiences* (Baltimore: John Hopkins University Press, 1976).

52. Messmer, quoted in Picard et al., *Histoire(s) de EDF,* 205–206.

53. Debeir et al., 199.

54. Jean-Jacques Salomon, "De la transparence," in Collège de la Prévention des Risques Technologiques, *Le risque technologique et la démocratie* (Paris: Documentation Française, 1994), 19–33.

55. Picard et al., 193.

56. Paul Bonnet, *Pourquoi l'energie nucléaire?* (Paris: Commissariat à l'Energie Atomique, 1982); Marceau Felden, *Energie: Le défi nucléaire* (Paris: Leson, 1976).

57. See the comprehensive analyses in Hecht, chaps. 2, 3, 5, and 8; and Jasper, chap. 5.

58. Hecht, chap. 8.

59. Hecht, chap. 8; Picard et al., chap. 12; Philippe Simonnot, *Les nucléocrates* (Grenoble: PUG, 1978), 187–201.

60. Jasper, 252–53.

61. Debeir et al., 211.

62. Groupement de Scientifiques pour l'Information sur l'Energie Nucléaire (GSIEN), *Plutonium sur Rhône* (Paris: Syros, 1981); and Dominique Finon, *L'Echec des surgénérateurs* (Grenoble: PUG, 1989).

63. See Parti Socialiste, *Energie: L'Autre politique* (Paris: Club Socialiste du Livre, 1980).

64. Jasper, chap. 13.

65. See the tabulation of fifteen years' opinion polls in Jasper, 261. Only in 1976 and 1977 did French public opinion tilt slightly against the nuclear power plants. Then, in 1978, the trend returned to a pro-nuclear ratio, becoming ever more strongly skewed in support of the nuclear program with each passing year.

66. Gérard Duménil, "Energie nucléaire et opinion publique," in Francis Fagnani and Alexandre Nicolon, eds., *Nucléopolis: Matériaux pour l'analyse d'une société nucléaire* (Grenoble: PUG, 1979), 324.

67. Charles Villeneuve, *Les Français et les centrales nucléaires,* transcript of television series (Europe 1/Sofedir, 1980). See also M. Marie, G. Masson, S. Mathieu, B. Ollivier, J. F. Ricard, and P. Weis, *L'Opinion publique face au nucléaire,* vol. 1, "Sondages," and vol. 2, "Entretiens" (Paris: Centre d'Etudes Sociologiques et Travaux de Recherches Appliquées, 1980).

68. Jacques Antoine and Véronique Popelin-Camus, *Nucléaire, écologie, environnement: L'Evolution de l'opinion publique française perçue à travers les sondages* (Paris: Centre d'Etudes Socio-Economiques et de Management, 1991); Organization for Economic Cooperation and Development, *L'Energie nucléaire et l'opinion publique* (Paris: OCDE, 1984).

69. Hecht, chaps. 6 and 7; Michèle Rivasi and Hélène Crié, *Ce nucléaire qu'on nous cache* (Paris: Albin Michel, 1998); Jean-François Viel, *La santé publique atomisée* (Paris: La Découverte, 1998); Jean-Pierre Pharabod and Jean-Paul Schapira, *Les jeux de l'atome et du hasard* (Paris: Calmann-Lévy, 1988).

70. Jasper, 242; Pierre Samuel, *Le nucléaire en questions* (Paris: Entente, 1975).

71. Françoise Zonabend, *The Nuclear Peninsula,* trans. J. A. Underwood (Cambridge: Cambridge University Press, 1993), 19–24; Alexandre Nicolon, "Analyse d'une opposition à un site nucléaire," in Fagnani and Nicolon, *Nucléopolis,* chap. 4; Jasper, 88.

72. Zonabend, chaps. 5 and 6; Finon, *L'Echec des surgénérateurs,* chap. 9; Pharabod and Schapira, *Les jeux de l'atome et du hasard;* Union Fédérale des Consommateurs, "Nucléaire: Le face-à-face," *Que Choisir* (numéro special, 1977).

73. Pierre Samuel, *Le nucléaire en questions;* Simonnot, *Les nucléocrates;* Jasper, 152–53.

74. Jasper, 163–64.

75. Samuel, *Le nucléaire en questions,* 56–63, 96–107.

76. Zonabend, chap. 3; Hecht, chaps. 6–7.

77. Quoted in Jasper, 176–77.

78. For an exhaustive statement of the pro-nuclear point of view, published under the auspices of the CEA, see Bonnet, *Pourquoi l'energie nucléaire?*

79. This argument recurs continually in the discourse of nuclear technocrats. See Simonnot, Part II; Debeir et al., chap. 11; Hecht, chaps. 6, 8; and Felden, *Energie: Le défi nucléaire.*

80. See the excellent overview in Jasper, chap. 13; see also Pronier and Jacques le Seigneur, chap. 2.

81. Brendan Prendiville, *Environmental Politics in France* (Boulder: Westview, 1994), 12–17.

82. Jasper, 239.

83. Quoted in Pronier and Jacques le Seigneur, 52.

84. Jasper, chap. 13; Collectif d'Enquête, *Aujourd'hui Malville, demain la France: Livre noir* (La pensée sauvage, 1978).

85. N. J. D. Lucas, *Energy in France: Planning, Politics, and Policy* (London: Europa, 1979), 209, cited in Jasper, 238–39.

86. Villeneuve, *Les Français et les centrales nucléaires.*

87. Jasper, 89.

88. Debeir et al., 204.

89. Debeir et al., 217.

90. Quoted in Debeir et al., 218.

91. Debeir et al., 218–19.

92. Faucher, *Les habits verts de la politique;* Jacob, *Histoire de l'écologie politique;* Bennahmias and Roche, *Des Verts de toutes les couleurs;* Sainteny, *Les Verts;* Simonnet, *L'Ecologisme.*

93. The best overviews of this process are given in Faucher, *Les habits verts de la politique;* Boy, Jacques le Seigneur, and Roche, *L'Ecologie au pouvoir;* and Sainteny, *Les Verts.*

94. Sainteny, 14–19.

95. Aujourd'hui L'Ecologie, ed., *Le pouvoir de vivre: Le projet des écologistes avec Brice Lalonde,* special edition of the journal *Ecologie* (Montargis: Ecologie Mensuel, March 1981).

96. Bennahmias and Roche, *Des verts de toutes les couleurs,* 62–64.

97. Sainteny, 19–25.

98. Pronier and Jacques le Seigneur, chap. 11.

99. Prendiville, *Environmental Politics in France,* 48.

100. Waechter, *Dessine-moi une planète.*

101. Bennahmias and Roche, 77–79.

102. Jerôme Strazzulla and Jean-Claude Zerbib, *Tchernobyl* (Paris: La Documentation Française, 1991), 49–80.

103. Quoted in Strazzulla and Zerbib, 22.

104. Quoted in Strazzulla and Zerbib, 31.

105. Antoine and Popelin-Camus, *Nucléaire, écologie, environnement,* 43.

106. Strazzulla and Zerbib, 81–88. See also the semi-official publication produced for French farmers by the Commissariat à l'Energie Atomique and the French Farmers' Association (FNSEA), *Agriculture, environnement, et nucléaire: Comment réagir en cas d'accident* (Paris: FNSEA, 1990). The document made explicit reference to the "cruel experience" of the Chernobyl aftermath, with its wild rumors and contradictory information.

107. The debate among the experts, meanwhile, continued to rage. See Bernard Wiesenfeld, *L'Atome écologique* (Les Ulis: EDP Sciences, 1998); and Rivasi and Crié, *Ce nucléaire qu'on nous cache.* See also chapter 11, note 57, below.

108. Philippe Ansel, *L'Attitude des Français à l'égard de l'energie nucléaire en 1992* (Paris: EDF, March 1993); and Commission des Communautés Européennes, *L'Opinion européenne et les questions énergétiques en 1991* (Brussels: CCE, 1992).

109. Prendiville, 45–51.

110. Roger Cans, *Tous verts! La surenchère écologique* (Paris: Calmann-Lévy, 1992).

111. Boy, Jacques le Seigneur, and Roche, *L'Ecologie au pouvoir,* chaps. 4–7.

112. Pronier and Jacques le Seigneur, chaps. 5–7.

113. Prendiville, 56–64.

114. Dominique Voynet, "Les Verts: Un Parti en Pleine Mutation," in Bernard Lefort, ed., *Le nouveau livre des Verts* (Paris: Editions du Félin, 1999), 11–17; Murielle Szac, *Dominique Voynet: Une vraie nature* (Paris: Plon, 1998).

115. See the exhaustive documentation provided on the Greens' website at http://www.verts.imaginet.fr/histoire.html.

116. Voynet, "Les Verts: Un Parti en Pleine Mutation," 11–17; see also the balance sheet on the following website: http://www.verts.imaginet.fr/documents/jbildep.html.

117. Jean-Marcel Bouguereau, "Dany Cohn-Bendit, est-il allemand ou français?" in Les Verts, *Numéro Unique: L'Europe: Nos désirs, nos débats, nos choix,* supplement to the journal *Vert Contact* (May–June 1999), 16.

118. Antoine Guiral, "Cohn-Bendit dope les Verts," *Libération* (June 14, 1999), available on the web at http://www.liberation.com/europeennes/actu/990614h.html. See also J.P., "Dany séduit les jeunes," *Libération* (June 17, 1999), 17.

119. Jean-Michel Thénard, "Un succès dérangeant pour Lionel Jospin," *Libération* (June 17, 1999), 16.

120. See the transcript of the January 1999 televised debate between Waechter and Cohn-Bendit at http://www.alsapresse.com/jdj/99/01/14/MA/article_1.html.

121. Alain Lipietz, *Green Hopes: The Future of Political Ecology,* trans. Malcolm Slater (Cambridge, England: Polity Press, 1995). See also the website at http://perso.club-internet.fr/lipietz/Index.htm.

CHAPTER FIVE

1. André Gorz, *Ecology as Politics,* trans. Patsy Vigderman and Jonathan Cloud (Boston: South End Press, 1980), 41.

2. Max Oelschlaeger, *The Idea of Wilderness: From Prehistory to the Age of Ecology* (New Haven: Yale University Press, 1991), 28.

3. I. G. Simmons, *Environmental History: A Concise Introduction* (Oxford: Blackwell, 1993), 3–29.

4. Peter Gay, *The Enlightenment: An Interpretation* (New York: Vintage, 1966).

5. Karl Marx and Friedrich Engels, *The Communist Manifesto* (New York: International Publishers, 1948), 13–14.

6. Statistics drawn from the website of the Department of Material Science and Engineering at the University of Illinois, Urbana/Champaign: http://matse1.mse.uiuc.edu/~tw/energy/prin.html.

7. Carolyn Merchant, *Radical Ecology* (New York: Routledge, 1992).

8. For a concise overview see Christian Brodhag, *Objectif terre* (Paris: Editions du Félin, 1990).

9. Roland de Miller, *Robert Hainard, peintre et philosophe de la nature* (Paris: Sang de la Terre, 1987); and Jean Jacob, *Histoire de l'écologie politique: Comment la gauche a redécouvert la nature* (Paris: Albin Michel, 1999).

10. Antoine Waechter, *Dessine-moi une planète* (Paris: Albin Michel, 1990). For a discussion of Waechter's leadership of the Greens, see Raymond Pronier and Vincent Jacques le Seigneur, *Génération Verte: Les écologistes en politique* (Paris: La Renaissance, 1992); and Jacob, *Histoire de l'écologie politique,* 136–61.

11. See the FNE website at www.multimania.com/fne/.

12. Georges Cingal, "Rapport D'Activités," *La Lettre du Herisson* 139bis (July–August 1992), 38–39.

13. Ivan Illich, *Tools for Conviviality,* taken from the web version of the text: http://www.la.psu.edu/philo/illich/tools/intro.html. For a brief overview of Illich's life and work, see http://www.cogsci.ed.ac.uk/~ira/illich/.

14. Jacques Ellul, *The Technological Bluff* (Grand Rapids: Eerdmans, 1990). For a discussion of Ellul's impact, see Victor Ferkiss, *Nature, Technology, and Society: Cultural Roots of the Current Environmental Crisis* (New York: New York University Press, 1993), chap. 12; and Paul Gagnon, "*La Vie Future:* Some French Responses to the Technological Society," *Journal of European Studies* 6 (1976): 172–89.

15. Ellul, *The Technological Society* (1964): this quotation is taken from the text reproduced on the website: http://www.regent.edu/acad/schcom/rojc/mdic/ellul1.html.

16. See for example the Greens' assessment of the Internet, on their website: http://www.verts.imaginet.fr/yc.html.

17. René Dumont, *L'Utopie ou la mort* (Paris: Seuil, 1974); Jean-Paul Besset, *René Dumont: Une vie saisie par l'écologie* (Paris: Stock, 1992).

18. Bernard Lefort, ed., *Le nouveau livre des Verts* (Paris: Editions du Félin, 1999), 69–77.

19. Institut Français de l'Environnement, ed., *L'Environnement en France, Edition 1999* (Paris: La Découverte, 1998), 150. Hereafter "Ifen."

20. Bernard Charbonneau, *Sauver nos régions: Ecologie et sociétés locales* (Paris: Sang de la Terre, 1991).

21. Daniel Boy, Vincent Jacques le Seigneur, and Agnès Roche, *L'Ecologie au pouvoir* (Paris: Presses de Sciences Po, 1995); Jacob, *Histoire de l'écologie politique;* Jean-Luc Bennahmias and Agnès Roche, *Des Verts de toutes les couleurs: Histoire et sociologie du mouvement écolo* (Paris: Albin Michel, 1992); Guillaume Sainteny, *Les Verts* (Paris: PUF, 1991); Dominique Simonnet, *L'Ecologisme,* 2d ed. (Paris: PUF, 1982).

22. Murielle Szac, *Dominique Voynet: Une vraie nature* (Paris: Plon, 1998).

23. Alain Lipietz, *Green Hopes: The Future of Political Ecology,* trans. Malcolm

Slater (Cambridge, England: Polity Press, 1995), 29. See also Lipietz's website at http://perso.club-internet.fr/lipietz/Index.htm.

24. Lipietz, *Green Hopes*, 7. I have slightly condensed the translation.

25. Lefort, ed., *Le nouveau livre des Verts*.

26. Interviews with Jean-Pierre Raffin, Paris, 1993.

27. Luc Ferry, *Le nouvel ordre écologique* (Paris: Grasset, 1992); *The New Ecological Order*, trans. Carol Volk (Chicago: University of Chicago Press, 1995).

28. Michel Serres, *Le contrat naturel* (Paris: Bourin, 1990).

29. Louis P. Pojman, ed., *Environmental Ethics* (Boston: Jones and Bartlett, 1994), 64–123, 155–85.

30. Ferry does not present these four propositions as explicitly as I do here in summarizing his argument.

31. François Terrasson, *La civilisation anti-nature* (Monaco: Editions du Rocher, 1994); Dominique Bourg, ed., *Les sentiments de la nature* (Paris: La Découverte, 1993); Jean Viard, *Le tiers espace: Essai sur la nature* (Paris, 1990); Roland De Miller, *Robert Hainard, peintre et philosophe de la nature* (Paris, 1987); Nicole Mathieu, "La notion de rural et les rapports ville-campagne en France: Des années cinquante aux années quatre-vingts," *Economie Rurale* 187 (May–June 1990): 35–41.; Jacques Baudry and Anne-Sophie Acx, eds., *Ecologie et friche dans les paysages agricoles* (Paris: Ministère de l'Environnement, 1993); Pierre Nora, ed., *Les lieux de mémoire*, vol. 2 (Paris: Gallimard, 1992).

32. France also shares with Italy another possible factor, namely, the traditions of the Catholic church, which, according to some scholars, may have influenced perceptions of nature by perpetuating traditions of other-worldliness, in contrast to Protestantism, which emphasized the individual's relation to the divine, and hence opened the door for a more direct involvement in the affairs of this earth. See Viard, *Le tiers espace*, 59–73.

33. Eric Hirsch and Michael O'Hanlon, eds., *The Anthropology of Landscape: Perspectives on Place and Space* (Oxford: Clarendon Press, 1995); Nicholas Green, *The Spectacle of Nature: Landscape and Bourgeois Culture in Nineteenth-Century France* (Manchester: Manchester University Press, 1990); and Simon Schama, *Landscape and Memory* (New York: Knopf, 1995).

34. Phillippe Collomb and France Guérin Pace, eds., *Les Français et l'environnement* (Paris: Institut National d'Etudes Demographiques, 1998), 83–84.

35. Waechter, *Dessine-moi une planète*, 96. See also 113.

36. Charbonneau, *Sauver nos régions*, 175.

37. Charbonneau, 178. I provide a condensed translation of Charbonneau's text here.

38. See Catherine Larrère and Raphaël Larrère, *Du bon usage de la nature: Pour une philosophie de l'environnement* (Paris: Aubier, 1997), chap. 2.

39. See the detailed discussion of the minuscule splinter group of "authoritarian greens" in Pronier and Jacques le Seigneur, *Génération Verte*, 189–218.

40. Lipietz, *Green Hopes*, 33.

41. Sainteny, *Les Verts*; Boy, Jacques le Seigneur, and Roche, eds., *L'Ecologie au pouvoir*.

42. Lefort, ed., *Le nouveau livre des Verts*, 159–68; see also Pronier and Jacques le

Seigneur, *Génération Verte,* 189–218; Florence Faucher, *Les habits verts de la politique* (Paris: Presses de Sciences Po, 1999), 191–269.

43. For a discussion of this right-wing ruralist tradition, see Michel Gervais, Marcel Jollivet, and Yves Tavernier, *La fin de la France paysanne: Depuis 1914,* vol. 4 of Georges Duby and Armand Wallon, eds., *Histoire de la France rurale* (Paris: Seuil, 1977), 452–79. See also René Rémond, *The Right Wing in France from 1815 to de Gaulle,* trans. James M. Laux (Philadelphia: University of Pennsylvania Press, 1969).

44. See the CPNT website at http://www.cpnt.asso.fr/. See also Sergio Dalla Bernardina, *L'Utopie de la nature: Chasseurs, écologistes, et touristes* (Paris: Imago, 1996); Lefort, ed., *Le nouveau livre des Verts,* 235–38.

45. Ferry, *The New Ecological Order,* 89–90.

46. Lefort, ed., *Le nouveau livre des Verts,* 111–16.

47. Jean-Marie Legay and Robert Barbault, eds., *La révolution technologique en écologie* (Paris: Masson, 1995).

48. Lefort, ed., *Le nouveau livre des Verts,* 214. I am providing a condensed translation here.

CHAPTER SIX

1. Bernard Charbonneau, *Sauver nos régions: Ecologie et sociétés locales* (Paris: Sang de la Terre, 1991), 27. I have slightly condensed the translation.

2. Bernard Lefort, ed., *Le nouveau livre des Verts* (Paris: Editions du Félin, 1999).

3. I have loosely based this concept of loan cars on a French experiment named Praxitèle, conducted in the mid-1990s in the town of Saint-Quentin-en-Yvelines, near Paris. It involved fifty electric Renaults, offered on a rotating system of public rentals. See the website at http://www-rocq.inria.fr/praxitele/historique.html.

4. The position of the Greens in their 1999 platform was that the only acceptable "universal language" would be Esperanto. I am here making the judgment that this position is too unrealistic (even for a utopia!), and hence draw from earlier Green electoral platforms, in which Esperanto was not mentioned. Dominique Foing, ed., *Le livre des Verts* (Paris: Editions du Félin, 1994).

5. The Greens' 1999 electoral platform aimed for 2030 as the year in which the last nuclear-fired electric power plant would be shut down. Judging from what most of France's scientific experts have written (even those who oppose nuclear energy and support the development of renewable energy sources), this date seems unrealistic (again, even for a utopia). In discussing energy issues here, I have therefore drawn from the more sober prognostications of France's "pro-Green" scientific experts, rather than from the overly sanguine presentation in the Greens' electoral platform. See Benjamin Dessus and François Pharabod, "Jérémie et Noé: Deux scénarios énergétiques mondiaux à long terme," *Revue de Energie* 421 (June 1990). See also Pierre Boisson, ed., *Energie 2010–2020: Les chemins d'une croissance sobre* (Paris: Documentation Française, 1998); Alain Liébard, Cédric Philibert, and Michel Rodot, *Du neuf sous le soleil* (Paris: Calmann-Lévy/Systèmes Solaires, 1991); Alexandre Herléa, ed., *L'Energie solaire en France* (Paris: CTHS, 1995).

6. Bruno Comby, *Le nucléaire, avenir de l'écologie?* (Paris: Editions de Guibert, 1994), 101. Comby is an engineer whom the greens would no doubt regard as an apologist for nuclear power. It is therefore significant that one finds the same type of observation in the writings of two energy experts who are also enthusiastic support-

ers of alternative energy sources: Benjamin Dessus and François Pharabod. According to them, if 15 percent of total world energy needs in the year 2100 will be met by solar technologies, these will have to cover a total area of approximately 100,000 square kilometers! Dessus and Pharabod, "Jérémie et Noé," 15. For another book that, like Comby's, portrays nuclear energy as the "truly" ecological alternative for the long haul, see Bernard Wiesenfeld, *L'Atome écologique* (Les Ulis: EDP Sciences, 1998).

7. I derive most of the information on wind turbines in this section from two excellent websites, one established by the U.S. government's Department of Energy (http://www.cren.doe.gov/wind/wttr.html), the other by the Danish Wind Turbine Manufacturer's Association (http://www.windpower.dk/tour/index.htm).

CHAPTER SEVEN

1. Richard White, "Are You an Environmentalist or Do You Work for a Living? Work and Nature," in William Cronon, ed., *Uncommon Ground: Toward Reinventing Nature* (New York: Norton, 1995), 183.

2. Although no single SNCF poster put it in these exact terms, this was the underlying message of the SNCF's advertising campaigns regarding the TGV over the years; it remains one of the principal arguments made by the SNCF today, as a way of demonstrating its commitment to protecting the environment. See the SNCF website: http://www.sncf.com/co/environ/htmlfr/part02.htm. See also the SNCF posters, such as the one entitled "Air Pur," held in the collection at the Centre de Documentation, Musée de la Publicité (Union des Arts Décoratifs), in Paris; and Veronique Puvilland, *Cent ans de publicité industrielle* (Paris: Editions L'Usine Nouvelle, 1991).

3. For the latest statistics and general information on the TGV, see the website of the TGV enthusiasts' organization, TGV Web, at http://mercurio.iet.unipi.it/tgv/tgvindex.html. For the history of the TGV, see Clive Lamming, *La grande aventure du TGV* (Paris: Larousse, 1987); and Jean-Michel Fourniau, *La genèse des grandes vitesses à la SNCF: De l'innovation à la décision du TGV Sud-est* (Paris: Institut National de Recherche sur les Transports et leur Sécurité, 1988).

4. For a listing of accidents (with pictures!) see the TGV Web website: http://mercurio.iet.unipi.it/tgv/wrecks.html#jun2000.

5. See, for example, the website of Bombardier Transportation, Inc., a Canadian company that manufactures rolling stock for the TGV: http://www.transportation.bombardier.com/htmen/pr_2_14.htm.

6. Daniel Eisenberg, "Amtrak's Last Train," *Time* (Dec. 4, 2000), 62.

7. Olivier Klein, *La genèse du TGV comme un instant de la crise du fordisme* (Lyon: Laboratoire d'Economie des Transports, 1999).

8. Lamming, *La grande aventure du TGV*, chap, 7

9. The train's designers also gave serious consideration to a system of tilting suspension, capable of banking the cars in curves; but in the end, they decided against it because it was too complex and expensive. In this they showed a great deal more realism than the Concorde's design team, which insisted on pushing the performance envelope to the limit, often to the detriment of practical considerations. Fourniau, *La genèse des grandes vitesses à la SNCF,* 66–94.

10. For technical diagrams of the TGV's most significant engineering innovations, see the TGV Web website at http://mercurio.iet.unipi.it/tgv/motrice.html.

11. Gérard Mathieu, *New High Speed Rail Developments: France's Master Plan* (Paris: SNCF, 1991), 5.

12. Jacques Ellul, *The Technological Bluff* (Grand Rapids: Eerdmans, 1990), chaps. 14–15.

13. The sense of *separateness*—of belonging to a place that was distinct from other places and possessed of its own history, habits, scenery, and culture—this was precisely what the streamlined electric behemoth was taking away. For Bernard Charbonneau, this powerful technology, whose very essence lay in prying open new spacial relations, would have an unintended and tragic effect: in the act itself of bringing the French regions more easily into contact with each other, it would shatter their millennial isolation, and rob them of the relative seclusion within which their distinctness had flourished. See Charbonneau, *Sauver nos régions: Ecologie et sociétés locales* (Paris: Sang de la Terre, 1991), chaps. 3 and 7; and "Accélération des transports et consommation de l'espace," *Combat Nature* 59 (December 1983): 16.

14. See the SNCF's official leaflet, *TGV-Méditerranée: Une grande ambition pour le sud* (Paris: 1990). See also the SNCF's elaborate website at http://www.tgvmediterranee.com/.

15. Gérard Perrier, "TGV-Méditeranée: Premières leçons d'un conflit," *Ecologie Politique* 6 (Spring 1993): 29–41. See also D.L., "Prendre le train de l'an 2000," *Le Provençal* (Feb. 8, 1993); Sophie Roquelle, "TGV-Méditeranée: la polémique relancée," *Le Figaro* (Aug. 22, 1992); Pierre Sorgue, "Bataille de ministres autour d'un tracé du TGV du Sud-Est," *Libération* (Aug. 26, 1992); Michele Cohen-Chabaud, "Barrages, tunnels, et grands chantiers bloqués par les croisés de l'écologie," *La Tribune de l'Expansion* (July 22, 1991); Eloi Martinez, "TGV-Méditerranée: Le projet de nouvelle ligne contesté en Avignon," *L'Humanité* (May 17, 1993). See also the transcript of the debate held on nationwide radio in August 1991: Philippe Lefevre (moderator), "La nouvelle bataille du rail," *France Inter* (Aug. 18, 1991, program aired at 1:15 P.M.); and the revealing interviews with national politicians conducted in April 1993 by the radio program and news magazine, "Grand Air" (*Grand Air* no. 8, April 1993).

16. Jean-Michel Fourniau, "La portée des contestations du TGV Méditerranée," *Ecologie et Politique* 21 (Autumn/Winter 1997): 61–75.

17. Bruno Latour, "Les limites de l'experience collective," *La Recherche* 306 (February 1998), available online at http://www.larecherche.fr/VIEW/306/03060881.html. As an example of this remarkable "glasnost" that the French government undertook during the 1990s, see the website at http://www.tgvbranchesud.org. This website, created by Réseau Ferré de France, the consortium responsible for building a new TGV line in northeastern France, offered the public an open platform for posting letters, ideas, objections, or suggestions regarding all aspects of the proposed new rail line. It provided exhaustive information regarding all aspects of the project, from the technical aspects to its environmental and cultural implications. Clearly, the technocrats had learned a lesson from all the sparks that had flown over the TGV-Méditerranée!

18. See the SNCF's website at http://www.tgvmediterranee.com/.

19. Some opponents of the TGV-Méditeranée even felt that the Greens, who should have been their natural allies in the campaign against the SNCF, had been excessively doctrinaire and unyielding in their defense of the high-speed train. Gérard

Perrier, "TGV-Méditeranée: Premières leçons d'un conflit," *Ecologie Politique* 6 (Spring 1993): 35–36. For a sampling of the general views expressed by French environmentalists about the TGV, see Dominique Foing, ed., *Le livre des Verts* (Paris: Editions du Félin, 1994), 143–52, 217–26; Bernard Lefort, ed., *Le nouveau livre des Verts* (Paris: Editions du Félin, 1999), 105–10, 117–24; Antoine Waechter, *Dessine-moi une planète* (Paris: Albin Michel, 1990), 41–56; and Pierre Samuel, *Les trains à grande vitesse* (Paris: Les Amis de la Terre, 1991). See also the website of Les Amis de la Terre: http://www.amisdelaterre.org/communique/1999/1999_06_02.html; and of Les Verts: http://www.verts.imaginet.fr/transp.html#DEPLAC.

20. Greens in the United States, Britain, and Germany, to name but a few Western nations, also tended to make guardedly favorable references to high-speed trains in their policy statements. See for example the positions on high-speed trains taken on the following websites: http://www.greenparty.org.uk/; http://www.gruene.de/index3.htm; http://www.greens.org/gpusa/. For a wider sampling, see the index of green sites at the following website: http://www.geocities.com/CapitolHill/Lobby/4192/greens.html.

21. Samuel, *Les trains à grande vitesse*.

22. Christian Bouchardy, *Le grand livre de la France sauvage* (Paris: Larousse-Bordas, 1998), 74–75.

23. See the official website at http://www.pointe-du-raz.com/. See also:http://www.ouest-france.com/tourisme-bretagne/sites/raz.htm and http://www.essi.fr/~medclec/bzh/Baie-Audierne/Raz/pointe-du-raz.html.

24. See the Conservatoire's website at http://www.conservatoire-du-littoral.fr/accueil.html. See also Raphaël Romi, *Droit et administration de l'environnement,* 3d ed. (Paris: Montchrestien, 1999), 225–31.

25. See http://www.pointe-du-raz.com/. See also Ifen (Institut Français de l'Environnement), ed., *L'Environnement en France, Edition 1999,* 387.

26. *Le Petit Larousse* (Paris: Larousse, 1992), 59.

27. Donna Haraway, "A Cyborg Manifesto: Science, Technology, and Socialist-Feminism in the Late Twentieth Century," in *Simians, Cyborgs, and Women: The Reinvention of Nature* (New York: Routledge, 1991).

CHAPTER EIGHT

1. Quoted in Danièle Léger and Bertrand Hervieu, *Le retour à la nature: Au fond de la forêt . . . l'état* (Paris: Seuil, 1979), 17.

2. For an illuminating discussion of the similarities and differences between the socialist tradition and the environmentalist tradition, see Alain Lipietz, *Green Hopes: The Future of Political Ecology,* trans. Malcolm Slater (Cambridge, England: Polity Press, 1995), chaps. 3, 4, 5. See also Alain Lipietz, "Les Verts: bleus, blancs, rouges . . . ou bruns?" and Alfred Grosser, "Faut-il avoir peur de l'écologie?" both in *Libération,* special edition, "Tout sur les écologistes" (March 1992): 64–65; Raymond Pronier and Vincent Jacques le Seigneur, *Génération Verte: Les écologistes en politique* (Paris: La Renaissance, 1992), chap. 8; and Bruno Latour, "Arrachement ou attachement à la nature?" *Ecologie Politique* 5 (Winter 1993): 15–26.

3. See, for example, the detailed discussion of this tension in Leszek Kolakowski, *Main Currents of Marxism,* 3 vols., trans. P. S. Falla (Oxford: Clarendon Press, 1978).

4. I am of course excluding here the danger of nuclear war, which (although it

certainly has immense ecological implications) falls more appropriately under the analytical categories of international politics and military history than environmental politics. For the purposes of my present argument, my point is that the fear of nuclear war failed to exert a mass-radicalizing effect on behalf of a swift and draconian ecological restructuring. See Michael Bess, *Realism, Utopia, and the Mushroom Cloud: Four Activist Intellectuals and their Strategies for Peace, 1945–1989* (Chicago: University of Chicago Press, 1993).

5. Quoted in Clarence J. Glacken, *Traces on the Rhodian Shore: Nature and Culture in Western Thought from Ancient Times to the End of the Eighteenth Century* (Berkeley: University of California Press, 1967), 31.

6. Quoted in Keith Thomas, *Man and the Natural World* (New York: Oxford University Press, 1983), 235–36.

7. Léger and Hervieu, *Le retour à la nature.*

8. This anecdote is drawn from John Ardagh, *France Today* (London: Penguin, 1995), 245. See also Léger and Hervieu, *Le retour à la nature;* and *Le Monde,* "La société française en mouvement" (Dossiers et Documents du *Monde,* October 1981), 49.

9. Ardagh, *France Today,* 241.

10. Léger and Hervieu, 7.

11. See the Nature et Progrès website at http://www.natpro.be/~natpro/Avant-Propos.htm. According to the political scientist Daniel Boy, the impact of this organization upon French agriculture and consumer society remained relatively marginal. Daniel Boy, "Les écologistes et l'agriculture" (Rapport no. 404), paper presented at the conference, "Les agriculteurs et la politique depuis 1970," held in December 1987 and organized by the Association Française de Science Politique.

12. Quoted in Roger Cans, *Tous Verts! La surenchère écologique* (Paris: Calmann-Lévy, 1992), 27. See also Béatrice D'Erceville, "A la recherche du rayon vert," *LSA* no. 1290 (Feb. 6, 1992): 80–82. A collection of some two hundred magazine and newspaper articles on the topic of business and the environment is available to researchers at the médiathèque of the Cité des Sciences et de l'Industrie at La Villette (Paris): see "Gérer L'Environnement," Call Number TI 5 3 Gérer.

13. Cans, *Tous Verts!,* 23–26.

14. Ifen (Institut Français de l'Environnement), ed., *L'Environnement en France, Edition 1999* (Paris: La Découverte, 1998), 279. This comprehensive survey is an indispensable book for any researcher working on the topic of environmentalism in France.

15. Ifen, 399.

16. Alexandre Vatimbella, *Le capitalisme vert* (Paris: Syros/Alternatives, 1992), 112.

17. Ifen, 268–69.

18. Ifen, 274–75.

19. Ifen, 269–75.

20. Ifen, 400.

21. Ifen, 190.

22. The figure for 1979 is given in Jean-Paul Meyronneinc, *Plaidoyer pour les déchets* (Rennes: Apogée, 1993), 23. The figure for 1996 is from Ifen, 184.

23. Pierre Boisson, ed., *Energie 2010–2020: Les chemins d'une croissance sobre* (Paris: Documentation Française, 1998), 159.

24. Boisson, 151–59.

25. Meyronneinc, *Plaidoyer pour les déchets,* chap. 2; see also Cyrille Harpet, *Du déchet: Philosophie des immondices* (Paris: L'Harmattan, 1998).

26. Cans, *Tous Verts!,* 29.

27. Cans, 162–63.

28. Ifen, 167–69.

29. Ifen, 366.

30. Ifen, chap. 22. To cite just a few of the myriad statistics: between 1994 and 1998, the average number of trips by car per person and per day rose by 23 percent; at the same time, it fell by 41 percent for bicycles and 36 percent for walking. The average speed of vehicle travel, and distance traveled per day, both went up 32 percent. Between 1985 and 1996 the number of passenger-kilometers traveled by car rose by 36 percent. Heavy truck transport rose by 15 percent between 1991 and 1996; during the same time the annual portion of freight shipped by rail declined by 36 percent, while air freight rose by 33 percent. In 1998, 33 percent of French households declared themselves to be disturbed by nearby road traffic.

31. Gérard Brun and Jean-Pierre Nicolas, eds., *Les transports et l'environnement: Vers un nouvel équilibre* (Paris: La Documentation Française, 1999).

32. Ifen, 371.

33. The city of La Rochelle maintains an informative website at http://www.ville-larochelle.fr/framefr.htm. See also the website devoted to Praxitèle, an experimental loan program for electric cars in the town of Saint-Quentin-en-Yvelines, at http://www.rocq.inria.fr/praxitele/.

34. Ifen, 371; see also the website maintained by Peugeot at http://www.psa.fr/electrique/01.html. A collection of some eighty-five magazine and newspaper articles on the topic of electric vehicles is available to researchers at the médiathèque of the Cité des Sciences et de l'Industrie at La Villette (Paris): see "La Voiture Electrique," call number TA 4 82.

35. On the implications of the new law on air pollution, see the Assemblée Nationale website: http://www.assemblee-nationale.mg/fr/actual/loi99/L99021.htm.

36. Edmond Maire, "Le Tourisme de Nature: Introduction," in Jacky Herbin, ed., *Tourisme et environnement* (Paris: La Documentation Française, 1992), 27–29.

37. Josy Dienot and Didier Theiller, "Les Nouvelles Pratiques Sportives de la Montagne," in Herbin, ed., *Tourisme et environnement,* 38.

38. Ifen, chap 23; Herbin, ed., *Tourisme et environnement,* 94–95. See also the richly informative website maintained by the French Ministry of Tourism at http://www.tourisme.gouv.fr/index.htm.

39. Ifen, 376.

40. Ifen, 380.

41. Ifen, 381.

42. Ifen, 382

43. Pierre Lascoumes, *L'Ecopouvoir: Environnements et politiques* (Paris: La Découverte, 1994), 37–96.

44. Ifen, 404.

45. Ifen, 404.

46. Thousands of school textbooks for France's highly centralized educational system, from the 1870s to the present, are stored in a well-organized archive in Paris,

at the Institut National de Recherche Pédagogique. I surveyed school textbooks for "Première" and "Terminale" students (approximately 16 and 17 years old, respectively), in the fields of Géographie and Sciences Naturelles, from the 1940s to the early 1990s. See also the pioneering discussions in Jeanne Daubois, *La nature et nos enfants* (Brussels: Casterman, 1973); and M. Vallée, *L'Ecologie dans l'enseignement du Second Degré* (Nantes: Annales du Centre Régional de Documentation Pédagogique de Nantes, 1970).

47. Christian Bock et al., *La nature et vous* (Paris: Hachette, 1978), 150–57.

48. In one popular geography textbook published in 1987, for example, one finds almost no reference to the word "ecology," or to negative environmental impacts of human activity on the French territory: Groupe de recherche pour l'enseignement de l'histoire et de la géographie, ed., *Géographie du temps présent* (Paris: Hachette, 1987).

49. Rémy Knafou, ed., *Géographie* (Paris: Bélin, 1989).

50. See the Ecole et Nature website at http://www.ecole-et-nature.org/accueil .htm. See also the article, "Associations: Les écoles buissonnières," *La Lettre du Hérisson* 135 (March 1992): 18–19.

51. Ifen, 403.

52. Joël de Rosnay, "Ecologie et éducation," and Jean-Yves Daniel, "L'Ecole et l'education à l'environnement," in Cité des Sciences et de l'Industrie, ed., *Les paradoxes de l'environnement* (Paris: Albin Michel, 1994), 111–136.

53. Cans, *Tous Verts!*, chap. 1; Vatimbella, *Le capitalisme vert*, chap. 5.

54. See the Blue Angel website at http://www.blauer-engel.de/. See also Eric Viardot, *L'Environnement dans l'entreprise* (Paris: L'Harmattan, 1997), 103–106.

55. Jacques Vigneron and Claude Burstein, eds., *Ecoproduit: Concepts et méthodologies* (Paris: Economica, 1993).

56. Antoine Blouet and Emmanuelle Rivoire, *L'Ecobilan* (Paris: Dunod, 1995), 15–17; the book also offers a sophisticated overview of the main methodological issues involved in such product life-cycle assessments.

57. Viardot, *L'Environnement dans l'entreprise*, 149; Blouet and Rivoire, *L'Ecobilan*, chaps. 1 and 2.

58. François Ramade, "Principales modalités par lesquelles les biens de consommation et les produits finis interfèrent avec l'environnement," in Vigneron and Burstein, eds., *Ecoproduit*, 51–60.

59. André Gorz, *Ecology as Politics*, trans. Patsy Vigderman and Jonathan Cloud (Boston: South End Press, 1980), 8–9. I am presenting here a condensed version of about a page and a half of Gorz's descriptive text.

CHAPTER NINE

1. Quoted in Danièle Léger and Bertrand Hervieu, *Le retour à la nature: Au fond de la forêt . . . l'état* (Paris: Seuil, 1979), back cover.

2. "Pourquoi nous irons au Larzac," *Lo Bramaïre*, special leaflet edition (Aug. 24–26, 1973), 2.

3. Aujourd'hui L'Ecologie, ed., *Le pouvoir de vivre: Le projet des écologistes avec Brice Lalonde* (Montargis: Ecologie Mensuel, March 1981), 269.

4. Alexandre Kiss, ed., *L'Ecologie et la loi: Le statut juridique de l'environnement* (Paris: L'Harmattan, 1989), 7.

5. Yves Jegouzo and Christophe Sanson, *Le guide de l'environnement* (Paris: Editions du Moniteur, 1990).

6. Jegouzo and Sanson, 43–49, 279–88; I have updated the information with references from Anne Bourgoin-Bareilles, *Guide de l'environnement* (Paris: Frison-Roche, 1998), 51–84.

7. Philippe Lebreton, *La nature en crise* (Paris: Sang de la Terre, 1988), 311–17; Antoine Waechter, *Dessine-moi une planète* (Paris: Albin Michel, 1990), 213–16.

8. Waechter, 216.

9. Florian Charvolin, "L'Invention de l'environnement en France (1960–1971): Les pratiques documentaires d'agrégation à l'origine du Ministère de la protection de la nature et de l'environnement" (dissertation in political science, Université Pierre Mendès-France de Grenoble and Ecole Nationale Supérieure des Mines de Paris [Centre de Sociologie de l'Innovation], 1993), chap. 7.

10. See, for example, Philippe Saint-Marc, *Socialisation de la nature* (Paris: Stock, 1975); René Dumont, *L'Utopie ou la mort* (Paris: Seuil, 1974); René Dubos, *Nous n'avons qu'une terre* (Paris: Denoël, 1972); André Gorz, *Ecology as Politics,* trans. Patsy Vigderman and Jonathan Cloud (Boston: South End Press, 1980); Brice Lalonde, Serge Moscovici, René Dumont, and Jean-Pierre Ribes, *Pourquoi les écologistes font-ils de la politique?* (Paris: Seuil, 1978). See also Florence Faucher, *Les habits verts de la politique* (Paris: Presses de Sciences Po, 1999); Jean Jacob, *Histoire de l'écologie politique: Comment la gauche a redécouvert la nature* (Paris: Albin Michel, 1999); Jean-Luc Bennahmias and Agnès Roche, *Des Verts de toutes les couleurs: Histoire et sociologie du mouvement écolo* (Paris: Albin Michel, 1992); Guillaume Sainteny, *Les Verts* (Paris: PUF, 1991); Dominique Simonnet, *L'Ecologisme,* 2d ed. (Paris: PUF, 1982); Raymond Pronier and Vincent Jacques le Seigneur, *Génération Verte: Les écologistes en politique* (Paris: La Renaissance, 1992).

11. Pierre Lascoumes, *L'Ecopouvoir: Environnements et politiques* (Paris: La Découverte, 1994), 97–105.

12. Jacques Theys, "Vingt Ans de politique Française de l'environnement: Les années 70–90," in Bernard Barraqué and Jacques Theys, eds., *Les politiques d'environnement: Evaluation de la première génération, 1971–1995* (Paris: Recherches, 1998), 28. Hereafter "Vingt Ans."

13. Theys, "Vingt Ans," 28.

14. Raphaël Romi, *Droit et administration de l'environnement,* 3d ed. (Paris: Montchrestien, 1999), 163–74.

15. Romi, 175–204.

16. See the website of the Parcs Naturels Régionaux: http://www.parcs-naturels-regionaux.tm.fr/un_parc/questions/index.html#jmpTOP

17. Ifen, 438; Nicole Questiaux, ed., *Données économiques de l'environnement* (Paris: Documentation Française, 1998).

18. Romi, 149–58; Dominique Guihal, *Droit répressif de l'environnement,* 2d ed. (Paris: Economica, 2000).

19. Ifen, 444–50; Eric Viardot, *L'Environnement dans l'entreprise* (Paris: L'Harmattan, 1997), 62–65.

20. See the Directorate's website: http://europa.eu.int/comm/dgs/environment/index_en.htm.

21. For an overview of this legislation, see the 739-page *Handbook on the Imple-*

mentation of EC Environmental Legislation, available in PDF format from the EU website: http://europa.eu.int/comm/environment/enlarg/handbook/handbook.pdf.

22. See the Life Programme site: http://europa.eu.int/comm/life/whatis.htm.

23. See the EEA website: http://www.eea.eu.int/.

24. Ifen, 449.

25. Ifen, 451.

26. For a partial listing of these treaties, see Ifen, 452.

27. See Pierre-Alain Muet, ed., *Fiscalité de l'environnement* (Paris: Documentation Française, 1998).

28. Caroline London, *Environnement et stratégie de l'entreprise* (Rennes: Apogée, 1993), 78–79. For a positive evaluation of this strategy, see Olivier Godard and Claude Henry, "Les instruments des politiques internationales de l'environnement: La prévention du risque climatique et les mécanismes de permis négociables," in Muet, ed., *Fiscalité de l'environnement,* 113–50.

29. Lascoumes, *L'Ecopouvoir,* 100–104.

30. Charvolin, "L'Invention de l'environnement en France," chaps. 4 and 5.

31. Lebreton, *La nature en crise,* 313.

32. Ifen, 438.

33. Theys, "Vingt Ans," 25; Lascoumes, 97–110.

34. Lascoumes, 140–50.

35. Rocard, quoted in Theys, "Vingt Ans," 28.

36. Pierre Lascoumes and Jean-Pierre Le Bourhis, *L'Environnement ou l'administration des possibles* (Paris: L'Harmattan, 1997), 77–116.

37. Jean-Pierre Raffin, "Historique de la Loi sur la Protection de la Nature," unpublished notes (Raffin personal archives); Roger Cans, "L'An X de la révolution verte," *Le Monde* (Oct. 7, 1986), 1, 12.

38. "Loi No. 76-629 du 10 Juillet 1976," *Journal Officiel* (July 13, 1976), 1.

39. Theys, "Vingt Ans," 26.

40. Cans, "L'An X de la révolution verte," 12.

41. Cans, "L'An X de la révolution verte," 1.

42. Gilles Martin and Martine Rèmond-Gouilloud, quoted in Theys, "Vingt Ans," 26.

43. Theys, "Vingt Ans," 27.

44. Lascoumes, 95–96, 140–41, 165–66.

45. Lascoumes, 141–61.

46. Lascoumes, 142.

47. Theys, "Vingt Ans," 32.

48. Lascoumes, 163–68.

49. *Ecologie et pouvoir* (Paris: Documentation Française, 1990).

50. Ifen, 437.

51. See the institute's website: http://www.ifen.fr/.

52. Lascoumes and Le Bourhis, *L'Environnement ou l'administration des possibles.*

53. Lascoumes and Le Bourhis, 185.

54. Lascoumes and Le Bourhis, 231–41.

55. See the Barnier website: http://www.erm.lu/barnier.htm.

56. Michel Barnier, *Le défi écologique* (Paris: Hachette, 1991), chaps. 5, 10.

57. For the full text of the Barnier law, see the French legislative website at: http://www.admi.net/jo/ENVX9400049L.html.

58. Romi, *Droit et administration de l'environnement*, 55–77.

59. See the *Handbook on the Implementation of EC Environmental Legislation*, available from the EU website: http://europa.eu.int/comm/environment/enlarg/handbook/handbook.pdf.

60. See "The Amsterdam Treaty: A Comprehensive Guide," at the EU website, http://europa.eu.int/scadplus/leg/en/lvb/a15000.htm.

61. See the European Union's website entitled, "A Strategy for Integrating the Environment into EU Policies:" http://europa.eu.int/scadplus/leg/en/lvb/l28075.htm.

62. Theys, "Vingt Ans," 39.

63. Detailed documentation on this struggle is provided on the website of the "Coordination Pour la Défense du Marais Poitevin," http://marais-poitevin.org/.

64. Correspondence between Michael Bess and Yves Le Quellec, one of the organizers of the "Coordination Pour la Défense du Marais Poitevin" (January 2001).

65. See the DATAR website: http://www.datar.gouv.fr/.

66. Murielle Szac, *Dominique Voynet: Une vraie nature* (Paris: Plon, 1998), chaps. 7 and 8.

67. Dominique Voynet, "Bilan de l'action du Ministère de l'Aménagement du Territoire et de l'Environnement de Juin 1997 à Avril 2000," speech before the members of France Nature Environnement (April 15, 2000), available from the Ministry of the Environment website: http://www.environnement.gouv.fr/actua/com2000/avril/17-bilan-97-2000.htm. Hereafter "Bilan."

68. Szac, 223–25.

69. On the TGAP, see Questiaux, ed., *Données économiques de l'environnement*, 21; and the Ministry of the Environment website: http://www.environnement.gouv.fr/lepoint/tgap.htm#2. See also Alain Lipietz, "Economie politique des écotaxes," in Muet, ed., *Fiscalité de l'environnement*, 9–40.

70. For the law's text see the French legislative website at: http://www.oree.org/ACTUALI/politique/projet_loadt.htm.

71. Voynet, "Bilan," 7.

72. Voynet, "Bilan," 2.

73. Voynet, "Bilan," 3, 24. The last sentence in the quotation comes from a separate part of Voynet's text.

CHAPTER TEN

1. Quoted in Alexandre Vatimbella, *Le capitalisme vert* (Paris: Syros/Alternatives, 1992), 131.

2. Christian Brodhag, *Objectif terre: Les Verts, de l'écologie à la politique* (Paris: Félin, 1990), 231–34.

3. For a judicious overview of this contentious subject, see Eric Viardot, *L'Environnement dans l'entreprise* (Paris: L'Harmattan, 1997).

4. Theys, "Vingt Ans," in Barraqué and Theys, eds., *Les politiques d'environnement*, 29. See also the statistics in Ifen, 327–44.

5. Roger Cans, *Tous verts! La surenchère écologique* (Paris: Calmann-Lévy, 1992), 157–73.

6. Viardot, 153–76.

7. For the report text, see OECD, "Examen des performances environnementales de la France: Conclusions et recommandations," available online at the website of the French Agronomy Institute, INRA: http://www.inra.fr/Internet/Produits/dpenv/ocde-c30.htm.

8. Ifen, 328–43.

9. Ifen, 339–40.

10. Ifen, 337.

11. Nicole Questiaux, ed., *Données économiques de l'environnement* (Paris: Documentation Française, 1998), 12.

12. For a detailed account of Nicoll's environmental retooling, see Eric Bezou, *Système de management environnemental* (Paris: Afnor, 1997), 195–97; see also the Nicoll website at http://www.nicoll.fr/.

13. Bezou, 15–17.

14. For discussions of the ISO-14000 and Eco-audit (known more commonly in English as "Emas"), see Bezou, *Système de management environnemental;* Caroline London, *Environnement et stratégie de l'entreprise* (Rennes: Apogée, 1993), 125–42; Raphaël Romi, *Droit et administration de l'environnement,* 3d ed. (Paris: Montchrestien, 1999), 379–96. See also the helpful overview at the Ministry of the Environment's website,http://www.environnement.gouv.fr/dossiers/managementenvironnemental/-2k1106managenvir.htm. See also the International Standards Organization's website at http://www.iso14000.com/; and the explanatory essay at http://iisd1.iisd.ca/greenstand/globlgrn.pdf essay on ISO-14000.

15. Ifen, 341.

16. Bezou, 273–74.

17. These statistics are taken from the Ministry of the Environment's website, at http://www.environnement.gouv.fr/dossiers/managementenvironnemental/2k1106-managenvir.htm; and from Pierre Lascoumes, *L'Ecopouvoir: Environnements et politiques* (Paris: La Découverte, 1994), 150–51.

18. Pierre Chapuy, in Ifen, 343.

19. Arnaud Comolet, "Le renouveau écologique: De l'éco-utopie à l'éco-capitalisme," *Futuribles* (Sept. 1991): 45.

20. Ifen, 408.

21. Ifen, 408–13.

22. Michel Mabit, *Les métiers de l'environnement: "Gagner sa vie en protégeant la Vie"* (Nantes: Éditions Opéra, 1998).

23. Ifen, 409; see also the company websites at http://www.eau.generale-des-eaux.com/ and at http://www.lyonnaise-des-eaux.fr/.

24. Ifen, 409–10.

25. Mabit, 30–31.

26. Ifen, 413–19.

CHAPTER ELEVEN

1. Herman Kahn, William Brown, Leon Martel, *The Next 200 Years* (New York: William Morrow, 1976), 1.

2. On the geographical diversity of France see Pierre Nora, ed., *Les lieux de mémoire,* vol. 2 (Paris: Gallimard, 1992); Philippe Pinchemel, *France: A Geographic, So-*

cial, and Economic Survey, trans. Dorothy Elkins with T. H. Elkins (Cambridge: Cambridge University Press, 1987); Xavier De Planhol, *Géographie historique de la France* (Paris: Fayard, 1988); Fernand Braudel, *The Identity of France,* trans. Siân Reynolds (New York: Harper Collins, 1990). On France's natural scenery see Christian Bouchardy, *Le grand livre de la France sauvage* (Paris: Larousse-Bordas, 1998); and Françoise Mosse, *À la découverte des réserves naturelles de France* (Paris: Nathan, 1996).

3. I. G. Simmons, *Environmental History: A Concise Introduction* (Oxford: Blackwell, 1993), 159.

4. Simmons, 82–88.

5. Groupe de recherche pour l'enseignement de l'histoire et de la géographie, ed., *Géographie du temps présent* (Paris: Hachette, 1987), 63.

6. Simmons, 87–88.

7. Ifen, 92.

8. Paul E. Waggoner, Jesse H. Ausubel, Iddo K. Wernick, "Lightening the Tread of Population on the Land: American Examples," *Population and Development Review* 22, no. 3 (Sept. 1996): 531–45, available online at http://phe.rockefeller.edu/tread/.

9. Ifen, 274–79.

10. OECD, "Examen des performances environnementales de la France : conclusions et recommandations," 1997, available at the French Agronomy Institute website: http://www.inra.fr/Internet/Produits/dpenv/ocde-c30.htm.

11. Ifen, 76–87.

12. Ifen, 93.

13. Ifen, 122–26.

14. This map is taken from Ifen, 123.

15. Jacques Theys, "Introduction," Ifen, 10.

16. Ifen, 126–28; 444–53.

17. See the U.S. National Park Service website at http://www.nature.nps.gov/wv/tbiodiv.htm.

18. Ifen, 93–99.

19. Ifen, 32.

20. Ifen, 41.

21. Ifen, 135.

22. Ifen, 137.

23. Ifen, 138; see also the Conservatoire's website at http://www.conservatoire-du-littoral.fr/.

24. Ifen, 84.

25. See the website of the Observatoire National des Zones Humides at http://www.ifen.fr/pages/4onzh.htm.

26. Ifen, 59–67.

27. See the 1998 French Senate report at the website: http://www.senat.fr/rap/r98-316/r98-3461.html.

28. See the websites of the organizations devoted to saving French wolves, at: http://www.loup.org/ and http://perso.club-internet.fr/e_faucon/loup/Relation.htm.

29. Dominique Voynet, "Bilan de l'action du Ministère de l'Aménagement du Territoire et de l'Environnement de Juin 1997 à Avril 2000," speech before the members of France Nature Environnement (April 15, 2000).

30. This exchange is reported in the following website: http://perso.club-internet.fr/e_faucon/loup/Relation.htm.

31. Ifen, 140.

32. Jean-Pierre Raffin, "La protection de l'ours brun (Ursus Arctos L.) dans les Pyrénées Françaises: Histoire d'une nonchalance institutionelle," in XIVème Colloque Francophone de Mammalogie de la SFEPM, *Introductions et réintroductions de mammifères sauvages* (Paris: Annales Biologiques du Centre, 1990), 81–90. See also the website of the "Save the Pyrenean Brown Bear" campaign, at: http://perso.wanadoo.fr/skizo.industrie/Ours-Presentation.htm.

33. Jean-Michel Guillot, "L'Ours des Pyrénées est condamné à disparaître," *Le Monde* (April 28, 1993), 10. See also the information on the documentary film, *Gardarem Lou Moussu,* at the "alternative cinema" website, Ciné Résistances: http://www.cine-resistances.com/catalogue1997/fichefilm/gardaremloumoussou.htm.

34. Ifen, 111.

35. Ifen, 112.

36. Ifen, 115-17. See for example the website of one Conservatoire Botanique National at http://www.mnhn.fr/mnhn/cbnbp/.

37. See the Ministry of Environment website at http://natura2000.environnement.gouv.fr/.

38. This latter number, well below the European average, was deemed insufficient by the European Commission, which returned the dossier to Paris for re-elaboration. As of 2001, the Ministry of the Environment was drawing up a new and considerably expanded list. See the documentation on the Ministry's website: http://natura2000.environnement.gouv.fr/10questions/question9.html.

39. Voynet, "Bilan," 15.

40. Jacques Theys, "Introduction," Ifen, 11.

41. John Pezzey, cited in Philippe Bontems and Gilles Rotillon, *Economie de l'environnement* (Paris: La Découverte, 1998), 98. See John Pezzey, *Sustainable Development Concepts: An Economic Analysis,* World Bank Environment Paper no. 2 (Washington, D.C.: World Bank, 1992).

42. For a summary of the Brundtland Report, see the website of Geneva International, a clearing-house for international organizations, at http://geneva-international.org/GVA/WelcomeKit/Environnement/chap_5.E.html.

43. Stephen Cotgrove, *Catastrophe or Cornucopia: The Environment, Politics, and the Future* (Chichester: Wiley, 1982).

44. Sylvie Faucheux and Jean-François Noël, *Economie des ressources naturelles et de l'environnement* (Paris: Armand Colin, 1995), 279–80.

45. Hans Jonas, *The Imperative of Responsibility : In Search of an Ethics for the Technological Age,* trans. Hans Jonas and David Herr (Chicago: University of Chicago Press, 1984).

46. See the Rio Declaration's text reproduced on the website of the United Nations Environmental Programme: http://www.unep.org/Documents/Default.asp?DocumentID=78&ArticleID=1163.

47. In the view of some scholars, the precautionary principle needed to be distinguished from the more general category of "risk management," because the concept of risk usually entailed dealing with relatively known and quantifiable probabilities. For example, the danger of malaria spreading through a human popu-

lation by means of mosquito bites fell under the purview of risk management: both the disease and its mechanisms of propagation were relatively well known, and were susceptible to mathematical modeling and prediction. By contrast, the danger of unleashing an unstoppable pandemic through genetic manipulation of microbes fell under the purview of the precautionary principle: it dealt with problems only dimly discernible in the present—a tangle of scientific variables and hypothetical assumptions based on observations in today's world, and projected to the best of contemporary abilities over the horizon of possible futures. Only the dire nature of the potential perils involved could justify this exercise of groping prognostication. In this sense, therefore, the precautionary principle lay outside the conceptual domain of risk management, and fell under a new and more intriguing category: "la gestion de l'attente d'information," or the "management of a situation in which society awaits further information." Nicolas Treich, "Vers une théorie économique de la précaution?" cited in Philippe Bontems and Gilles Rotillon, *Economie de l'environnement* (Paris: La Découverte, 1998), 108. On the concept of risk see Denis Duclos, *La peur et le savoir: La société face à la science, la technique, et leurs dangers* (Paris: La Découverte, 1989).

48. Al Gore, *Earth in the Balance: Ecology and the Human Spirit* (New York: Plume, 1993).

49. Ifen, 443–54; Christian Brodhag, *Objectif terre: Les Verts, de l'écologie à la politique* (Paris: Félin, 1990), 247–56.

50. For foreign aid statistics see the *Columbia Encyclopedia* article at the following website: http://www.bartleby.com/65/fo/foreignai.html; and the article on foreign aid reproduced on the website of Third World Traveler, a clearing-house for information on development issues: http://www.thirdworldtraveler.com/US_ThirdWorld/US_aid_95.html.

51. For a definition of dynamic equilibrium in the field of chemistry, see the science information website maintained by "Room 103," an organization of Cal Tech graduates: http://www.room103.com/archive/q_dynamicequil.htm. The gist goes as follows:

"Equilibrium is the point at which a chemical reaction is balanced. This does not mean that chemical transformations have ceased. Chemists acknowledge this by prefacing 'equilibrium' with the word 'dynamic.' On the microscopic level, this means that the concentrations of the materials allow the rate of the forward reaction to equal the rate of the reverse reaction."

52. Faucheux and Noël, *Economie des ressources naturelles et de l'environnement*, 282–99.

53. Pierre Boisson, ed., *Energie 2010–2020: Les chemins d'une croissance sobre* (Paris: Documentation Française, 1998), 159.

54. Ifen, 319.

55. Ifen, 303.

56. Ifen, 285–98.

57. Jean-Jacques Salomon, "De la transparence," in Collège de la Prévention des Risques Technologiques, *Le risque technologique et la démocratie* (Paris: Documentation Française, 1994), 19–33. For recent relatively optimistic assessments of the security of the nuclear industrial cycle, see Bruno Comby, *Le nucléaire, avenir de l'écologie?* (Paris: Editions de Guibert, 1994); Bernard Wiesenfeld, *L'Atome écologique*

(Les Ulis: EDP Sciences, 1998); Jean-Yves Le Déaut, *Le système français de radioprotection, de contrôle, et de sécurité nucléaire* (Paris: Documentatin Française, 1998); and Georges Charpak and Richard L. Garwin, *Feux follets et champignons nucléaires* (Paris: Odile Jacob, 1997). For relatively pessimistic assessments, see Michèle Rivasi and Hélène Crié, *Ce nucléaire qu'on nous cache* (Paris: Albin Michel, 1998); Jean-François Viel, *La santé publique atomisée* (Paris: La Découverte, 1998); and Jean-Pierre Pharabod and Jean-Paul Schapira, *Les jeux de l'atome et du hasard* (Paris: Calmann-Lévy, 1988).

58. Jean-Paul Meyronneinc, *Plaidoyer pour les déchets* (Rennes: Apogée, 1993), 23; Ifen, 184.

59. Phillippe Collomb and France Guérin-Pace, eds, *Les Français et l'environnement* (Paris: Institut National d'Etudes Demographiques, 1998); René Neboit-Guilhot and Lucette Davy, eds., *Les Français dans leur environnement* (Paris: Nathan, 1996); Bruno Maresca and Pascale Hébel, eds., *L'Environnement: ce qu'en disent les Français* (Paris: Documentation Française, 1999); Jean-Marc Besse and Isabelle Roussel, eds., *Environnement: Représentations et concepts de la nature* (Paris: L'Harmattan, 1997).

CHAPTER TWELVE

1. Paul Valéry, *Regards sur le monde actuel* (Paris: Stock, 1931), 35.

2. For a listing of books and articles, some of them comparative, on the green movements of a wide variety of nations, see chapter 4, note 30.

3. Valéry, 35 (emphasis in original).

4. Bill McKibben, *The End of Nature* (New York: Random House, 1989).

CHAPTER THIRTEEN

1. Pierre Teilhard de Chardin, *The Phenomenon of Man* (New York: Harper and Row, 1965), excerpted on the following website: http://www.webcom.com/gaia/tdc.html.

2. Pierre Lascoumes, *L'Ecopouvoir: Environnements et politiques* (Paris: La Découverte, 1994), 312–13.

3. Al Gore, *Earth in the Balance: Ecology and the Human Spirit* (New York: Plume, 1993), 32–33.

4. B. L. Turner, ed., *The Earth as Transformed by Human Action: Global and Regional Changes in the Biosphere over the past 300 Years* (Cambridge: Cambridge University Press, 1990); William L. Thomas, Jr., ed., *Man's Role in Changing the Face of the Earth* (Chicago: University of Chicago Press, 1955); George Perkins Marsh, *The Earth as Modified by Human Action* (New York: Arno, 1970 [first published in 1864 as *Man and Nature; or, Physical Geography as Modified by Human Action*]). See also the discussion given by Robert E. Ricklefs in the introduction to his textbook on the science of ecology: *Ecology,* 3d ed. (New York: W. H. Freeman, 1990), 3–7; Eric Hobsbawm, *The Age of Extremes* (New York: Vintage, 1994), 568–70.

5. J. R. McNeill, *Something New Under the Sun: An Environmental History of the Twentieth-Century World* (New York: Norton, 2000), 360–61.

6. McNeill, 4–5.

7. David R. Headrick, "Technological Change," in Turner, ed., *The Earth as Transformed by Human Action,* 55–68. See also Victor Ferkiss, *Nature, Technology, and Soci-*

ety: Cultural Roots of the Current Environmental Crisis (New York: New York University Press, 1993), chap. 11; and Richard D. North, *Life on a Modern Planet* (Manchester: Manchester University Press, 1995), chap. 10.

8. For an English-language description of the "fishberry" achievement see the article by Thomas Caceci, one of the scientists who holds a patent on it, at the following website: http://www.vetmed.vt.edu/Publications/News/newsrel/00110.html. A fine French book on the subject's broader implications is Arnaud Apoteker, *Du poisson dans les fraises: Notre alimentation manipulée* (Paris: La Découverte, 1999).

9. Daniel Boy, "Les biotechnologies et l'opinion publique européenne," *Futuribles* 238 (January 1999): 47–53.

10. Boy, "Les biotechnologies," 53–54.

11. Ifen, 218–19.

12. Ifen, 219.

13. Ifen, 218.

14. Louis-Marie Houdebine, *Les biotechnologies animales: Nécessité ou révolution inutile* (Paris: Editions France Agricole, 1998).

15. Ifen, 218.

16. Jean-Marie Pelt, *Plantes et aliments transgéniques* (Paris: Fayard, 1998); Bertrand Jordan, *Génétique et génome: La fin de l'innocence* (Paris: Flammarion, 1996); Comité consultatif national d'éthique pour les sciences de la vie et de la santé, eds., *Ethique et recherche biomédicale* (Paris: La Documentation Française, 1997); Apoteker, *Du poisson dans les fraises;* François Gros and Gérard Huber, eds., *Vers un anti-destin? Patrimoine génétique et droits de l'humanité* (Paris: Odile Jacob, 1992); Michel Tibon-Cornillot, *Les corps transfigurés: Mécanisation du vivant et imaginaire de la biologie* (Paris: Seuil, 1992).

17. The most forceful advocate of these positions is Jean-Marie Pelt, in his *Plantes et aliments transgéniques.*

18. See the account in Boy, "Les biotechnologies," 54–55.

19. See Noel Keith Roberts, *From Piltdown Man to Point Omega: The Evolutionary Theory of Teilhard de Chardin* (New York: Lang, 2000); Jennifer Cobb Kreisberg, "A Globe, Clothing Itself with a Brain," in *Wired,* available at: http://www2.gol.com/users/coynerhm/teilhard.html. See also the following websites devoted to Teilhard's life and work: http://www.mnhn.fr/teilhard/, and http://www.cruzio.com/~cscp/teilhard.htm.

20. Frank E. Manuel and Fritzie P. Manuel, *Utopian Thought in the Western World* (Cambridge, Mass.: Belknap Press, 1979).

21. Lascoumes, *L'Ecopouvoir;* and Pierre Lascoumes and Jean-Pierre Le Bourhis, *L'Environnement ou l'administration des possibles* (Paris: L'Harmattan, 1997).

22. Lascoumes, *L'Ecopouvoir,* 312–13.

23. Stephen Jay Gould, "The Golden Rule: A Proper Scale for our Environmental Crisis," in Louis P. Pojman, ed., *Environmental Ethics* (Boston: Jones and Bartlett, 1994), 168.

24. Markus Krummenacker and James Lewis, eds., *Prospects in Nanotechnology: Toward Molecular Manufacturing* (New York: Wiley, 1995); B. C. Crandall, ed., *Nanotechnology: Molecular Speculations on Global Abundance* (Cambridge, Mass.: MIT Press, 1996); K. Eric Drexler, *Nanosystems: Molecular Machinery, Manufacturing, and Computation* (New York: Wiley, 1992); Hans Moravec, *Mind Children: The Future of Robot and Human Intelligence* (Cambridge, Mass.: Harvard University Press, 1988).

25. Bill Joy, "Why the Future Doesn't Need Us," in *Wired* (April 2000), available at: http://www.wired.com/wired/archive/8.04/joy_pr.html.

CHAPTER FOURTEEN

1. William Cronon, "The Trouble with Wilderness," in William Cronon, ed., *Uncommon Ground: Toward Reinventing Nature* (New York: Norton, 1995), 79.

2. Robert Elliot, *Faking Nature: The Ethics of Environmental Restoration* (New York: Routledge, 1997), 76–97, 130–33. The thought-experiment, as presented here, is an abbreviated amalgam of several points and examples offered by Elliot in a longer and more detailed set of arguments; I have tried to remain as close as possible to the underlying spirit of Elliot's reasoning.

3. Bill McKibben, *The End of Nature* (New York: Random House, 1989), 48.

4. Donald Worster, "A Country Without Secrets," in *Under Western Skies: Nature and History in the American West* (New York: Oxford University Press, 1992), 238–54; and Cronon, "Introduction," and "The Trouble with Wilderness," in Cronon, ed., *Uncommon Ground.*

5. See Bruno Latour, *Nous n'avons jamais été modernes* (Paris: La Découverte, 1991), translated by Catherine Porter as *We Have Never Been Modern* (Cambridge: Harvard University Press, 1993); Bruno Latour, *Politiques de la nature: Comment faire entrer les sciences en démocratie* (Paris: La Découverte, 1999); Bruno Latour, "Arrachement ou attachement à la nature?" *Ecologie Politique* 5 (Winter 1993): 1–26; Michel Serres, *Le contrat naturel* (Paris: Bourin, 1990); Claus Emmeche, *The Garden in the Machine: The Emerging Science of Artificial Life* (Princeton: Princeton University Press, 1994); Donna Haraway, "A Cyborg Manifesto: Science, Technology, and Socialist-Feminism in the Late Twentieth Century," in *Simians, Cyborgs, and Women: The Reinvention of Nature* (New York: Routledge, 1991); Richard White, *The Organic Machine: The Remaking of the Columbia River* (New York: Hill and Wang, 1995); N. Katherine Hayles, "Simulated Nature and Natural Simulations: Rethinking the Relation between the Beholder and the World," in Cronon, ed., *Uncommon Ground;* and N. Katherine Hayles, *How We Became Posthuman* (Chicago: University of Chicago Press, 1999).

6. White, *The Organic Machine.*

7. Hayles, "Simulated Nature and Natural Simulations," in Cronon, ed., *Uncommon Ground,* 456.

8. Cronon, "The Trouble with Wilderness," 88–89.

9. Latour, *Politiques de la nature.* Like Hegel in the nineteenth century and Whitehead in the twentieth, Latour proposes to get around the major dualisms of Western philosophy by means of the underlying concept of *process.*

10. A. N. Whitehead articulated the same issue in the following way in 1929: "All modern philosophy hinges round the difficulty of describing the world in terms of subject and predicate, substance and quality, particular and universal. The result always does violence to that immediate experience which we express in our actions, our hopes, our sympathies, our purposes, and which we enjoy in spite of our lack of phrases for its verbal analysis. We find ourselves in a buzzing world, amid a democracy of fellow creatures; whereas, under some disguise or other, orthodox philosophy can only introduce us to solitary substances, each enjoying an illusory experience: 'O Bottom, thou are changed! What do I see on thee?'" Alfred North Whitehead, *Process and Reality* (New York: Free Press, 1929), 64.

11. Latour, *Politiques de la nature,* 156.

12. In the old world of Western philosophy, Latour argues, citizens and political leaders had to rely on the authority of scientists and other "experts" before taking action; but this authority was shaky from the start, since the scientists and experts often disagreed vehemently about the nature of the phenomena they were discovering or inventing. Thus, in the old way of thinking, the governance of science was "short-circuited" (Latour's term) in two distinct ways: the scientists themselves could not provide the clear and definitive knowledge that was being demanded of them; and the citizens were cut off from real decision-making by their own lack of commensurate knowledge and authority. In the new, process-based mode of thinking, Latour contends, this would no longer be the case. Everyone has a say; a provisional consensus is sought (such consensus being relatively easier to negotiate because the participants know that it is provisional); appropriate action is taken; then the process repeats: it adds up to a democratic, inclusive, open-ended cycle.

13. Louis Badré, *Histoire de la forêt française* (Paris: Arthaud, 1983); Pierre Bazire and Jean Gadant, *La forêt en France* (Paris: Documentation Française, 1991).

14. Kalaora and Savoye, "La protection des régions de montagne au XIXe siècle," in A. Cadoret, ed., *Protection de la nature: Histoire et idéologie: De la nature à l'environnement* (Paris: L'Harmattan, 1985); Andrée Corvol, *L'Homme aux bois: Histoire des relations de l'homme et de la forêt, XVIIe-XXe siècle* (Paris. Fayard, 1987); Tamara L. Whited, *Forests and Peasant Politics in Modern France* (New Haven: Yale University Press, 2000); Nicole Demesse, Alain Persuy, Jean Cauwet, and Roger Fischer, *France, ta forêt fout le camp!* (Paris: Stock, 1976).

15. For good overviews of the Landes forestry enterprise see the website of Sotrafor at: http://perso.wanadoo.fr/sotrafor/index.htm and the website of the Observatoire National des Forêts at: http://perso.wanadoo.fr/earthfirst/landes.html.

16. Christian Bouchardy, *Le grand livre de la France sauvage* (Paris: Larousse-Bordas, 1998), 63–64; Philippe Lebreton, *La nature en crise* (Paris: Sang de la Terre, 1988). See also the website of the organization devoted to saving the marais Poitevin, at http://marais-poitevin.org/ and the website of the French Vendée region, at http://www.vendee.com/french.sites.marais_p.htm.

17. Jean Carlier, *Vanoise: Victoire pour demain* (Paris: Calmann-Lévy, 1972). See also the park's official website at: http://www.vanoise.com/pnv_fi.htm.

18. Some environmentalists tend to link the idea of stewardship directly to Christian traditions derived from the book of Genesis, in which God appoints man as caretaker of the physical world. This religious definition is not the one I am using here, for it is too often grounded in a homocentric ethics—protecting nature simply because nature is useful and beneficial to humans. However, the concept of stewardship by no means necessarily entails this kind of homocentric stance; on the contrary, it is perfectly compatible with other strains of environmental ethics in which the natural world and its inhabitants are accorded intrinsic value. Thus, I will use the term "stewardship" in its broader and secular sense, to signify a generalized attitude of respect for the natural world, and a concern about how best to preserve those qualities that are essential to its "naturalness." See Roger S. Gottlieb, ed., *This Sacred Earth: Religion, Nature, Environment* (New York: Routledge, 1996).

19. This phrase is taken from the website maintained by Sotrafor, one of the Landes' largest forestry companies: http://perso.wanadoo.fr/sotrafor/landes/foret/l_index.htm.

20. See the park's website, http://www.vanoise.com/pnv_fr.htm, under the heading "patrimoine."

21. See Oelschlaeger; Glacken; Worster, *Nature's Economy.*

22. Cronon, "The Trouble with Wilderness," 79–80.

23. The text of Wittgenstein's Ethics Lecture is available at the following website: http://groups.yahoo.com/group/wittgenstein-dialognet/message/55. It was also published as Ludwig Wittgenstein, "A Lecture on Ethics," *Philosophical Occasions 1912–1951,* ed. James C. Klagge and Alfred Nordmann (Indianapolis and Cambridge: Hackett, 1993), 37–44.

24. Holmes Rolston III, "The Preservation of Natural Value in the Solar System," in Eugene Hargrove, ed., *Beyond Spaceship Earth: Environmental Ethics and the Solar System* (San Francisco: Sierra Club, 1987). See also Elliot, *Faking Nature,* 130–42.

25. Cronon, "The Trouble with Wilderness," 88.

CHAPTER FIFTEEN

1. Bruno Latour, *Nous n'avons jamais été modernes* (Paris: La Découverte, 1991), 9; my translation.

2. Richard White, "Are You an Environmentalist or Do You Work for a Living?" in William Cronon, ed., *Uncommon Ground: Toward Reinventing Nature* (New York: Norton, 1995), 183–84. For purposes of brevity, I have edited this passage, eliminating an ongoing comparison that White makes with the work and thought of Bill McKibben.

3. I derive the dual image of Breakdown and Gridwork from an offhand remark made back in the 1970s by my anthropology professor at Reed College, Gail Kelly. Most modern social theorists, she said, can be seen as falling into two categories. On one side, we find those whose deepest fear is that society is falling apart: their underlying aim is therefore to figure out how citizens can be more effectively knitted together. These are the thinkers like Durkheim, Geertz, or Habermas. On the other side, we find those whose deepest fear is that society is becoming *too* closely integrated, too restrictive and monolithic: they spend their time trying to find ways to loosen the grip of institutions, rules, and internalized norms, carving a frail space for individual freedom. These are the thinkers like Nietzsche or Foucault.

The image made an impression on me: agoraphobia or claustrophobia? Are we living in a perpetually falling-down edifice, whose walls we must continually build and rebuild? Or is something very different the case: do we live in a perpetually rising prison, whose shifting and encircling walls we must continually learn to evade? Are we forever on the brink of being entombed within a structure of our own making? Over the years, I have come to think of this problem more in the manner of a Zen koan, one of those inherently unanswerable queries whose nagging presence nonetheless keeps us alive and on our toes.

4. Antoine Waechter, *Dessine-moi une planète* (Paris: Albin Michel, 1990), 157–58. I give a condensed translation of Waechter's text here.

CHAPTER SIXTEEN

1. The lyrics to Young's song, "After the Goldrush," are available on the following website: http://gunther.simplenet.com/v/data/afterthe.htm.

2. If one takes for example two of the main green periodicals in France, *Ecologie*

Politique and *Combat Nature,* and scrutinizes them for references to outer space, one finds nearly nothing, year after year. The same can be said for the writings of France's most prominent ecological leaders and intellectuals, such as Brice Lalonde, Antoine Waechter, Alain Lipietz, or Bernard Charbonneau. Only one book exists in English—albeit an excellent one—on the environmental implications of outer space exploration: Eugene Hargrove, ed., *Beyond Spaceship Earth: Environmental Ethics and the Solar System* (San Francisco: Sierra Club, 1987). For a broader discussion that touches peripherally on the environmentalists' lack of interest in space and space technology, see Victor Ferkiss, *Nature, Technology, and Society: Cultural Roots of the Current Environmental Crisis* (New York: New York University Press, 1993), chap. 11.

3. A good place to start is Peter Redfield, *Space in the Tropics: From Convicts to Rockets in French Guiana* (Berkeley: University of California Press, 2000), which provides an excellent overview of the French space program's history and a highly original analysis of its significance. See also the official website of the European Space Agency, available at: http://www.esa.int/export/esaCP/GGGZM2D3KCC_index_0.html. I have drawn for my analysis on the following official publications by the European Space Agency (all of them issued by European Space Agency, Publications Division, Noordwijk, The Netherlands): *Columbus: An Expedition to Space* (1991); *European Space: For Exclusively Peaceful Purposes* (1992); *The ESRO-ESA Space Science Story: Twenty-Five Years of European Cooperation* (1990); *Europe into Space: The Auger Years (1959–1967)* (1993); *Reaching for the Skies: The Ariane Family Story and Beyond* (1988). For discussions of the philosophical significance of Europe's space missions, see Heinz Wismann, "Etre ou ne pas être dans l'espace?" *Libération* (June 2, 1993), 35; and R. M. Bonnet, "Pourquoi les missions spatiales?" speech at colloquium on "Ethics and Environment," Boulogne (March 11, 1993). See also Martine Castello, *La grande aventure d'Ariane* (Paris: Larousse, 1987); and Bernard Chabbert, *Les fils d'Ariane* (Paris: Plon, 1986). For a broad-ranging discussion of space exploration from an American perspective, see Walter A. McDougall, *The Heavens and the Earth: A Political History of the Space Age* (New York: Basic Books, 1985).

4. On the long-term prospects and visions concerning human activities in space, see Redfield, *Space in the Tropics,* chaps. 5 and 6; Académie Nationale de l'Air et de l'Espace, ed., *Actes de L'Atelier-débat, "Les Apports de la Conquête Spatiale à l'Humanité"* (Paris: Cépaduès, 1992); André Lebeau, *L'Espace en héritage* (Paris: Odile Jacob, 1989); Pierre-Marie Martin, *Droit des activités spatiales* (Paris: Masson, 1992); Guy Pignolet de Sainte Rose, *La conquête industrielle du système solaire* (Paris: Le Rocher, 1986). English-language studies include: Thomas R. McDonough, *Space: The Next Twenty-Five Years* (New York: Wiley, 1987); Arthur C. Clarke, *By Space Possessed* (London: Gollancz, 1993); Michael A. G. Michaud, *Reaching for the High Frontier: The American Pro-Space Movement, 1972–84* (New York: Praeger, 1986); Roy Gibson, *Space* (Oxford: Clarendon, 1992); Guy Collins, *Europe in Space* (New York: St. Martin's, 1990); Eugene F. Mallove and Gregory L. Matloff, *The Starflight Handbook: A Pioneer's Guide to Interstellar Travel* (New York: Wiley, 1989); Frederick I. Ordway III and Randy Liebermann, eds., *Blueprint for Space* (Washington: Smithsonian Institution, 1992).

5. European Space Agency, *Satellites at the Service of the Environment and Development* (Paris: ESA, 1992); Chabbert, *Les fils d'Ariane.* For an overview in English see Gibson, *Space,* chap. 7.

6. See for example Christian Brodhag, *Objectif terre: Les Verts, de l'écologie à la politique* (Paris: Félin, 1990), 20–21. In English, see J. Baird Callicott, "Moral Considerability and Extraterrestrial Life," and William K. Hartmann, "Space Exploration and Environmental Issues," in Hargrove, ed., *Beyond Spaceship Earth*, 227–61 and 119–39 respectively; and Donald Worster, *Nature's Economy: A History of Ecological Ideas,* 2d ed. (Cambridge: Cambridge University Press, 1994), 358–59.

7. See the discussion of this tendency in Callicott, "Moral Considerability and Extraterrestrial Life."

8. Thus, on one of the few occasions in which we find a French environmentalist leader actually taking a position on outer space, here is the language that we encounter: "Seen from the dark and frozen emptiness of space, the Earth appears as a colored marble with countless iridescences, on the surface of which fluffy sheep seem to be chasing one another. All the other planets are nothing but cold and lifeless mineral substance." Antoine Waechter, *Dessine-moi une planète* (Paris: Albin Michel, 1990), 123.

9. Hartmann, "Space Exploration and Environmental Issues."

10. Jules Verne, *De la terre à la lune* (Paris: Hachette, 1928 [first ed. 1865]); Camille Flammarion, *La fin du monde* (Paris: Flammarion, 1894).

11. Lebeau, *L'Espace en heritage,* back cover.

12. Two perceptive discussions of the cultural notion of "wild frontier" are John Rennie Short, *Imagined Country: Environment, Culture and Society* (London: Routledge, 1991), especially chaps. 1 and 8; and Donald Worster, *Under Western Skies: Nature and History in the American West* (New York: Oxford University Press, 1992).

13. Collins, *Europe in Space.* For a large and well-organized dossier of French press clippings on the subject of space, spanning a wide range of media perspectives, see the médiathèque of the Cité des Sciences et de l'Industrie at La Villette (Paris), under the heading, "Espace."

14. See Redfield, *Space in the Tropics,* chaps. 5 and 6.

15. Guy Pignolet de Sainte Rose, *La conquête industrielle du système solaire* (Paris: Le Rocher, 1986). For a provocative article in English, see Jesco von Puttkamer, "The Industrialization of Space: Transcending the Limits to Growth," *Futurist* 13 (June 1979): 192–201.

16. The term is used explicitly in Roger M. Bonnet, "Pourquoi les missions spatiales?," speech at colloquium on "Ethics and Environment," Boulogne (March 11, 1993).

17. Martin, *Droit des activités spatiales.*

18. See Frank B. Golley, "Environmental Ethics and Extraterrestrial Ecosystems," in Hargrove, ed., *Beyond Spaceship Earth*, 211–25; and Jacqueline Switzer, *Green Backlash: The History and Politics of Environmental Opposition in the U.S.* (Boulder: Lynne Rienner, 1997). For a bibliographic overview of the broad literature about nature conservation and the "wise use" concept, see Worster, *Nature's Economy,* 486–91.

19. Henry Michel, "Ce que l'espace apporte à la Terre: Aspects militaires," in Académie Nationale de l'Air et de l'Espace, ed., *Actes de L'Atelier-débat, "Les Apports de la Conquête Spatiale à l'Humanité"*; Lebeau, *L'Espace en heritage;* Bonnet, "Pourquoi les missions spatiales?"; *Europe into Space: The Auger Years, 1959–1967.* For an English-language discussion of the profound link between national military ambitions and the conquest of space, see Walter A. McDougall, *The Heavens and the Earth;* and Michaud, *Reaching for the High Frontier.*

20. Martine Castello, in her history of the Ariane rocket series, sums up the military stakes in these terms: "It wasn't until 1953 that the French Directorate for Research and Manufacture of Armaments, well aware that the nation would require advanced space technology if it desired to maintain its rank among the great powers, finally managed to convince France's politicians that 'something had to be urgently done' in this domain. It would take many years before these pioneering lobbyists would succeed in their campaign; but they were helped considerably by the giant steps being taken by the superpowers, which made France's leaders increasingly nervous." Castello, *La grande aventure d'Ariane,* 8.

21. Roger Bonnet, the European Space Agency's Director of Scientific Programs, even went one step further during a conference in 1993: "Humankind can only appropriate space for itself if it establishes and follows a code of good conduct: in practice this means making sure that space remains a patrimony that belongs not only to all human beings, but to all the potential inhabitants of the solar system. It is our common heritage." R. M. Bonnet, "Pourquoi les missions spatiales?" According to one of the official publications of the European Space Agency, "The ESA's main objective, set out by the thirteen full member states, is to provide for and to promote, for exclusively peaceful purposes, cooperation among European states in space research and technology and their space applications." European Space Agency, *European Space: For Exclusively Peaceful Purposes.*

22. André Lebeau, an official with the European Space Agency, summed up this ambiguous situation in a book published in 1989: "Two forces have fueled the development of space technology thus far: the search for profit and the preparation for war. The great question before us is whether human beings will learn in time how to pool their efforts in a truly global undertaking among the stars—just as, five centuries ago, the conquest of the oceans mobilized our ancestors and transformed out civilization." Lebeau, *L'Espace en heritage,* 376.

23. See Holmes Rolston III, "The Preservation of Natural Value in the Solar System," and Paul F. Uhlir and William P. Bishop, "Wilderness and Space," in Hargrove, ed., *Beyond Spaceship Earth,* 140–82 and 183–210 respectively; and Redfield, *Space in the Tropics,* chaps. 5 and 6.

24. Cousteau himself often noted the striking parallels between his undersea adventures and the exploration of outer space. For example, the narration of his award-winning 1956 film, *The Silent World,* opened with the words, "Divers are true spacemen." Richard Munson, *Cousteau: The Captain and his World* (New York: Morrow, 1989), 16.

25. This question implicitly points toward a remarkable concept that has now passed from science fiction into the common parlance of space scientists and engineers: the notion of "terraforming," or refashioning the entirety of another planet in earth's image, using colossal machines to render the environment of that planet habitable for earth creatures without life-support systems. A terraformed Mars—with a manufactured atmosphere and imported trees, birds, and rivers—would this be a natural place or a giant planetary artifact? Clearly, the problem of artificialization would not go away, simply because our species has left the earth behind; however, the infinitude of space would no doubt alter the implications of this phenomenon considerably. A science fiction novel giving a detailed depiction of the terraforming of Mars is Kim Stanley Robinson, *Red Mars* (New York: Bantam, 1993); the sequel is entitled, quite appropriately, *Green Mars.* See also Lebeau, part III, chap. 2. For a harshly

critical French perspective on the concept of terraforming, portraying it as an arrogant and reckless defilement of a pristine natural realm, see the ESA's scientific director Roger M. Bonnet, "Pourquoi les missions spatiales?" For English-language scholarly discussions of terraforming and related technological mega-visions, see James E. Oberg, *Mission to Mars: Plans and Concepts for the First Manned Landing* (Harrisburg, Pa.: Stackpole Books, 1982), 193; McDonough, *Space: The Next Twenty-Five Years,* chap. 15; Clarke, *By Space Possessed;* Mallove and Matloff, *The Starflight Handbook;* and Ordway and Liebermann, eds., *Blueprint for Space.*

26. On the shifting meanings of the word "wind," for example, see the nonfiction essay by Arthur C. Clarke, "The Winds of Space," in his *By Space Possessed,* chap. 11.

CONCLUSION

1. William Morris, *The Dream of John Ball,* quoted in E. P. Thompson, *The Poverty of Theory and Other Essays* (London: Monthly Review Press, 1978), 88.

2. Antoine Waechter, *Dessine-moi une planète* (Paris: Albin Michel, 1990), 156.

BIBLIOGRAPHY

1. UNPUBLISHED SOURCES

I conducted the field research for this project over several phases between 1992 and 2000, with a seven-month stay in Paris during 1992–93. During that time I conducted interviews with the following persons: Alain Beltran, Jean-Luc Benhammias, Jean Carlier, Brice Lalonde, Laurence Mermet, Théodore Monod, Jacques Noettinger, Sylvie Pétin, François Pharabod, Jean-Pierre Raffin, Pierre Samuel, and Antoine Waechter.

The most valuable archival resource for me proved to be the immense personal files of three veteran environmental activists: Jean Carlier, Jean-Pierre Raffin, and Pierre Samuel. In particular, Jean-Pierre Raffin has amassed a staggeringly detailed and comprehensive archive on all aspects of French environmental matters, spanning the entire period from the 1960s to the present. This archive, well-organized in some two hundred file boxes, includes newspaper clippings, internal documents and correspondence of major environmental organizations, European Parliamentary records, official French government documents and reports, scientific studies and papers, records of legal proceedings, and exhaustive personal notes. To my amazement, Raffin simply handed me the keys to this trove and said: "There's a photocopying store around the corner: have at it!" (Needless to say, I thereupon proceeded to give myself a "xerox tan.")

I made extensive use of the document collections maintained by a wide variety of public and private organizations: Agence de l'Environnement et de la Maîtrise de l'Énergie (ADEME); Les Amis de la Terre; Aérospatiale Corporation, Bibliothèque de

Documentation Internationale Contemporaine (Nanterre); Equipe Cousteau; Centre National d'Etudes Spatiales; Electricité de France; European Space Agency; press archives of the news magazine *L'Express;* France Nature Environnement; France Tele- com; Génération Ecologie; Institut National de Recherche Pédagogique; Institut d'Histoire du Temps Présent; Institut Français d'Opinion Publique; press archives of the newspaper *Libération;* Ministère de l'Environnement; Musée de la Publicité (Union des Arts Décoratifs); Muséum National d'Histoire Naturelle; Musée de l'Air et de l'Espace; Organisation de Coopération et Développement Economiques (OECD); Peugeot Corporation; Renault Corporation; Société Nationale de Protection de la Na- ture; Société Nationale des Chemins de Fer; Les Verts; Médiathèque, Cité des Sci- ences et de l'Industrie at La Villette.

For film and other visual media, I found a veritable treasury at the Cinémathèque of the Ministère de l'Agriculture et du Développement Rural. This archive is open to all researchers; a catalogue listing hundreds of titles is available.

2. WEB-BASED SOURCES

At first, the French were slow to jump on the Internet bandwagon—perhaps be- cause their own pioneering Minitel network had seemed adequate, or perhaps be- cause this new technology struck them as yet another Anglo-Saxon Trojan Horse. At any rate, they have now "gone virtual" with a vengeance. By 2001, the web had be- come the single most powerful research tool at my disposal for this project: the whole nation, at every level, seems to be wired and open for online contact. From the bud- getary deliberations of the Vanoise Park's governing body, to the grassroots mobiliza- tion efforts on behalf of wolves, to the legal statutes making their way through parliamentary committees—everything is there, instantly, on screen.

The best place to start a French web search is through a sophisticated search en- gine like Google.com; typing quotations around key phrases proves particularly ef- fective. The websites of the European Union, French government, Ministry of the Environment, Les Verts, and various French newspapers provide particularly rich documentation.

3. PRINTED SOURCES

I have divided this portion of the bibliography into two parts: Environmental Top- ics and General (non-environmental) Topics. However, I have not attempted to make the traditional scholarly distinction between primary and secondary sources: with a contemporary subject like this one, the line between the two is simply too hazy to be of much use.

3.1. Environmental Topics

Abélès, Marc, ed. *Le défi écologiste*. Paris: L'Harmattan, 1993.
Abram, David. *The Spell of the Sensuous*. New York: Vintage Books, 1996.
Acot, Pascal. *Histoire de l'écologie*. Paris: PUF, 1988.
Aguesse, Pierre. *Clefs pour l'écologie*. Paris: Séghers, 1971.
Allègre, Claude. *Ecologie des villes, écologie des champs*. Paris: Fayard, 1993.
Alphandéry, Pierre, Pierre Bitoun, and Yves Dupont. *Les champs du départ*. Paris: La Découverte, 1989.

————. *L'Equivoque écologique*. Paris: La Découverte, 1991.

Anger, Didier. *Chronique d'une lutte: Le combat antinucléaire à Flamanville et dans La Hague*. Paris: Simoën, 1978.

Ansel, Philippe. *L'Attitude des Français à l'égard de l'energie nucléaire en 1992*. Paris: EDF [Direction de la Communication], March 1993.

Antoine, Jacques, and Véronique Popelin-Camus. *Nucléaire, écologie, environnement. L'Evolution de l'opinion publique française perçue à travers les sondages*. Paris: Centre d'Etudes Socio-Economiques et de Management, 1991.

Apoteker, Arnaud. *Du poisson dans les fraises: Notre alimentation manipulée*. Paris: La Découverte, 1999.

"Associations: Les écoles buissonnières." *La Lettre du Hérisson* 135 (March 1992): 18–19.

Aubert, Francis, and Jean-Pierre Sylvestre. *Ecologie et société*. Dijon: Educagri, 1998.

Aujourd'hui l'Ecologie, ed. *Le pouvoir de vivre: Le projet des écologistes avec Brice Lalonde*. Montargis: Ecologie Mensuel, March 1981.

Bachelet, Michel. *L'Ingérence écologique*. Paris: Frison-Roche, 1995.

Badré, Louis. *Histoire de la forêt française*. Paris: Arthaud, 1983.

Barnier, Michel. *Le défi écologique: Chacun pour tous*. Paris: Hachette, 1991.

Barraqué, Bernard, and Jacques Theys, eds. *Les politiques d'environnement: Evaluation de la première génération, 1971–1995*. Paris: Recherches, 1998.

Baudrillard, Jean. *La société de consommation: Ses mythes, ses structures*. Paris: Denoël, 1970.

Baudry, Jacques, and Anne-Sophie Acx, eds. *Ecologie et friche dans les paysages agricoles*. Paris: Ministère de l'Environnement, 1993.

Bazire, Pierre, and Jean Gadant. *La forêt en France*. Paris: Documentation Française, 1991.

Beck, Corinne, and Robert Delort. *Pour une histoire de l'environnement*. Paris: CNRS Editions, 1993.

Bennahmias, Jean-Luc, and Agnès Roche. *Des Verts de toutes les couleurs: Histoire et sociologie du mouvement écolo*. Paris: Albin Michel, 1992.

Bess, Michael. "Ecology and Artifice: Shifting Perceptions of Nature and High Technology in Postwar France." *Technology and Culture*, vol. 36, no. 4 (October 1995): 830–62.

————. "Ecology and the Crisis of Agriculture in Postwar France." *French Politics and Society*. 13. no. 4 (Fall 1995): 33–50.

————. "Greening the Mainstream: Paradoxes of Anti-Statism and Anti-Consumerism in the French Environmental Movement." *Environmental History* 5, no. 1 (January 2000): 6–26.

————. "France." In Mark Cioc, ed., "Environmental History Writing in Southern Europe." *Environmental History* 5, no. 4 (October 2000): 545–56.

Besse, Jean-Marc, and Isabelle Roussel, eds. *Environnements: Représentations et concepts de la nature*. Paris: L'Harmattan, 1997.

Besset, Jean-Paul. *René Dumont: Une vie saisie par l'écologie*. Paris: Stock, 1992.

Bezou, Eric. *Système de management environnemental*. Paris: Afnor, 1997.

Bigot, François. *L'Urbanisme au défi de l'environnement*. Rennes: Apogée, 1994.

Blouet, Antoine, and Emmanuelle Rivoire. *L'Ecobilan*. Paris: Dunod, 1995.

Bock, Christian, et al. *La nature et vous*. Paris: Hachette, 1978.

Boisson, Pierre, ed. *Energie 2010–2020: Les chemins d'une croissance sobre*. Paris: Documentation Française, 1998.

Boniface, Pascal, and Jean-François Gribinski. *Les écologistes et la défense*. Paris: Dunod, 1994.

Bonnefous, Edouard. *Réconcilier l'homme et la nature*. Paris: PUF, 1990.

Bonnet, Paul. *Pourquoi l'energie nucléaire?* Paris: Commissariat à l'Energie Atomique, 1982.

Bonnieux, François, and Brigitte Desaigues. *Economie et politiques de l'environnement*. Paris: Dalloz, 1998.

Bontems, Philippe, and Gilles Rotillon. *Economie de l'environnement*. Paris: La Découverte, 1998.

Bouchardy, Christian. *Le grand livre de la France sauvage*. Paris: Larousse-Bordas, 1998.

Bouguereau, Jean-Marcel. "Dany Cohn-Bendit, est-il allemand ou français?" In *Les Verts, Numéro Unique: L'Europe: Nos désirs, nos débats, nos choix*, supplement to the journal *Vert Contact* (May–June 1999).

Bourg, Dominique. *Les scénarios de l'écologie*. Paris: Hachette, 1996.

Bourg, Dominique, ed. *Les sentiments de la nature*. Paris: La Découverte, 1993.

Bourgoin-Bareilles, Anne. *Guide de l'environnement*. Paris: Frison-Roche, 1998.

Boy, Daniel. "Les écologistes en France." *French Politics and Society* 10, no. 3 (Summer 1992): 1–25.

———. "Les biotechnologies et l'opinion publique européenne." *Futuribles* 238 (January 1999): 47–53.

Boy, Daniel, Vincent Jacques le Seigneur, and Agnès Roche. *L'écologie au pouvoir*. Paris: Presses de Sciences Po, 1995.

Brodhag, Christian. *Objectif terre: Les Verts, de l'écologie à la politique*. Paris: Félin, 1990.

Brun, Gérard, and Jean-Pierre Nicolas, eds. *Les transports et l'environnement: Vers un nouvel équilibre*. Paris: La Documentation Française, 1999.

C. R. "Greenpeace-France se saborde." *Le Monde*, Dec. 15, 1987: 15.

Cadoret, A., ed. *Protection de la nature: Histoire et idéologie: De la nature à l'environnement*. Paris: L'Harmattan, 1985.

Callenbach, Ernest. *Ecotopia*. New York: Bantam, 1975.

Cans, Roger. "L'an X de la révolution verte." *Le Monde*, Oct. 7, 1986: 1, 12.

———. *Tous verts! La surenchère écologique*. Paris: Calmann-Lévy, 1992.

Capul, Jean-Yves, ed. *L'Etat de la décentralisation*. Cahiers Français no. 256. Paris: Documentation Française, 1992.

Carbiener, Didier. *Les arbres qui cachent le forêt: La gestion forestière à l'épreuve de l'écologie*. Aix-en-Provence: Edisud, 1995.

Carlier, Jean. *Vanoise: Victoire pour demain*. Paris: Calmann-Lévy, 1972.

Charbonneau, Bernard. "Accélération des transports et consommation de l'espace." *Combat Nature* 59 (December 1983): 16.

———. *Sauver nos régions: Ecologie et sociétés locales*. Paris: Sang de la Terre, 1991.

Charvolin, Florian. "L'invention de l'environnement en France (1960–1971): Les pratiques documentaires d'agrégation à l'origine du Ministère de la protection de la nature et de l'environnement." Dissertation in political science, Université

Pierre Mendès-France de Grenoble and Ecole Nationale Supérieure des Mines de Paris (Centre de Sociologie de l'Innovation), 1993.

Chérèque, Jacques, ed. *Une nouvelle étape pour l'aménagement du territoire.* Paris: Documentation Française, 1990.

Chevrillon, Olivier. "Pouvoir: Silence, on flotte." *Le Point* no. 680 (Sept. 30, 1985): 69.

Cingal, Georges. "Rapport D'Activités." *La Lettre du Herisson* 139bis (Juillet-Août 1992): 38–39.

Cité des Sciences et de l'Industrie, ed. *Les paradoxes de l'environnement.* Paris: Albin Michel, 1994.

Clébant, Marcel. *Croisade pour la mer.* Paris: Fayard, 1972.

Club CRIN "Environnement," ed. *Surveillance de l'environnement.* Paris: ECRIN, 1998.

Cohen-Chabaud, Michele. "Barrages, tunnels, et grands chantiers bloqués par les croisés de l'écologie." *La Tribune de l'Expansion,* July 22, 1991.

Collectif d'Enquête. *Aujourd'hui Malville, demain la France: Livre noir.* N.p.: La pensée sauvage, 1978.

Collomb, Phillippe, and France Guérin-Pace, eds. *Les Français et l'environnement.* Paris: Institut National d'Etudes Demographiques, 1998.

Colomès, Michel. "Presse étrangère: Quand les autres parlent France." *Le Point* no. 680 (Sept. 30, 1985): 68.

Comby, Bruno. *Le nucléaire, avenir de l'écologie?* Paris: Editions de Guibert, 1994.

Comité consultatif national d'éthique pour les sciences de la vie et de la santé, eds. *Ethique et recherche biomédicale.* Paris: La Documentation Française, 1997.

Commissariat à l'Energie Atomique and FNSEA. *Agriculture, environnement, et nucléaire: Comment réagir en cas d'accident.* Paris: FNSEA, 1990.

Commission des Communautés Européennes. *L'Opinion européenne et les questions énergétiques en 1991.* Brussels: CCE, 1992.

Commoner, Barry. *Quelle terre laisserons-nous à nos enfants?* Paris: Seuil, 1969.

Comolet, Arnaud. "Le renouveau écologique: De l'éco-utopie à l'éco-capitalisme." *Futuribles* 157 (Sept. 1991): 45.

Confédération Paysanne. *L'Agriculture Paysanne.* Paris: Confédération Paysanne, 1990.

Corbin, Alain. *The Lure of the Sea: The Discovery of the Seaside in the Western World, 1750–1840.* Translated Jocelyn Phelps. Berkeley: University of California Press, 1994.

Corvol, Andrée. *L'Homme aux bois: Histoire des relations de l'homme et de la forêt, XVIIe–XXe siècle.* Paris: Fayard, 1987.

Cotgrove, Stephen. *Catastrophe or Cornucopia: The Environment, Politics, and the Future.* Chichester: Wiley, 1982.

Courtet, Laurent, Pascal Gateaud, and Bernard Stephan. *La Loire en sursis: Croisade pour le dernier fleuve sauvage d'Europe.* Paris: Sang de la Terre, 1991.

Cousteau, Jacques-Yves. "Mes premiers soixante-quinze ans." *Calypso Log* no. 37, French edition (June 1985): 4–11.

———. "Water is an Embracing Medium." *Calypso Log* 12, no. 2, English-language edition (June 1985): 24.

Cronon, William, ed. *Uncommon Ground: Toward Reinventing Nature.* New York: Norton, 1995.

Dalla Bernardina, Sergio. *L'Utopie de la nature: Chasseurs, écologistes, et touristes.* Paris: Imago, 1996.

Dalton, Russell J. *The Green Rainbow: Environmental Groups in Western Europe.* New Haven: Yale University Press, 1994.

Daubois, Jeanne. *La nature et nos enfants.* Brussels: Casterman, 1973.

De Beaulieu, François. *Les dents du progrès: La marée noire.* Paris: Le Sycomore, 1978.

Debeir, Jean-Claude, Jean-Paul Deléage, and Daniel Hémery. *In the Servitude of Power: Energy and Civilization through the Ages.* Translated by John Barzman. London: Zed, 1991.

Deléage, Jean-Paul. *Histoire de l'ecologie.* Paris: La Découverte, 1991.

Demesse, Nicole, Alain Persuy, Jean Cauwet, and Roger Fischer. *France, ta forêt fout le camp!* Paris: Stock, 1976.

De Miller, Roland. *Robert Hainard, peintre et philosophe de la nature.* Paris, 1987.

De Roo, Priscilla, and Jean-Paul Laborie, eds. *Atlas de l'aménagement du territoir.* Paris: DATAR/Documentation Française, 1988.

Desbrosses, Philippe. *L'Intelligence verte: L'Agriculture de demain.* Paris: Editions du Rocher, 1999.

Dessus, Benjamin, and François Pharabod. "Jérémie et Noé: Deux scénarios énergétiques mondiaux à long terme." *Revue de l'Energie* no. 421 (June 1990): 3–19.

Diani, Mario. *The Green Connection: Structures of Environmental Action in Italy.* Edinburgh: Edinburgh University Press, 1994.

Di Castri, Francesco. *L'Ecologie: Les défis d'une science en temps de crise.* Paris: Documentation Française, 1983.

Dominick, Raymond. *The Environmental Movement in Germany.* Bloomington: Indiana University Press, 1993.

Dorst, Jean. *Avant que nature meure.* Paris: Delachaux et Niestlé, 1965.

Drouet, Dominique. *L'Industrie de l'environnement en France.* Paris: Armand Colin, 1997.

Dubos, René. *Nous n'avons qu'une terre.* Paris: Denoël, 1972.

Dubost, Françoise. *Vert patrimoine.* Paris: Editions de la Maison des Sciences de l'Homme, 1994.

Duclos, Denis. *La peur et le savoir: La société face à la science, la technique, et leurs dangers.* Paris: La Découverte, 1989.

Dumont, René. *L'Utopie ou la mort.* Paris: Seuil, 1974.

Elliott, Robert. *Faking Nature: The Ethics of Environmental Restoration.* New York: Routledge, 1997.

Ellul, Jacques. *The Technological Bluff.* Grand Rapids: Eerdmans, 1990.

Emmeche, Claus. *The Garden in the Machine: The Emerging Science of Artificial Life.* Princeton: Princeton University Press, 1994.

D'Erceville, Béatrice. "A la recherche du rayon vert." *LSA* no. 1290 (Feb. 6, 1992).

"Fabius accable Hernu et Lacoste." *Le Figaro,* Sept. 26, 1985: 1.

Fagnani, Francis, and Alexandre Nicolon, eds. *Nucléopolis: Matériaux pour l'analyse d'une société nucléaire.* Grenoble: Presses Universitaires de Grenoble, 1979.

Faucher, Florence. *Les habits verts de la politique.* Paris: Presses de Sciences Po, 1999.

Faucheux, Sylvie, and Jean-François Noël. *Economie des ressources naturelles et de l'environnement.* Paris: Armand Colin, 1995.

Felden, Marceau. *Energie: Le défi nucléaire*. Paris: Leson, 1976.

Ferkiss, Victor. *Nature, Technology, and Society: Cultural Roots of the Current Environmental Crisis*. New York: New York University Press, 1993.

Ferry, Luc. *Le nouvel ordre écologique*. Paris: Grasset, 1992. *The New Ecological Order*. Translated by Carol Volk. Chicago: University of Chicago Press, 1995.

Finon, Dominique. *L'Echec des surgénérateurs*. Grenoble: PUG, 1989.

Foing, Dominique, ed. *Le livre des Verts*. Paris: Editions du Félin, 1994.

Fourniau, Jean-Michel. "La portée des contestations du TGV Méditerranée." *Ecologie et Politique* 21 (Autumn/Winter 1997): 61–75.

Frost, Robert L. "Mechanical Dreams: Democracy and Technological Discourse in Twentieth-Century France." In Langdon Winner, ed., *Democracy in a Technological Society*, 51–80. Dordrecht, The Netherlands: Kluwer, 1992.

Gagnon, Paul. "*La Vie Future*: Some French Responses to the Technological Society." *Journal of European Studies* 6, no. 23 (Sept. 1976): 172–89.

Génot, Jean-Claude. *Ecologiquement correct ou protection contre nature?* Aix-en-Provence: Edisud, 1998.

George, Pierre. *L'Environnement*. Paris: PUF, 1971.

Glacken, Clarence J. *Traces on the Rhodian Shore: Nature and Culture in Western Thought from Ancient Times to the End of the Eighteenth Century*. Berkeley: University of California Press, 1967.

"Going Green." *The Economist* 322, no. 7748 (February 29, 1992): 52.

Gore, Al. *Earth in the Balance: Ecology and the Human Spirit*. New York: Plume, 1993.

Gorz, André. *Ecology as Politics*. Translated by Patsy Vigderman and Jonathan Cloud. Boston: South End Press, 1980.

Gottlieb, Roger S., ed. *This Sacred Earth: Religion, Nature, Environment*. New York: Routledge, 1996.

Gouzien, Annie, and Patrick Le Louarn, eds. *Environnement et politique: Constructions juridico-politiques et usages sociaux*. Rennes: Presses Universitaires de Rennes, 1996.

Green, Nicholas. *The Spectacle of Nature: Landscape and Bourgeois Culture in Nineteenth-Century France*. Manchester: Manchester University Press, 1990.

Grenon, Michel. *La pomme nucléaire et l'orange solaire*. Paris: Robert Laffont, 1978.

Grillet, Thierry, and Daniel Le Conte Des Floris, eds. *Les natures du vert*. Paris: Autrement, 1986.

Gros, François, and Gérard Huber, eds. *Vers un anti-destin? Patrimoine génétique et droits de l'humanité*. Paris: Odile Jacob, 1992.

Grosser, Alfred. "Faut-il avoir peur de l'écologie?" In *Libération*, special edition, "Tout sur les écologistes," March 1992: 64–65.

Groupement de Scientifiques pour l'Information sur l'Energie Nucléaire (GSIEN). *Plutonium sur Rhône*. Paris: Syros, 1981.

Grove, Richard. *Green Imperialism: Colonial Expansion, Tropical Island Edens and the Origins of Environmentalism, 1600–1860*. Cambridge: Cambridge University Press, 1995.

Gruvel, A. *Deuxième Congrès International pour la Protection de la Nature: Procès-verbaux, rapports, et voeux*. Paris: Société d'Editions, 1932.

Guattari, Félix. *Les trois écologies*. Paris: Galilée, 1989.

Guihal, Dominique. *Droit répressif de l'environnement.* 2d ed. Paris: Economica, 2000.

Guillot, Jean-Michel. "L'Ours des Pyrénées est condamné à disparaître." *Le Monde,* April 28, 1993: 10.

Guillot, Pascal. "Données historiques de l'environnement et perspectives d'avenir." Unpublished manuscript, Université des Sciences et Techniques de Lille, 1988.

Guiral, Antoine. "Cohn-Bendit dope les Verts." *Libération,* June 14, 1999.

Haraway, Donna. "A Cyborg Manifesto: Science, Technology, and Socialist-Feminism in the Late Twentieth Century." In *Simians, Cyborgs, and Women: The Reinvention of Nature,* 149–81. New York: Routledge, 1991.

Hargrove, Eugene, ed. *Beyond Spaceship Earth: Environmental Ethics and the Solar System.* San Francisco: Sierra Club, 1987.

Harpet, Cyrille. *Du déchet: Philosophie des immondices.* Paris: L'Harmattan, 1998.

Hascoët, Guy. *Le pouvoir est ailleurs.* Arles: Actes Sud, 1999.

Hecht, Gabrielle. *The Radiance of France: Nuclear Power and National Identity after World War II.* Cambridge, Mass.: MIT Press, 1998.

Heim, Roger. *Destruction et protection de la nature.* Paris: Armand Colin, 1952.

Herbin, Jacky, ed. *Tourisme et environnement.* Paris: La Documentation Française, 1992.

Herléa, Alexandre, ed. *L'Energie solaire en France.* Paris: CTHS, 1995.

Hillairet, J. "Thémis, La Centrale Solaire." *Entropie* 18, no. 103 (1982): 4–20.

Hirsch, Eric, and Michael O'Hanlon, eds. *The Anthropology of Landscape: Perspectives on Place and Space.* Oxford: Clarendon Press, 1995.

Houdebine, Louis-Marie. *Les biotechnologies animales: Nécessité ou révolution inutile.* Paris: Editions France Agricole, 1998.

Howorth, Jolyon. "HiroChirac and the French Nuclear Testing Conundrum: A Testing Time for the Pursuit of Grandeur." *French Politics and Society* 13, no. 3 (Summer 1995): 1–17.

Hülsberg, Werner. *The German Greens.* Translated by Gus Fagan. London: Verso, 1988.

Hunter, Robert. *The Greenpeace Chronicle.* New York: Picador, 1982.

Ifen (Institut Français de l'Environnement), ed. *L'Environnement en France, Edition 1999.* Paris: La Découverte, 1998.

Illich, Ivan. *Energie et équité.* Paris: Seuil, 1973.

———. *La convivialité.* Paris: Seuil, 1974.

Jacob, Jean. *Histoire de l'écologie politique: Comment la gauche a redécouvert la nature.* Paris: Albin Michel, 1999.

Jasper, James. *Nuclear Politics: Energy and the State in the United States, Sweden, and France.* Princeton: Princeton University Press, 1990.

Jegouzo, Yves, and Christophe Sanson. *Le guide de l'environnement.* Paris: Editions du Moniteur, 1990.

Jenson, Jane. "From *Baba Cool* to a *Vote Utile:* The Trajectory of the French *Verts.*" *French Politics and Society* 7, no. 4 (Fall 1989): 1–15.

Jonas, Hans. *The Imperative of Responsibility: In Search of an Ethics for the Technological Age.* Translated by Hans Jonas and David Herr. Chicago: University of Chicago Press, 1984.

Jordan, Bertrand. *Génétique et génome: La fin de l'innocence.* Paris: Flammarion, 1996.

Jouve, Henry, ed. *Les espaces naturels, un capital pour l'avenir.* Paris: Documentation Française, 1991.

Kahn, Herman, and Julian Simon, eds. *The Resourceful Earth.* Oxford: Oxford University Press, 1984.

Kalaora, Bernard. *Au-delà de la nature l'environnement: L'Observation sociale de l'environnement.* Paris: L'Harmattan, 1998.

King, Michael. *Death of the Rainbow Warrior.* Harmondsworth: Penguin, 1986.

Kiss, Alexandre, ed. *L'Ecologie et la loi: Le statut juridique de l'environnement.* Paris: L'Harmattan, 1989.

Kitschelt, Herbert. *The Logics of Party Formation: Ecological Politics in Belgium and West Germany.* Ithaca, N.Y.: Cornell University Press, 1989.

Lacoste, André-Claude, et al. *Croissance et environnement: Les conditions de la qualité de la vie.* Paris: Documentation Française, 1993.

Lalonde, Brice. *Sur la vague verte.* Paris: Laffont, 1981.

Lalonde, Brice, Serge Moscovici, René Dumont, and Jean-Pierre Ribes. *Pourquoi les écologistes font-ils de la politique?* Paris: Seuil, 1978.

Lapoix, François. *Sauver la ville: Ecologie du milieu urbain.* Paris: Sang de la Terre, 1991.

Larrère, Catherine, and Raphaël Larrère. *Du bon usage de la nature: Pour une philosophie de l'environnement.* Paris: Aubier, 1997.

Lascoumes, Pierre. *L'Ecopouvoir: Environnements et politiques.* Paris: La Découverte, 1994.

Lascoumes, Pierre, and Jean-Pierre Le Bourhis. *L'Environnement ou l'administration des possibles.* Paris: L'Harmattan, 1997.

Latour, Bruno. *Nous n'avons jamais été modernes.* Paris: La Découverte, 1991. *We Have Never Been Modern.* Translated by Catherine Porter. Cambridge: Harvard University Press, 1993.

———. "Arrachement ou attachement à la nature?" *Ecologie Politique* 5 (Winter 1993): 15–26.

———. "Les limites de l'experience collective." *La Recherche* 306 (February 1998).

———. *Politiques de la nature: Comment faire entrer les sciences en démocratie.* Paris: La Découverte, 1999.

Lebreton, Philippe. *La nature en crise.* Paris: Sang de la Terre, 1988.

——— [pseud. Prof. Mollo-Mollo]. *L'Energie, c'est vous.* Paris: Stock, 1974.

Le Déaut, Jean-Yves. *Le système français de radioprotection, de contrôle, et de sécurité nucléaire.* Paris: Documentation Française, 1998.

Lefevre, Philippe, moderator. "La nouvelle bataille du rail." *France Inter* (radio program), Aug. 18, 1991.

Lefort, Bernard, ed. *Le nouveau livre des Verts.* Paris: Editions du Félin, 1999.

Legay, Jean-Marie, and Robert Barbault, eds. *La révolution technologique en écologie.* Paris: Masson, 1995.

Le Gendre, Bertrand. "Quand M. Hernu niait le sabotage." *Le Monde,* Nov. 5, 1987.

Léger, Danièle, and Bertrand Hervieu. *Le retour à la nature: Au fond de la forêt... l'état.* Paris: Seuil, 1979.

Lenoble, Robert. *Esquisse d'une histoire de l'idée de nature.* Paris: Albin Michel, 1969.

Lequenne, Philippe. *Dans les coulisses de Greenpeace.* Paris: L'Harmattan, 1997.

Liébard, Alain, Cédric Philibert, and Michel Rodot. *Du neuf sous le soleil.* Paris: Calmann-Lévy/Systèmes Solaires, 1991.

Lipietz, Alain. "Les Verts: bleus, blancs, rouges . . . ou bruns?" In *Libération,* special edition, "Tout sur les écologistes," March 1992: 64–65.

————. *Green Hopes: The Future of Political Ecology.* Translated by Malcolm Slater. Cambridge, England: Polity Press, 1995.

"Loi No. 76–629 du 10 Juillet 1976." *Journal Officiel,* July 13, 1976: 1.

London, Caroline. *Environnement et stratégie de l'entreprise.* Rennes: Apogée, 1993.

Lowe, Philip, and Jane Goyder. *Environmental Groups in Politics.* London: Allen and Unwin, 1983.

Lucas, N. J. D. *Energy in France: Planning, Politics, and Policy.* London: Europa, 1979.

Mabit, Michel. *Les métiers de l'environnement: "Gagner sa vie en protégeant la Vie."* Nantes: Editions Opéra, 1998.

Magoc, Chris J. *Yellowstone: The Creation and Selling of an American Landscape, 1870–1903.* Albuquerque: University of New Mexico Press, 1999.

Marie, M., G. Masson, S. Mathieu, B. Ollivier, J. F. Ricard, and P. Weis. *L'Opinion publique face au nucléaire.* Paris: Centre d'Etudes Sociologiques et Travaux de Recherches Appliquées, 1980.

Marsh, George Perkins. *The Earth as Modified by Human Action.* New York: Arno, 1970. First published in 1864 as *Man and Nature; or, Physical Geography as Modified by Human Action.*

Martinez, Eloi. "TGV-Méditerranée: Le projet de nouvelle ligne contesté en Avignon." *L'Humanité,* May 17, 1993.

Mathieu, Nicole. "La notion de rural et les rapports ville-campagne en France: Des années cinquante aux années quatre-vingts." *Economie Rurale* no. 187 (May–June 1990): 35– 41.

McKibben, Bill. *The End of Nature.* New York: Random House, 1989.

McNeill, J. R. *Something New Under the Sun: An Environmental History of the Twentieth-Century World.* New York: Norton, 2000.

Meadows, Donella H., et al. *The Limits to Growth: A Report for the Club of Rome's Project on the Predicament of Mankind.* New York: Universe Books, 1972.

Merchant, Carolyn. *Radical Ecology.* New York: Routledge, 1992.

Meyronneinc, Jean-Paul. *Plaidoyer pour les déchets.* Rennes: Apogée, 1993.

Ministère de l'Environnement, ed. *Ethique et environnement: Colloque.* Paris: Documentation Française, 1997.

Monod, Théodore. *Sortie de secours.* Paris: Seghers, 1991.

Morgan, Robin, and Brian Whitaker. *Rainbow Warrior: The French Attempt to Sink Greenpeace.* London: Arrow, 1986.

Moscovici, Serge. *La société contre nature.* Paris: Union Générale d'Editions, 1972.

Mosse, Françoise. *À la découverte des réserves naturelles de France.* Paris: Nathan, 1996.

Muet, Pierre-Alain, ed. *Fiscalité de l'environnement.* Paris: Documentation Française, 1998.

Müller-Rommel, Ferdinand, ed. *New Politics in Western Europe.* Boulder: Westview Press, 1989.

Munson, Richard. *Cousteau: The Captain and his World.* New York: Morrow, 1989.

Nash, Roderick. *The Rights of Nature: A History of Environmental Ethics.* Madison: University of Wisconsin Press, 1989.

Neboit-Guilhot, René, and Lucette Davy, eds. *Les Français dans leur environnement.* Paris: Nathan, 1996.

Nelkin, Dorothy, and Michael Pollak. *The Atom Besieged: Extraparliamentary Dissent in France and Germany.* Cambridge: MIT Press, 1981.

Nicolino, Fabrice. *Le tour de France d'un écologiste*. Paris: Seuil, 1993.

North, Richard D. *Life on a Modern Planet*. Manchester: Manchester University Press, 1995.

Oelschlaeger, Max. *The Idea of Wilderness: From Prehistory to the Age of Ecology*. New Haven: Yale University Press, 1991.

Osborne, Michael. *Nature, the Exotic, and the Science of French Colonialism*. Bloomington: Indiana University Press, 1994.

Ost, François. *La nature hors la loi: L'Ecologie à l'épreuve du droit*. Paris: La Découverte, 1995.

P.J. "Dany séduit les jeunes." *Libération*, June 17, 1999: 17.

Parkin, Sara. *Green Parties: An International Guide*. London: Heretic Books, 1989.

Parti Socialiste, ed. *Energie: L'Autre politique*. Paris: Club Socialiste du Livre, 1980.

—. *Ecologie et pouvoir*. Paris: Documentation Française, 1990.

Pecqueur, M. Michel. *Bilan et perspectives des activités industrielles liées à la protection de l'environnement en France*. Paris: Journal Officiel, 1992.

Pelt, Jean-Marie. *Plantes et aliments transgéniques*. Paris: Fayard, 1998.

Peninou, Jean-Louis. "Comment Paris a sauvé les Turenge." *Libération*, Nov. 5, 1985: 1.

Perrier, Gérard. "TGV-Méditeranée: Premières leçons d'un conflit." *Ecologie Politique* 6 (Spring 1993): 29–41.

Pestel, Eduard. *Beyond the Limits to Growth*. New York: Universe Books, 1989.

Pezzey, John. *Sustainable Development Concepts: An Economic Analysis*. World Bank Environment Paper No. 2. Washington, D.C.: World Bank, 1992.

Pharabod, Jean-Pierre, and Jean-Paul Schapira. *Les jeux de l'atome et du hasard*. Paris: Calmann-Lévy, 1988.

Picard, Jean-François, Alain Beltran, and Martine Bungener. *Histoire(s) de l'EDF: Comment se sont prises les décisions de 1946 à nos jours*. Paris: Dunod, 1985.

Piétrasanta, Yves. *L'Ecologie, clé de la politique*. Paris: L'Harmattan, 1998.

Pojman, Louis P., ed. *Environmental Ethics*. Boston: Jones and Bartlett, 1994.

Poujade, Robert. *Le ministère de l'impossible*. Paris: Calmann-Lévy, 1975.

"Pourquoi nous irons au Larzac." *La Bramaïre*, special leaflet edition, Aug. 24–26, 1973: 2.

Prendiville, Brendan. *Environmental Politics in France*. Boulder: Westview, 1994.

Pritchard, Sara B. "'Le nouveau Rhône est né' (Donzère-Mondragon)." In Robert Belot, Michel Cotte, and Pierre Lamard, eds., *La technologie au risque de l'histoire*, 77–86. Belfort: Université de Technologie de Belfort-Montbéliard, 2000.

—. "Hydroelectric Development in Postwar France." In Char Miller, Mark Cioc, and Kate Showers, eds., *Water and the Environment Since 1945: Global Perspectives*, 93–95. New York: St. James Press/Gale Publications, 2001.

—. "Recreating the Rhône: Nature and Technology in France Since World War II." Ph.D. diss., Department of History, Stanford University, 2001.

Pronier, Raymond, and Vincent Jacques le Seigneur. *Génération Verte: Les écologistes en politique*. Paris: La Renaissance, 1992.

Pujol, Jean-Luc, and Dominique Dron, eds. *Agriculture, monde rural, et environnement. Qualité oblige*. Paris: Documentation Française, 1998.

Questiaux, Nicole, ed. *Données économiques de l'environnement*. Paris: Documentation Française, 1998.

Raffin, Jean-Pierre. "La protection de l'ours brun (Ursus Arctos L.) dans les Pyrénées

Françaises: Histoire d'une nonchalance institutionelle." In XIVème Colloque Francophone de Mammalogie de la SFEPM, *Introductions et réintroductions de mammifères sauvages,* 81–90. Paris: Annales Biologiques du Centre, 1990.

Ricklefs, Robert E. *Ecology.* 3d ed.. New York: W. H. Freeman, 1990.

Rivasi, Michèle, and Hélène Crié. *Ce nucléaire qu'on nous cache.* Paris: Albin Michel, 1998.

Roditi, David, and André Joffre. *Tecsol: Equipement Solaire Thermique en Europe.* Brussels: Commission des Communautés Européennes, 1992.

Romi, Raphaël. *Droit et administration de l'environnement.* 3d ed.. Paris: Montchrestien, 1999.

Roquelle, Sophie. "TGV-Méditeranée: La polémique relancée." *Le Figaro,* Aug. 22, 1992.

Rostagnat, Michel. *Les nouvelles frontières de l'environnement.* Rodez: Editions du Rouergue, 1993.

Royal, Ségolène. *Pays, paysans, paysages: La réconciliation est-elle possible?* Paris: Laffont, 1993.

Rudolf, Florence. *L'Environnement: Une construction sociale: Pratiques et discours sur l'environnement en Allemagne et en France.* Strasbourg: Presses Universitaires de Strasbourg, 1998.

Ruffat, Michèle. *Commerce, consumérisme, protection de l'environnement.* Paris: Institut du Commerce et de la Consommation, 1991.

Saint-Marc, Philippe. *Socialisation de la nature.* Paris: Stock, 1975.

Sainteny, Guillaume. *Les Verts.* Paris: PUF, 1991.

Salomon, Jean-Jacques. "De la transparence." In Collège de la Prévention des Risques Technologiques, *Le risque technologique et la démocratie,* 19–33. Paris: Documentation Française, 1994.

Samuel, Pierre. *Le nucléaire en questions.* Paris: Entente, 1975.

———. *Les trains à grande vitesse.* Paris: Les Amis de la Terre, 1991.

Schama, Simon. *Landscape and Memory.* New York: Knopf, 1995.

Scheffer, Victor. *The Shaping of Environmentalism in America.* Seattle: University of Washington Press, 1991.

Schubert, Katherine, and Paul Zagamé, eds. *L'Environnement: Une nouvelle dimension de l'analyse économique.* Paris: Vuibert, 1998.

Serres, Michel. *Le contrat naturel.* Paris: Bourin, 1990.

Shull, Tad. "The Ecologists in the Regional Elections: Strategies Behind the Split." *French Politics and Society* 10, no. 2 (Spring 1992): 13–19.

Simonnet, Dominique. *L'Ecologisme.* 2d ed. Paris: PUF, 1982.

Simonnot, Philippe. *Les nucléocrates.* Grenoble: Presses Universitaires de Grenoble, 1978.

Simons, Marlise. "Paris Can No Longer Hide a Dirty Secret: Pollution." *International Herald Tribune,* July 15–16, 1995: 2.

Singleton, Fred, ed. *Environmental Problems in the Soviet Union and Eastern Europe.* Boulder: Lynne Rienner, 1987.

Smil, Vaclav. *The Bad Earth: Environmental Degradation in China.* New York: M. E. Sharpe, 1984.

SNCF. *TGV-Méditerranée: Une grande ambition pour le sud.* Paris: SNCF, 1990.

Shabecoff, Philip. *A Fierce Green Fire: The American Environmental Movement.* New York: Hill and Wang, 1993.

Short, John Rennie. *Imagined Country: Environment, Culture and Society.* London: Routledge, 1991.

Simmons, I. G. *Environmental History: A Concise Introduction.* Oxford: Blackwell, 1993.

Sorgue, Pierre. "Bataille de ministres autour d'un tracé du TGV du Sud-Est." *Libération,* Aug. 26, 1992.

"Spécial Marée Noire: Les Bretons se mobilisent devant le fléau qui vient de la mer." *Paris Match,* April 22, 1967.

Stengers, Isabelle. *Cosmopolitiques,* vol. 6, *La vie et l'artifice: Visages de l'émergence.* Paris: La Découverte, 1997.

Strazzulla, Jérôme, and Jean-Claude Zerbib. *Tchernobyl.* Paris: Documentation Française, 1991.

Switzer, Jacqueline. *Green Backlash: The History and Politics of Environmental Opposition in the U.S.* Boulder: Lynne Rienner, 1997.

Szac, Murielle. *Dominique Voynet: Une vraie nature.* Paris: Plon, 1998.

Taylor, Bron, ed. *Ecological Resistance Movements: The Global Emergence of Radical and Popular Environmentalism.* Albany: State University of New York Press, 1995.

Terrasson, François. *La civilisation anti-nature.* Monaco: Editions du Rocher, 1994.

Thénard, Jean-Michel. "Un succès dérangeant pour Lionel Jospin." *Libération,* June 17, 1999: 16.

Tibon-Cornillot, Michel. *Les corps transfigurés: Mécanisation du vivant et imaginaire de la biologie.* Paris: Seuil, 1992.

Thomas, Keith. *Man and the Natural World.* New York: Oxford University Press, 1983.

Thomas, William L., Jr., ed. *Man's Role in Changing the Face of the Earth.* Chicago: University of Chicago Press, 1955.

Turner, B. L., ed. *The Earth as Transformed by Human Action: Global and Regional Changes in the Biosphere over the past 300 Years.* Cambridge: Cambridge University Press, 1990.

Union Fédérale des Consommateurs. "Nucléaire: Le face-à-face." *Que Choisir,* special number, 1977.

Vallée, M. *L'Ecologie dans l'enseignement du Second Degré.* Nantes: Annales du Centre Régional de Documentation Pédagogique de Nantes, 1970.

Vatimbella, Alexandre. *Le capitalisme vert.* Paris: Syros/Alternatives, 1992.

Vermont, Olivier. *La face cachée de Greenpeace.* Paris: Albin Michel, 1997.

Vernier, Jacques. *La bataille de l'environnement.* Paris: Laffont, 1971.

Viard, Jean. *Le tiers espace: Essai sur la nature.* Paris: Méridiens Klincksieck, 1990.

Viardot, Eric. *L'Environnement dans l'entreprise.* Paris: L'Harmattan, 1997.

Viel, Jean-François. *La santé publique atomisée.* Paris: La Découverte, 1998.

Vigneron, Jacques, and Frédéric Malaval. *Les innovations des éco-industries.* Paris: Economica, 1998.

Vigneron, Jacques, and Claude Burstein, eds. *Ecoproduit: Concepts et méthodologies.* Paris: Economica, 1993.

Villeneuve, Charles. *Les Français et les centrales nucléaires.* Transcript of television series. Europe 1/Sofedir, 1980.

Voynet, Dominique. "Bilan de l'action du Ministère de l'Aménagement du Territoire et de l'Environnement de Juin 1997 à Avril 2000." Speech before the members of France Nature Environnement (April 15, 2000), available from the Ministry of the Environment website: http://www.environnement.gouv.fr/actua/com2000/avril/17-bilan-97-2000.htm.

Waechter, Antoine. *Dessine-moi une planète.* Paris: Albin Michel, 1990.

Waggoner, Paul E., Jesse H. Ausubel, Iddo K. Wernick. "Lightening the Tread of Population on the Land: American Examples." *Population and Development Review* 22, no. 3 (September 1996): 531–45.

White, Richard. *The Organic Machine: The Remaking of the Columbia River.* New York: Hill and Wang, 1995.

Whited, Tamara L. *Forests and Peasant Politics in Modern France.* New Haven: Yale University Press, 2000.

Wiesenfeld, Bernard. *L'Atome écologique.* Les Ulis: EDP Sciences, 1998.

Worster, Donald. *Under Western Skies: Nature and History in the American West.* New York: Oxford University Press, 1992.

———. *Nature's Economy: A History of Ecological Ideas.* 2d ed. Cambridge: Cambridge University Press, 1994.

Yost, David S. "Nuclear Debates in France." *Survival* 36, no. 4 (Winter 1994–95): 113–39.

Zonabend, Françoise. *The Nuclear Peninsula.* Translated by J. A. Underwood. Cambridge: Cambridge University Press, 1993.

3.2. General (non-environmental) Topics

Académie Nationale de l'Air et de l'Espace, ed. *Actes de L'atelier-débat, "Les Apports de la Conquête Spatiale à l'Humanité."* Paris: Cépaduès, 1992.

Adenauer, Konrad. "Germany and Europe." *Foreign Affairs* 31, no. 3 (April 1953): 361–66.

Ailleret, Charles. *L'Aventure atomique française.* Paris: Grasset, 1968.

Aldrich, Robert, and John Connell, eds. *France in World Politics.* London: Routledge, 1989.

Alexander, Richard D. *Darwinism and Human Affairs.* Seattle: University of Washington Press, 1979.

Appel, Toby A. *The Cuvier-Geoffroy Debate: French Biology in the Decades Before Darwin.* New York: Oxford University Press, 1987.

Ardagh, John. *France Today.* London: Penguin, 1995.

Aron, Raymond. *Le grand débat: Initiation à la stratégie atomique.* Paris: Calmann-Lévy, 1963. *The Great Debate.* Translated by Ernst Pawel. New York: Doubleday, 1965.

———. *Progress and Disillusion: The Dialectics of Modern Society.* New York: Praeger, 1968.

Barsanti, Giulio. *La mappa della vita: Teorie della natura e teorie dell'uomo in Francia, 1750–1850.* Naples: Guida, 1983.

Beaufre, André. *L'OTAN et l'Europe.* Paris: Calmann-Lévy, 1966.

Belot, Robert, Michel Cotte, and Pierre Lamard, eds. *La technologie au risque de l'histoire.* Paris: Berg/Université de Technologie de Belfort-Montbéliard, 2000.

Bernstein, Serge. *La France de l'expansion.* Paris: Seuil, 1989.

Bertrand, Maurice. *Pour une doctrine militaire française.* Paris: Gallimard, 1965.

Bess, Michael. *Realism, Utopia, and the Mushroom Cloud: Four Activist Intellectuals and their Strategies for Peace, 1945–1989.* Chicago: University of Chicago Press, 1993.

Bonnet, Roger M. "Pourquoi les missions spatiales?" Speech at colloquium on "Ethique et Environnement," Boulogne, March 11, 1993.

Bourdet, Claude. *L'aventure incertaine: De la résistance à la restauration.* Paris: Stock, 1975.

Braillard, Philippe, and Alain Demant. *Eureka et l'Europe technologique.* Brussels: Axes/ Bruylant 1991.

Braudel, Fernand. *The Mediterranean and the Mediterranean World in the Age of Philip II.* Translated by Siân Reynolds. New York: Harper and Row, 1972. First French ed. 1949.

———. *The Identity of France.* Translated by Siân Reynolds. New York: Harper Collins, 1990.

Brissaud, Jean-Marc. *Eléments pour une nouvelle politique étrangère.* Pau: Front National, Université d'été, September 1985.

Buhler, Alain. *Petit dictionnaire de la révolution étudiante.* Paris: Didier, 1968.

Burrell, Raymond E. *The French Communist Party, Nuclear Weapons, and National Defense: Issues of the 1978 Election Campaign.* Washington: U.S. Government Printing Office, 1979.

Cairns, John C., ed. *Contemporary France: Illusion, Conflict, and Regeneration.* New York: New Viewpoints, 1978.

Carré, Jean-Jacques, Paul Dubois, Edmond Malinvaud. *French Economic Growth.* Translated by John P. Hatfield. Stanford: Stanford University Press, 1975.

Castello, Martine. *La grande aventure d'Ariane.* Paris: Larousse, 1987.

Caute, David. *The Year of the Barricades: A Journey Through 1968.* New York: Harper and Row, 1988.

Cerny, Philip G., ed. *Social Movements and Protest in France.* New York: St. Martin's, 1982.

Cerny, Philip G., and Martin A. Schain, eds. *French Politics and Public Policy.* New York: St. Martin's, 1980.

Chabbert, Bernard. *Les fils d'Ariane.* Paris: Plon, 1986.

Chapman, Herrick. *State Capitalism and Working-Class Radicalism in the French Aircraft Industry.* Berkeley: University of California Press, 1991.

Charpak, Georges, and Richard L. Garwin. *Feux follets et champignons nucléaires.* Paris: Odile Jacob, 1997.

Chesneaux, Jean, and Nic Maclellan. *La France dans le Pacifique: De Bougainville à Mururoa.* Paris: La Découverte, 1992.

"Cinémas Paysans." *CinémAction,* no. 16 (1982).

Clark, Linda L. *Social Darwinism in France.* University, Ala.: University of Alabama Press, 1984.

Clarke, Arthur C. *By Space Possessed.* London: Gollancz, 1993.

Cogan, Charles G. *Charles de Gaulle: A Brief Biography with Documents.* New York: St. Martin's, 1996.

Cohen, Elie. *Le Colbertisme "high-tech."* Paris: Hachette, 1992.

Collins, Guy. *Europe in Space.* New York: St. Martin's, 1990.

Colson, René. *Un paysan face à l'avenir rural.* Paris: Epi, 1976.

Commissariat Général du Plan. *France rurale: Un nouveau contrat.* Préparation du

XIème Plan, Commission "Agriculture, Alimentation, et Développement Rural," présidée par Philippe Mangin. Paris: Documentation Française, 1993.

"Concorde Assassiné par les Américains?" *Paris-Match* no. 1234 (Dec. 30, 1972).

Crandall, B. C., ed. *Nanotechnology: Molecular Speculations on Global Abundance.* Cambridge, Mass.: MIT Press, 1996.

Dansette, Adrien. *Mai 1968.* Paris: Plon, 1971.

Debatisse, Michel. *La révolution silencieuse.* Paris: Calmann-Lévy, 1963.

Debbasch, Charles, and Jean-Marie Pontier. *La société française.* Paris: Dalloz, 1989.

Denarié, Paul. *L'aventure de Concorde.* Paris: Presses Noires, 1969.

De Planhol, Xavier. *Géographie historique de la France.* Paris: Fayard, 1988.

Digeon, Claude. *La crise allemande de la pensée française, 1870–1914.* Paris: PUF, 1959.

Dollfuss, Daniel. *La force de frappe.* Paris: Julliard, 1960.

Drexler, K. Eric. *Nanosystems: Molecular Machinery, Manufacturing, and Computation.* New York: Wiley, 1992.

Duhamel, Alain. *Les peurs françaises.* Paris: Flammarion, 1993.

Duvigneau, Michel. "Les communautés villageoises de Maurice Failevic." *CinémAction* no 36 (1986): 124–28.

Eichenberg, Richard C. *Public Opinion and National Security in Western Europe.* Ithaca: Cornell University Press, 1989.

Eisenberg, Daniel. "Amtrak's Last Train." *Time,* Dec. 4, 2000: 62.

Estienne, Pierre. *Terres d'abandon? La population des montagnes françaises: Hier, aujourd'hui, demain.* Clermont-Ferrand: Institut d'Etudes du Massif Central, 1988.

European Space Agency. *Reaching for the Skies: The Ariane Family Story and Beyond.* Noordwijk, The Netherlands: European Space Agency Publications, 1988.

———. *The ESRO-ESA Space Science Story: Twenty-Five Years of European Cooperation.* Noordwijk, The Netherlands: European Space Agency Publications, 1990.

———. *Columbus: An Expedition to Space.* Noordwijk, The Netherlands: European Space Agency Publications, 1991.

———. *European Space: For Exclusively Peaceful Purposes.* Noordwijk, The Netherlands: European Space Agency Publications, 1992.

———. *Satellites at the Service of the Environment and Development.* Paris: European Space Agency, 1992.

———. *Europe into Space: The Auger Years (1959–1967).* Noordwijk, The Netherlands: European Space Agency Publications, 1993.

Fabre-Luce, Alfred. *L'Or et la Bombe.* Paris: Calmann-Lévy, 1968.

Failevic, Maurice. *Le cheval vapeur.* 16mm. film, 97 mins. Antenne 2/S.F.P., 1980.

Faligot, Roger, and Pascal Krop. *La Piscine: The French Secret Service since 1944.* Translated by W. D. Halls. London: Basil Blackwell, 1989.

Faure, Guy. "Le M.I.T.I., ou la politique à longue terme." *Revue française de gestion* (special number, "Le Japon mode ou modèle?"), nos. 27–28 (Sept.-Oct. 1980).

Feigenbaum, Harvey B. *The Politics of Public Enterprise: Oil and the French State.* Princeton: Princeton University Press, 1985.

Feldman, Elliott J. *Concorde and Dissent: Explaining High Technology Project Failures in Britain and France.* Cambridge: Cambridge University Press, 1985.

Flammarion, Camille. *La fin du monde.* Paris: Flammarion, 1894.

Flockton, Christopher, and Eleonore Kofman. *France.* London: PCP, 1989.

Flynn, Gregory, and Hans Rattinger, eds. *The Public and Atlantic Defense.* London: Rowman and Allanheld, 1985.

Fohlen, Claude. *La France de l'entre-deux-guerres.* Paris: Casterman, 1966.

Forster, Robert, and Orest Ranum, eds. *Rural Society in France.* Baltimore: Johns Hopkins University Press, 1977.

Fourastié, Jean. *Les trente glorieuses.* Paris: Fayard, 1979.

Fourniau, Jean-Michel. *La genèse des grandes vitesses à la SNCF: De l'innovation à la décision du TGV Sud-est.* Paris: Institut National de Recherche sur les Transports et leur Sécurité, 1988.

Frost, Robert L. *Alternating Currents: Nationalized Power in France, 1946–1970.* Ithaca: Cornell University Press, 1991.

Gallois, Pierre. *Le renoncement: De la France défendue à l'Europe protégée.* Paris: Plon, 1977.

Gaspard, Françoise. *A Small City in France.* Translated by Arthur Goldhammer. Cambridge: Harvard University Press, 1995.

Gay, Peter. *The Enlightenment: An Interpretation.* New York: Vintage, 1966.

Gervais, Michel, Marcel Jollivet, and Yves Tavernier. *La fin de la France paysanne: Depuis 1914,* vol. 4 of Georges Duby and Armand Wallon, eds., *Histoire de la France rurale.* Paris: Seuil, 1977.

Gibson, Roy. *Space.* Oxford: Clarendon, 1992.

Gilpin, Robert. *France in the Age of the Scientific State.* Princeton: Princeton University Press, 1968.

Gitlin, Todd. *The Sixties: Years of Hope, Days of Rage.* New York: Bantam, 1987.

Goodell, Rae. *The Visible Scientists.* Boston: Little, Brown, 1975.

Gordon, Philip H. *A Certain Idea of France: French Security Policy and the Gaullist Legacy.* Princeton: Princeton University Press, 1993.

Gravier, Jean-François. *Paris et le désert français.* Paris: Le Portulan, 1947.

Greilsammer, Alain. *Les mouvements fédéralistes en France de 1945 à 1974.* Paris: Presses D'Europe, 1975.

Groupe de recherche pour l'enseignement de l'histoire et de la géographie, ed. *Géographie du temps présent.* Paris: Hachette, 1987.

Hanley, D. L., and A. P. Kerr, eds. *May '68: Coming of Age.* London: Macmillan, 1989.

Harrison, Michael. *The Reluctant Ally: France and Atlantic Security.* Baltimore: Johns Hopkins Press, 1981.

Hayles, N. Katherine. *How We Became Posthuman.* Chicago: University of Chicago Press, 1999.

Hébrard, Frédérique. *Le château des oliviers.* Paris: Flammarion, 1993.

Henningham, Stephen. *France and the South Pacific.* Honolulu: University of Hawaii Press, 1992.

Hennion, Blandine. *Le Front National: L'Argent et l'establishment.* Paris: La Découverte, 1993.

Hobsbawm, Eric. *The Age of Extremes.* New York: Vintage, 1994.

Hoffmann, Stanley. "Obstinate or Obsolete? The Fate of the Nation-State and the Case for Western Europe." *Daedalus* 95, no. 3 (Summer 1966): 862–915.

———. *Decline or Renewal? France Since the 1930s.* New York: Viking, 1974.

———. "Fragments Floating in the Here and Now." *Daedalus* 108, no. 1 (Winter 1979): 1–26.

Hoffmann, Stanley, ed. *In Search of France.* Cambridge, Mass.: Harvard University Press, 1963.

Hollifield, James F., and George Ross, eds. *Searching for the New France*. New York: Routledge, 1991.

Howorth, Jolyon, and Patricia Chilton, eds. *Defence and Dissent in Contemporary France*. London: Croom Helm, 1984.

Hughes, Thomas P. *American Genesis: A Century of Invention and Technological Enthusiasm, 1870–1970*. New York: Viking, 1989.

Inglehart, Ronald. *Culture Shift in Advanced Industrial Society*. Princeton: Princeton University Press, 1990.

Institut Français d'Opinion Publique. "L'Avion Concorde." *Sondages* nos. 3 and 4 (1975).

———. *Les mutations idéologiques en France au cours des cinquante dernières années vues à travers les sondages de l'IFOP*. Paris: IFOP, 1991.

Joffrin, Laurent. *Mai 68*. Paris: Seuil, 1988.

Johnstone, Diana. *The Politics of Euromissiles: Europe's Role in America's World*. London: Verso, 1984.

Joy, Bill. "Why the Future Doesn't Need Us." *Wired*, April 2000.

Judt, Tony. *Past Imperfect: French Intellectuals, 1944–1956*. Berkeley: University of California Press, 1992.

Kahn, Herman, William Brown, and Leon Martel. *The Next 200 Years*. New York: William Morrow, 1976.

Kindleberger, Charles P. *Economic Growth in France and Britain, 1851–1950*. New York: Simon and Schuster, 1964.

Klein, Olivier. *La genèse du TGV comme un instant de la crise du fordisme*. Lyon: Laboratoire d'Economie des Transports, 1999.

Knafou, Rémy, ed. *Géographie*. Paris: Bélin, 1989.

Kocs, Stephen A. *Autonomy or Power? The Franco-German Relationship and Europe's Strategic Choices, 1955–1995*. Westport, Conn.: Praeger, 1995.

Kolakowski, Leszek. *Main Currents of Marxism*. 3 vols. Translated by P. S. Falla. Oxford: Clarendon Press, 1978.

Krummenacker, Markus, and James Lewis, eds. *Prospects in Nanotechnology: Toward Molecular Manufacturing*. New York: Wiley, 1995.

Kuisel, Richard F. *Capitalism and the State in Modern France: Renovation and Economic Management in the Twentieth Century*. Cambridge: Cambridge University Press, 1981.

———. *Seducing the French: the Dilemma of Americanization*. Berkeley: University of California Press, 1993.

L.D. "Prendre le train de l'an 2000." *Le Provençal*, Feb. 8, 1993.

Lacouture, Jean. *De Gaulle: The Ruler, 1945–1970*. Translated by Alan Sheridan. New York: Norton, 1993.

Laird, Robbin F., ed. *French Security Policy: From Independence to Interdependence*. Boulder: Westview, 1986.

Lamming, Clive. *La grande aventure du TGV*. Paris: Larousse, 1987.

Lebeau, André. *Choix stratégiques et grands programmes civils*. Paris: Economica, 1987.

———. *L'Espace en heritage*. Paris: Odile Jacob, 1989.

Le Monde. "La société française en mouvement" (Dossiers et Documents du *Monde*, October 1981).

Le Prestre, Philippe G., ed. *French Security Policy in a Disarming World: Domestic Challenges and International Constraints*. Boulder: Rienner, 1989.

Le Roy Ladurie, Emmanuel. *Montaillou: The Promised Land of Error.* Translated by Barbara Bray. New York: G. Braziller, 1978.

Lerner, Daniel, and Raymond Aron, eds. *France Defeats EDC.* New York: Praeger, 1957.

Lewino, Walter. *L'Imagination au pouvoir.* Paris: Eric Losfeld, 1968.

Luizet, François. "Comment va Concorde." *Le Figaro,* Feb. 24, 1985.

Mallove, Eugene F., and Gregory L. Matloff. *The Starflight Handbook: A Pioneer's Guide to Interstellar Travel.* New York: Wiley, 1989.

Manuel, Frank E., and Fritzie P. Manuel. *Utopian Thought in the Western World.* Cambridge, Mass.: Belknap Press, 1979.

Marcus, John T. *Neutralism and Nationalism in France.* New York: Bookman, 1958.

Marcus, Jonathan. *The National Front and French Politics.* Houndmills, England: Macmillan, 1995.

Martin, Pierre-Marie. *Droit des activités spatiales.* Paris: Masson, 1992.

Marwick, Arthur. *The Sixties.* New York: Oxford University Press, 1998.

Marx, Karl, and Friedrich Engels. *The Communist Manifesto.* New York: International Publishers, 1948.

Mathieu, Gérard. *New High Speed Rail Developments: France's Master Plan.* Paris: SNCF, 1991.

Mayer, Nonna, and Pascal Perrineau, eds. *Le Front National a découvert.* Paris: Fondation Nationale des Sciences Politiques, 1989.

Mazarr, Michael J., and Alexander T. Lennon, eds. *Toward a Nuclear Peace: The Future of Nuclear Weapons.* New York: St. Martin's, 1994.

McDonough, Thomas R. *Space: The Next Twenty-Five Years.* New York: Wiley, 1987.

McDougall, Walter A. *France's Rhineland Diplomacy, 1914–1924.* Princeton: Princeton University Press, 1978.

———. *The Heavens and the Earth.* New York: Basic Books, 1985.

Mendershausen, Horst. *Coping with the Oil Crisis: French and German Experiences.* Baltimore: John Hopkins University Press, 1976.

Mendl, Wolf. *Deterrence and Persuasion: French Nuclear Armament in the Context of National Policy, 1945–1969.* New York: Praeger, 1970.

Mendras, Henri. *The Vanishing Peasant.* Translated by Jean Lerner. Cambridge, Mass.: MIT Press, 1970.

Michaud, Michael A. G. *Reaching for the High Frontier: The American Pro-Space Movement, 1972–84.* New York: Praeger, 1986.

Ministère de l'Agriculture et de la Forêt. *Catalogue de films.* 1990.

Mitchell, Allan. *Victors and Vanquished: The German Influence on Army and Church in France after 1870.* Chapel Hill: University of North Carolina Press, 1984.

Moravec, Hans. *Mind Children: The Future of Robot and Human Intelligence.* Cambridge, Mass.: Harvard University Press, 1988.

Nora, Pierre, ed. *Les lieux de mémoire.* 2 vols. Paris: Gallimard, 1992.

"Nouveau Programme Français: La Super-Caravelle." *Informations Aéronautiques,* supplément no. 64 au no. 502 (Dec. 14, 1961).

Nugent, Neill, and David Lowe. *The Left in France.* New York: St. Martin's, 1982.

Oberg, James E. *Mission to Mars: Plans and Concepts for the First Manned Landing.* Harrisburg, Pa.: Stackpole Books, 1982.

Ordway, Frederick I., III, and Randy Liebermann, eds. *Blueprint for Space.* Washington: Smithsonian Institution, 1992.

Pignolet de Sainte Rose, Guy. *La conquête industrielle du système solaire.* Paris: Le Rocher, 1986.

Pinchemel, Philippe. *France: A Geographic, Social, and Economic Survey.* Translated by Dorothy Elkins with T. H. Elkins. Cambridge: Cambridge University Press, 1987.

Pompidou, Georges. *Entretiens et discours, 1968–1974.* Paris: Flammarion, 1984.

Porch, Douglas. *The French Secret Services: From the Dreyfus Affair to the Gulf War.* New York: Farrar, Straus and Giroux, 1995.

Posner, Theodore Robert. *Current French Security Policy: The Gaullist Legacy.* New York: Greenwood Press, 1991.

Puchala, Donald J. "Integration and Disintegration in Franco-German Relations, 1954–1965." *International Organization* 24, no. 2 (Spring 1970): 183–208.

"La prodigieuse histoire de Concorde." *France-Soir,* March 6–7, 1977.

Puvilland, Veronique. *Cent ans de publicité industrielle.* Paris: Editions L'Usine Nouvelle, 1991.

Reader, Keith A., ed. *The May 1968 Events in France: Reproductions and Interpretations.* New York: St. Martin's, 1993.

Redfield, Peter. *Space in the Tropics: From Convicts to Rockets in French Guiana.* Berkeley: University of California Press, 2000.

Rémond, René. *The Right Wing in France from 1815 to de Gaulle.* Translated by James M. Laux. Philadelphia: University of Pennsylvania Press, 1969.

Rhodes, Richard. *The Making of the Atomic Bomb.* New York: Simon and Schuster, 1986.

Rioux, Jean-Pierre. *La France de la Quatrième République.* 2 vols. Paris: Seuil, 1980 (vol. 1), 1983 (vol. 2).

Rioux, Jean-Pierre. "Vive la consommation." *L'Histoire* no. 102 (July–August 1987).

Roberts, Noel Keith. *From Piltdown Man to Point Omega: The Evolutionary Theory of Teilhard de Chardin.* New York: Lang, 2000.

Robinson, Kim Stanley. *Red Mars.* New York: Bantam, 1993.

Roger, Jacques. *The Life Sciences in Eighteenth-Century French Thought.* Stanford: Stanford University Press, 1997.

Rogers, Susan Carol. *Shaping Modern Times in Rural France.* Princeton: Princeton University Press, 1991.

Rouquier, Georges. *Farrebique.* 16mm. film, 90 mins. L'Ecran Français. Films Etienne Lallier, 1947.

Rousso, Henry. *De Monnet à Massé: Enjeux politiques et objectifs économiques dans le cadre des quatre premiers Plans (1946–1965).* Paris: Editions du CNRS, 1986.

Salomon, Jean-Jacques. *Le gaulois, le cow-boy, et le samouraï: La politique française de la technologie.* Paris: Economica, 1986.

Saint-Exupéry, Antoine de. *Wind, Sand, and Stars.* Translated by Lewis Galantière. London: Heinemann, 1939.

Sanguinetti, Alexandre. *La France et l'arme atomique.* Paris: Julliard, 1964.

Scheinman, Lawrence. *Atomic Energy Policy in France under the Fourth Republic.* Princeton: Princeton University Press, 1965.

Schiff, Stacy. *Saint-Exupéry.* New York: Knopf, 1994.

Schnapp, Alain, and Pierre Vidal-Naquet. *The French Student Uprising, November 1967–June 1968: An Analytical Record.* Translated by Maria Jolas. Boston: Beacon, 1971.

Semmel, Bernard. *Imperialism and Social Reform.* London: Allen and Unwin, 1968.

Séris, Jean-Pierre. *La technique.* Paris: PUF, 1994.

Servan-Schreiber, Jean-Jacques. *Le défi américain.* Paris: Denoël, 1967.

"Le seul rival: le Tupolev 144 'Concordsky.'" *La Dépêche du Midi,* March 2, 1989.

Simmons, Harvey G. *The French National Front.* Boulder: Westview, 1996.

Stern, Fritz. *The Politics of Cultural Despair: A Study in the Rise of the Germanic Ideology.* New York: Doubleday, 1961.

Swart, Koenraad W. *The Sense of Decadence in Nineteenth-Century France.* The Hague: Nijhoff, 1964.

Tacet, Daniel. *Un monde sans paysans.* Paris: Hachette, 1992.

Teilhard de Chardin, Pierre. *The Phenomenon of Man.* New York: Harper and Row, 1965.

Thompson, E. P. *The Poverty of Theory and Other Essays.* London: Monthly Review Press, 1978.

Todd, Daniel, and Jamie Simpson. *The World Aircraft Industry.* London: Croom Helm, 1986.

Touraine, Alain. *The May Movement.* Translated by Leonard F. X. Mayhew. New York: Random House, 1971.

Turcat, André. *Concorde: Essais et batailles.* Paris: Stock, 1977.

Valéry, Paul. *Regards sur le monde actuel.* Paris: Stock, 1931.

Verne, Jules. *De la terre à la lune.* 1865. Paris: Hachette, 1928.

Von Puttkamer, Jesco. "The Industrialization of Space: Transcending the Limits to Growth." *Futurist* 13 (June 1979): 192–201.

Wakeman, Rosemary. *Modernizing the Provincial City: Toulouse, 1945–1975.* Cambridge, Mass.: Harvard University Press, 1997.

Wall, Irwin. *The United States and the Making of Postwar France, 1945–1954.* Cambridge: Cambridge University Press, 1991.

Weart, Spencer R. *Scientists in Power.* Cambridge, Mass.: Harvard University Press, 1979.

Weber, Eugen. *Peasants into Frenchmen.* Stanford: Stanford University Press, 1976.

Whitehead, Alfred North. *Process and Reality.* New York: Free Press, 1929.

Wilson, Andrew. *The Concorde Fiasco.* Harmondsworth: Penguin, 1973.

Winchester, Hilary P. M. *Contemporary France.* Harlow: Longman, 1993.

Wismann, Heinz. "Etre ou ne pas être dans l'espace?" *Libération,* June 2, 1993: 35.

Wittgenstein, Ludwig. "A Lecture on Ethics." In *Philosophical Occasions 1912–1951,* ed. James C. Klagge and Alfred Nordmann, 37–44. Indianapolis and Cambridge: Hackett, 1993.

Yonnet, Paul. *Jeux, modes, et masses: La société française et le moderne, 1945–1985.* Paris: Gallimard, 1985.

Yost, David S. *France's Deterrent Posture and Security in Europe.* Adelphi Papers no. 194. London: International Institute for Strategic Studies, 1984.

Zeldin, Theodore. *France, 1848–1945,* vol. 2, *Intellect, Taste, and Anxiety.* Oxford: Clarendon Press, 1977.

Zysman, John. *Political Strategies for Industrial Order: State, Market, and Industry in France.* Berkeley: University of California Press, 1977.